Masterpieces of
Rijksmuseum Volkenkunde

AF361370

Masterpieces of
Rijksmuseum Volkenkunde

Collection Series
Rijksmuseum Volkenkunde
National Museum of Ethnology

This book attests to 175 years of collecting and exploring by
the Rijksmuseum Volkenkunde / National Museum of Ethnology.
Out of a collection of 240,000 objects, more than 100 masterpieces were selected following diverse criteria. Some objects were
chosen because of their aesthetic qualities, others because of their
age, rarity, collection history or historical relevance. You will
experience the pinnacle of world heritage including artistic
masterpieces, products of ingenious craftsmanship, works with a
religious or spiritual significance, or things that excel through
their functional simplicity.

The masterpieces reflect the collecting history of the museum,
starting from 1837 up to the present day. The vignettes and
contextual histories procure an insight into human behaviour,
the way people give sense to their lives, craftsmanship and
creativity. In so doing, you are making an inspiring journey
through the whole world.

Discover the Nvich fish skin coat, the Tibetan human bone dance
girdle, the Congolese power figure, the Inca knotted cord and
so much more.

1837 1863 1868 1873 1878 1883 1888 1893 1898 1903 1908 1913 1918 1923 1928 1933

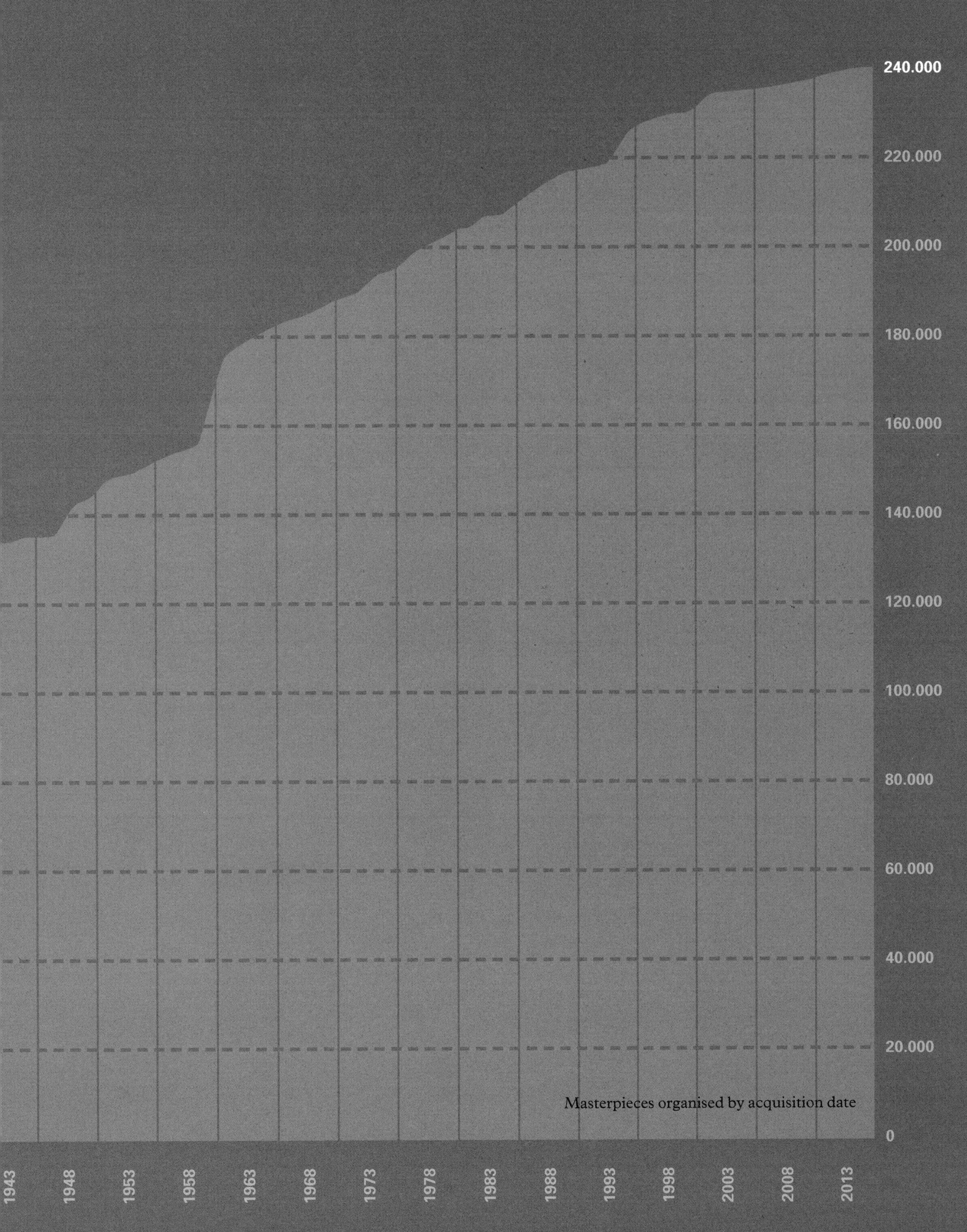

240.000
220.000
200.000
180.000
160.000
140.000
120.000
100.000
80.000
60.000
40.000
20.000
0
Masterpieces organised by acquisition date
1943
1948
1953
1958
1963
1968
1973
1978
1983
1988
1993
1998
2003
2008
2013

Masterpieces organised by acquisition date

1837

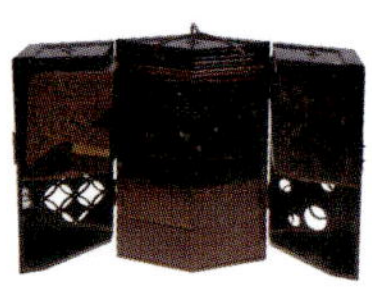

p. 10
Luxury picnic set (*Bentōbako*)
Japan

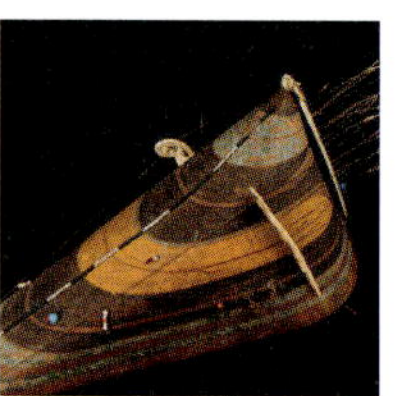

p. 12
Hunting hat
Alaska

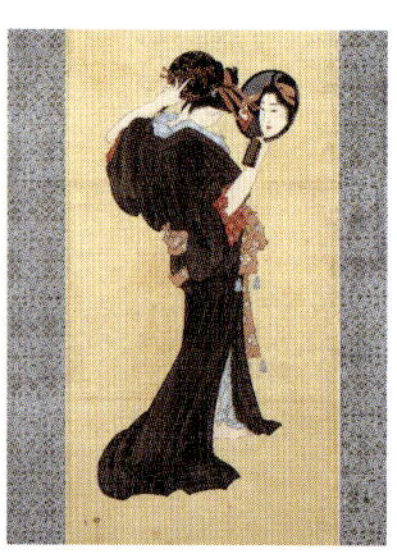

p. 14
Courtesan inspects her coiffure
Japan

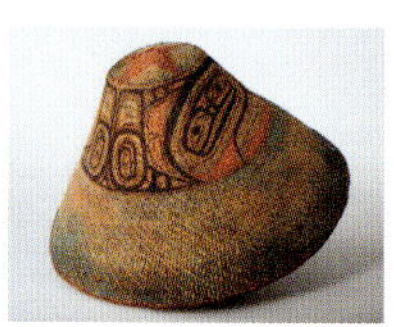

p. 16
Clan hat
United States

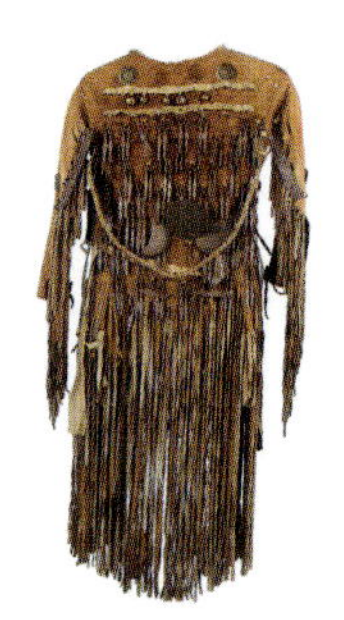

p. 18
Shaman's coat
Siberia

1856

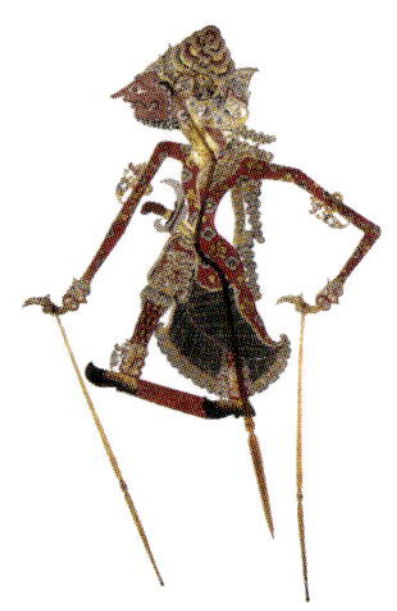

p. 20
Wayang kulit
Batara Guru, Brahma and Vishnu
Indonesia

1867

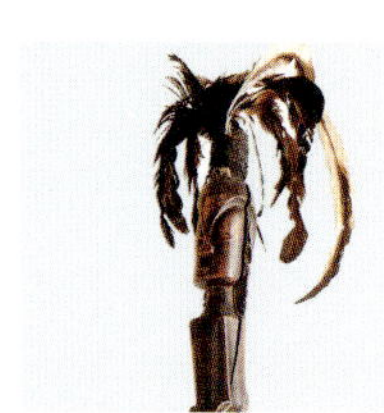

p. 22
Magic staff (*Tunggal panaluan*)
Indonesia

1878

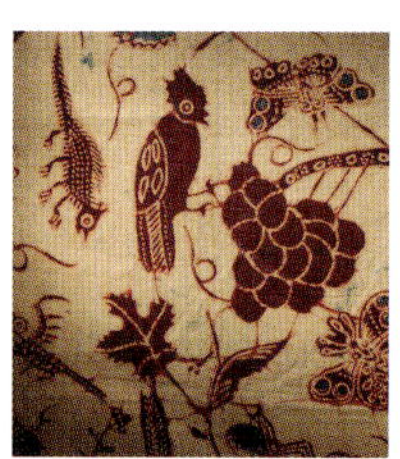

p. 24
Sarong (*Sarung*)
Indonesia

1881

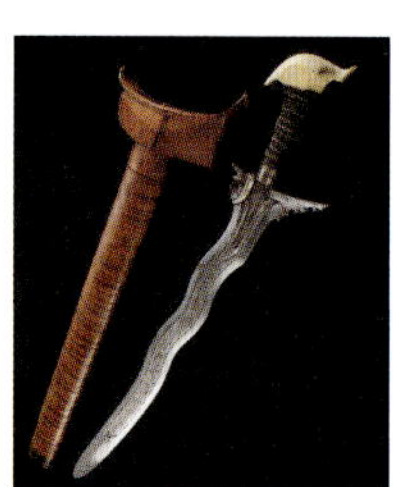

p. 26
Kris and shoulder cloth
Brunei Darussalam

1882

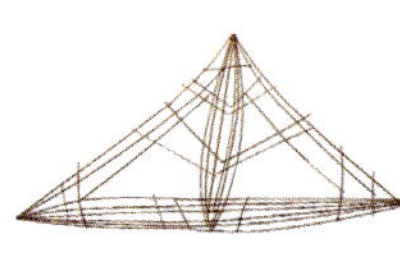

p. 28
Sea chart (*Meddo*)
Marshall Islands

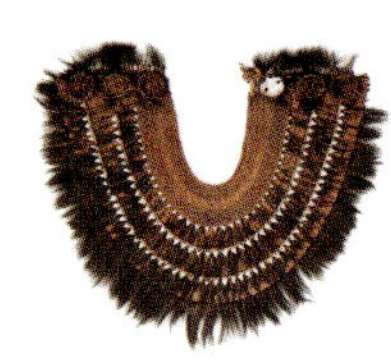

p. 30
Gorget (*Taumi*)
French Polynesia

1883

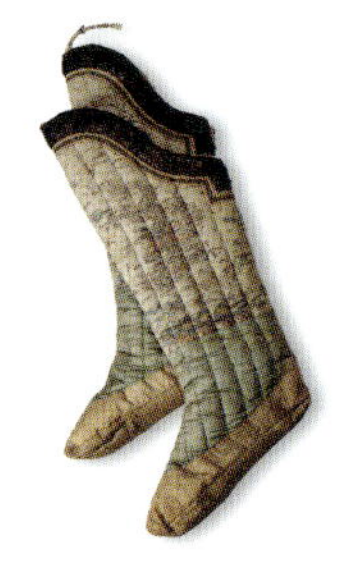

p. 32
Boot liners
China

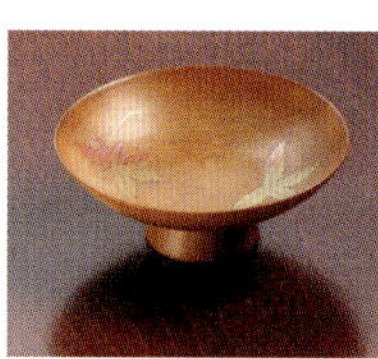

p. 34
Sake bowl
Japan

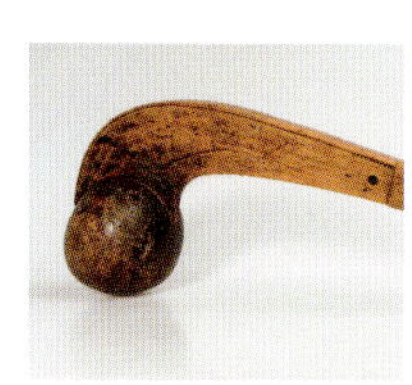

p. 36
War club
United States

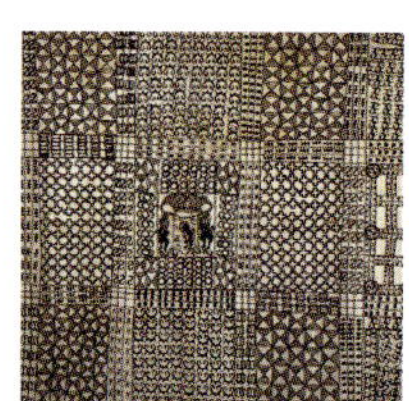

p. 38
Adinkra cloth
Ghana

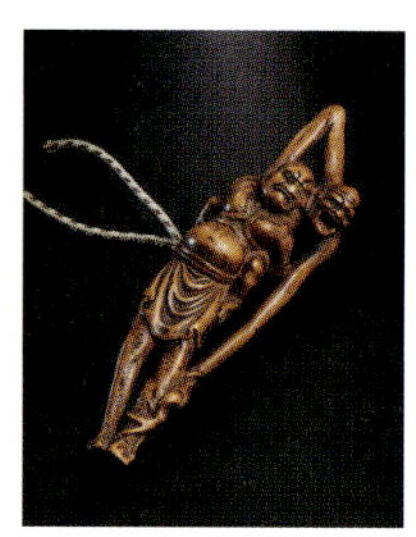

p. 40
Tenaga and Ashinaga (*Netsuke*)
Japan

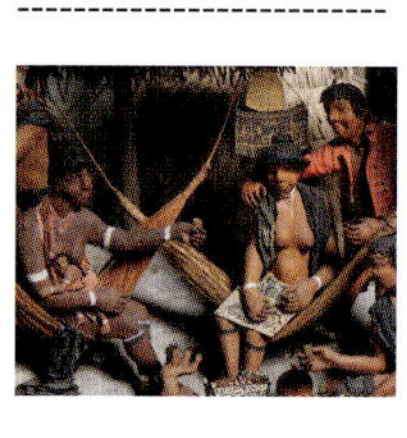

p. 42
Diorama
Suriname

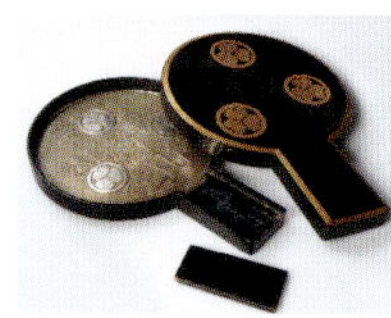

p. 44
Magic mirror (*Makkyō*)
Japan

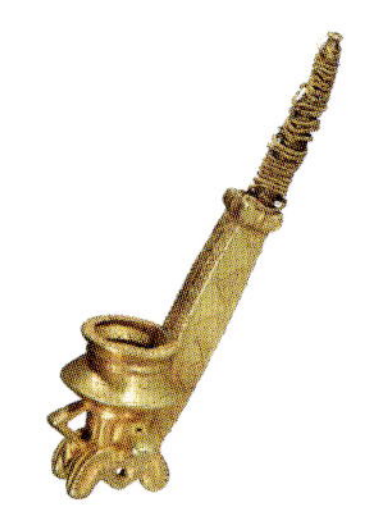

p. 46
Gold pipe
Ghana

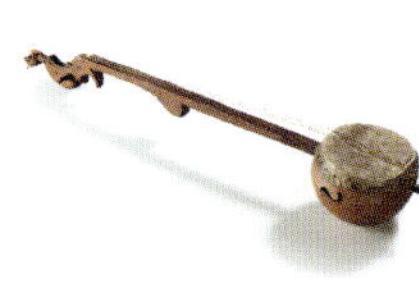

p. 48
Banjo
Suriname

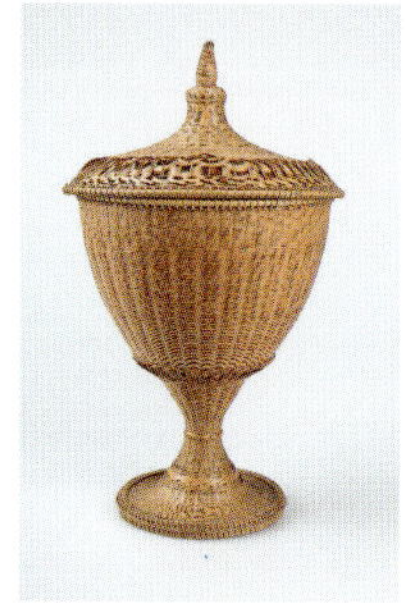

p. 50
Cake dish
Japan

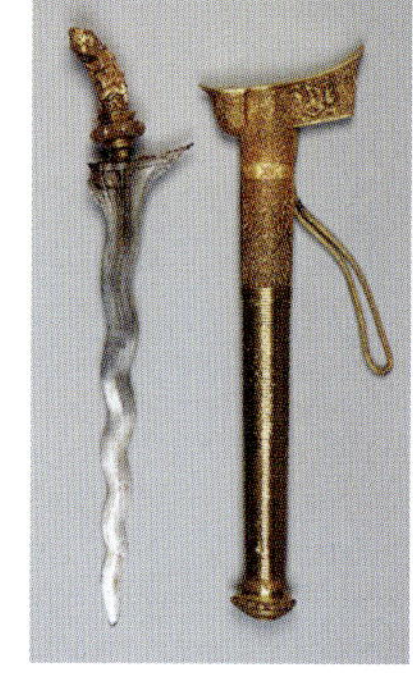

p. 52
Ceremonial kris
Indonesia

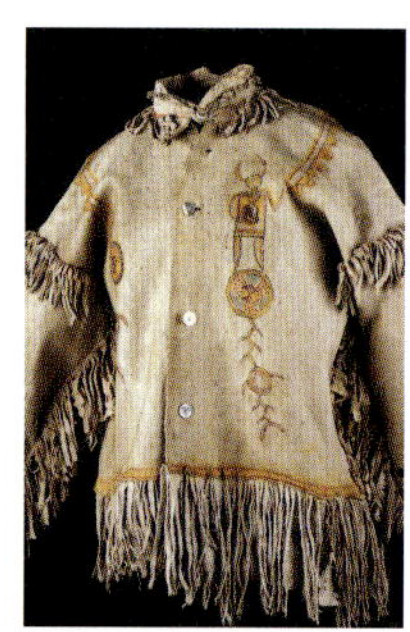

p. 54
War shirt
United States

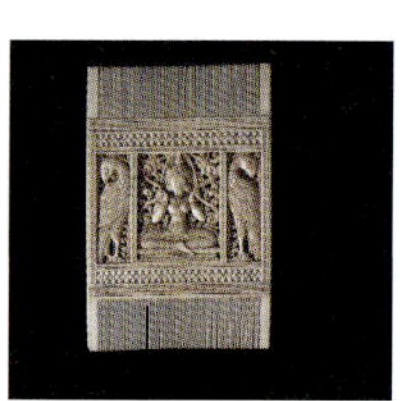

p. 56
Ivory comb with goddess
Sri Lanka

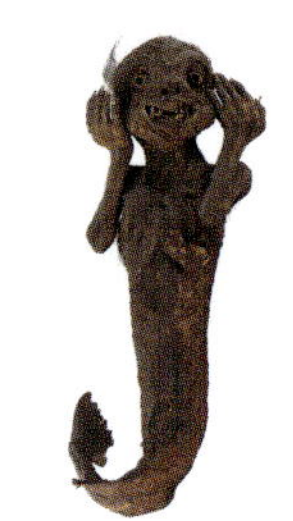

p. 58
Siren or mermaid (*Ningyo*)
Japan

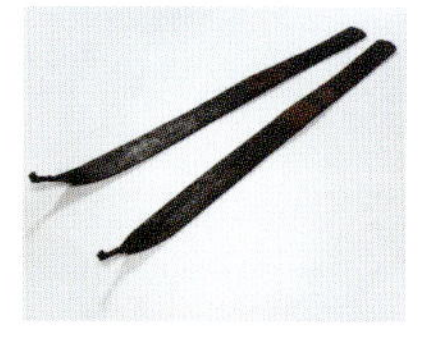

p. 60
Skis
Scandinavia

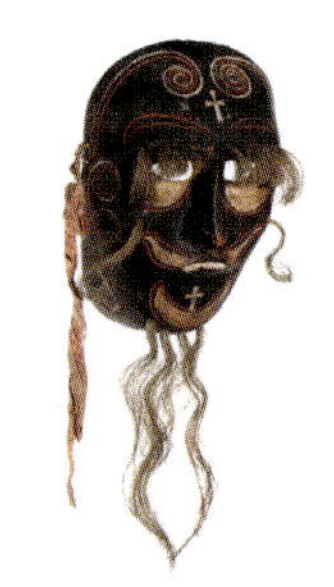

p. 62
Mask
United States

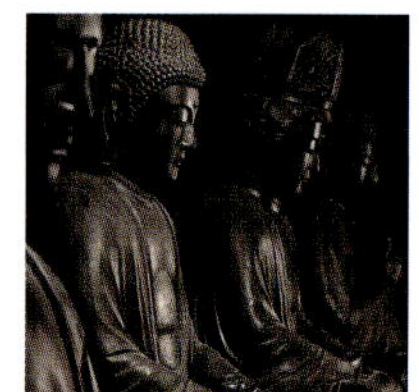

p. 64
Three bronze Buddhas
Japan

Masterpieces organised by acquisition date

1919

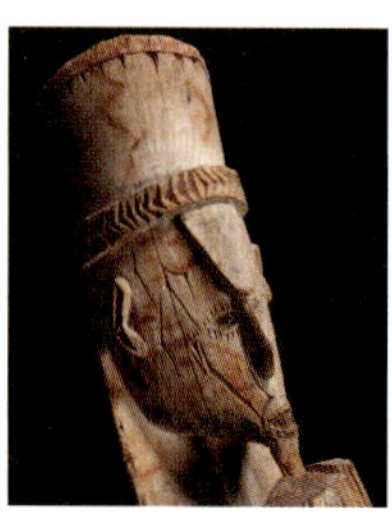

p. 122
Statue of a
pregnant woman
Indonesia

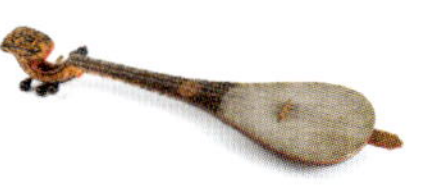

p. 124
Lute (*Qabus*)
Pakistan

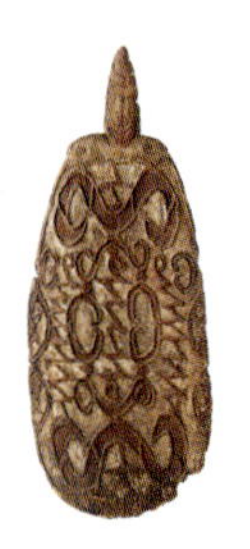

p. 126
Shield
Indonesia

1920

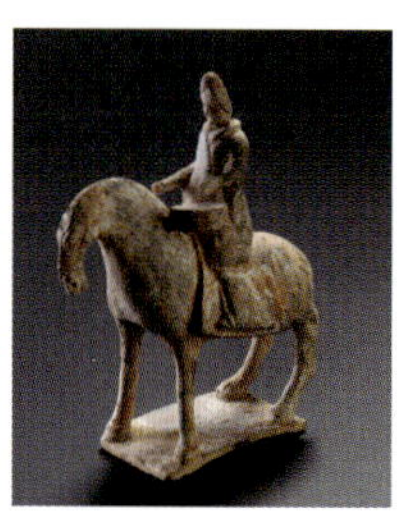

pag. 128
Tomb model
China

1922

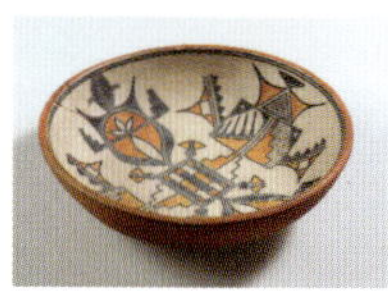

p. 130
Dish
United States

1926

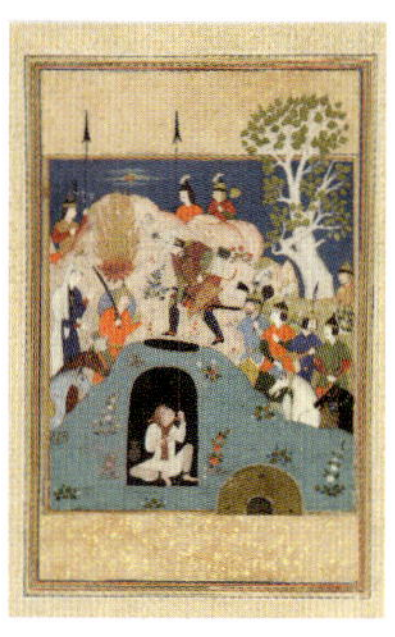

p. 132
Two miniatures from
the *Shahnameh*
Persia

1930

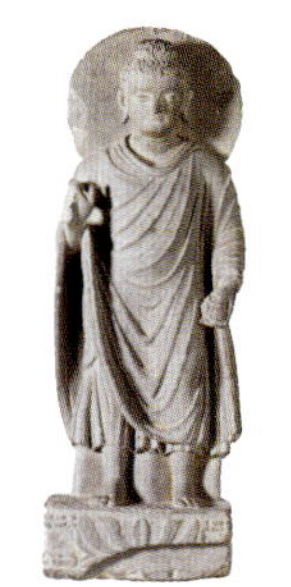

p. 134
Standing Buddha
Pakistan

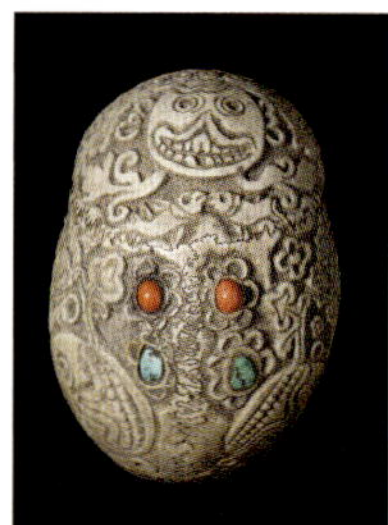

p. 136
Skull cup
Tibet

1933

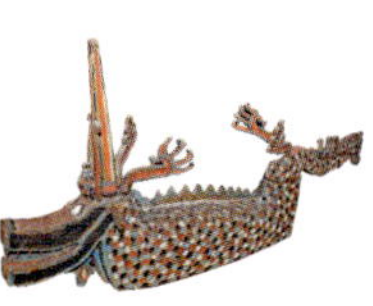

p. 138
Snake statue
Indonesia

1938

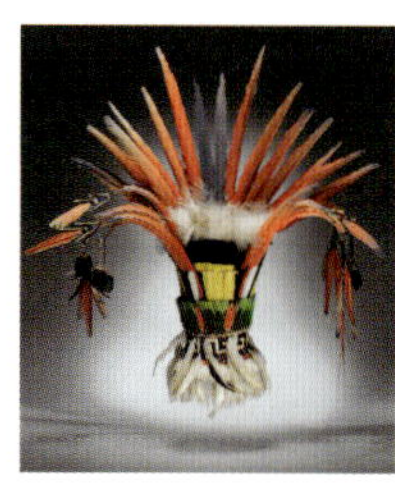

p. 140
Headdress (*Olok*)
Suriname

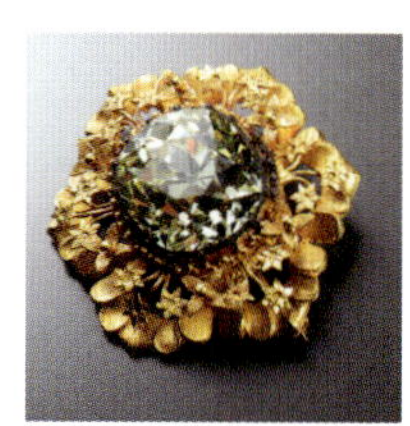

p. 142
Lombok treasure
Indonesia

1940

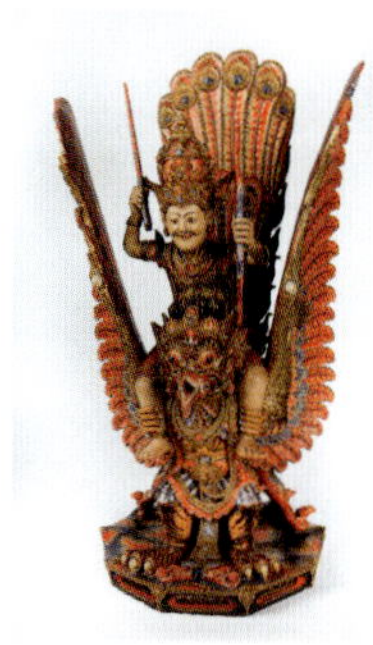

p. 146
Statue of Garuda
wth Rama
Indonesia

1947

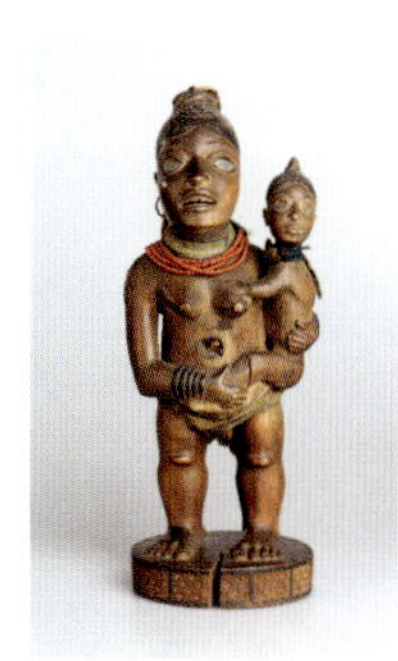

p. 148
Figure of mother
and child (*Phemba*)
Democratic
Republic of Congo

p. 150
Amoghapasha
Lokeshvara and
his retinue
Indonesia

p. 152
Throwing knife
Africa

1950

p. 154
Ritual bone
apron
Tibet

1951

p. 156
Bodhisattva
Manjushri
Himalayas

1952

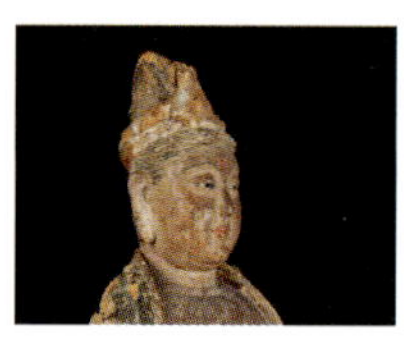

p. 158
Bodhisattva
China

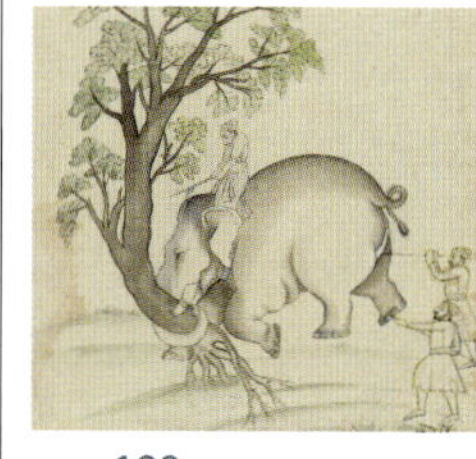

p. 160
Indian miniature
drawing with
elephant
India

1953

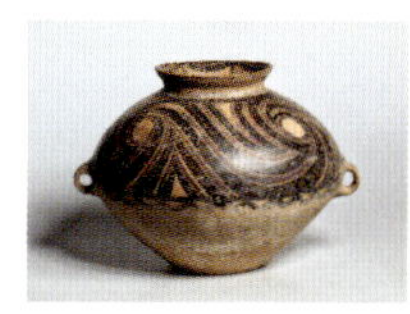

p. 162
Jar (*Guan*)
China

1954

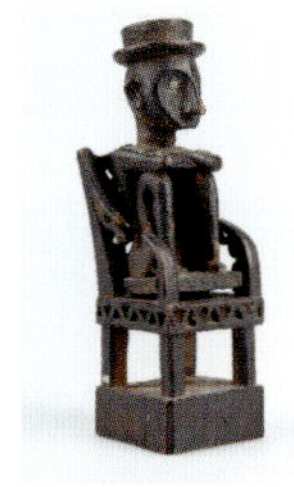

p. 164
Ancestral figurine
Indonesia

1956

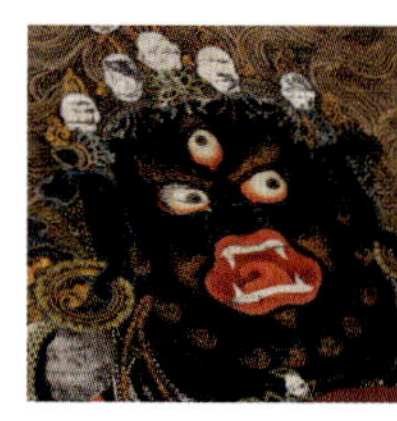

p. 166
Thangka with
Mahakala
Tibet

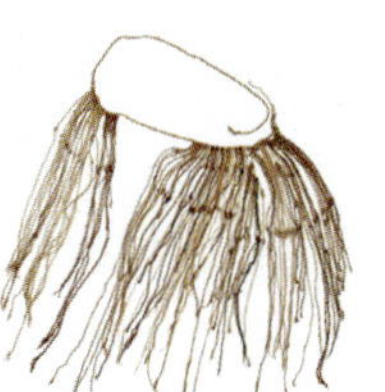

p. 168
Knotted cord
(*Khipu*)
Peru

1958

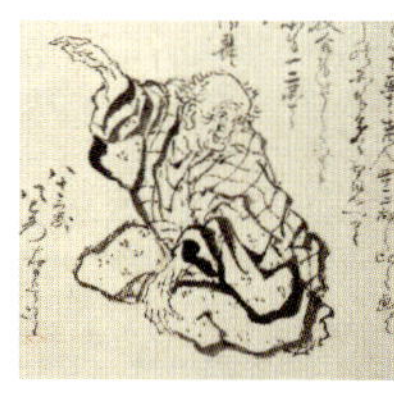

p. 170
Self-portrait at
83 years of age
Japan

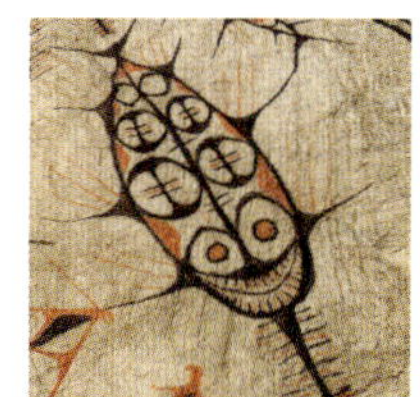

p. 172
Barkcloth
Indonesia

1959

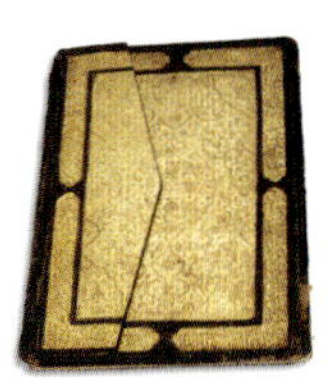

p. 174
1/30th part of
the Qur'an with
binding
Persia

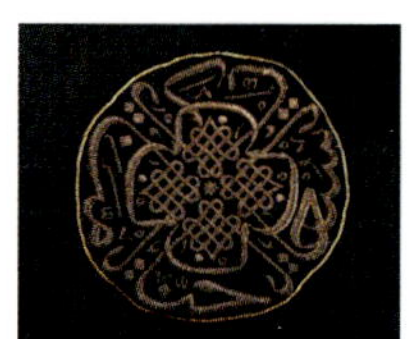

p. 176
Fragment of the
textile covering
the Ka'ba (*Kiswa*)
Egypt

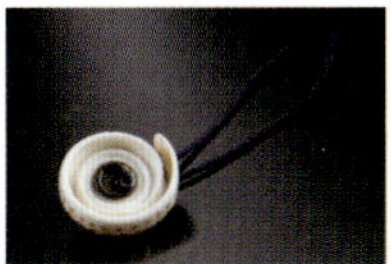

1962

p. 178
Mitsu tomoe mounted in a cone shell (*Netsuke*)
Japan

1963

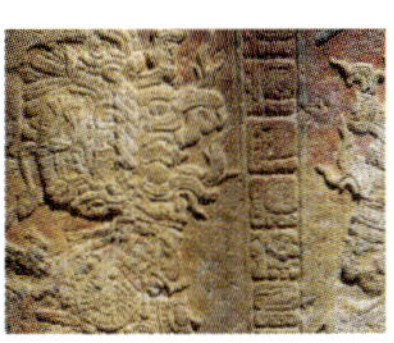

p. 180
Relief depicting the Bird Jaguar blood sacrifice
Guatemala

1964

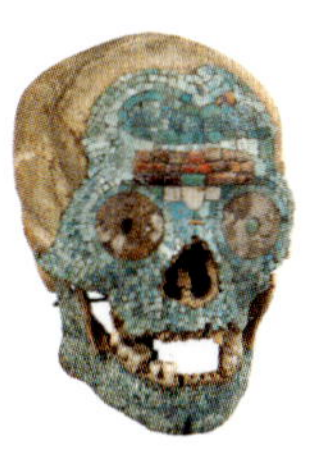

p. 182
Ancestor skull
Mexico

1967

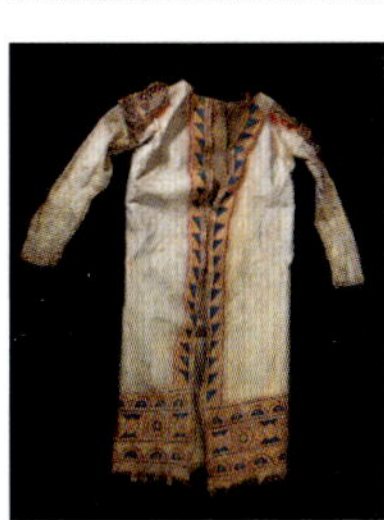

p. 184
Coat
Canada

1969

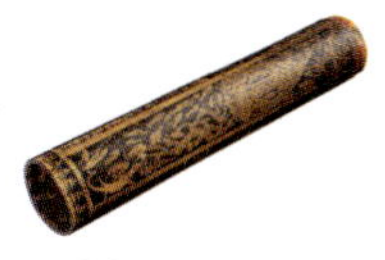

p. 186
Bamboo tube (*Solep*)
Indonesia

1972

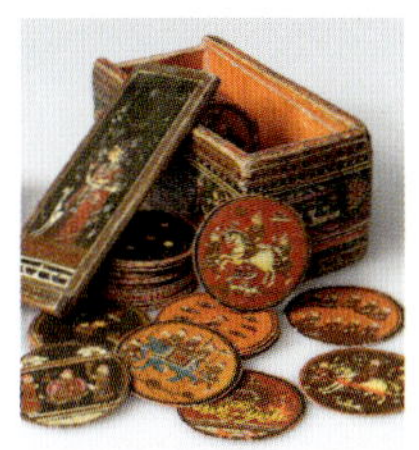

p. 188
Board game (*Ganjifa*)
India

1973

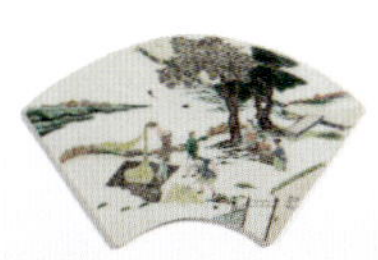

p. 190
Porcelain panels
China

1975

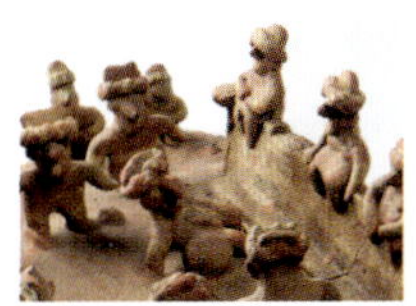

p. 192
Model of a ball court
Mexico

1977

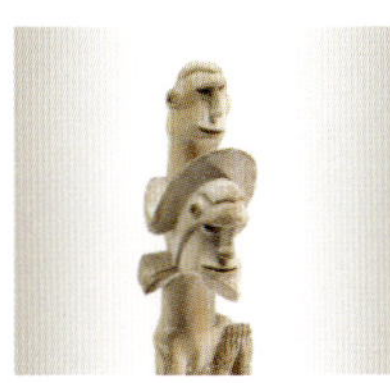

p. 194
Mother-and-child figure
Indonesia

1982

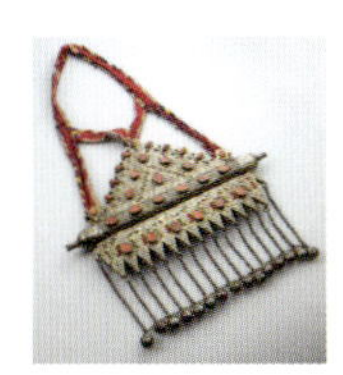

p. 196
Amulet holder in the form of a pendant
Turkmenistan

1985

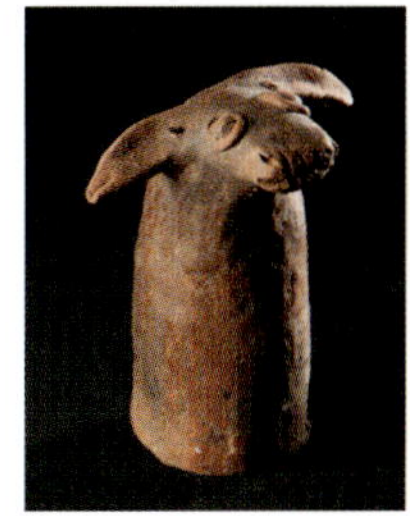

p. 198
Vedic fire sacrifice set
India

1991

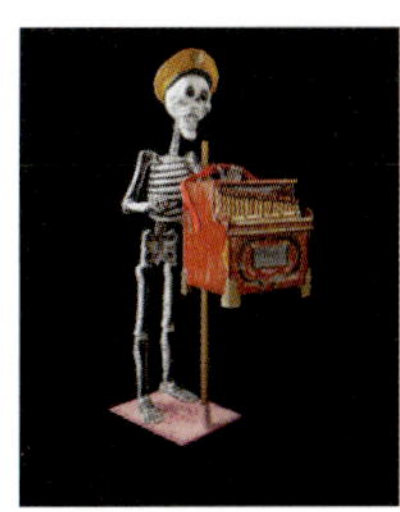

p. 200
Figure of an organ-grinder (*Calavera*)
Mexico

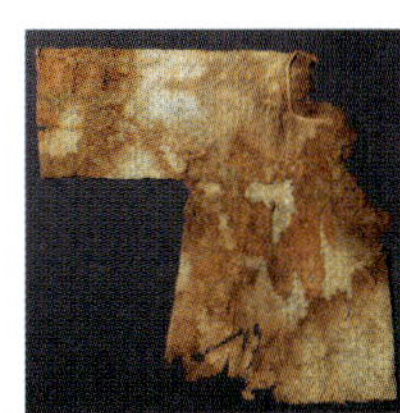

p. 202
Mediaeval Tellem cotton
Mali

1993

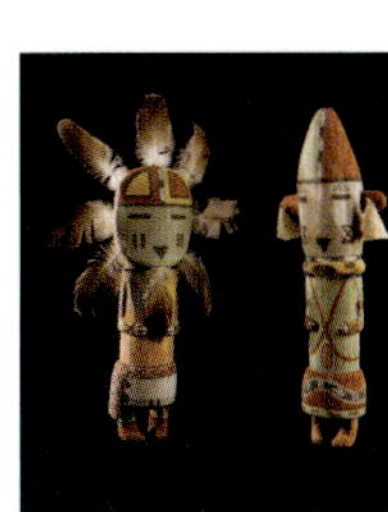

p. 204
Katsinum: Aholi and Dawa
United States

1997

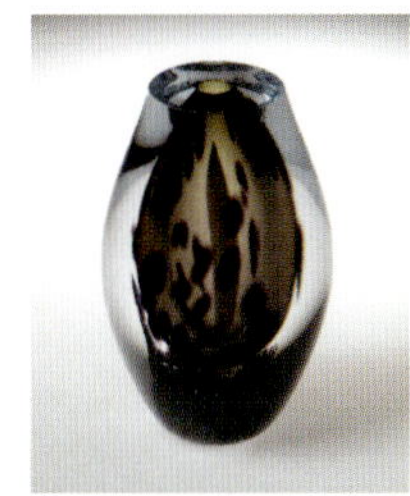

p. 206
Vase
Greenland

1998

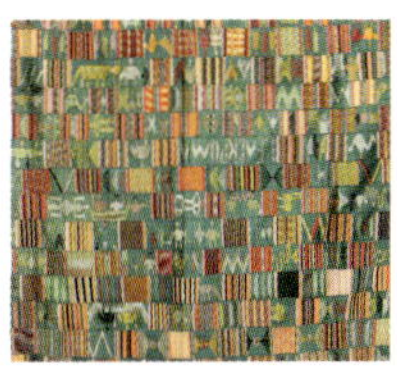

p. 208
Kente cloth
Ghana

1999

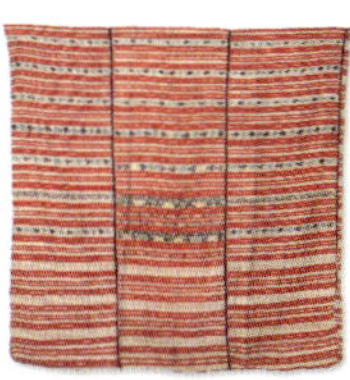

p. 210
Garment (*Huipil de tapar*)
Mexico

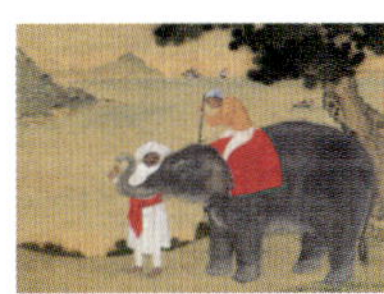

p. 212
Elephant with its attendant
Japan

2001

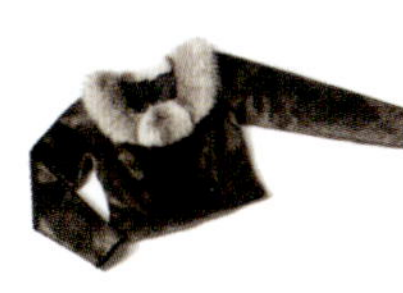

p. 214
Woman's blouse
Greenland

2002

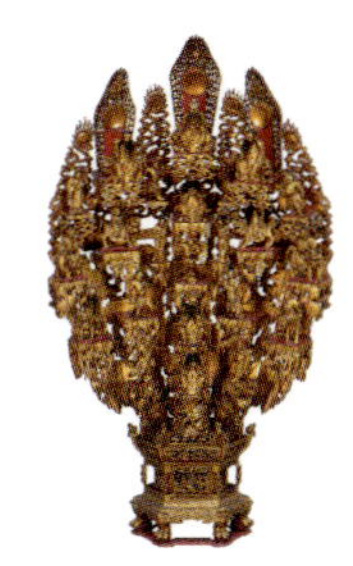

p. 216
Mountain of immortals (*Xianshan*)
China

2008

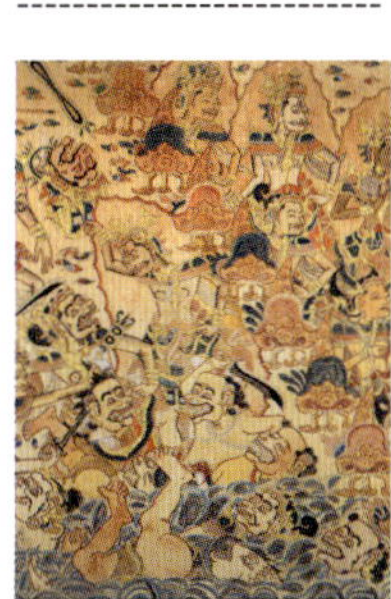

p. 216
Painting
Indonesia

2009

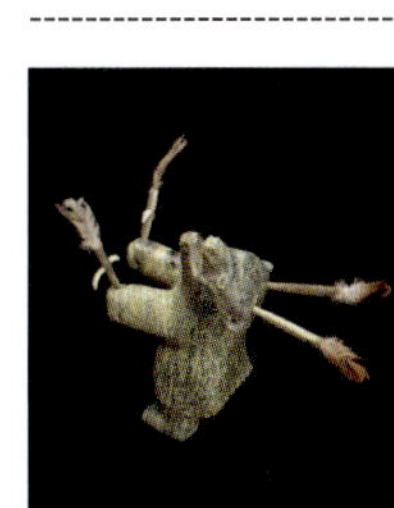

p. 222
'Shaman bear'
Canada

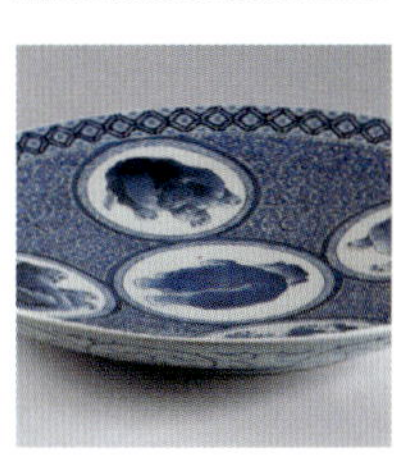

p. 224
Porcelain serving dish
Japan

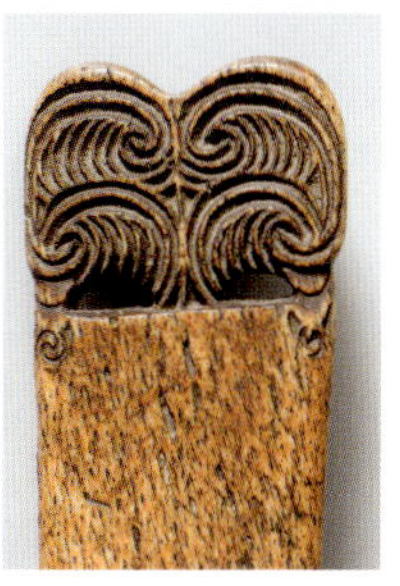

p. 226
Staff (*Hoeroa*)
New Zealand

2010

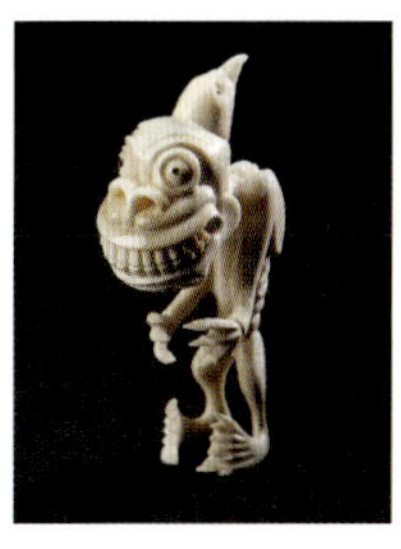

p. 228
Figurine (*Tupilak*)
Greenland

2011

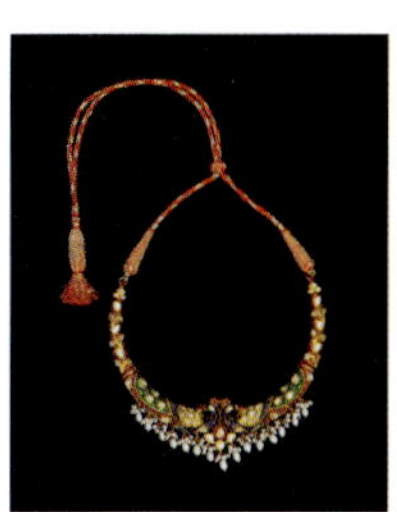

p. 230
Necklace (*Hasli*)
India

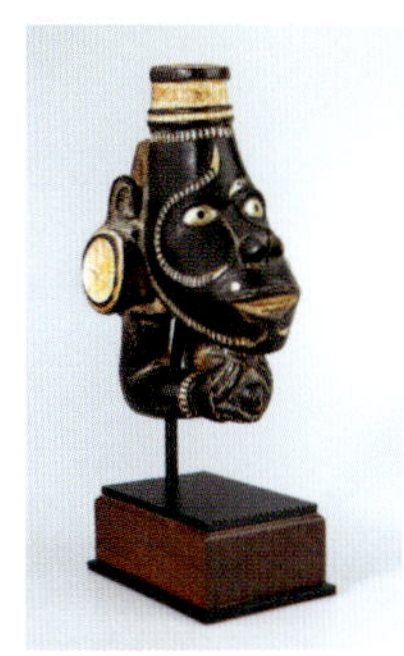

p. 232
Prow ornament (*Isu, Nguzu nguzu* of *Musu musu*)
Solomon Islands

Luxury picnic set (*Bentōbako*)

Edo period, Japan
before 1826
26,6 x 28,5 x 24,8 cm
wood, lacquer, mother-of-pearl, metal, bronze
RMV 1-543 (1837)

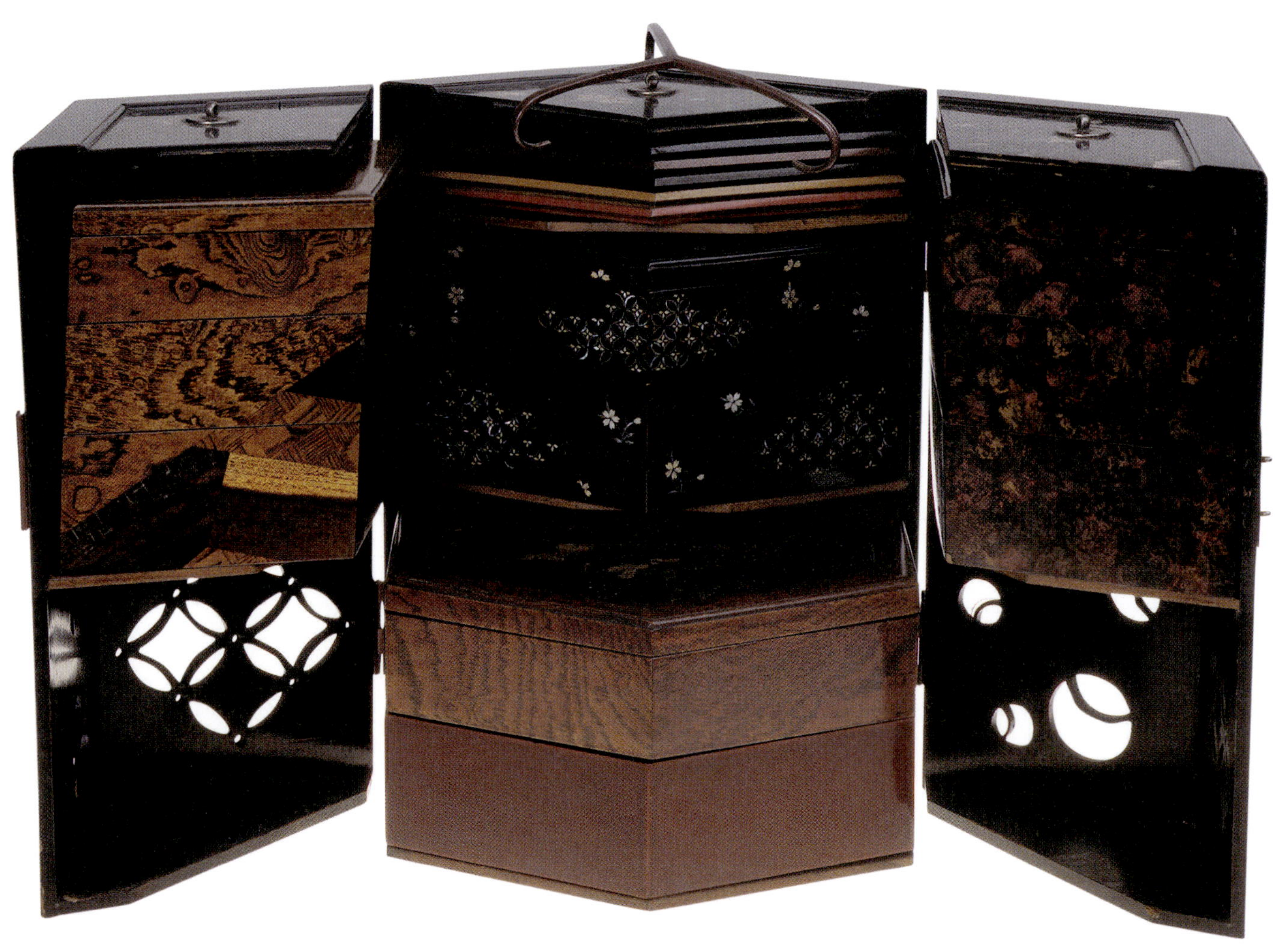

Picnic set

This luxury picnic set or *bentōbako* is an outstanding example of compact refinement. The set consists of three fold-out compartments and contains a number of wooden boxes, finished in red, black or transparent lacquer. Some of the boxes are beautifully inlaid with mother-of-pearl or made of different types of wood in a marquetry technique. The little dishes are in the middle compartment at the top. The outer case is decorated with openwork *shippō* motifs (overlapping circles arranged to form lozenges and ovals) and *tsubo* motifs (interlocking circles or 'manhole' motif). A bronze handle ingeniously holds the compartments together when the set is being transported.

Picnics in Japan

Picnic sets are indispensable on day trips to admire the cherry blossom, a popular Japanese activity during the third month of the lunar year (usually in April). They are also used on countless summer occasions, including the parties in the eighth month, when people go off into the countryside and sit on benches to enjoy the autumn moon. The picnic box does not accommodate *sake*, which had to be taken along separately. The little trays and boxes are only to be used for fish, shellfish, and vegetables, possibly with the addition of rice in the large box.

Hakone marquetry

This picnic set is a variegated mix of local techniques, typical of the gaudy taste of the Japanese middle class. The *yosegisaiku* or marquetry is characteristic of the area surrounding Hakone, which is three days' walking distance from Edo. In this region, people had been producing bowls and dishes, boxes, trays and miscellaneous cheap souvenirs known as *hikimonosaiku* since the late eighteenth century. In the early nineteenth century, the technique of marquetry was developed, in which pieces of different kinds of timber were made into an integrated whole, thin layers being removed using a plane and glued to the outer surface of a box as a veneer.

Mix of local techniques

The collectors Jan Cock Blomhoff and J.F. van Overmeer Fisscher record in their travel journals that the Hakone region was also well known for its lacquerware. The red and transparent lacquered boxes in the middle section probably come from that region. The fine mother-of-pearl inlaid work in the central boxes, however, is more likely to have been made in Kyoto. The case with its *ajour* decoration, on the other hand, may well originate from Hakone. All in all, this picnic set is a fine example of a mix of selected local techniques. The commissioner probably ordered the parts from different places.

View of Edo

This picnic set was undoubtedly purchased by the collector Philipp Franz von Siebold during the court journey he made in 1826 in the retinue of the chief Dutch official or Opperhoofd De Sturler. This was a journey undertaken every four years by the delegation of the *Opperhoofd* of Deshima, the Dutch trading post in Japan, to the *shōgun's* court in the capital, Edo. Items were frequently reserved and ordered on the outward journey and collected on the way back. For collectors such as Blomhoff, Fisscher and von Siebold, the court journey was an ideal opportunity to expand their collections with objects that they would never have been able to purchase from Deshima. Their collections (now in the Rijksmuseum Volkenkunde) uniquely illuminate numerous local products that are virtually unknown in present-day Japan.

Hunting hat

Unangan (Aleut), Aleutian Islands, Alaska
late 18th to early 19th century
20 x 44,5 cm
wood, bone, ivory, sea lion whiskers, sinew thread, glass beads
RMV 1-1409 (1837)

Between Russia and America

This early nineteenth-century hunting hat is beautifully decorated with a stripe motif, carved ivory figurines, bead embellishment and sea lion whiskers. The small ivory bird figure on the top has become damaged. The flattened piece at the front is characteristic of the hats of the Aleutian Islands. Experts have linked the hunting hats to the Okvik or Old Bering Sea culture of 300 BC. Earlier examples are preserved in museums in Russia, Alaska, America and Europe. Some are over 350 years old, most of them collected by Russian whalers and colonists. The Aleutian Islands were part of the Russian Empire from 1741 until 1867, when they were sold to the United States.

Steaming and bending

Unangan and Yup'ik hunting hats were carved from thin sections of wood that were bent into a curved shape and sewn together (at the back of the head) using sinew thread. The wood would be bent by being held over steam from boiling water or soaked in water until it was pliable. Nowadays, the Yup'ik sometimes bend wood by biting it; this is probably an ancient method. Sometimes an elongated piece of bone or ivory is used to camouflage a joint. In some cases, a hat might be carved from a hollowed-out, solid piece of wood. A very common decorative feature is a stripe motif ending in a meandering geometrical pattern.

Protection and enticement

On the Aleutian Islands, a hunting hat was an indispensable element of hunting gear. It protected the wearer from reflected sunlight from the water and ice, and could also serve as camouflage. A Yup'ik hunter explained that they used to rub white clay or *urasqaq* into the hats, enabling them to get as close as possible to seals when hunting on ice. The decorations on the hat helped to conjure up magical forces and evil spirits to entice their prey.

Hunters and their hats

Whaling was surrounded by mysterious rituals and secrecy. Few men were whalers, and these few were often the most important leaders. Their hats were rare, expensive, mysterious, and were kept concealed. Hunting hats often reflected the wearer's status. For instance, decorations such as whiskers indicated the number of walruses or other great sea creatures a hunter had caught.

Clear vision

Numerous geometrical motifs refer to elements from the animal kingdom. The muzzle, snout, beak, nose and eyes are particularly prominent features. Many of the animal motifs are related to birds of prey, or birds that have very keen sight, or can fly very high or fast, swoop or dive deep under water: from eagles and falcons to great northern divers, guillemots, sea gulls, puffins, and cormorants. The bird motif stands for crossing boundaries: the dividing line between human and animal, the visible and the concealed, high and low, land and sea, life and death, killing and surviving, man and woman, young and old. Certain bird motifs allude to the mythical thunderbirds, which can kill human beings as well as walruses and caribou. The bird's eye represents supernatural sight, but it also represents the hunter's clarity of vision or insight. The beak stands for lethal power. It sometimes has a phallic shape, in which case it is a fertility symbol.

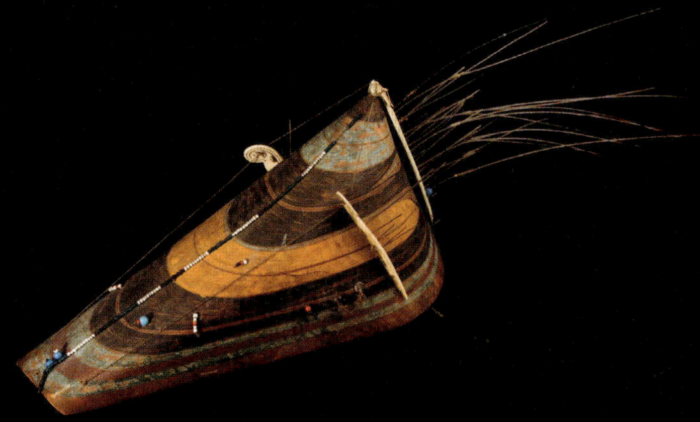

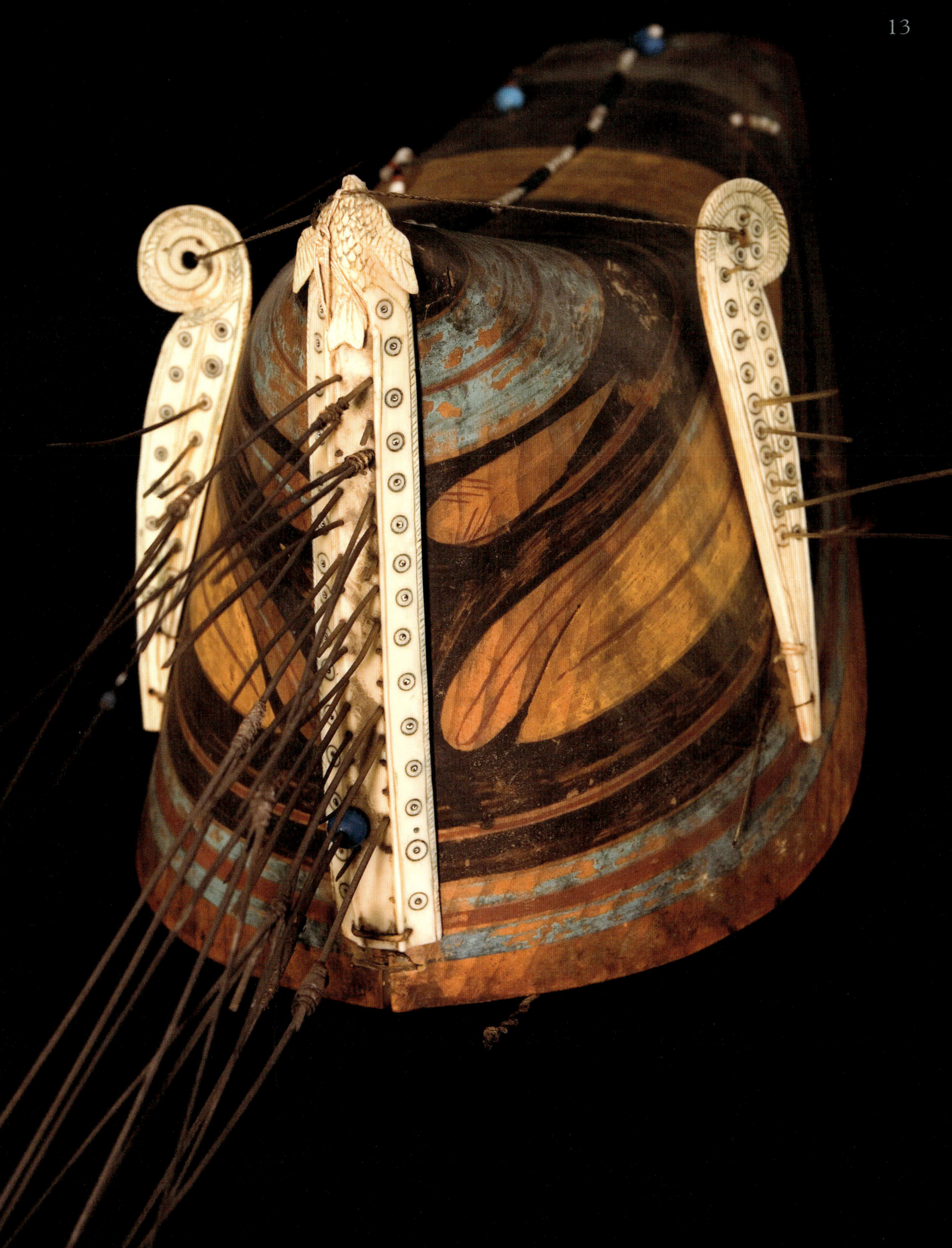

Courtesan inspects her coiffure

Katsushika Hokusai, Edo period, Japan
1822-1826
86,3 x 31,2 cm
silk, ink *(sumi)*, pigment, mounted as a hanging scroll (*kakejiku*)
RMV 1-1164 (1837)

The elegance of the courtesan

A courtesan inspects the back of her coiffure with the aid of two mirrors. She is dressed in a slightly translucent black kimono over a red and light-blue under-kimono, fastened with a mauve *obi*. This is tied at the front, a fashion exclusive to courtesans. The elegance of the slightly backward-leaning figure is emphasised by details such as the raised left arm and her décolleté: the hairline in her neck corresponds to the silhouette of Mount Fuji, an image of ideal beauty in Japan. The face of the woman, which we see only in the raised mirror, is characteristic of Hokusai's style in this period.

Seventeen paintings

Besides eleven paintings on Dutch paper, Siebold also acquired four paintings made for him by Hokkei, one of Hokusai's pupils, as well as two large paintings on silk. Siebold continued with his penny-pinching approach. He had the latter two mounted in Nagasaki as scroll paintings, thus opting for the cheaper solution of mounting them on patterned paper instead of the customary silk with brocade trimmings.

Siebold insults Hokusai

In 1826, it was *Opperhoofd* De Sturler who made the court journey. This time, Siebold accompanied the procession. Various personal details can be distilled from surviving letters and notes. For instance, we know that Hokusai came to Hotel Nagasakiya during the Dutchmen's stay in Edo on 30 April, bringing the paintings that Blomhoff had ordered. While *Opperhoofd* De Sturler paid the agreed sum of money without a murmur, Siebold had second thoughts, and protested that the price was too high. After all, as a physician he earned far less than his travelling companion. Hokusai refused to accept a lower price, and returned to his studio, taking the paintings with him. When De Sturler learned of von Siebold's behaviour, he flew into a rage, since it had been agreed that in all trade with Japan, it was the Japanese who set the price. He summoned Hokusai again and paid him the agreed sum for his work.

Lively illustrations

How this painting by Katsushika Hokusai (1760-1849) ended up in Siebold's collection is unclear. We know, however, that *Opperhoofd* Jan Cock Blomhoff and the clerk Johan van Overmeer Fisscher purchased a large number of small volumes with scenes of everyday life drawn by Hokusai while they were in Edo during the court journey of 1822. These lively illustrations appealed to them more than portraits of courtesans from Edo's brothel district or scenes from the *kabuki* theatre, with which they were probably unfamiliar.

Ordered from Hokusai

Perhaps Blomhoff and Fisscher were so enchanted by the pictures they had purchased that they wanted to meet the artist. For it seems that Blomhoff gave Hokusai some Dutch paper during this meeting, since we know that not long after that, Hokusai made a painting on this paper, dated 1824. In any case, the visit led to an order of a large number of paintings, which Hokusai was to come and deliver in the course of the following court journey, in 1826.

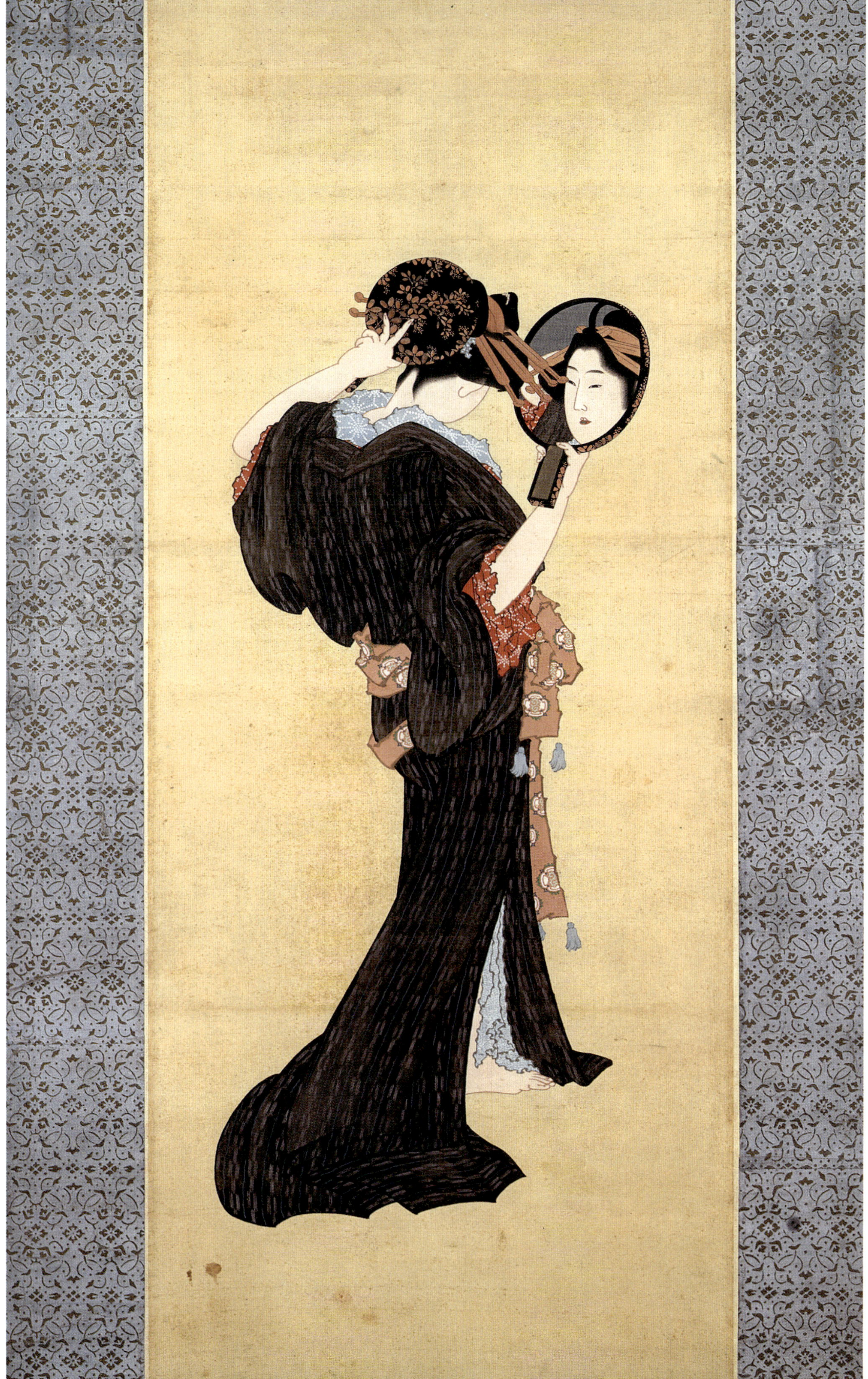

Clan hat

Tlingit, Northwest Coast, United States
1790-1830
h. 16 cm, d. 29 cm
spruce roots, dyes
RMV 1-1412 (1837)

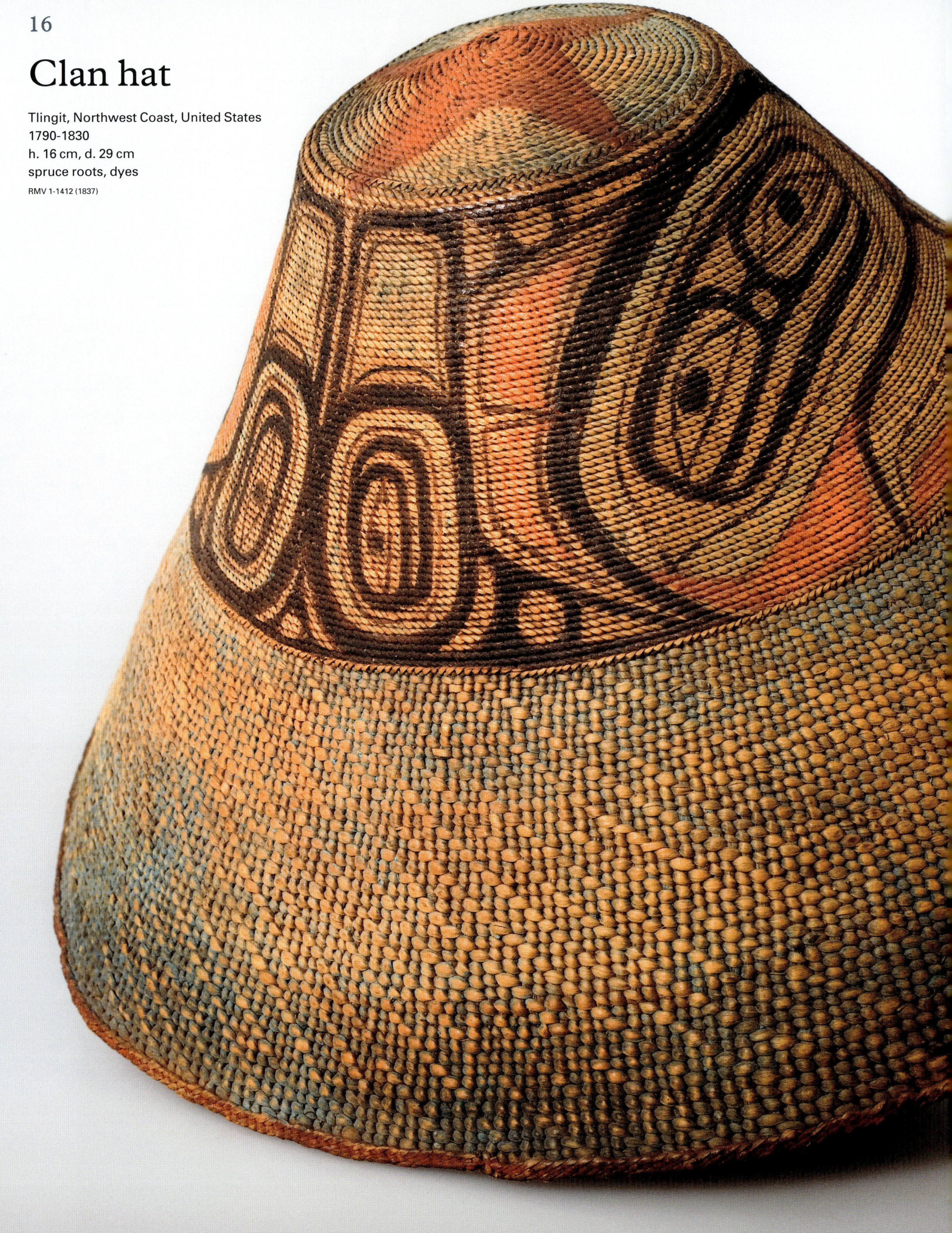

Spruce roots

In the rainy, humid climate of the Northwest Pacific Coast, spruce root hats were far from frivolous luxuries. Spruce roots made perfect material for woven hats, partly because of their water-repellent properties, and partly because of the strong but pliable structure of their fibres. After the fine and many-branched bunches of roots were first dried over a fire, they would be peeled and split into fine strands. The flat-topped conical hats were worn by young and old alike. Plain ones were for everyday use, while painted ones were worn by clan chiefs, most notably on special social and ceremonial occasions.

Status

The Indian communities of the Northwest Pacific Coast had a hierarchical class system. At the top was the clan chief, the standard-bearer. Clan chiefs displayed their status with clan symbols in woodcarvings and paintings on totem poles, the façade of their house, screens, furniture, and clothing. They also displayed them on their hats. Some hats had several cylinders of woven spruce roots topping the crown. The number of rings probably represents the number of potlatches (festive occasions on which objects were given away to guests) that these wealthy families had hosted.

Weaving and painting

Hats worn to indicate high status were generally made using two distinct weaving techniques. For the underside, a technique was used that would yield a fine surface relief, making it possible to produce a variety of patterns. The top section was woven as flat as possible using a twining technique, so that the surface could be painted. Painting hats that denoted high status was the prerogative of men who were entitled to reproduce clan symbols. The basic colours for the motifs depicting supernatural beings from mythology were black and red, sometimes with the addition of bluish-green, as in this case. The painter of this hat reveals himself to be a master of the Tlingit version of the 'form line' style that is typical of the Northwest Coast. The precise identity of the painted figures is hard to determine because of the high degree of abstraction, but those who are familiar with this art will recognise salmon trout heads within a larger motif of a water creature with eyes, ears, and fins.

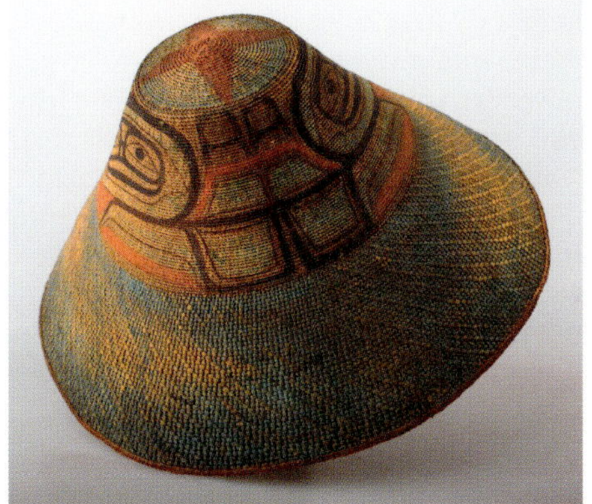

Dating

These conical woven hats were primarily characteristic of tribes of the northern Northwest Coast. It has been suggested that hats of this type derived from the headgear worn by Chinese sailors working on the ship of John Meares, who visited this coastal region in 1788. However, similar hats have also been excavated in prehistoric settlements, which confirms their indigenous development. Many early hats are stylistically related to northern ethnic groups such as the Aleuts and Inuit. The painting of this hat suggests a more southerly provenance. It was probably made between 1790 and 1830 in southeast Alaska, the tribal territory of the Tlingit.

Signature

Some painters of woven hats denoting high status signed them, generally on the flattened tops, and often in the form of a star. The star's colour and the number of points identified the maker. Tom Price (Haida) used a five-pointed red star; Charles Edenshaw (Haida) had a four-pointed star, divided into red and black sections on the hats that had been woven by his wife Isabella. This Tlingit hat bears a four-pointed red star. The identity of the artist who used this mark is unknown.

Shaman's coat

Yakut, Siberia
early 19th century (c. 1800)
150 x 68 cm
hide, iron, sinew thread
RMV 1-1582 (1837)

From heavy metal to esoteric lightness

This shaman's coat belongs to the collection of Philipp Franz von Siebold (1796–1866), who probably bought it in Russia between 1831 and 1837. It belonged to 'a collection of Siberian rarities'. The entire surface of this reindeer-hide coat is studded with pieces of metal. Four metal disks are attached to the back, beneath which are bells, elongated metal appendages, and a cord. The front of the coat also has countless metal embellishments. The coat has an open front in which a panel or long 'apron' was worn. This matching garment was also embellished with metal ornaments full of symbolic and magical significance.

Siberian shamans

Siberian shamans mediated between different realms, between the spirit world and that of living beings. Besides conjuring up spirits, shamans could also establish contact with the countless gods, influence the weather, lure game for the hunt, make predictions, and heal.

Becoming a shaman

A few long strips on the back of the coat probably represent ribs. This skeleton motif evoked death as a rite of passage, in which a person was reborn as a shaman. Only someone chosen by a predecessor shaman or by the spirits could become a shaman. Omens would manifest themselves in dreams or natural phenomena. Traumatic events such as serious illness or near-death experiences were frequently seen as signifying that someone had been chosen. After this, the person's supernatural powers, such as clairvoyance, would often be revealed. The shaman's work could often be extremely dangerous, as indicated by the cord dangling from the back of the coat. A villager, acting as his or her assistant, could pull this cord to prevent the shaman from going so far away, while taking action, that returning to this earthly existence became impossible. In some cases, the assistant would literally have to hang from the cord to exert enough resistance.

Magical practices

The metal pendants generally represented the shaman's personal spirit helpers. These were often creatures, which might range from insects to large, powerful animals such as bears. The iron and brass disks or 'mirrors' are passages leading to a different world or universe. The fringes along the sleeves correspond to the wings of a bird and enable the shaman to 'fly'. Shamans would travel, pursuing a supernatural path on their quest to discover the reasons for misfortune, starvation, disease or death. Their task was to reverse these calamities, for which purpose they employed their supernatural powers.

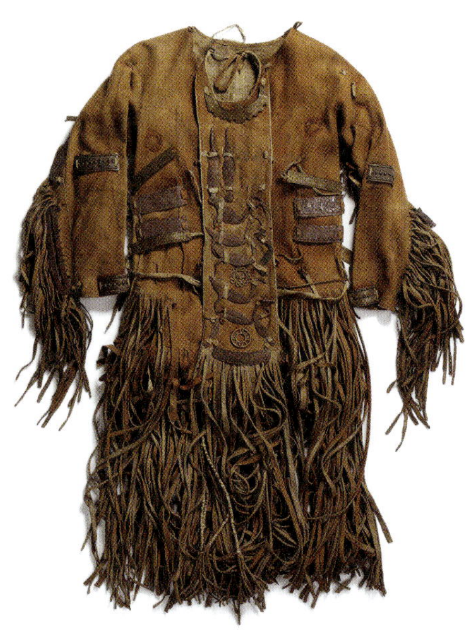

The invention of a tradition

Russian domination and seventy years of communism wrought immense harm, in both cultural and human terms. Shamans were prosecuted as *kulaks*, the rich. Many of them perished in Russian prisons. Their drums and coats were burned or taken to major museums. Today, Siberian minorities are endeavouring to revive their old traditions. Some possess the supernatural powers of their great-grandparents, shamans whom they never knew. In Tuva, and other parts of Siberia, clinics have been opened providing shamanist medical and psychological treatment.

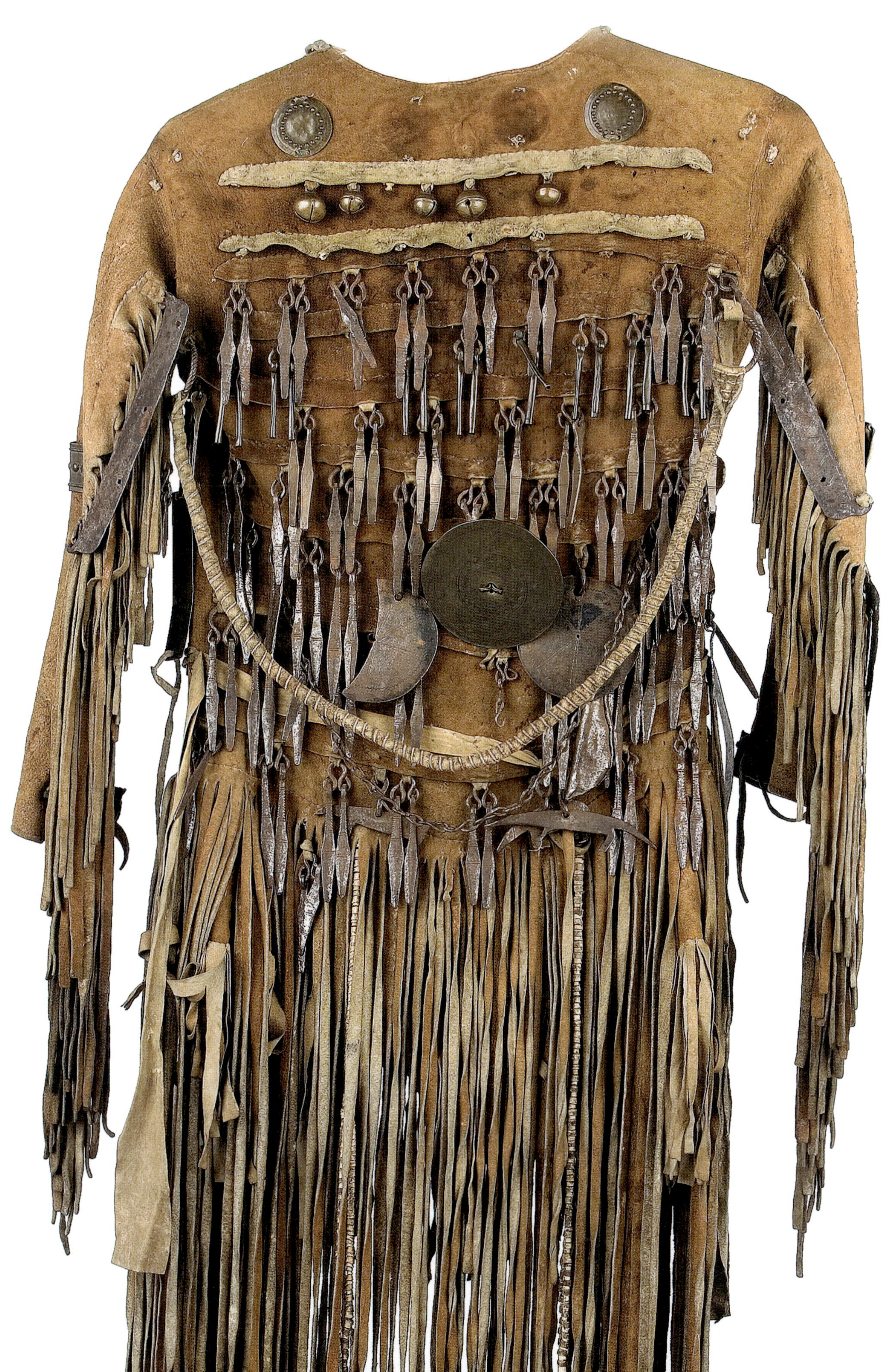

Wayang kulit Batara Guru, Brahma and Vishnu

Surakarta, Central Java, Indonesia
1856
h. 70 cm, 59 cm, 50 cm
leather, horn, paint, gold leaf
RMV 37- 726, RMV 37- 729, RMV 37- 730 (1856)

Divine puppets

The shapes of these three *wayang* puppets show that they represent important divinities. Their features are refined – with narrow lips, eyes and nose – and they wear richly decorated garments and a wealth of gold jewellery. Another characteristic accessory of a god's clothing is a crown with a protective bird's head motif (*garuda mungkur*) at the back. In addition, divine figures usually wear a long coat, a shoulder cloth, and long trousers. Their jewellery consists of ankle bracelets, rings on arms and fingers, necklaces and ear jewels.

Internal Administration

In 1856, the *controleur* (senior civil servant) W.L.A.H. Harloff in Surakarta, Central Java, ordered a large number of *wayang* puppets for use as educational material for prospective colonial officials, students at the Internal Administration course at the Royal Academy in Delft. After this institution was closed in 1864, the ethnography collection was moved to the Rijksmuseum Volkenkunde

Shadow puppets

Wayang is a kind of theatre that can be performed by human actors or puppets. *Wayang kulit* is played using leather puppets; accompanied by gamelan instruments, the puppeteer or dalang sits behind a screen and creates a shadow show on the spectators' side of the screen. *Wayang kulit* is most common on Java, but also occurs in other regions. A full *wayang kulit* set consists of hundreds of puppets, representing gods and demons, princes and servants, humans and animals. All *wayang* plays are about the struggle between good and evil. There is always a disruption of the cosmic equilibrium, but by the end of the performance, which may last for many hours, the balance has been restored.

Wayang purwa

Old myths and legends and the great Indian epic poems *Mahabharata* and *Ramayana* are acted out in *wayang purwa*. But *wayang* shows also depict local traditions and tales relating to Islam or to recent political developments. Hindu gods only play a role in the *wayang purwa* repertoire, for instance in Abiasa. In this story or *lakon*, the gods help the protagonist Raden Abiasa to press his claim to the throne of the realm of Astina.

Life cycle

The three puppets depict prominent Hindu gods: Brahma, Vishnu and Batara Guru. As Creator, Sustainer of Life, and Destroyer (making way for new life), respectively, the three gods (*Trimurti*) are collectively responsible for the life cycles on earth. Batara Guru, the Divine Teacher, is a manifestation of the supreme deity Shiva. Unlike the other two, his upper body is nude and he has four arms that cannot move. He stands on his mount, the bull Nandi. As supreme deity, the colour of his body is gold, and he wears a snake necklace. To his left stands a trident, while in his right hand he holds a lance tapering into a fly whisk at the top. Brahma's face and coat are red, since he is associated with fire. He is impatient by temperament, and therefore has rounder eyes than the other gods. The black colour that is associated with Vishnu recurs in his face and coat. Like Brahma, he wears a dagger or kris in his belt.

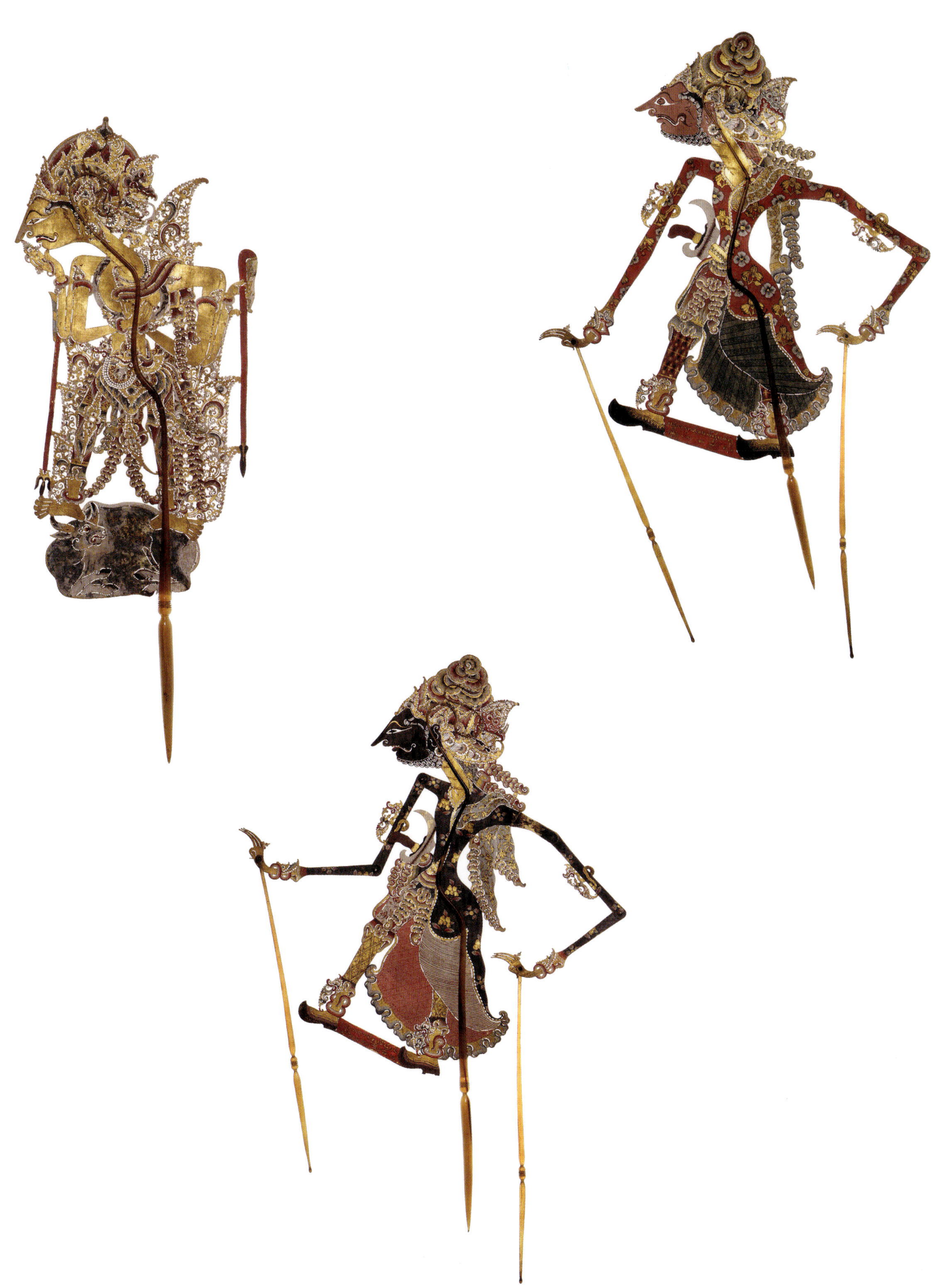

Magic staff (*Tunggal panaluan*)

Toba Batak; Northern Sumatra, Indonesia
1st half of 19th century
l. 2 m
wood, thread, cocks' feathers, iron
RMV 79-3 (1867)

A German baron

The collector of the oldest magic staff in the museum collection, Carl Benjamin Hermann Baron von Rosenberg (1817-1888), set sail for Sumatra in 1839 as a soldier. In the service of the Dutch East Indies Army, he was appointed as assistant to the naturalist Franz Junghuhn. In this capacity he built up a varied ethnography collection. He acquired this staff, which he donated to the museum in 1867, in the village of Huta Tinggi during an expedition in the Batak regions, in July 1843. In 1859 Von Rosenberg became a government researcher, after which he conducted scientific and ethnographic research in Sulawesi, the Lesser Sunda Islands, and the Moluccas.

The priest's attributes

In the traditional religion of the Batak, relations with the gods, spirits, and ancestors were maintained by a priest or *datu*, who was also a magical healer. His sacred knowledge of rituals was contained in divination books made from beaten bark (*pustaha*), which enabled him to determine favourable times for important events. He also owned a small jar containing magical ingredients or *pupuk* and diverse amulets. He himself cut the magic staff or *tunggal panaluan* from hard wood, ritually invested it with spiritual power and 'fed' it with sacrifices. The staff had an iron tip, with which it would be driven into the ground during rituals

Mix of religions

Most communities on the island of Sumatra are Muslim, but the Batak are an exception. The Toba, one of the six Batak ethnic groups, inhabit the heart of the Batak region, near Lake Toba. This is also the birthplace of the common mythological ancestor of the Batak peoples. The original religion of the Batak includes many Hindu influences, which arose through trading contacts with India and Hindu-Buddhist Sumatran and Javanese principalities. At the end of the seventeenth century, the Dutch established a trading post on the west coast of northern Sumatra. In the mid-nineteenth century, the first Christian missionaries settled in the Batak regions. As a result, Christianity is widespread among the Batak to this day.

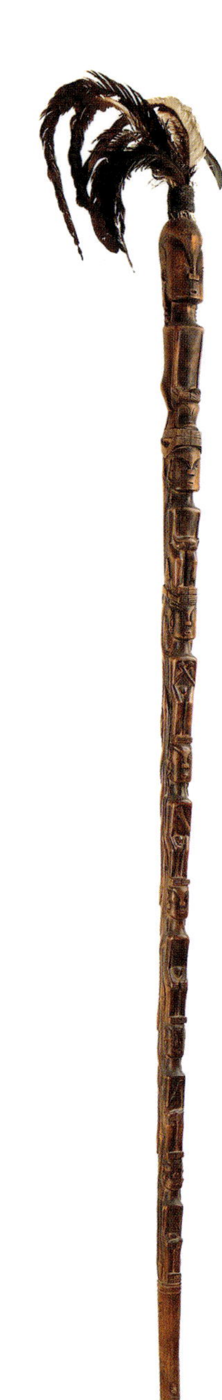

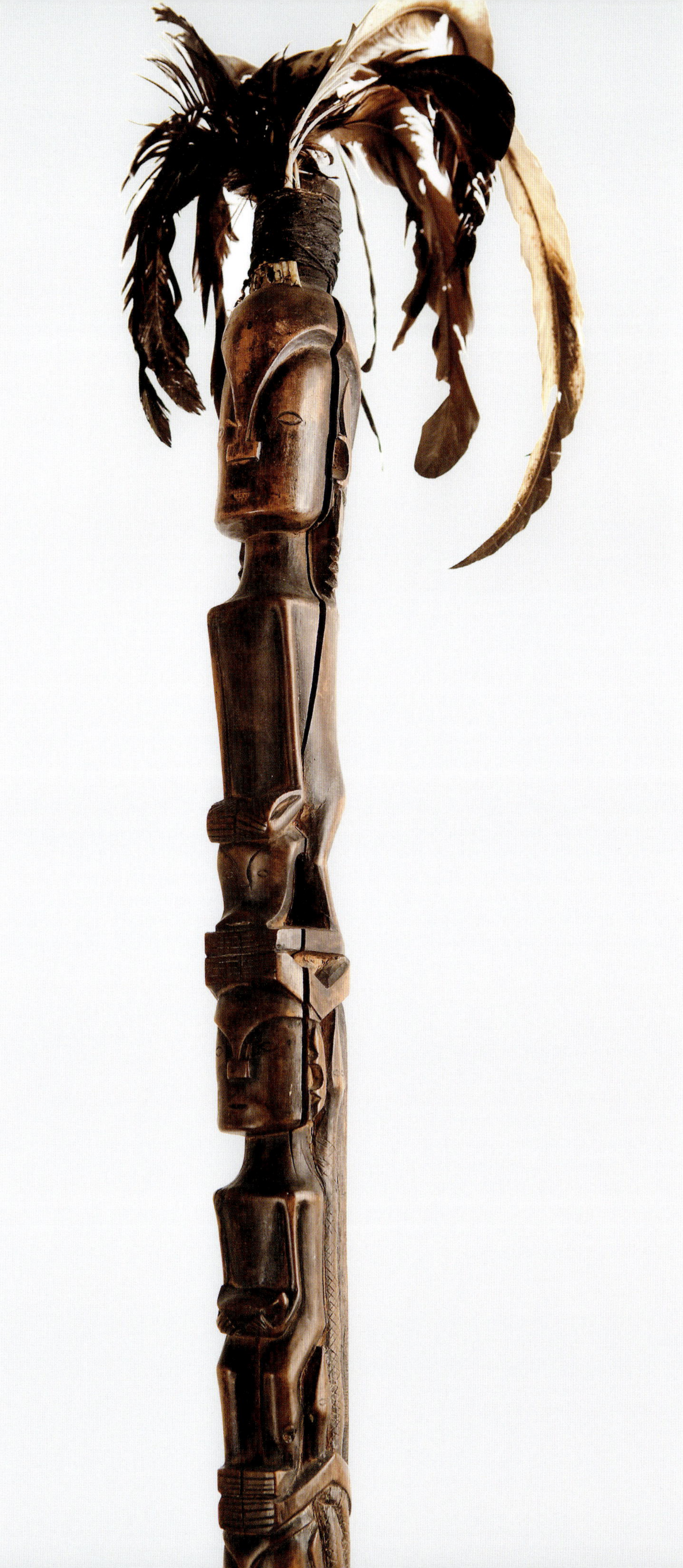

Clan property

The magic staffs probably originate from the region surrounding the mountain Pusuk Buhit, in the territory of the Toba Batak. Although the magic staff was among the *datu's* most important attributes, he did not own it. The staff belonged to a patrilineal group or clan (*marga*). This ownership was reflected in its use: priests used the *tunggal panaluan* in rituals pertaining to the community as a whole, thus safeguarding the continuity of the society. Examples include rituals enacted to ward off rain, war ceremonies, and rituals to suppress epidemics.

Incestuous twins

Like most other old *tunggal panaluan*, this staff widens somewhat towards the top, displaying seven human figures, standing one on top of the other. The man at the top has a headdress made of cocks' feathers. According to a creation myth, these figures depict twins who were turned into wood in punishment for their incestuous love, along with five followers and animal helpers. Carved into the back are entwined snakes and a lizard. In the Bataks' conceptual universe, the mythical snake supports the underworld; the name of the lizard, Boraspati, like Naga, is of Indian origin.

Sarong (*Sarung*)

Indo-European; Java, Indonesia
before 1878
216 x 112 cm
cotton, natural dyes
RMV 300-364 (1878)

Presentation of the colony in Paris

This batik cloth belongs to a large series of objects that was donated to the Rijksmuseum Volkenkunde in 1878 after the end of the Paris World's Fair. At this exhibition, the Netherlands presented itself by constructing a colonial pavilion, which focused on the latest developments in cottage industries in the archipelago. The Javanese batik industry was one of these. Indonesia is still proud of its batik production today. Like wayang, batik is on UNESCO's cultural world heritage list.

Entrepreneurship and conversion

The sarong was made in Banyumas (West Java), and comes from Van Oosterom's batik workshop. These *Batik Panastroman*, as they were called, were known primarily in West Java. The Indo-European craftswoman Catharina Carolina Van Oosterom-Philips was born in Salatiga in 1816. Widowed at an early age and obliged to earn her own living, Catharina van Oosterom started up a batik company in Banyumas, where she had celebrated her marriage in 1832. Besides being a highly successful entrepreneur, she was also eager to propagate the Christian faith among the local population. She used to read to her batik employees from the Bible as they worked.

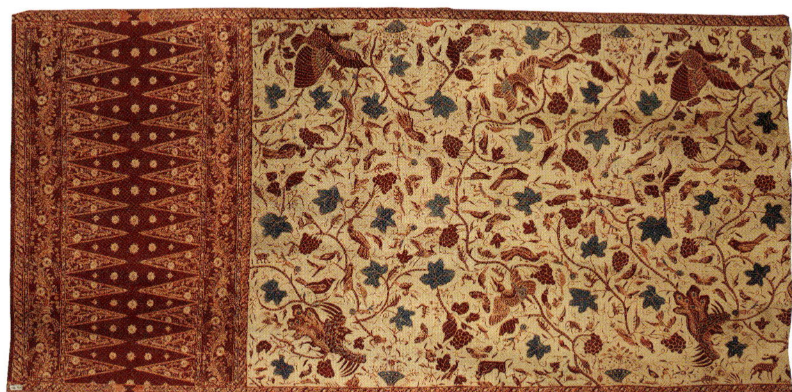

Drawn in wax

The typical Javanese technique used to decorate this cloth is called batik. In batik, the motifs are created by placing liquid wax on certain parts of the cloth, so that when the cloth is immersed in a basin of dye, these sections are not coloured. This process is repeated using different colours, and the wax is removed by boiling. This cloth has been decorated by the technique of *batik tulis* ('written batik'); the wax has been applied using a *canting*, a small spouted container. Wax motifs can also be stamped onto the cloth, in a technique known as *batik cap*.

Batik Belanda

This cloth is a fine example of Batik Belanda, cloths that were made for sale by Indo-European companies. The motifs were inspired in part by indigenous patterns and in part by European motifs. A combination of diverse animals, as on this cloth, is called in Javanese *alas-alasan*, 'all kinds of creatures in the forest', and represents cosmic totality. The bunches of grapes and vine leaves are typically European. The colours of the cloth are also significant. The white background signifies that the sarong must be worn in the evening, and the bright red with few blue accents indicates that the cloth is intended to be worn by young brides.

Batik hip cloth

When the two ends of this elongated cloth are sewn together, the result is a cylindrical skirt or *sarung*, a garment that is wound around the hips. The central section of the cloth, with a pattern of red and blue birds, four-footed creatures, butterflies, vine leaves, and bunches of grapes against a white background, is called the *badan* (body). The *badan* is always enclosed by a narrow border with small motifs, the *pinggir*. The end, consisting of two rows of triangles, filled with 'young bamboo shoots' (*pucuk rebung*), is called the *kepala* (head). The rectangles on either side of the triangles, likewise filled with floral motifs, are called the *papan* (board).

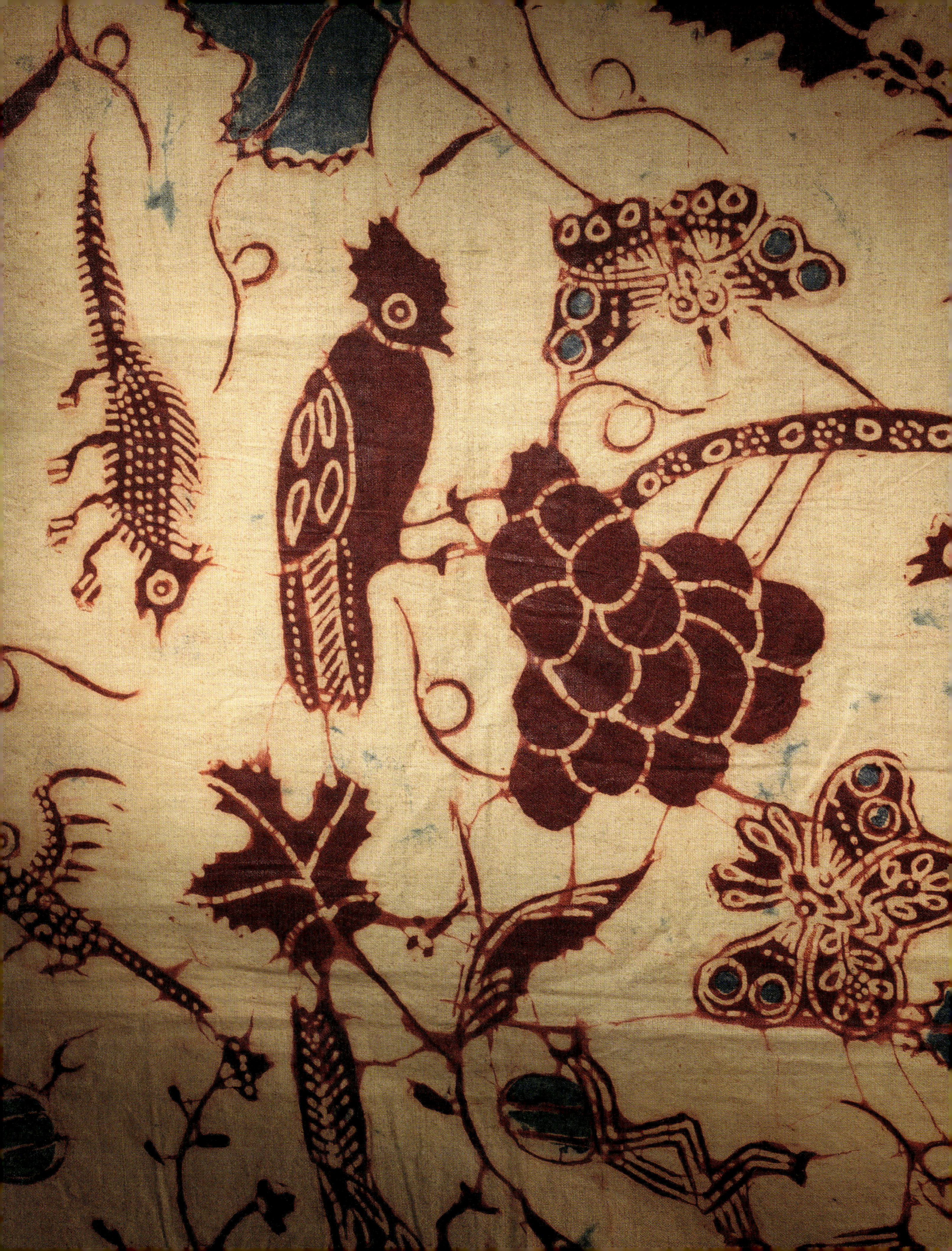

Kris and shoulder cloth

Sulu Archipelago and Sultanate Brunei Darussalam
1st half of 19th century
kris: l. 67 cm, blade: l. 50 cm; scabbard: l. 53 cm; fabric: 236 x 79 cm
kris: iron, nickel, silver; scabbard: ivory, horn; fabric: silk, gold thread

RMV 261-1, RMV 261-4 (1881)

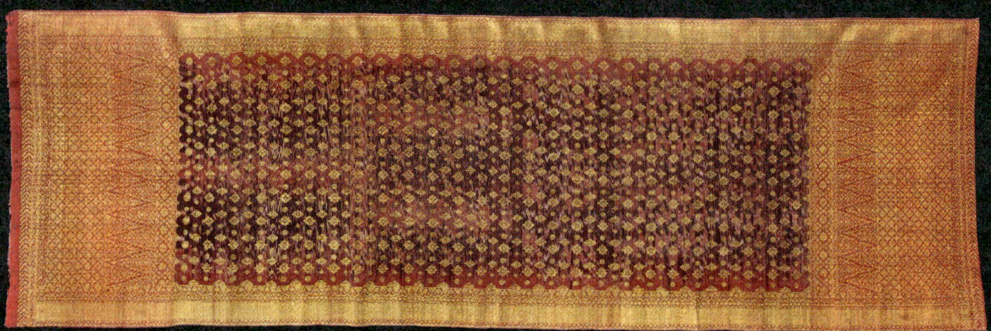

Letter from the Minister
The following letter from the museum archives explains how series 264 entered the museum's collection.

"To curator Mr L. Serrurier in charge of the management of the National Ethnographic Museum, regarding gifts from the Sultan of Brunei

The Hague, 3 January 1881

According to information received from my colleague, the Minister of Colonies, His Majesty's Steamship Atjeh visited the north coast of Borneo in May last year, and, as is customary in such meetings with native rulers in the Eastern Archipelago, certain gifts were offered to the Sultan of Brunei (Borneo Proper) on behalf of the government of the Dutch East Indies. The Sultan in his turn presented the following gifts:
1. Two kains (native garments) made in Brunei, interwoven with gold thread,
2. A Soloh kris (native dagger), and
3. A parang (large native knife).
I have the honour to send you herewith these objects, which I received from my said fellow minister and which are rightly destined, pursuant to the royal decree issued by government missive no. 46 of 23 December 1880, to be placed in the State Museum of Ethnography, with the request to incorporate them into the collection and to notify me that they have been duly received.

Secretary General of the Interior
For the Minister of the Interior'

Kris from the Sulu Archipelago
The 'Soloh kris (native dagger)' comes from the Sulu Archipelago, now part of the Philippines, which lies to the north of Brunei and was part of this sultanate until 1888. The blade of this ceremonial weapon has five curves, and the *pamor* – the pattern that arises as a result of the forging of iron and nickel together – is wavy. The scabbard is made of reddish brown burnished wood, combined with black horn. The ivory upper side of the hilt is carved in the shape of a stylised bird's head, a characteristic feature of krisses from this region.

Shoulder cloth from Brunei
The 'native garment made in Brunei' is a red silk cloth worn over the shoulder, woven with a rich quantity of gold thread, in the *songket* technique. In this technique, threads wound around with gold are inserted in between the weft threads of the fabric during the weaving process, following a pattern determined in advance, to form the decorative motifs. In the past, this intricate process was practised primarily at the royal courts in Southeast Asia. The silk and the gold thread originated from China. The central section of the cloth is decorated with star figures, while the gold thread pattern at either end consists of a row of triangles and small lozenges known as *mas-masan* ('golden').

Male and female
In the cultural region of Southeast Asia, rulers and other dignitaries frequently exchanged gifts to affirm and maintain good relations. Decorative weapons were popular gifts, usually in combination with beautifully decorated fabrics. In the conceptual universe of many ethnic groups inhabiting the islands of Southeast Asia, weapons and metal objects represent the male aspect of society, while fabrics or garments represent the female aspect. These two categories of objects were made by men and women respectively. The combination of weapons and cloths, as in this gift from the Sultan of Brunei, therefore constitutes a harmonious, unified whole.

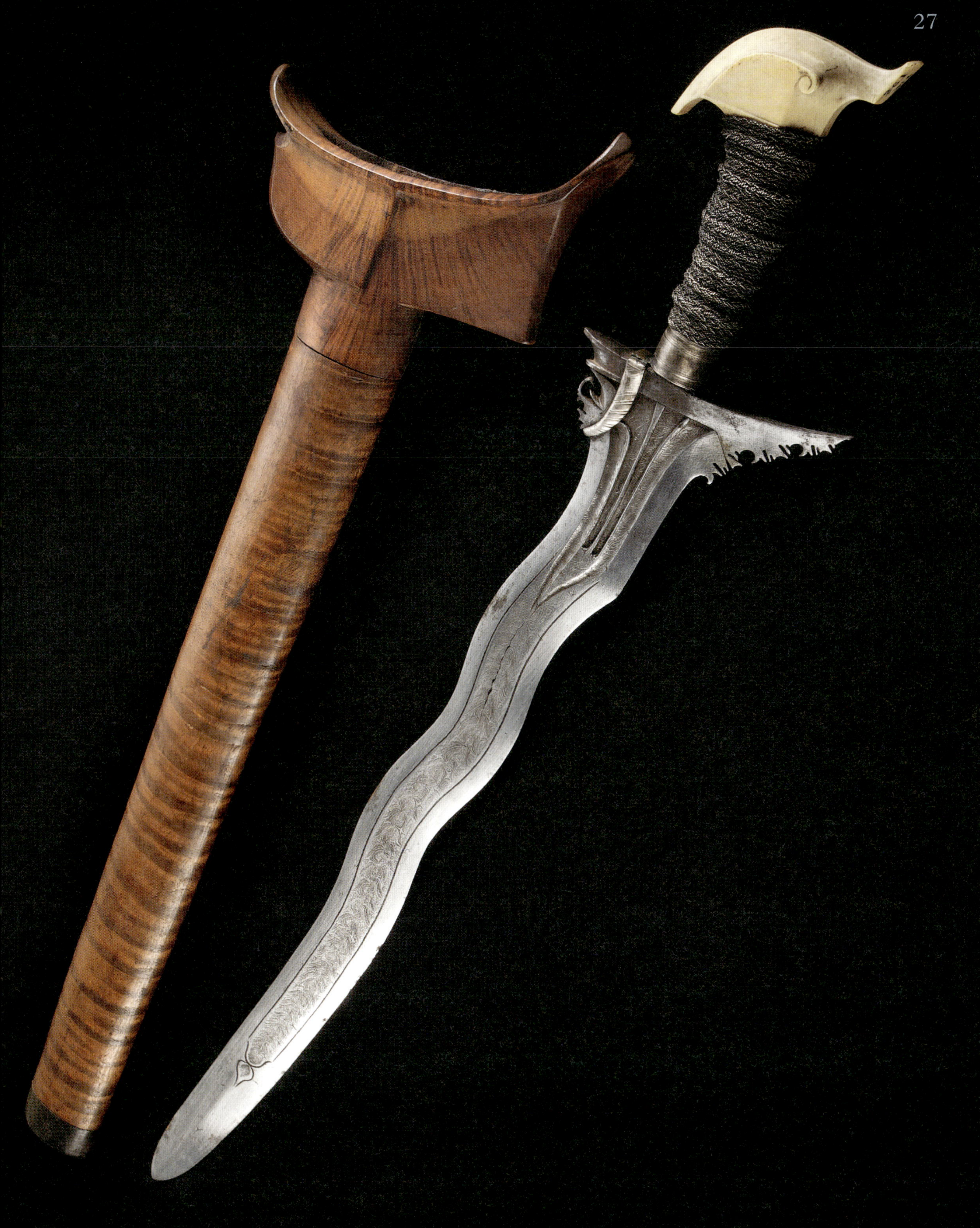

Sea chart (*Meddo*)

Marshall Islands
before 1882
149 x 78,5 cm
bamboo, tree bark, coconut fibre
RMV 316-94 (1882)

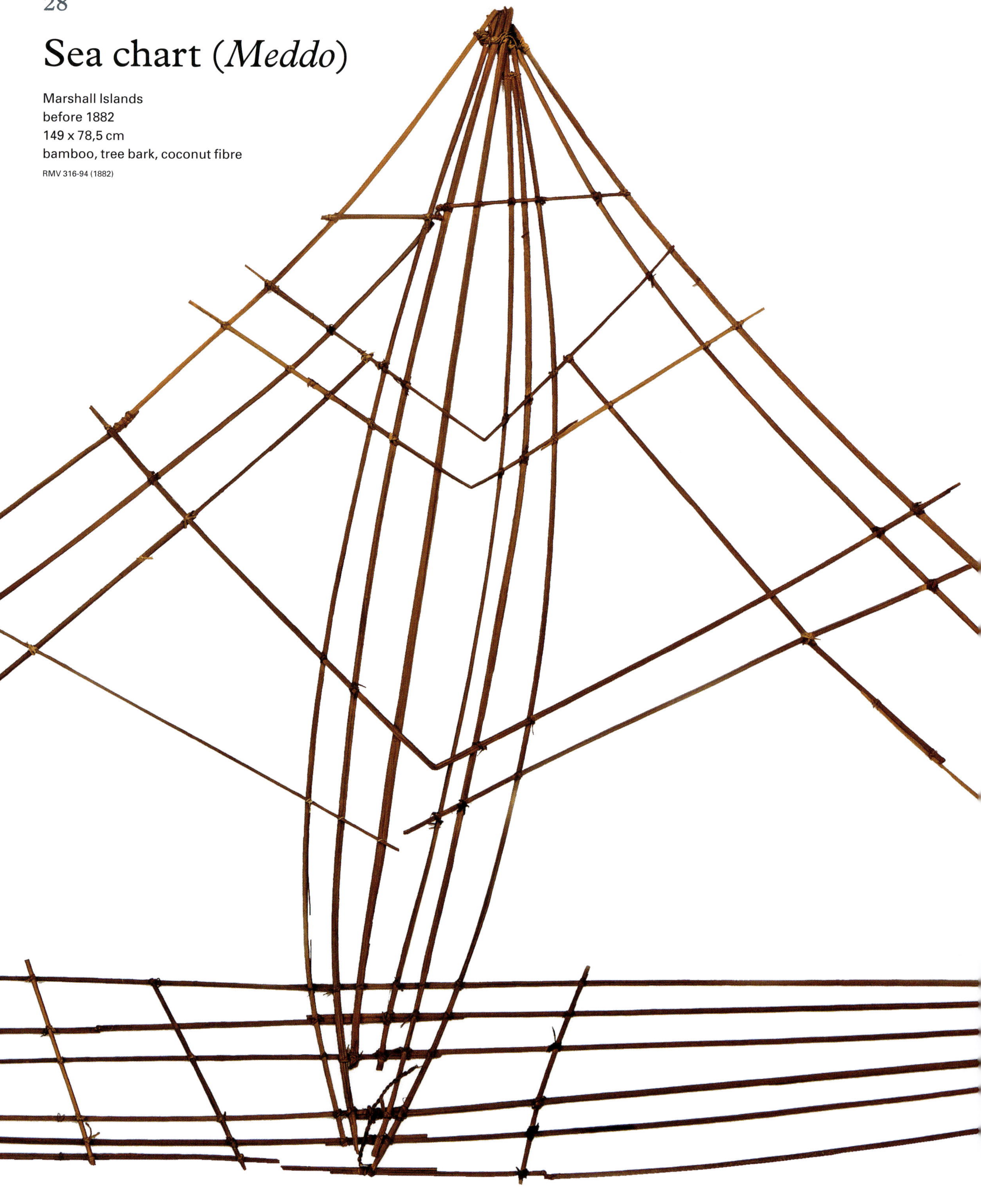

Stick chart

This sea chart or *meddo* from the Marshall Islands is composed of thin bamboo sticks bound together with bark fibre. Long and short sticks are used to represent swells, sea currents and waves, while the coconut fibre knots indicate islands. It is more common, however, for islands to be denoted by shells. The absence of shells makes this chart highly unusual.

Mnemonic device

Sea charts from the Marshall Islands were not used in the same way as Western charts, but instead served as mnemonic devices. Before undertaking a sea voyage, sailors would commit to memory the swell patterns, sea currents, and islands depicted on the chart. Since a *meddo* places the islands as they should be seen in relation to the sea currents, it disregards the actual distance between the islands. Charts were made as the need arose, and only the maker could interpret them. Even experienced seamen could not make anything of the chart without the maker's explanation.

Unique documentation

The first Westerner to write about the use of these sea charts was the missionary Luther Halsey Gulick Sr, in 1862. When this sea chart was donated in 1882 by J. Rohlfs and Captain F. Rohlfs of Hamburg, it was accompanied by exceptionally good documentation. From this we know the names of the islands depicted on the chart, for instance: the coral atolls of Namorik, Jaluit, Kili, Ebon and Ailinglaplap, all of which lie in the Ralik Archipelago of the Marshall Islands.

Secret knowledge

Anyone embarking on a sea voyage needed to have a sound knowledge of the art of navigation. This knowledge, distilled from the careful observation of marine phenomena, was a well-guarded secret, which was only passed on within certain prominent families. How do swells change closer to land? How do two sea currents react to each other in the vicinity of an island? Other elements to be taken into account included the refraction and reflection of light by the surface of the water, the formation of shadows, and the behaviour of waves. Expert masters of the art of navigation therefore enjoyed great prestige and high status within the community.

Queen of palms

The small islands are denoted by knots in the coconut fibre. The coconut palm is a versatile plant that is used for a variety of purposes. The juice of unripe coconuts is a refreshing beverage, the flesh can be converted into soap, oil, and a variety of culinary ingredients, while the hard outer shell can be turned into a bowl or burned as firewood. Ropes are twined from coconut fibre. The trunk is used as a beam, a mast, for water drainage, and to make furniture. The leaves can serve as roofing material or be woven into baskets. Coconuts also have a range of medicinal applications.

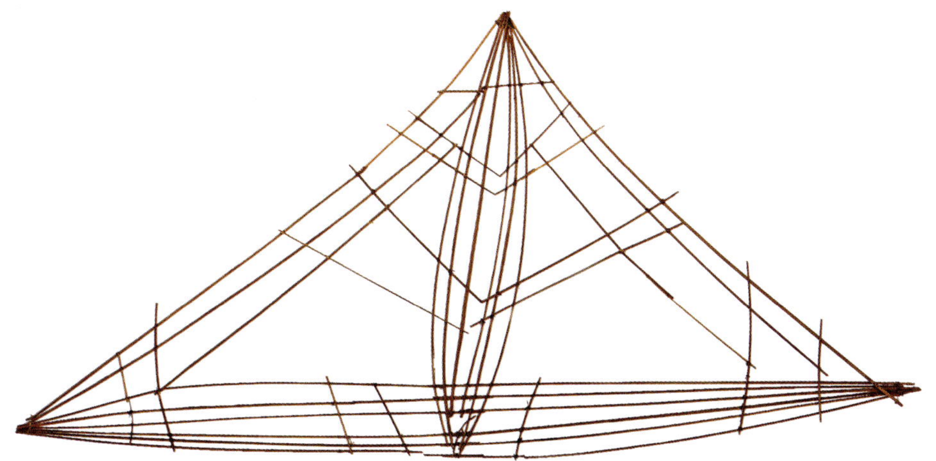

Gorget (*Taumi*)

Society Islands, French Polynesia
before 1882
53 x 62 x 2,5 cm
vegetable fibres, shark teeth, dog hair, feathers
RMV 330-5 (1882)

Composite object
This U-shaped gorget or *taumi* has been made from numerous different materials. Against a background of woven plant fibres, three rows of black feathers have been attached, each with a hem of shark teeth. Encircling the object are tufts of Polynesian dog hair. One of the six original mother-of-pearl discs is still present.

Scientific expedition
The naturalist Henry Nottidge Moseley sold this object to the Rijksmuseum Volkenkunde in 1882. He probably acquired it during the scientific expedition of *HMS Challenger*, which made a long sea voyage for the purpose of studying the oceans between 1872 and 1876. From 18 September to 3 October 1875 the team of scientists stayed in Tahiti to research the water and sea creatures there. Von Willemoes Suhm died on this voyage. He was a former pupil of Philipp Franz Balthasar von Siebold, the founder of the Rijksmuseum Volkenkunde

Revenge and power
In Polynesia, war played an important part in maintaining leaders' power and prestige. Wars were sometimes motivated by a desire for revenge, or sprang from ceremonial rivalries between villages. This gorget from Tahiti, a prestigious object, was presented as a tribute to the ruling *ali'i*, the most important chiefs. These leaders were believed to embody ancestral gods.

The power of the shark
The gorget was worn by Tahitian military leaders and their foremost warriors. The U-shape may possibly have been intended to represent a shark's jaws, so that the wearer would take on the shark's powers by putting it around his neck. Some researchers believe that a *taumi* was also used as a shield in single combat. Others see the gorget rather as protection for the chest and shoulders, shielding the vital organs from assaults by stones and other projectiles. In any case, the gorget was an emblem of the wearer's aristocratic status, and would be seized by the victors as part of the spoils of war.

On dogs, shells, sharks and birds
According to early eye-witness accounts, the dog hair and mother-of-pearl shells came from the Tuamotu Archipelago, and probably reached Tahiti in the magnificent double hull canoes that were built by the masterful Tuamotu carpenters and joiners. Well into the nineteenth century, far-flung trading networks linked the Marquesas Islands, the Tuamotus and Mangareva to the Society Islands. In addition to shark teeth, feathers too were highly prestigious materials, not least because people believed that a deity that alighted on sanctuaries in the form of a bird was closely connected with mortal leaders.

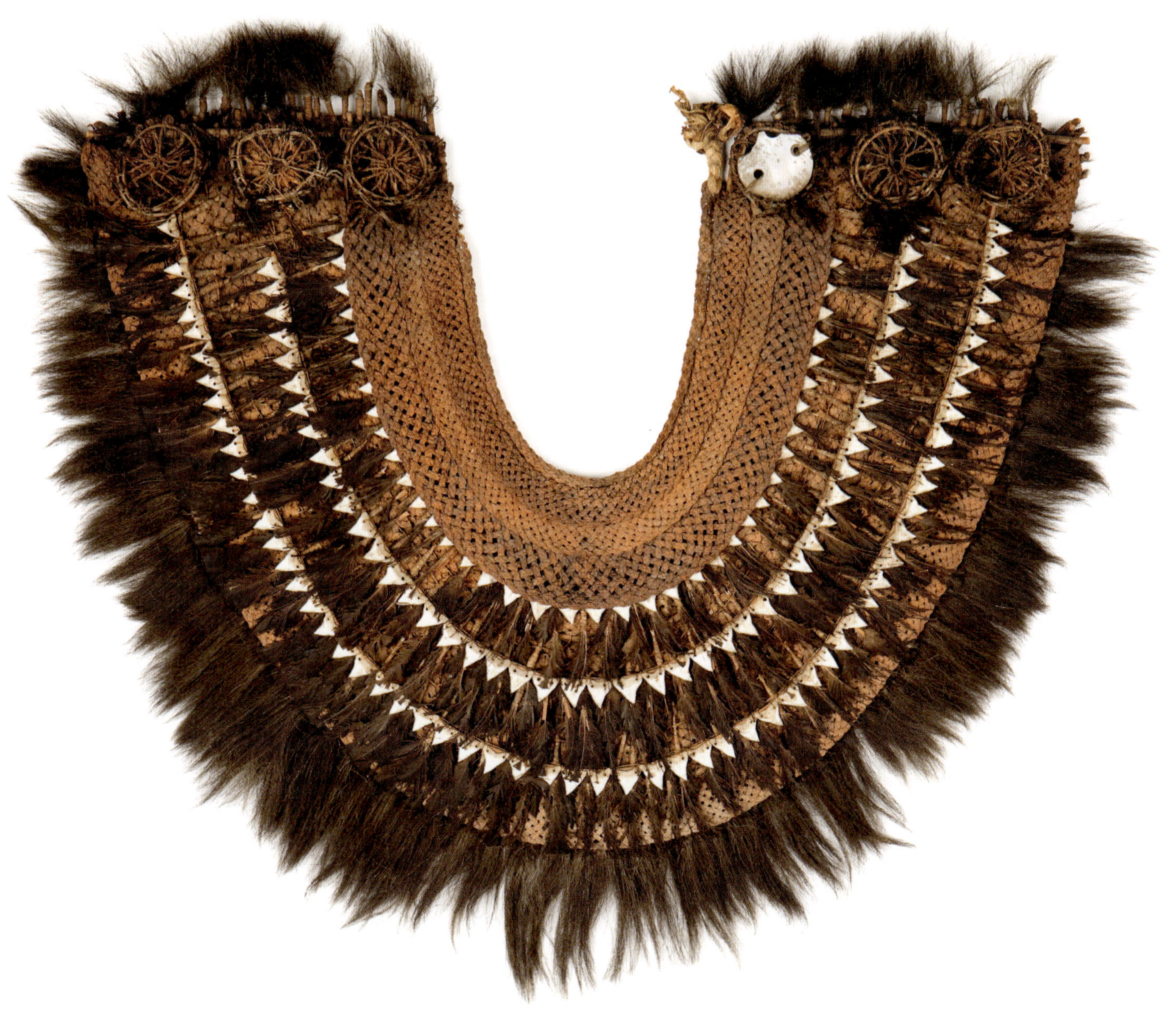

Boot liners

China
18th century
l. 50 cm
satin, cotton, ink and colour pigments
RMV 360 609 (1883)

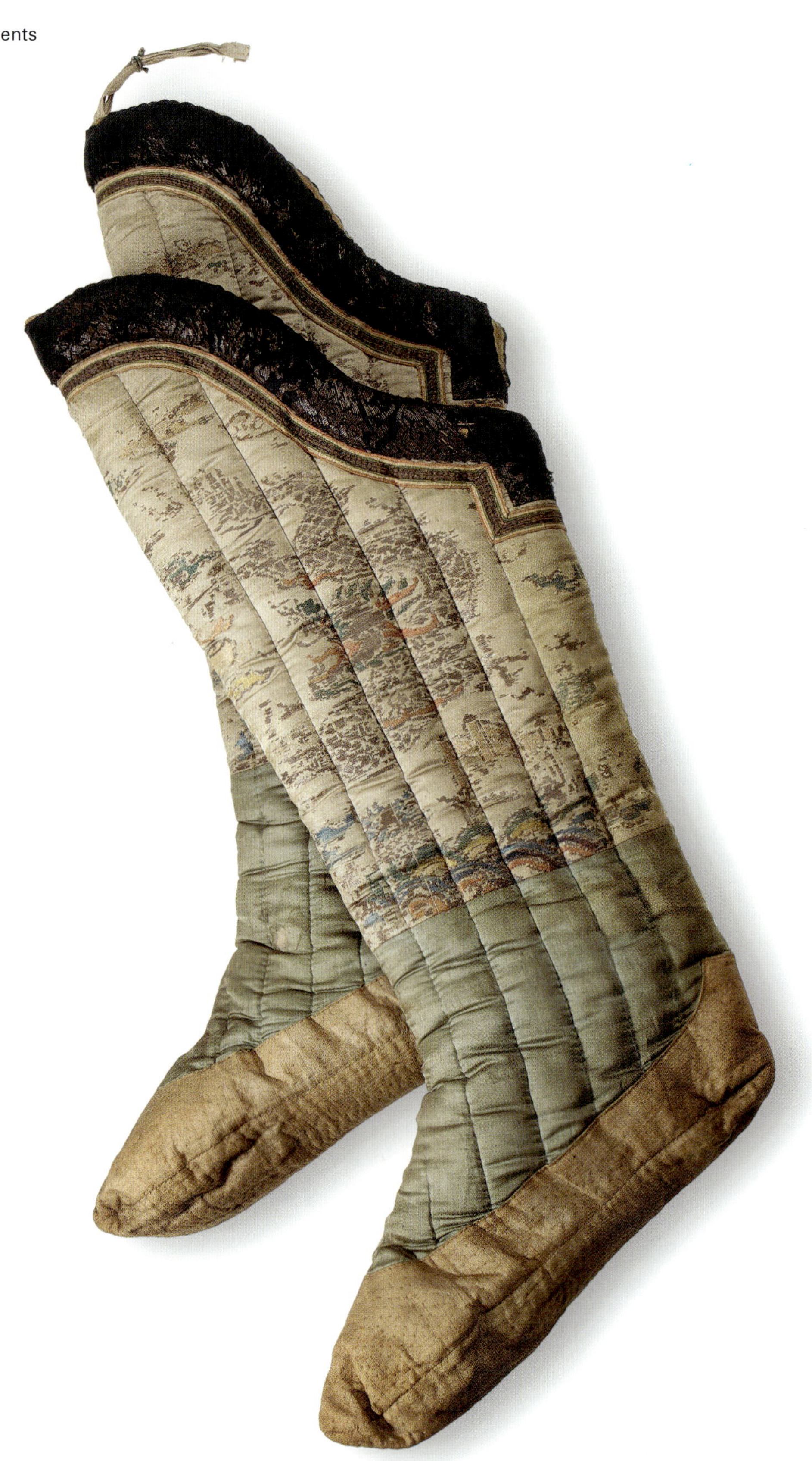

A landscape on your feet

These liners for boots rise along their front edge in line with the style of boots into which they fitted. Boot liners, which insulated the feet like socks, were a category of winter wear for high-class men. Although faced with satin, the liners' insulation was provided by padded cotton (now mostly lost), a manufacture that all classes of Chinese society used in one form or another during the cold season. Remarkably, however, these liners are also embroidered with a landscape.

A widow's gift

The first known Dutch collector of these boot liners was the Dutch lawyer Jean Theodore Royer (1737-1807). Royer did not visit China, but he devoted huge energy to learn the Chinese language and to compile a lexicon of its words based sometimes on objects in his collection. Eventually, Royer's widow presented his collection of Chinese curiosities to Willem I. In an accompanying inventory, she describes the liners: "a pair of sewn men's socks of coloured satin". Although accurate, this description of a female art does not take into account that its inspiration was the predominantly male practice of landscape painting.

Intriguing the court

Royer's suppliers of objects were usually involved in trade with China. Those who actually sailed there probably purchased exotica in the great trading port of Canton (Guangzhou). Whoever acquired these boot liners secured a sartorial expression of elegance central to the self image of the Chinese elite whose language so fascinated Royer. It is possible that when Royer conducted Tan Assoy, a Chinese visitor to The Netherlands, to meet Stadhouder Willem V and Princess Wilhelmina of Prussia – in a classic live performance of ethnography – he may have persuaded Tan to wear this footwear in order to intrigue and instruct also the Dutch court.

Matching status with clothing

These liners belonged no doubt to an official – or to a man who wished to appear as such – whose status dictated certain grades of clothing. Even though horses were hardly a feature of life in the more populous south, boots denoted the equestrian life and its association with ruling-class status. Liners materialized a personal statement safely hidden from view during contact with the outside world. At less formal moments indoors, the painted fabric might be on show, especially if the wearer sat on furniture that revealed his fashionably dressed shins to best advantage.

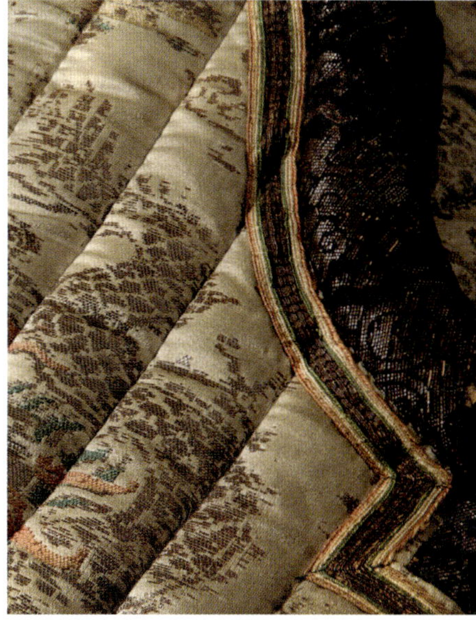

Cultural pursuits of the elites

This embroidery reveals the extent to which both the genre of landscape and a representational medium, directly inspired by painting, were deemed fit forms of decoration for the body. Moreover, a reference to painting – the cultural pursuit of many educated men and a smaller number of women – complicates the social history of clothing. Since most preserved clothing in the late imperial period was embroidered predominantly by women, the notion of painting proposes an art for the body done by either men or women on behalf of men. The suggested role of a painter also enhanced the liners' status as an unique edition.

Sake bowl

Edo period, Japan
1800-1823
bowl: diam. 8.4 cm, h. 3.3 cm; ring-shaped stand: diam. 3.2 cm, h. 1.2 cm
wood (maple), gold lacquer, turned work
RMV 360-2048 (1883)

A sake bowl for autumn

This sake bowl, *sakazuki*, was turned on a lathe or *rokuro* from maple wood. The inside is decorated with two maple leaves in autumn colours, applied in flat lacquerware. Because of its fine, red-coloured leaves, the maple or *momiji* is directly associated with autumn, which is enhanced in this bowl by the gold lacquer decorations with a hint of red. For those who had refined taste and liked to display it, this little bowl was ideally suited to *tsukimi*, festivals held in the eighth month, in which groups of friends would gather to sit on benches and enjoy the full moon – with a bottle of sake, of course.

Made in Kyoto

We know from a note written by Fisscher that the people of the Hakone mountain region, which the Dutchmen passed through on their court journey, specialised in turned work. Fisscher writes: 'It is in this place [Hakone] and in these mountains, that the finest works of art are made in lacquerware, carvings and turned work; and no one can resist the temptation to buy them, when entering the storehouses here'. The quality of the lacquerware, however, indicates that this piece was actually made in Kyoto. This theory is supported by an inscription in gold lacquer on the foot of the dish, stating that it was 'made from the wood of a maple from Takao in Heian', the classical name for Kyoto.

Blomhoff's sake bowls

In the catalogue of his Japanese collection, Blomhoff listed this bowl under the heading 'Section 30: Domestic items', as 'Eight different Sackysike [=*sakazuki*] or drinking bowls, most of them in red lacquer with gold figures, figurines, flowers etc., including one in yellow lacquer and one very large one'. Nine of the ten sake bowls in the Rijksmuseum Volkenkunde's Blomhoff collection are indeed in red lacquer, and some have gold lacquer. The yellow lacquer bowl is evidently this small bowl, in transparent lacquer. The 'very large one' is unfortunately missing. We do know, however, that it was 15.5 cm in diameter – indeed much bigger than the rest, which all have diameters ranging between 8.3 and 9.8 cm.

Bowls for New Year's celebrations

Most of the bowls are particularly suitable for use around the New Year, because of their decorations, with motifs such as *minogame* or 'ten-thousand-year-old tortoises'. Ancient toadstools and cranes at the waterside beneath an old pine tree also symbolise long life, as do young pines in the fog, alluding to the classical custom of going into the countryside on New Year's Day to pick young pines.

Maple wood

The *momiji* is one of the twenty-odd varieties of the maple species known in Japan. In contrast to European and American varieties, Japanese maple trees do not grow much above twelve metres in height. Their beautiful red autumn leaves make these trees popular in parks around houses and in temple gardens. Their gleaming, silky, yellowish-white wood displays clear growth rings and has very delicate, dense grain. It makes excellent wood for carving, turning or bending, and is ideally suited to small items of furniture such as tables and cabinets.

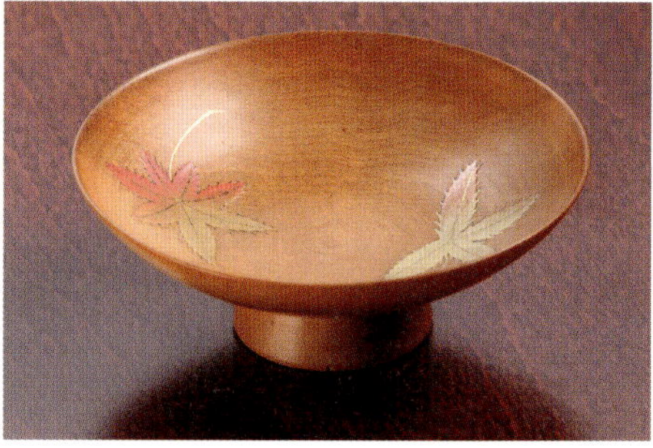

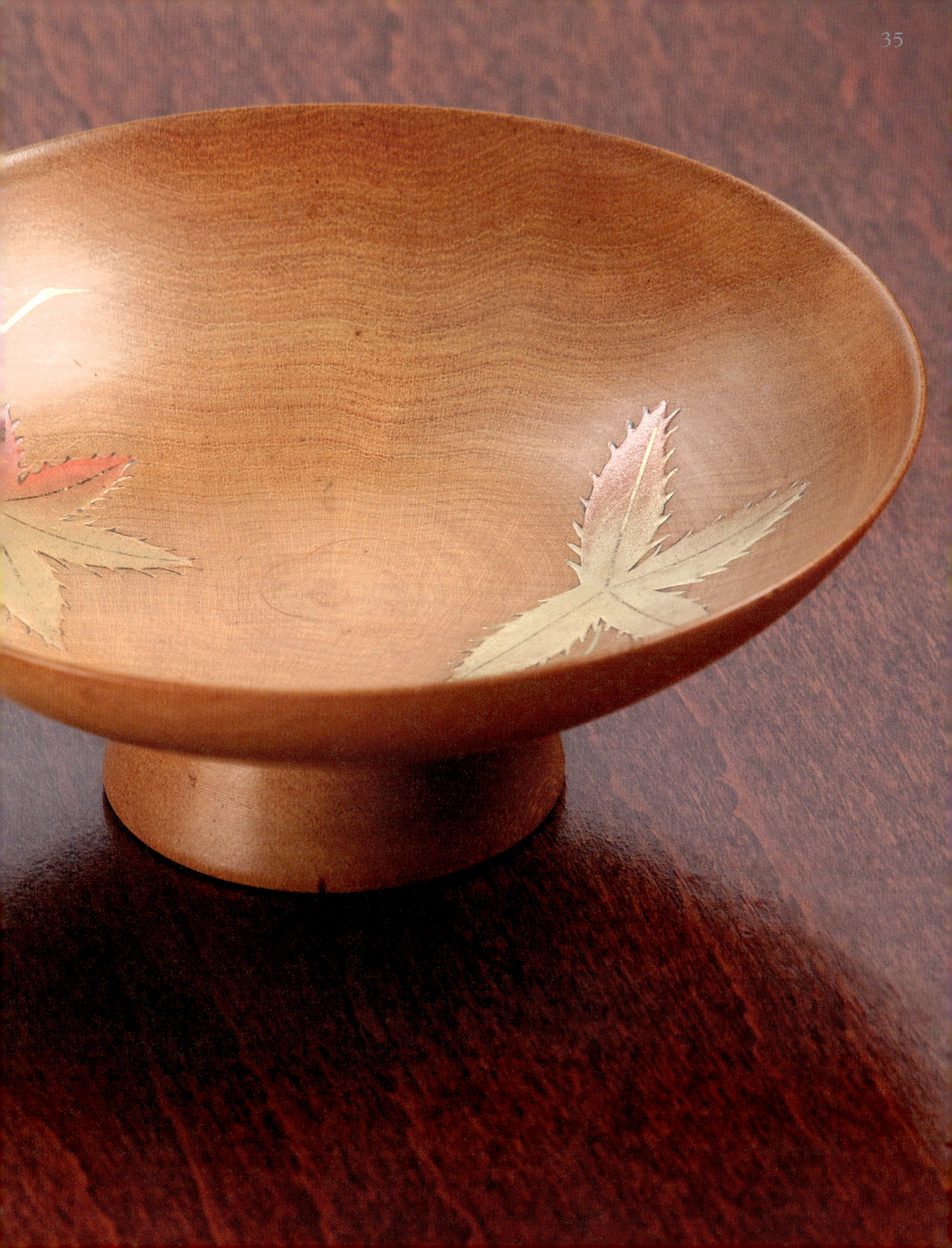

War club

Algonquin; Delaware, United States
c. 1650
l. 55,5 cm
maple wood
RMV 360-1579 (1883)

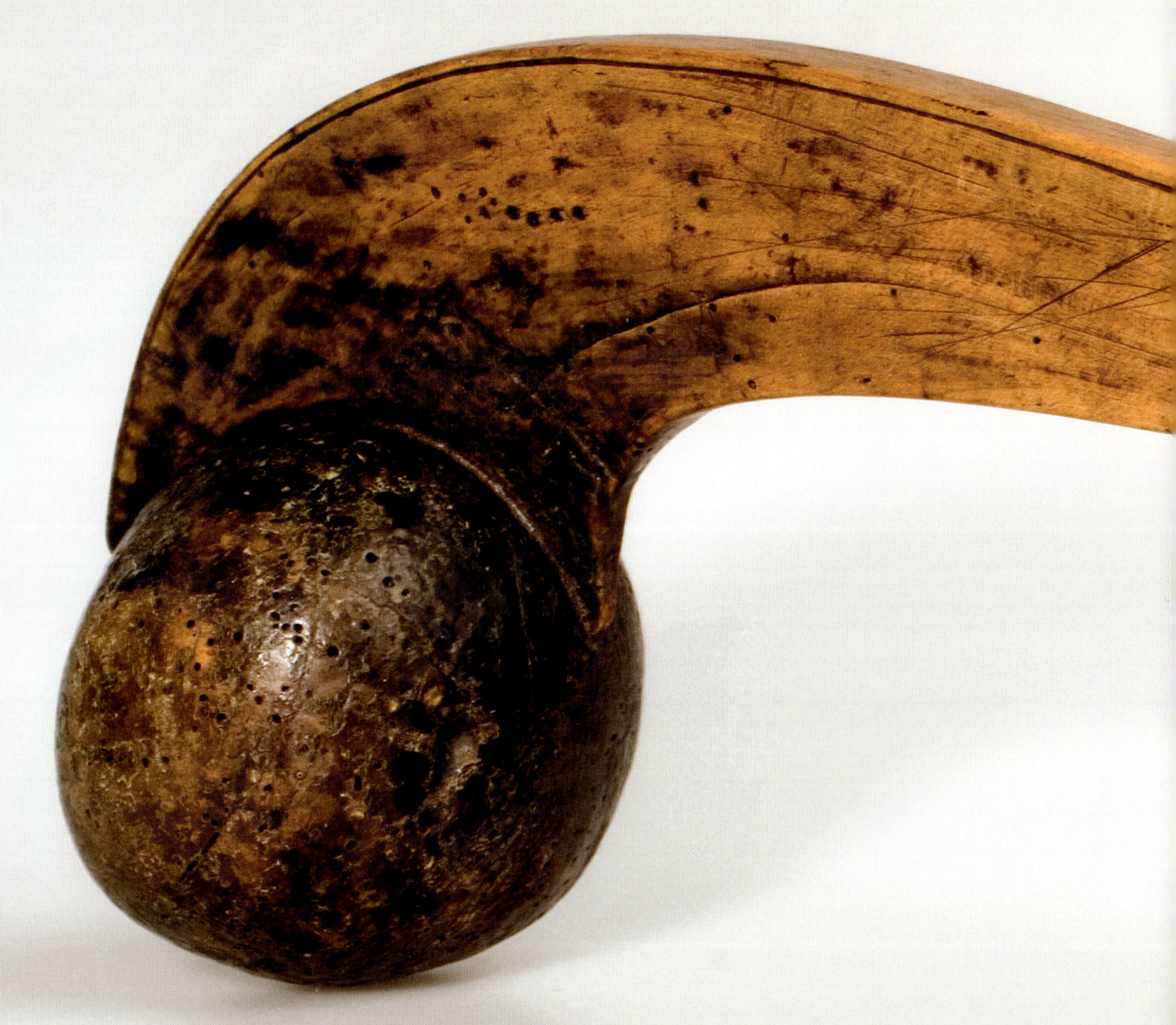

Unique

This is possibly the only Native American object to have been preserved in the Netherlands from the period of the Dutch colonisation of the region along the North American Hudson and Delaware Rivers (1609-1664). Others – such as garments made of hide and fur and woven belts with wampum shells that ended up in the Netherlands in that period – either perished with the ravages of time or vanished. For numerous collections were sold abroad after the owner's death, and the provenance details were generally lost.

Collections

The origin of this club can be established with a degree of probability verging on certainty, on the basis of historical documents. Before 1681 it was in the anatomy collection of the University of Leiden, which also contained a number of objects of ethnography. When it disappeared from the inventory of that collection, an identical club suddenly appeared in the Royal Cabinet of Rarities in The Hague. It can be assumed that this is the same object, partly because ethnographic objects frequently changed hands. In 1883 the club was transferred to the Rijksmuseum Volkenkunde, along with other ethnographic specimens.

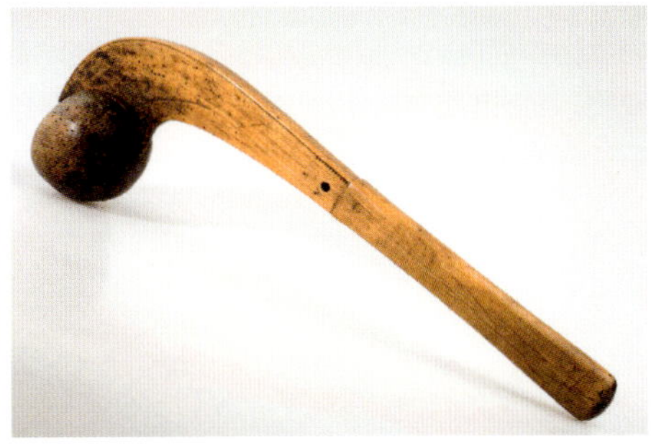

Weapons

Dutch chroniclers with first-hand experience of New Netherland and its indigenous population frequently referred to the weapons that were used. Thus, the Reverend Johannes Megapolensis (1651) discussed the use of bows and arrows, stone axes, and wooden war hammers. Adriaen van der Donck, who visited the Mohawk tribe in 1655, saw warriors with war clubs and rectangular shields. He noted that guns and iron battle-axes were starting to replace traditional weapons. From these chronicles, we know that the small triangular notches along the top of the club, from the haft, were more common on the seventeenth-century war clubs of the Algonquins and Iroquois.

War and peace

The club is a remnant from a raw history between Native Americans and Dutch in New Netherland, a period of maladministration and armed conflict. The struggle for farmland and violent incidents triggered by heavy drinking caused tensions to run high. The club probably came from a group of Esopus Indians who attacked Wiltwyck on 7 June 1663 in revenge for the deportation of Indian prisoners of war to Curaçao by the governor, Peter Stuyvesant. The Dutch mounted a counter-attack, in which almost all the Esopus were killed. It was probably from one of these battles that Blom acquired the war club. Subsequently a new peace treaty was signed, and the few surviving Esopus joined the neighbouring Wappinger tribe.

Reverend Blom

Herman Blom, a Protestant minister in Woubrugge, donated a Native American war club and a North American giant crab to Leiden's anatomy collection after returning in 1668 from New Netherland, the Dutch colony on the east coast of North America. From 1660 onwards he had worked as the Church minister of Wiltwyck, a village of Dutch immigrants on the Hudson River. The name of Wiltwyck (from the Dutch for 'wild neighbourhood') derived from the presence of hostile American Indians, the Esopus, in that district. The Dutch settlement was sometimes referred to by that Indian name. The Esopus were a Delaware tribe, and this nation's northernmost representatives.

Adinkra cloth

Asante, Ghana
before 1825
271 x 212 cm
cotton
RMV 360-1700 (1883)

The oldest known *adinkra* cloth

This cotton cloth, decorated with black lines and symbols, is one of the oldest known pieces of textile – along with one dating from 1817 in the British Museum – to have been printed and painted in the *adinkra* technique.
No old fabrics of this kind can be found, unfortunately, in museums or cultural institutions in Ghana. It used to be extremely difficult to conserve them: Ghana's climatic conditions are highly detrimental to textiles. For this reason, old textiles produced here are extremely rare.

St George d'Elmina Castle

On 23 September 1825, the Interim Commander of the Dutch possessions on the Coast of Guinea, Major F.F.L.U. Last, despatched this textile from St George d'Elmina Castle on the Gold Coast (now Ghana) to the Royal Cabinet of Rarities in The Hague. Little is known about the background of this superb cloth, but the interim commander probably commissioned it as a gift for King William I. This hypothesis is supported by the striking painted symbol in the middle, which greatly resembles the Netherlands' national coat of arms. Still, this coat of arms is the only unusual element; the other motifs are customary in older *adinkras*.

Adinkra printing technique

In the *adinkra* technique, bark from trees is boiled down, after which crushed ferriferous stone is added, creating the black ink that is used to print the cotton fabric. A grid of lines is applied, after which the resulting rectangles are filled in using stamps. These stamps are generally made from gourds, from which the maker carves or gouges out motifs. Many of the motifs represent everyday utensils such as combs or ladders. Sometimes, the artist may produce a piece of textile in accordance with a customer's instructions, including everything from colour and design to the use of symbols. Printed cotton fabrics are named adinkras after the printing technique.

Adinkra garments

Adinkra garments are mainly seen at funerals, but depending on their colour they may be worn on festive occasions (if the background colour is white) or as everyday dress. All garments are customer-made; *prêt-à-porter* collections do not exist. The Asante made clothing from a variety of materials. Besides *adinkra* garments, *kente* cloths are also worn (see RMV 5899-10). Men wear *adinkra* cloths wrapped around the body, leaving one shoulder uncovered. Smaller cloths may be wrapped around the hips..

You are what you wear

In *adinkra* textiles, the more intricate the pattern or design, the more expensive the cloth. Wearing adinkras was once the prerogative of a select élite, but today they may be worn by anyone who can afford them. The *adinkra* technique has been used for making garments since the nineteenth century. In recent years, new production methods such as machine printing and wax-print have been adapted for *adinkra* and *kente* textiles, alongside the older, traditional modes of craftsmanship.

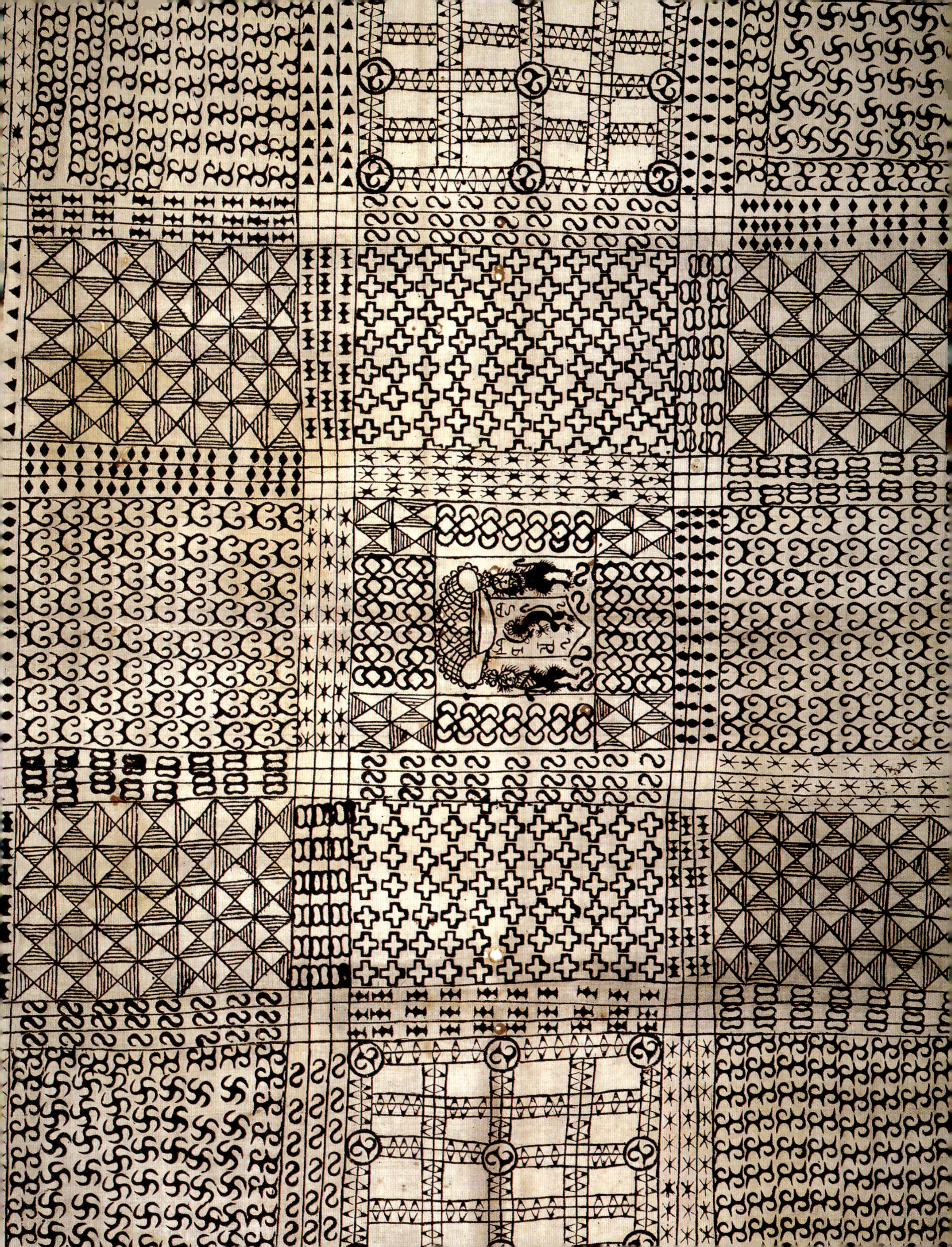

Tenaga and Ashinaga (*Netsuke*)

Gesshō, Edo-period, Japan
1780-1823
10,9 x 3 cm
wood (palm), carving
RMV 360-2193 (1883)

Long Legs and Long Arms go fishing
A *netsuke* carved as a figurine representing 'Long Arms', Tenaga, sitting on the back of a grimacing 'Long Legs', Ashinaga, who has been seized by an octopus while fishing. These mythological creatures symbolise the cooperation between two people, each of whom is inferior in some way, but who cooperate to overcome their frailties. And so it happens: Long Arms uses his unusual limbs to grasp the octopus and release his comrade from its grip. This theme is often depicted in *netsuke*, but seldom with such beauty and boldness as in this piece.

The 'root attacher'
Netsuke are often described as 'belt toggles', but the literal translation of the word is 'root attacher'. This is an apter term for an object that cannot slide away behind your belt and hence ensures that your smoking pouch or medicine box is always within reach, while leaving your hands free. *Netsuke* are often seen as a natural development arising from the fashion of carrying about one's person *inrō*, lacquered medicine boxes, or tobacco, which the Spanish had introduced from the Philippines around 1600.

The invention of *netsuke*
The literal translation 'root attacher' recalls the way in which these items were invented: by land labourers on their way to their fields, leading an ox by a rope with one hand, with a hoe slung over their shoulder, and carrying a lunch bag and a drinking gourd in the other hand. When the ox walks around the wrong side of a tree for the umpteenth time, it is a wonderful thing to have at least one hand free. If you take a piece of tree-root and use it to tie your knapsack and gourd to your belt, you will have at least one hand free, and behold: the *netsuke* was invented.

No smoking in public
Lacquered medicine boxes are associated with warrior nobles and the affluent middle classes, but tobacco pouches were for anyone who could afford the indulgence. Smoking was initially confined to the home, tea houses, and restaurants that provided smoking sets for general use. Smoking in the street was certainly frowned on, and aside from farmers and hunters, no one would carry around their own smoking set, tobacco pouch and pipe. This custom did not take hold in the major cities until around 1760-70.

Gesshō's craftsmanship
Netsuke must not damage the clothing and must feel delightful in the hand. This means that they must be compact, without projecting bits on which your sleeve might snag. But the theme of Long Legs and Long Arms obviously calls for these features to be emphasised. Furthermore, that Long Arm's arm is actually carved almost completely free from Long Leg's body attests to the carver's great boldness, and still more to his immense skill. The risk of the thin free arm breaking off must almost have compelled the buyer to enquire whether he might receive a guarantee. The *netsuke* carver Gesshō will have reassured him, confident of his craftsmanship, but it must have been a gamble all the same.

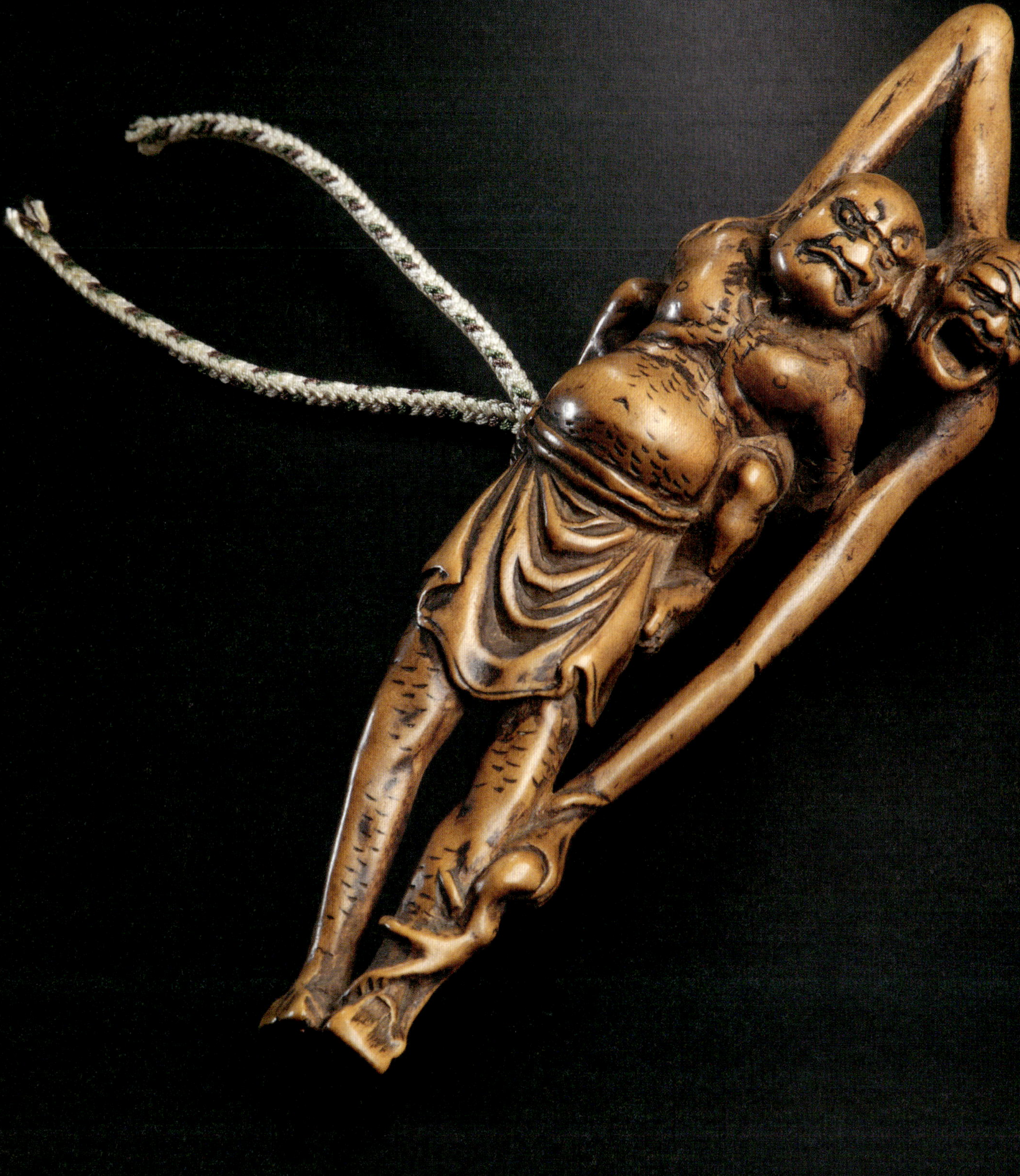

Diorama

Colonial period; Suriname (former Dutch Guiana)
1827
51,5 x 79,5 x 24 cm
wood, paper, glue, fibres, gouache
RMV 360-5139d (1883)

An Arawak village

This diorama depicts a moment in the life of the Lokono (Arawak) Indians of Suriname, around 1820. The diorama is divided into two parts. There is a party in progress in the house on the left, as shown by the five dancing men in festive apparel. In the right-hand house we see figures including a man returning from hunting, someone making fire, and a woman with a baby. All the figures, not just the human figures but also the dogs, birds, and pots, are hollow and open at the back. Between the two buildings stands a *tokai*, a shaman's hut, into which the shaman can retreat with patients to heal them.

Arawaks or Caribs?

In the left-hand part of the dwelling, people are dancing to the music of bamboo flutes. The woman at the front on the left, sitting on a little bench, is straining pressed cassava over an earthenware pot. She is making *kasiri*, a festive alcoholic beverage. The central woman in the right-hand side of the dwelling is weaving a *kwejoe* or pubic apron from beads. The people depicted here are probably Lokono (Arawak), since pubic aprons are worn only by Lokono women, not by the women of the other indigenous coast-dwellers, the Kari'na (Caribs). The man in the red coat behind her is probably a captain, an administrator appointed by the colonial authorities.

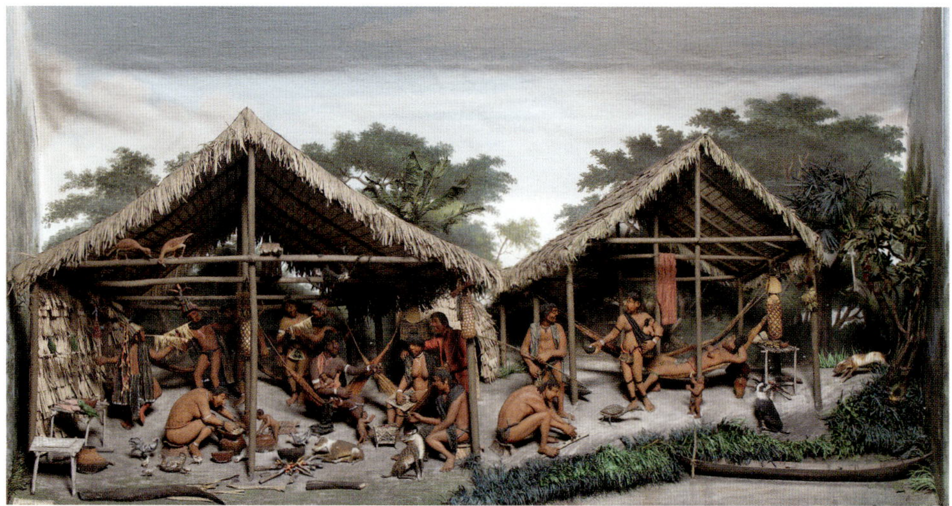

Gerrit Schouten

This is one of the few of Gerrit Schouten's dioramas to be owned by a Dutch museum. Gerrit Schouten (1779-1839) was the most important nineteenth-century artist in Suriname. He grew up in a rich cultural milieu: his father was a poet, actor, and founder of the society the Surinamese Friends of Literature (*De Surinaamse Lettervrinden*). Since the colonial territory had no art school in this period, Schouten trained himself, becoming the first Creole painter in Suriname and probably the first mixed-race person to establish a reputation as an artist. King Willem I of the Netherlands awarded him a gold medal for his work in 1828. Schouten made dozens of dioramas between 1810 and 1839. They can be divided into four groups, by subject-matter: Paramaribo, the plantations, slave dances, and the indigenous population. This diorama is a superb example of the fourth group.

Perspective

The perspective of this diorama is ingeniously constructed. First, the artist has adopted an ideal vantage point, just below the centre of the box. From any other point of view, it would be impossible to see all the parts of the image at the same time. To enhance the perspective, the rear wall, with its painted trees, meets the 'roof' not in a right angle but in a curved surface.

Souvenirs

Most dioramas were made and sold to tourists or people returning from the colony to the Netherlands, as unusual souvenirs. This one was ordered from Schouten in 1826 by the director of the Royal Cabinet of Rarities (KKZ) in The Hague through the agency of A.F. Lammens, president of the colony's Court of Justice. Lammens furnished the diorama with a detailed description before sending it to the KKZ. When he completed it, he signed the diorama 'G. Schouten fecit 1827 te Suriname'.

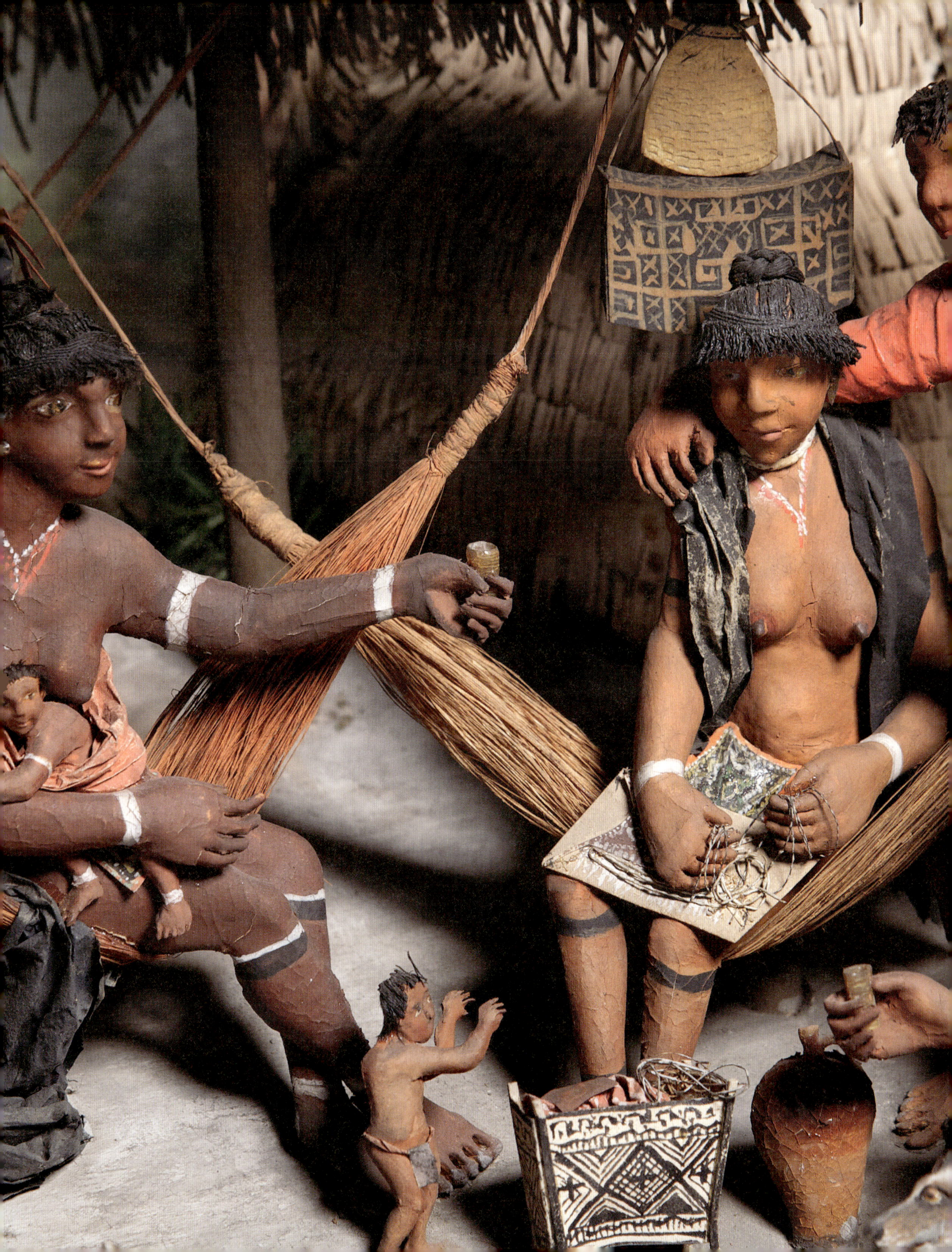

Magic mirror (*Makkyō*)

Edo period, Japan
1800-1823
mirror: diam. 25.8 cm; lacquered box: l. 37.8 cm
mirror: bronze, bamboo; box: wood, lacquer
RMV 360-3136a (1883)

Magic mirror

Although the collector Blomhoff does not say so anywhere, he must have received this mirror as a gift during one of the two court journeys undertaken in 1818 and 1822. He did provide a fine description of the mirror, listing it under the heading 'Section 12: Japanese accessories for men and women, for everyday use and as luxury items'. What Blomhoff apparently failed to realise, or had perhaps forgotten by the time he compiled his catalogue, was that this is a magic mirror or *makkyō*. A *makkyō* is a mirror that can reflect an image concealed in its surface on the wall, in this case a family coat of arms.

The Tokugawa family

The family coat of arms belongs to the Tokugawa family, the military rulers who governed Japan from 1603 to 1868. They were one of the most powerful families in Japan. In the Edo period, they supplied all the shōguns, in addition to numerous provincial administrators or *daimyō*. It was not uncommon in this period to display the family coat of arms on utensils and accessories. Luxury articles such as this mirror were generally commissioned from the maker. The silver of the mirror had to be burnished regularly, to remove tarnishing deposits. It was not until the nineteenth century, under European influence, that glass mirrors became more common.

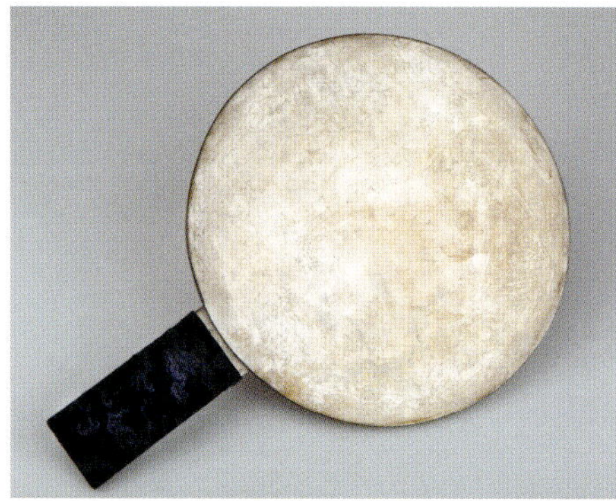

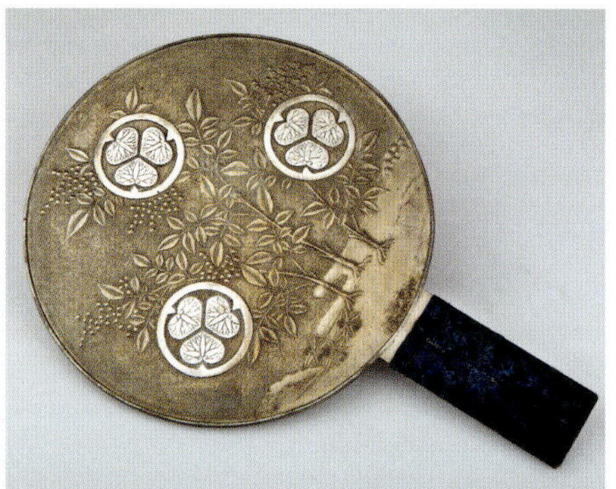

Family coat of arms

On the mirror box, three times within a circle, is the *aoimon*, a family coat of arms, applied in *hiramakie*, gold lacquer. The lid is set off with a gold line along the edge. The same family coat of arms (three hollyhock leaves) is also applied three times in the metal back of the mirror, using a special metal alloy, against a blooming lespedeza, Japanese clover or *hagi*. The reflecting side is made of a thin layer of silver.

Metallurgical production process

In this case, the reflection is the family coat of arms, which is achieved by means of an extremely complex metallurgical production process. The technology used to create magic mirrors was developed in the Edo period, but the process has only recently been studied and 'reinvented'.

Concealed crucifix

Magic mirrors of this kind were obviously ideal for the projection of signs that were not supposed to be seen in public. Thus, a magic mirror is known in which the reflection displays a crucifix, while the outside of the mirror exhibits completely unremarkable decorative motifs: cranes, long-tailed tortoises, and an old pine tree. The mirror was probably used during Holy Communion by Christians who had to practice their religion in secrecy; Christianity was prohibited in Japan from 1620 onwards.

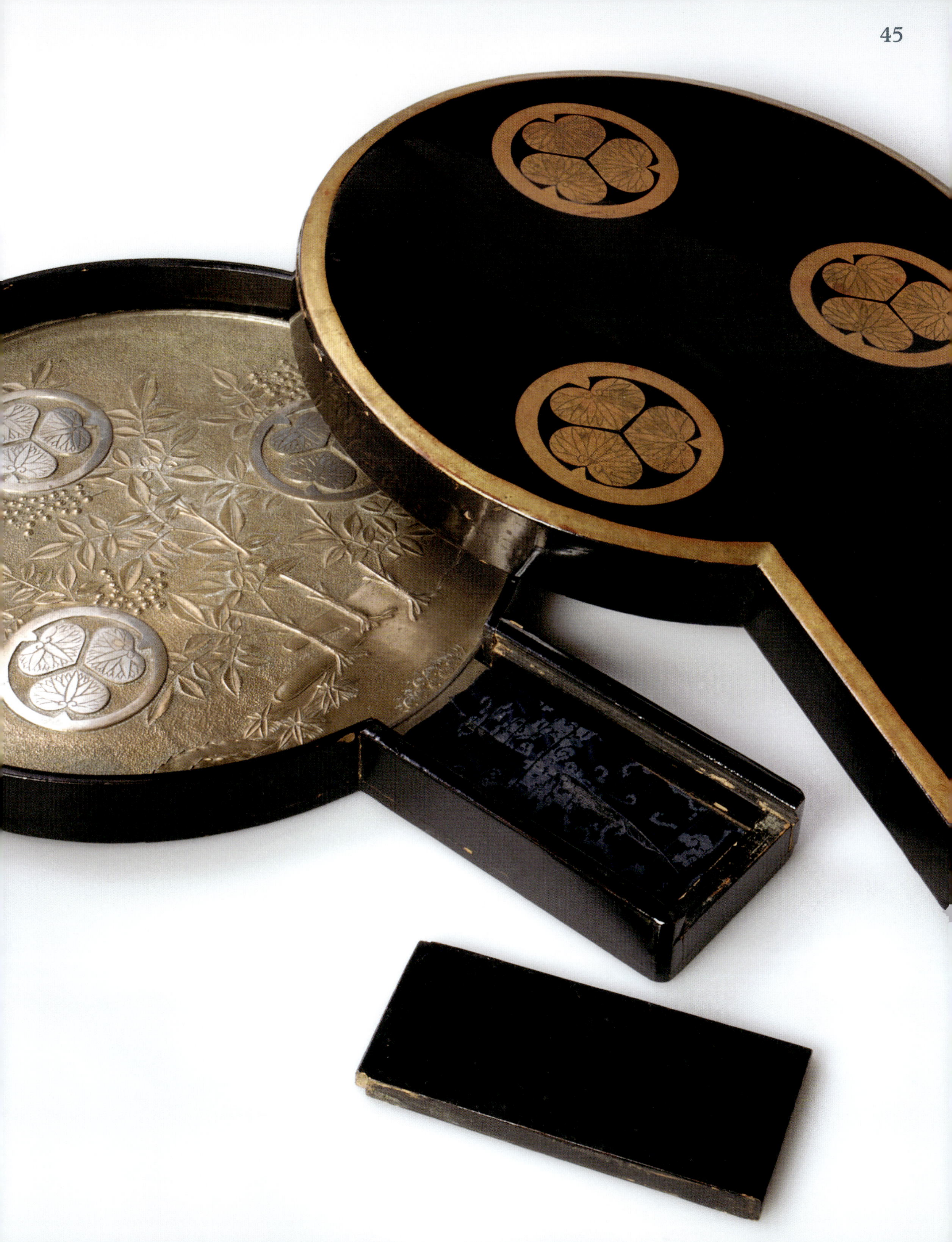

Gold pipe

Asante, Ghana
before 1837
15,5 x 4,3 x 4 cm
gold
RMV 360-5211 (1883)

Gold

Before Columbus discovered America, most of the gold that circulated in Europe came from West Africa: present-day Ghana was formerly known as the Gold Coast because of this trade. However, gold occurred only in relatively small quantities in river sediments, and its extraction was time-consuming and labour-intensive. After the banning of the slave trade in 1814, gold remained an important trade product, which the Asante sold to the Dutch.

Diplomatic gift

The king of the Asante of Ghana gave this gold pipe to King William I in 1837. It was specially made for the king in Kumasi, the capital of the ancient Asante Kingdom. Ghanaian kings frequently presented gold and silver pipes as gifts to visiting dignitaries. It was Major General Verveer who accepted the pipe from 'the king of Ashanti' on behalf of William I. In the Netherlands, it was transferred to the Royal Cabinet of Rarities. Exchanging precious objects was an important part of maintaining good trade relations. It is not known what gift was offered by the Dutch in exchange for the pipe.

Peace pipe

Other rulers were also presented with gold pipes. The king of the Asante, Asantehene Opoku Ware, had presented ambassador Dupuis with a gold pipe intended for the King of Great Britain back in 1820. Dupuis made the following entry in his report: 'The king desired me to report that, having himself smoked the pipe, the great white king might do the same, and then it should be considered a symbol of peace and friendship between them. It was a proper custom, he said, and grateful to his gods, who, when two people made friends that way, watched over the lives and prosperity of both'.

Smoking

Tobacco originates from the continent of America, and European merchants marketed it in the rest of the world in the seventeenth century. In Africa, it was often used to barter with the local population. The earliest pipes are frequently based on European models. Decorative ceremonial pipes in this African style were probably not intro-duced until the eighteenth century, when the Asante culture flourished, possibly in response to the decorated pipes with motifs representing images from Europe and America. This pipe, with its unique design, was made using the 'lost-wax' technique (see also p. 90-91).

Regalia

The king of the Asante is depicted with his gold pipes in a number of nineteenth-century photographs from the mission-aries' archives in Basel. The pipes have an exceedingly long stem and belong to the king's personal regalia. They were status symbols and a royal prerogative. Today, we no longer encounter gold pipes among the king's possessions. This may imply a decrease in the value attached to the possession of gold pipes; the pipes may have been melted down to make other objects.

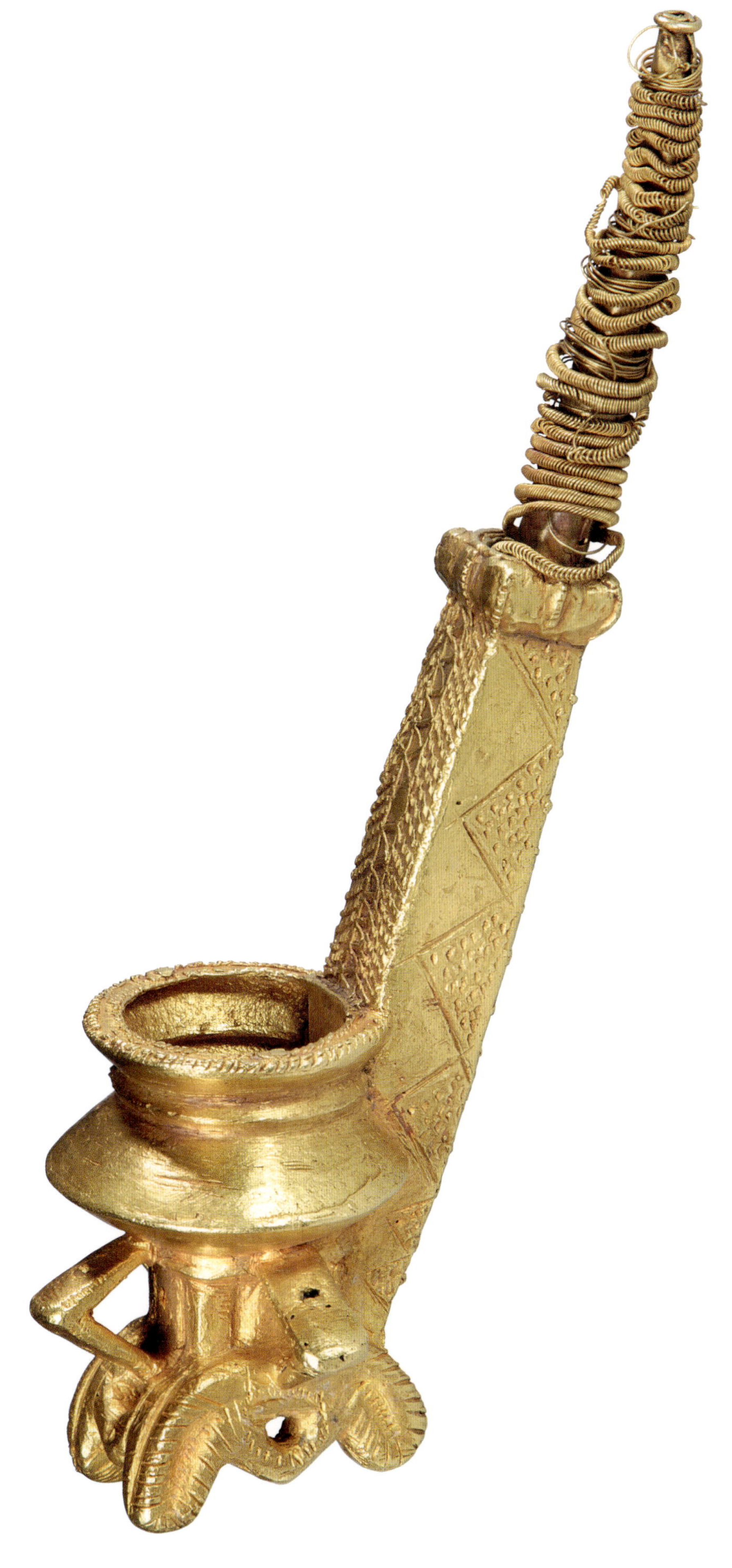

Banjo

Colonial period; Suriname (former Dutch Guiana)
c. 1770
81 x 16 x 13 cm
gourd, wood, sheepskin, iron
RMV 360-5696 (1883)

The oldest banjo

This is the oldest known banjo in the continent of America. It was made by a slave in Suriname and acquired by John Gabriel Stedman in the 1770s. The banjo's body is made from a gourd, over which a sheepskin is stretched. The instrument has four iron strings, the shortest of which serves as the bass. The instrument has a wooden neck. Since every gourd is different, there were no standard sizes for the different parts, and each gourd banjo is unique.

African origins

Musical instruments of this kind probably originated in Africa, having been brought to America by slaves who were transported there. Since the European rulers prohibited instruments deemed to be too closely related to African culture, like drums and wind instruments, quite early in colonial times, musicians took up the banjo instead. This string instrument was intended for use indoors, for the mutual entertainment of slaves. Today's musicians play modern banjos rather than the old gourd types.

'A very agreeable sound'

Stedman himself described the banjo as follows: 'The Creole-bania . . is like a mandolin or guitar, being made of a gourd covered with a sheepskin, to which is fixed a very long neck or handle; this instrument has but four strings, three long and one short, which is thick and serves for a bass: it is played by the fingers, and has a very agreeable sound, more so when accompanied with a song.'

Music as a form of escape

Music and singing played an important part in the debate surrounding the abolition of slavery. Writers who advocated the continuation of slavery claimed that the fact that slaves sang a great deal, made music and danced, proved that they were cheerful, that slaves were not treated badly, and that there was hence no need to abolish slavery. In 1827 a slave named Aaron replied to this argument, saying: 'cheerfulness is a way of putting one's cares aside, not proof of happiness.'

John Gabriël Stedman

John Gabriël Stedman (1744-1798) was a Dutch-Scottish captain in the Dutch colonial army unit of Colonel Fourgeoud, who had been sent to the colonies to suppress a slave uprising. Stedman led military expeditions against runaway slaves or 'maroons'. In 1796 he published his book *Narrative of a Five Years' Expedition, Against the Revolted Negros of Surinam*, in which he criticized Surinamese society, especially the treatment of slaves. His story, written in the manner of an exciting novel, is a journalistic account with detailed descriptions of the region's natural history. Stedman discusses his love for the slave Joanna, the difficulties of meeting her, and his efforts to purchase the freedom of Joanna and her son. Stedman's book provides an incisive picture of Suriname in the age of slavery. It is illustrated with dozens of engravings, made after the author's own sketches.

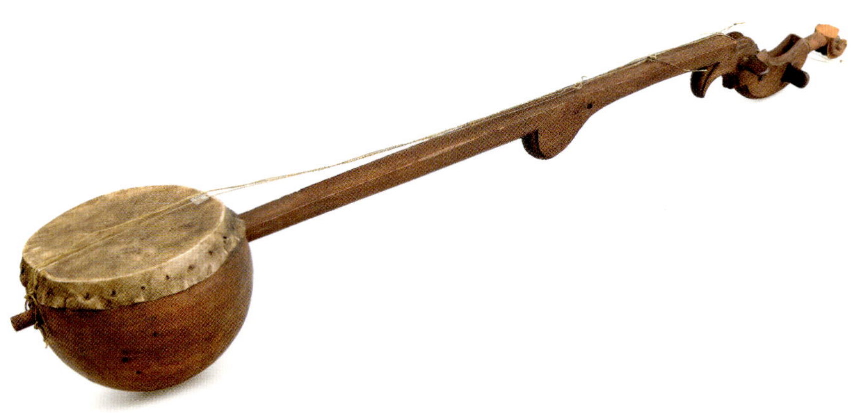

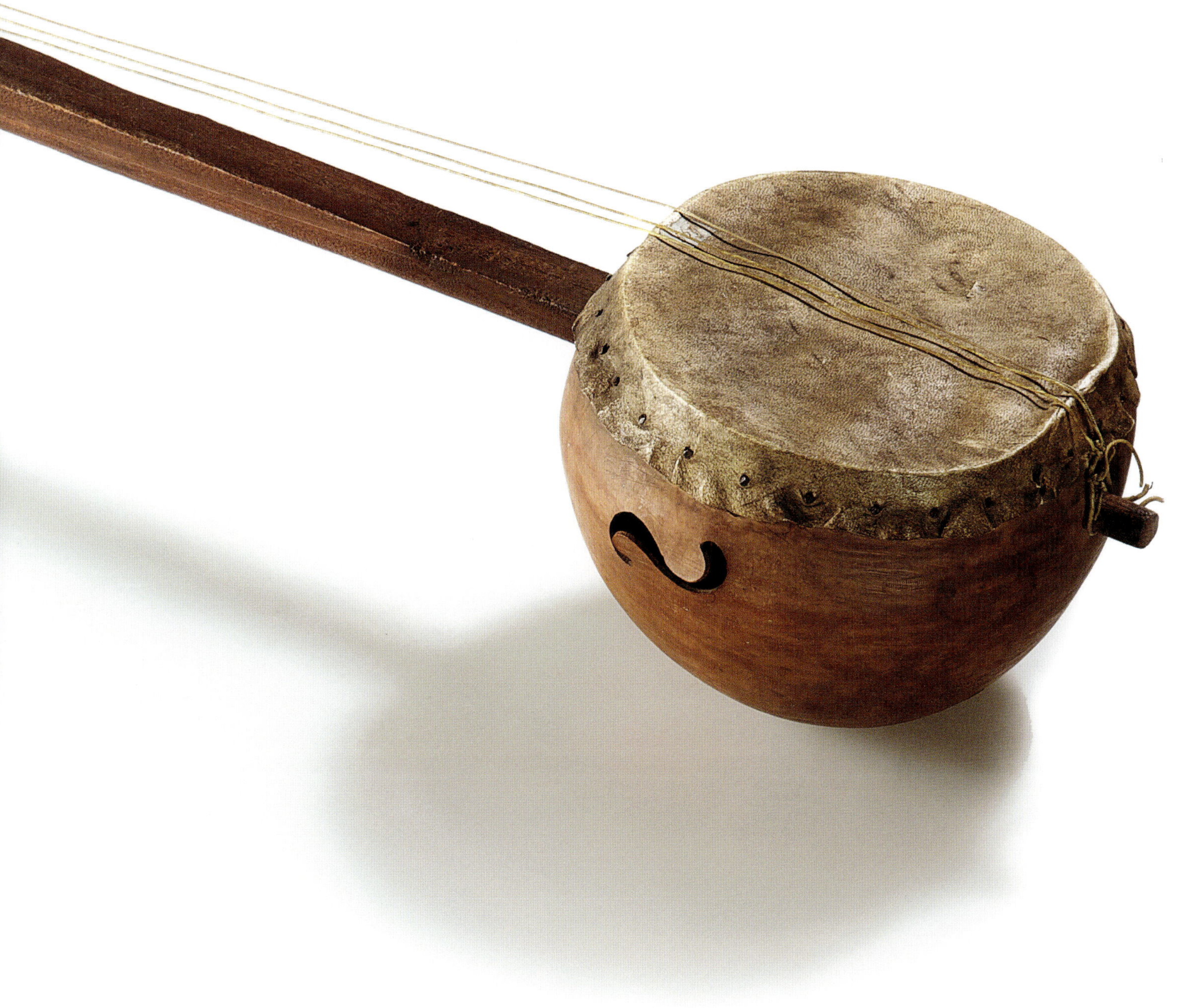

Cake dish

Edo period, Japan
1820-1822
h. 35 cm, diam. 20 cm
bamboo, lacquer, wickerwork
RMV 360-4871 (1883)

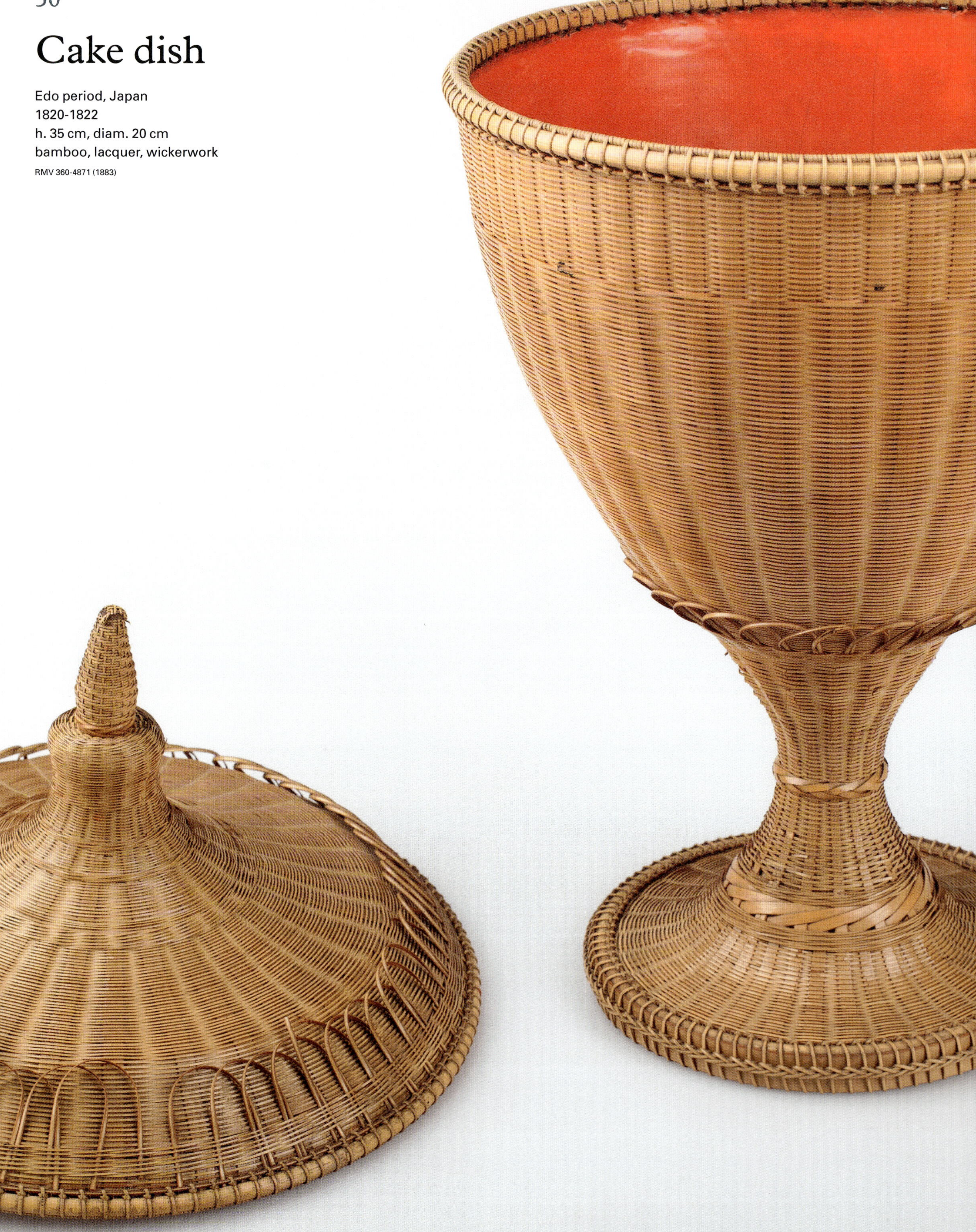

Unique cake dish

This refined cake dish has been woven from bamboo. Both on the wide, flared base and on the outer rim of the lid, decorative loops, made from very fine strips, have been added. The changeable weaving pattern prevents any dullness or monotony. The interiors of the dish and lid are both lacquered in bright red. In the catalogue of his collection, the collector Fisscher writes that the dish is used 'for serving cake'. The dish is unique in the world. In Japan itself, all cake dishes of this kind have been lost.

Collecting during the court journeys

The dish was purchased during Fisscher's 1822 court journey in the retinue of Opperhoofd Blomhoff. It is not known precisely where the object was bought. In any case, it was not in Fuchū. On 21 March, Fisscher was travelling along the Tōkaidō, the main road between Kyoto and Edo, and he wrote: 'This city [Fuchū] is a renowned manufacturing centre for all types of fine wickerwork, turned work and lacquerware, and of artistically crafted baskets, boxes, and Japanese implements in bamboo and wood. The merchants crammed the room with the most exquisite collections . . . but after we had chosen some items, we were unable to agree on the price, especially since we knew from previous occasions that the prices were set much too high, and as a result they departed very late at night, having done virtually no trade'.

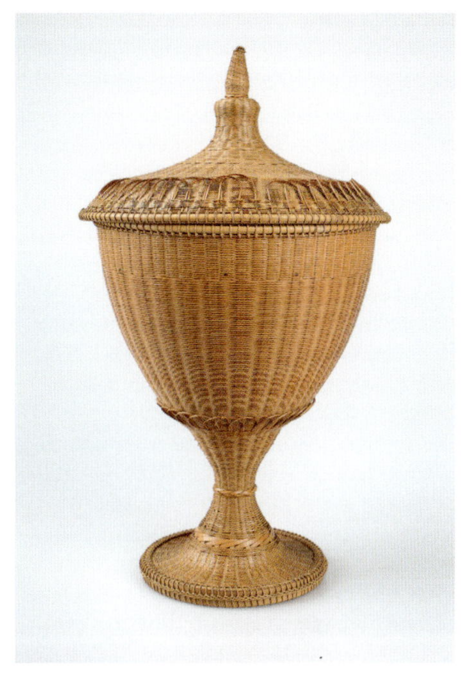

Dutch influence?

Since the objects were purchased new, we can assume that the dish was made in 1821. The shape of this dish is fairly unique for Japan. It was probably inspired by European glasses, which were quite well known in Japan at the time. Drinking glasses were also made in this region, woven from bamboo with red lacquer on the inside, and these are known to have been inspired directly by Western examples. The museum possesses eight examples of these glasses, also purchased by Fisscher, possibly in the same shop.

Second chance

A few days later, on 24 March, on the way from Numazu to Odawara, there was a second chance. Perhaps it was then that this dish was purchased: 'A few miles past Hakone, we arrived at [the place of business of] one of the leading merchants in Hatta, and then at that of yūmoto, which were specially arranged to receive the great gentlemen who pass by on their journeys, and to have them served tea, pastries and other refreshments by beautiful girls, according to the country's custom. We found the prices more reasonable here than in Fuchū, and purchased diverse mosaics as well as beautifully worked Japanese basketry and lacquerware'.

Great gentlemen

The great gentlemen mentioned by Fisscher are the numerous travelling *daimyō*, provincial administrators who were obliged to keep moving, alternating between a year governing their own province and a year in the capital, Edo. They often travelled with a company of several hundred samurai. Partly thanks to this busy traffic, many cities along the Tōkaidō flourished and developed local specialities, such as the marquetry or *yosegisaiku* produced in Hakone (see p. 10-11), which Fisscher here calls 'mosaics'.

Ceremonial kris

Makassar; South Sulawesi, Indonesia
17th century
scabbard: 2.5 x 13 x 44 cm; blade: 4.5 x 9 x 46 cm
gold, precious stones, iron, nickel, wood
RMV 360-6021 (1883)

Stadholder's property
This precious ceremonial kris, decorated with gold and precious stones, belonged to Stadholder Willem IV (1711- 1751), who served from 1749 onwards as President of the Council of the *Heeren Zeventien* and Director-General of the Dutch East India Company (VOC). It is the oldest known Indonesian object belonging to the Orange family to have been preserved. Willem IV was an enthusiastic scholar, with a particular interest in the East Indies. He built up a Collection of Rare Naturalia and Artificialia, which was later incorporated into the Royal Cabinet of Curiosities.

Vassals of Majapahit
Although the kris as a type of weapon is originally Javanese, we also find these daggers on other Indonesian islands, especially in South Sulawesi, since nickel-containing iron occurs in that region. The art of forging krisses spread from the powerful Hindu realm of Majapahit, which influenced much of the archipelago from East Java, most notably in the fourteenth century. This influence extended to the principalities of Gowa and Bone, with their Makassarese and Buginese populations. These two principalities were vassal states of Majapahit until the sixteenth century. In the mid-sixteenth century, Gowa and Bone were converted to Islam from Giri (Gresik) on East Java.

Cultural gifts
Royal weapons were eagerly seized as war booty, but they also frequently changed hands since they were presented as cultural gifts. This seventeenth-century kris, from the kingdom of Gowa in South Sulawesi, was probably given to Stadholder Willem IV in the eighteenth century, but the precious object may have been in the possession of the VOC before then. In 1653 there were clashes between Gowa and the VOC, and in 1667 Cornelis Speelman defeated the army of Makassaar. Under the terms of the Treaty of Bongaya, the ruler had to submit to VOC rule. The VOC may have acquired the kris at that time; alternatively, it may have acquired it in 1739, when the army of the neighbouring state of Bone ousted the ruler of Gowa, after which it was defeated by the VOC.

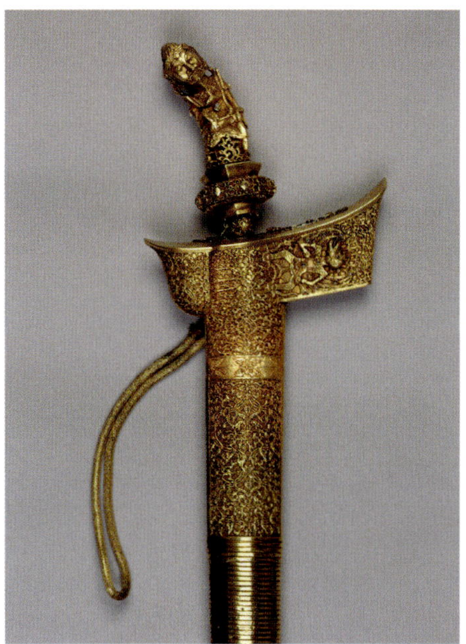

The power of a kris
Forged in fire from iron and nickel (sometimes originating from meteorites), a kris, a two-edged dagger, unites powerful cosmic forces. During the forging process, the kris smith or empu applies motifs (*pamor*) to the blade, which give the kris its soul. The blade is compared to a snake, which coils if the kris blade has wavy lines (*luk*), and rests if the blade is straight. The hilt of a kris is frequently shaped like a figure that protects the owner. A kris is not always intended to serve as a weapon; many were worn as signs of rank.

Garuda and Bima
Besides being known as fine sailors and merchants, the Makassarese and Buginese were also known as highly skilled goldsmiths; work in precious metals was practised to a high standard at the royal courts of Gowa and Bone. The loop of gold thread on the scabbard is typical of krisses from South Sulawesi; the motifs reflect the Hindu influence of Majapahit. Depicted on the chased gold scabbard, standing, is Garuda, the mount of the Hindu god Vishnu. The gold hilt of this kris, shaped like a curved wayang figure, is the hero Bima, who features in the epic *Mahabharata*.

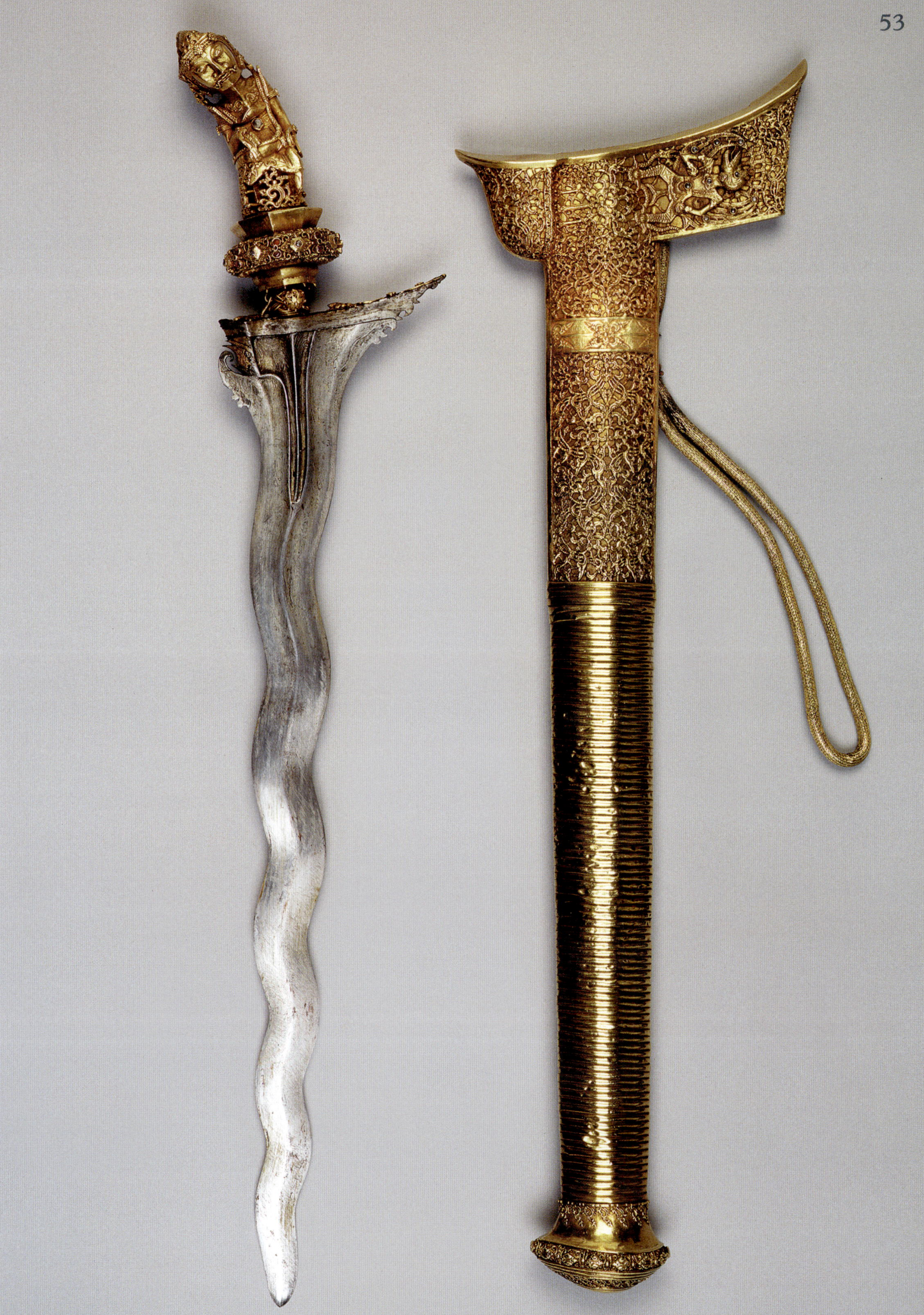

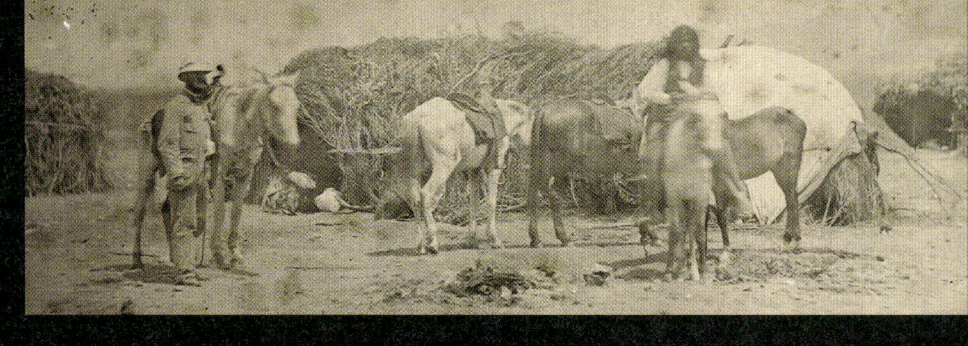

Legendary

No Native American tribe appealed to the imagination of young European readers more than the Apaches. Around the year 1900, novelists depicted them as a legendary warrior tribe that was utterly fearless and could survive amid the most wretched conditions. As a young boy, Herman ten Kate had devoured adventure stories set in the Wild West with breathless excitement. After his visit to Indian reservations in Arizona, he wrote in his diary in 1883: 'I cannot help but feel a certain admiration for that handful of savages, who carved out a path from the icy north to the hot deserts of Mexico, always fighting and always on the move, never giving in to defeat, always persevering to the end . . . Their name will endure, long after the last of their warriors has departed to the "blessed hunting grounds".'

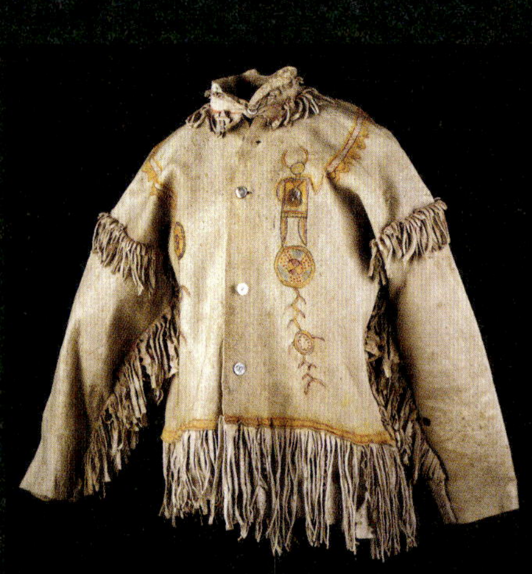

Model

Ten Kate paid ten dollars for this painted shirt of a young Apache warrior, possibly his most expensive purchase on this trip. The shirts of Native American men from the American and Canadian West were initially cut in traditional style: the animal pelt was used as such, with its contours left intact. Later on, leather shirts were modelled on army coats, but decorated with traditional elements such as fringes and beads, and sometimes with silver buttons made by Westerners or Indians. Such coats were worn primarily by Apache scouts employed by the army.

Motifs

Although the precise meaning of these motifs can no longer be ascertained, they can be interpreted on the basis of other, documented, examples. Alan Ferg of the Arizona State Museum believes that the horseshoe motif may represent the rainbow, while the zigzag lines stand for lightning and the quartered circles with points are mountains with rain. These motifs allude to the power of lightning, the strongest power that a medicine man can possess. One thing that can be stated with certainty is that the horned anthropoid figure represents a Sacred Being. The figure wears a pendant made from an abalone shell. A similar piece of shell has been applied at the same height on the back of the shirt, to give the wearer supernatural protection. The colours black, blue, red and yellow imbue the motifs with added sacred significance.

A unique opportunity

The Apaches were the tribe that continued the longest and the most effectively to resist white domination and the loss of their mother country. Only by making an enormous concentrated effort did the American army finally succeed in forcing small groups to surrender and to settle in reservations. Many Apaches kept up their armed resistance, employing clever guerrilla tactics, under leaders such as Cochise, Victorio, Loco, and Geronimo. The young anthropologist Ten Kate arrived in Tucson in the period when General Crook was returning from Mexico with a large group of Apaches who had laid down their arms. Crook gave him permission to visit the Indians in the reservations assigned to them in southeast Arizona. Ten Kate hired the French photographer C. Duhem to accompany him and take photographs.

Medicine man

This shirt is remarkable for the traditional painting on it. Perhaps it was captured from a scout by a warrior and then painted. According to the Apache expert Alan Ferg of the Arizona State Museum, the motifs indicate that the painting was done by, or according to the instructions of, a medicine man. Medicine men were in contact with Sacred Beings with supernatural powers and used painted motifs to attract their attention in supplications for protection or healing.

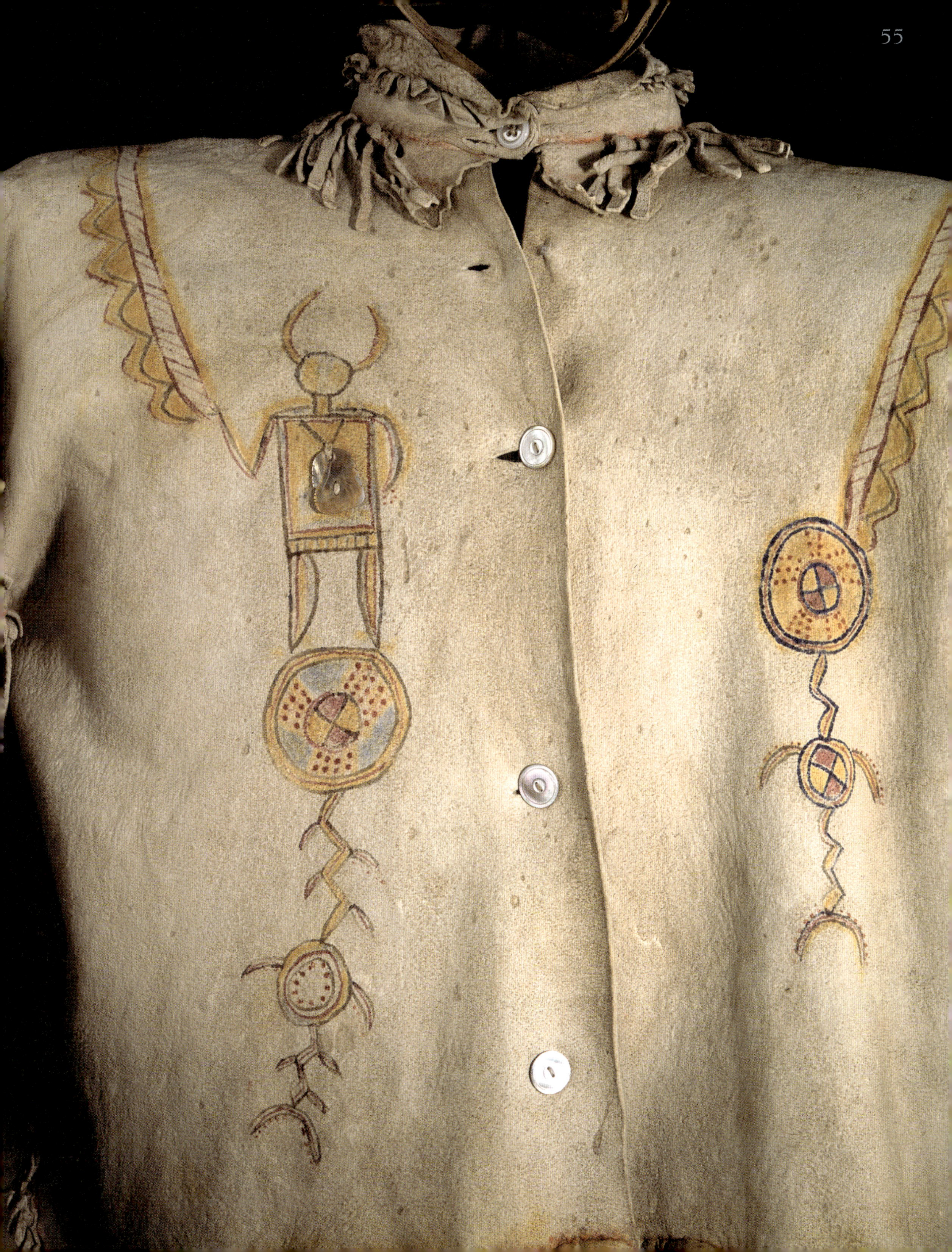

Ivory comb with goddess

Kandy period, Sri Lanka
1750-1880
16 x 10 cm
ivory

RMV 360-6127 (1883)

Conundrum

The identity of the goddess depicted here is something of a conundrum. The goddess is shown on a lotus seat. She holds the stems of two lotus flowers in her hand, an allusion to Lakshmi, the goddess of prosperity and beauty. The three panels, bounded by pearl frames, represent a pond with lotus blossoms, the most popular setting for Lakshmi. However, the goddess is also flanked by two geese (*hamsa*), which could identify her as Sarasvati. Hamsa is known as the mount of Sarasvati's husband, the supreme deity Brahma, but Sarasvati herself is also sometimes depicted with a goose. Sarasvati symbolises beauty and fertility, and she is the patron of the arts.

Cinnamon from Ceylon

In the seventeenth century, when European powers discovered that the island of Ceylon (present-day Sri Lanka) possessed the best cinnamon trees in the world, they saw profit. A struggle erupted for the best trading position, culminating in a protracted armed conflict between Portugal and the Netherlands. In 1658, Portugal was finally defeated when the Netherlands concluded an alliance with the Ceylonese kingdom of Kandy, and the VOC secured a monopoly on trade in the precious commodity of cinnamon. Ceylon also had large numbers of elephants, which were seen as another valuable 'commodity', partly because of their ivory, and also because of their usefulness as strong plantation workers.

Luxury articles

Among the Ceylonese élite, carved ivory combs, fans and jewellery boxes were coveted luxury articles, which were often decorated with images of Hindu and Buddhist gods. For instance, combs displaying an image of the god of love Kama were popular wedding gifts. This comb was probably presented as a gift to a Dutch merchant or diplomat. From the sixteenth century onwards, the Ceylonese court presented ivory show-pieces to esteemed European visitors.

Breathing of the soul

Ancient Indian texts praise the goose for its elegant flight. The graceful movements of its wings stand for beauty and grace, while its white feathers symbolise wisdom. For Brahma's mount personifies a deep layer of spirituality, namely cosmic breath. Hamsa symbolises the life force that can release the believer from the cycle of reincarnations and lead the soul to the path of ultimate liberation and bliss.

Royal Cabinet of Rarities

The comb comes from the Royal Cabinet of Rarities. King William I was an active collector of curiosities, as were many others in the aristocratic and learned circles of the eighteenth and nineteenth centuries. Especially at the beginning of his reign, he frequently dispatched scholars to purchase fascinating objects from overseas territories in order to display them to interested parties 'for their delight and edification'. Exactly how this comb ended up in the Cabinet is unknown. The Cabinet closed in 1883, with part of its collection going to the Rijksmuseum and part to the precursor institution (the Rijks Ethnografisch Museum) of the Rijksmuseum Volkenkunde.

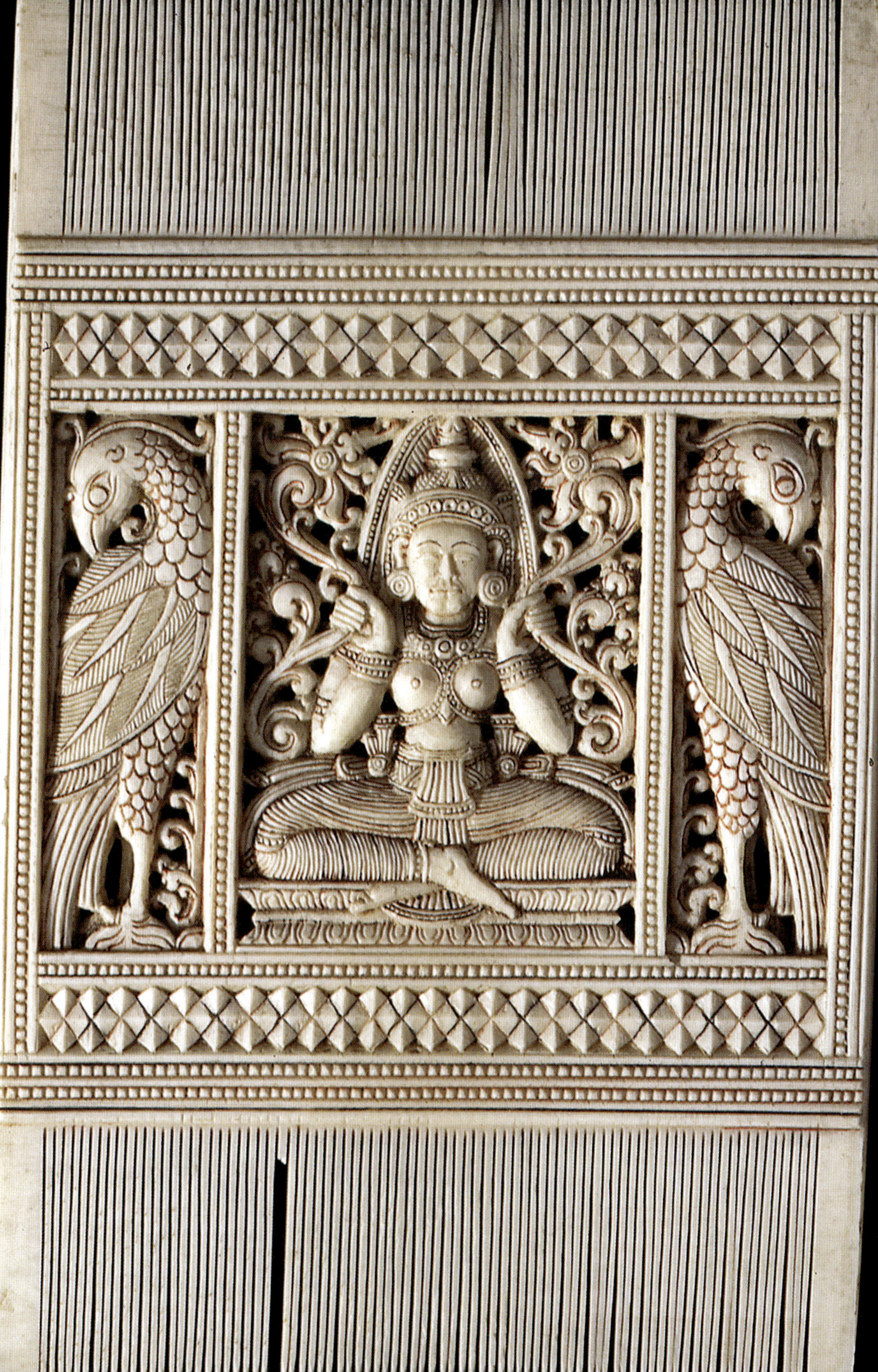

Siren or mermaid (*Ningyo*)

Edo period, Japan
early 19th century
58 x 21 x 22 cm
papier-mâché, cotton, wood, gut (ox), hide (monkey), nail, jaw (dog), vertebra (fish), skin (salmon)
RMV 360-10410 (1883)

The *ningyo* or 'human fish'

A monster representing a mermaid is known as a *ningyo* or 'human fish'. This piece was produced by Japanese craftsmen in the early nineteenth century. The upper torso is partly that of a monkey, but has a dog's jaw. The lower part of the body is that of a fish, probably a salmon. Such creatures were produced to be displayed, primarily by itinerant showmen who often hired circus tents or *misemonokoya* in squares or at busy intersections near bridges.

Exhibitions of curiosities in Japan

Exhibitions of all kinds of unusual and rare items are known from as far back as the early seventeenth century, and had their heyday in the late eighteenth and early nineteenth centuries. In Edo they were often held at the Ryōgoku Bridge, in the main street of Ueno and in Asakusa Okuyama. Items displayed included strange objects made out of shells, straw or paper, but they also included life-sized dolls depicting historical scenes or strange creatures such as 'Long Arms' and 'Long Legs'. It was believed that they had decided to leave the island where they lived to settle in the great cities of Japan.

Blomhoff's mermaid

The mermaid was already a curiosity in the eighteenth century. Thus, we know from the diary kept by an inhabitant of Edo that a mermaid was exhibited in the district of Asakusa in 1777. The collector Fisscher writes in one of his publications about the enormous sensation created by a mermaid 'that had been purchased a few months before by Mr Cock Blomhoff, and when this first Mermaid was displayed on the island of Deshima, and later became the property of the Dutchmen, there was a great influx of Japanese every day to see this monster, and none of them had the slightest doubt concerning the specimen's authenticity.' Blomhoff paid sixty guilders for this mermaid, evidently enough to ensure a regular supply of such figures for several years. For the Rijksmuseum Volkenkunde possesses the largest collection of nineteenth-century Japanese monsters in the world – twelve specimens in all.

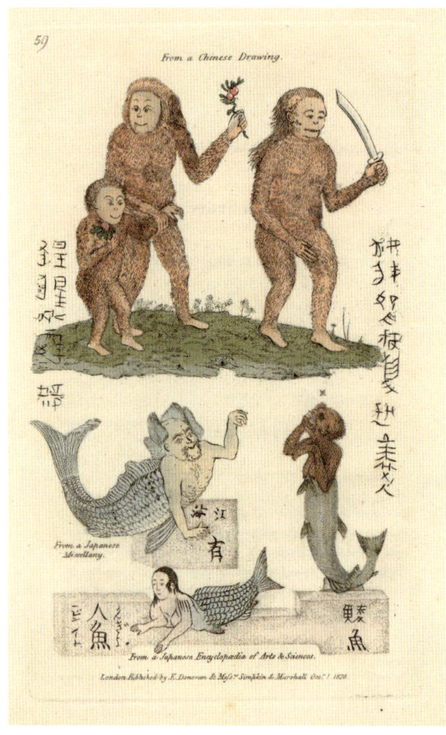

From messengers of doom to protectors

Mermaids are mentioned quite early in Japanese writings, but they do not really play an important role until the late seventeenth century. They were initially seen as disseminators or harbingers of doom, but after a while this belief reversed into the conviction that they actually possessed the power to prevent disaster, and that eating a mermaid could confer immortality. Mermaid oil was even developed, an oil that would burn eternally, and that, spread on someone's body, would supposedly make it totally impermeable to water. The belief in these salutary properties increased especially in the late eighteenth and early nineteenth centuries: a mermaid's bones were believed to be effective antidotes to poison as well as curing many other disorders.

The Feejee Mermaid scandal

Although Fisscher was living in the fairly isolated place of Deshima, it had apparently not escaped his notice that Japanese 'sirens or mermaids' were also being exhibited in Paris and London in 1822 and 1823. Fisscher was probably referring to the London 'Feejee mermaid'. The storm of indignation that this exhibition unleashed probably did much to contribute to its success among the general public. As far as is known, this was the first introduction of a Japanese product of this kind in Europe.

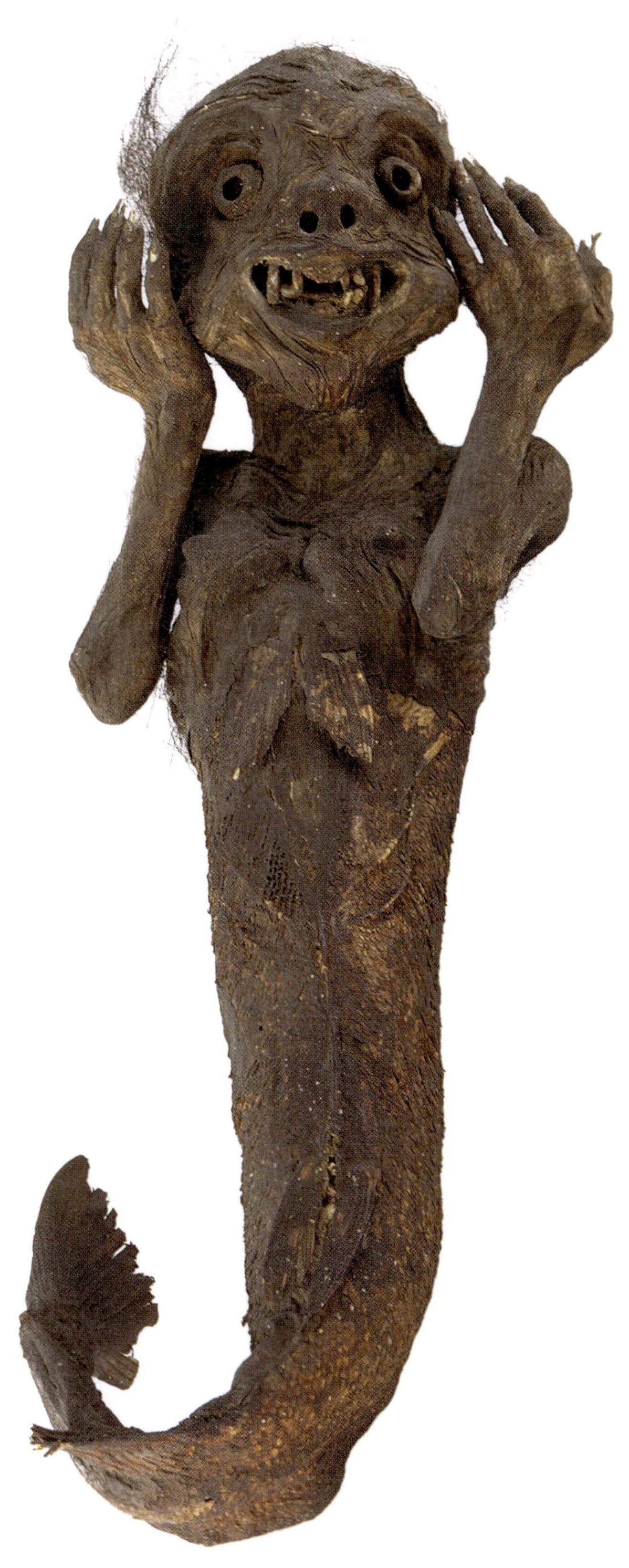

Skis

Sámi, Sápmi (Lapland), Northern Scandinavia
before 1797
10.5 x 160 x 10 cm
ash
RMV 360-7466, RMV 360-7467 (1883)

In the Leiden collection
These skis were collected between
1791 and 1797 by Cornelis de Jong van
Rodenburgh (1762–1838), commander
of the frigate Scipio, and donated to the
collection of the Royal Cabinet of
Rarities in 1816. In 1883 they were in
the collection that was transferred to the
Rijksmuseum Volkenkunde. They have
belonged to the Leiden collection for
almost two hundred years.

History from Sápmi (Lapland)
The skis probably date from around
1790 but may be older still. Scholars
believe that people first attached skis to
their shoes some 6,000 to 8,000 years
ago in northern Scandinavia, and
possibly even earlier in Siberia. Some
have been found in the marshes and
peat bogs of Scandinavia that date from
3,000 to 4,000 BC, and skis are depicted in prehistoric cave drawings
(*hellerisninger*) in northern Scandinavia,
in the Sámi region. This means of
transport was invented by Arctic
hunters, somewhere between Sápmi
(Lapland) in the west and Chukotka in
the Siberian eastern shores of the Bering
Straits. One old Norwegian farmer
associated the Sámi so strongly with skis
that he called them 'Skiing Finns'. We
find a similar expression, *skrithifinnoi*,
in the fifth century AD in the writings
of a Greek historian, and the term was
repeated by the Swedish scholar
Schefferus in 1682.

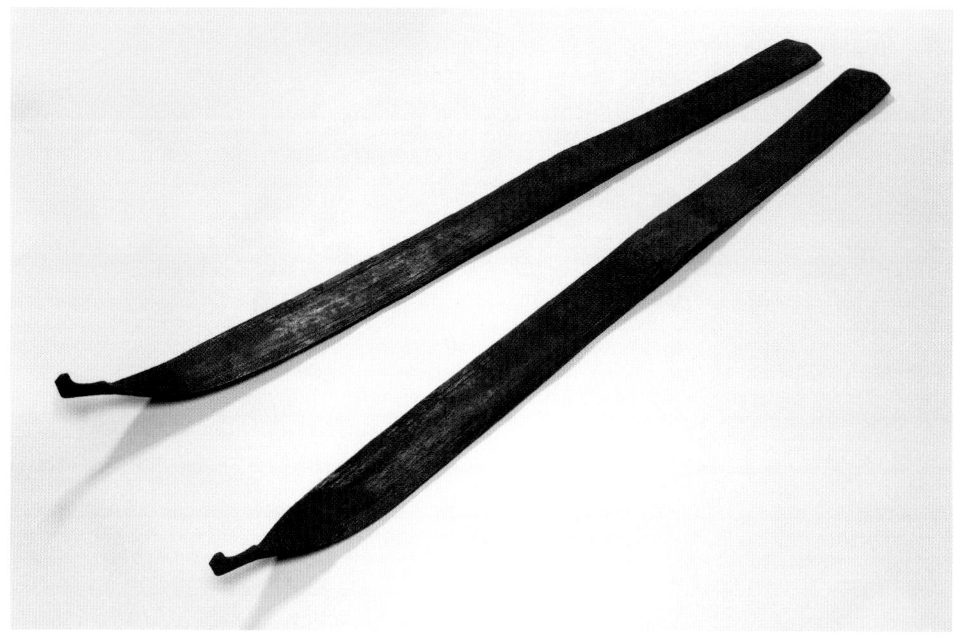

Smooth strips
The skis are made from ash, and the
slightly upward curve of the point tapers
into a knob. Figures are engraved just in
front of the feet, possibly the owner's
identifying marks. A space is hollowed
out underneath to allow for the bindings
to be attached.

Slats in all sorts and sizes
Skis prevented people from sinking up
to their waist in the snow even when
straying off the well-trodden paths.
They were made in different types and
in a range of lengths and breadths to suit
the wearer's size. Most were covered
with hide on the gliding side to provide a
better grip on the snow. Hunting on skis
was particularly effective because the
hunter could distribute his weight
forwards and backwards and between
the skis. Meanwhile, the prey, moving
on paws, would sink ever deeper into the
snow, which slowed it down. This effect
was especially marked when the top
layer of snow was lightly frozen.

Superb skiers
When the Norwegian army needed
outstanding alpine and cross-country
skiers in the Second World War to
defend the country, they employed
Sámi. The Sámi frequently used skis
when caring for their reindeer herds well
into the 1970s. These days, many of
them have snow scooters, and heli-
copters are sometimes used in reindeer
farming. Skis remain practical and
enjoyable accessories in the snow-
covered north.

Curl tip
The simplest and possibly oldest type of
ski is the 'boat type'. The front curves
upwards slightly and ends in a knob or
curl that is highly reminiscent of the
prow of an old boat. This shape is also
common in sleds. It has a hole in the
middle for the bindings, which generally
consist of a simple leather strap for the
foot. The Sámi of southern regions
sometimes added a heel strap.

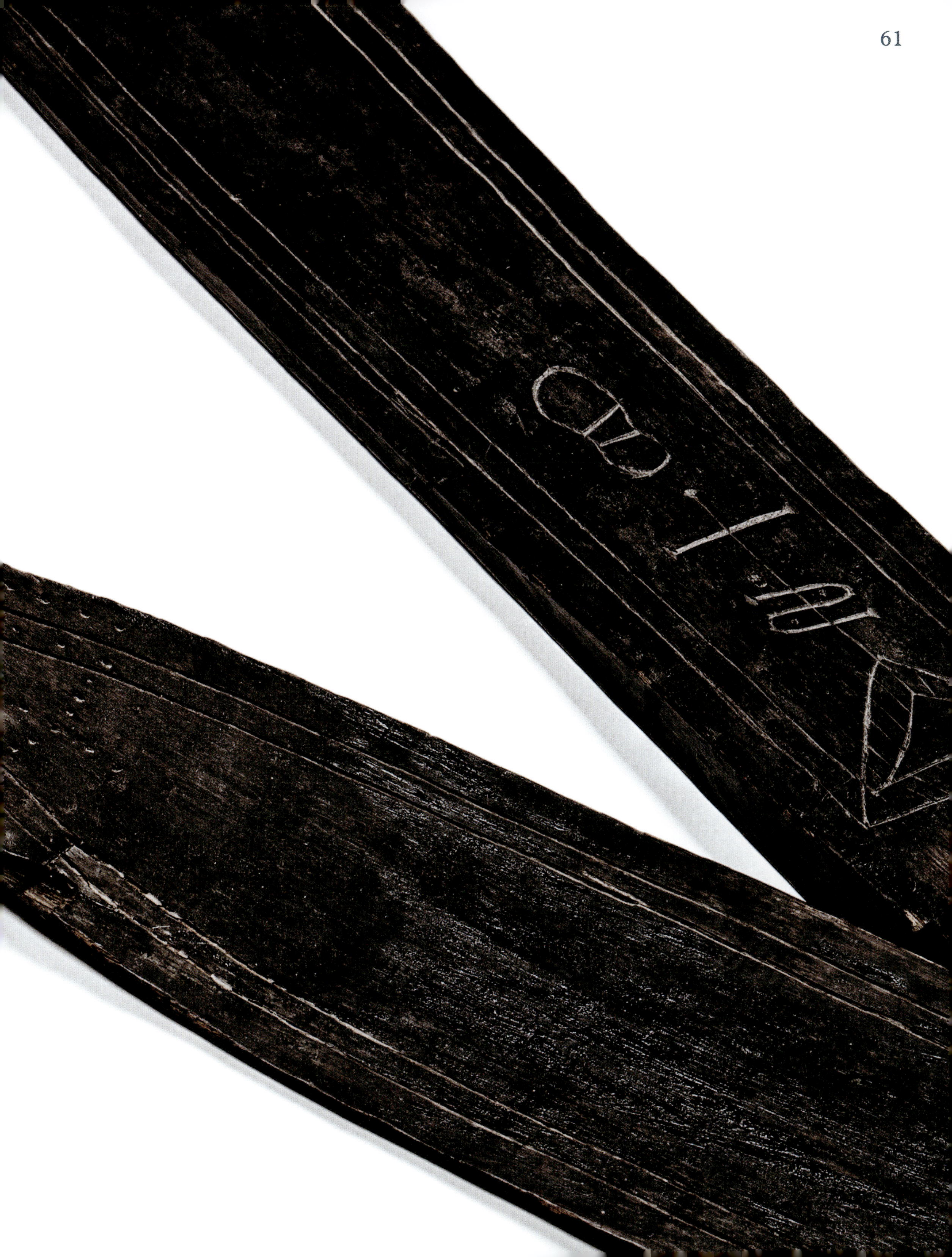

Mask

Yoeme, United States
before 1883
h. 20 cm, w. 14 cm
wood, dyes, horse hair, cotton
RMV 362-56 (1883)

Yoeme (Yaqui)
This dance mask was purchased by the Dutch traveller and anthropologist Ten Kate, when he visited the Yoeme Indians in 1883. The Yoeme lived on the mainland to the east of the Gulf of California. They had been driven out of part of the coastal region by Spaniards and Mexicans, but for a long time they continued to hold sway in the inland areas. Belém on the Rio Muerto was their most important centre, but it was inaccessible because the Yoeme successfully resisted further encroachment into their territory.

Rubbish dumps
Some of the Yoeme lived in the city of Guaymas, which was then Mexico's most important coastal city. Several groups lived near large rubbish dumps, in ramshackle huts. Strong, healthy adults worked as day labourers in the city or the docks, while others became domestic servants in the homes of the well-to-do. Many of the Yoeme provided for themselves by retrieving items of value from the rubbish dumps and selling them. Widespread disease and death resulted from this work.

Eyewitness account
Ten Kate's travel account includes a brief description of the dance: 'The pascóla is danced by a single man to the music of a violin and a flute. The dancer is almost naked, only a loincloth covers his hips. The face is hidden by a wooden mask, painted black with white figures, among them a cross. In his right hand, he holds a *sonagé*, an elongated tambourine, which he beats from time to time with the palm of his left hand. Around his ankles he wears a *teneboi* which makes a rushing sound when he moves, not unlike the sound of a rattlesnake . . . Although the dancer moves his body and his extremities very vigorously, he hardly changes place.'

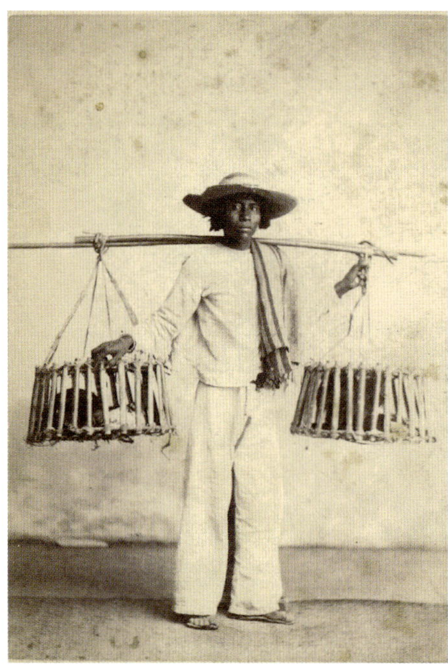

Easter and *pascola*
Herman ten Kate visited the Yoeme of Guaymas in 1883, shortly before Easter, and saw the *pascola* dance performed there. The name comes from the Cáhita language and means 'the old man of the fiesta'. This figure is a cross between a venerable old man and a demon. The pascola is a remnant of dances that were performed by masked ritual clowns. It belongs to the Yoeme's ancient beliefs, which were sometimes referred to as the 'religion of the woods'. In the later *pascola*, Indian and Christian elements were mixed. The pascola is still one of the most important ritual and social events of the Yoeme Indians in Sonora (Mexico) and Arizona (USA).

Photography
It was forbidden to photograph the dance. Ten Kate also wanted to photograph individual members of the Yoeme, but most Indians were afraid that allowing a white man to possess their image placed their lives in immediate peril. Only a few allowed themselves to be persuaded, with money and tobacco, to pose for the photographer Alfredo Laurent, whom the Dutch anthropologist had hired for the occasion.

Collecting
Ten Kate succeeded in buying a virtually new *pascola* mask. This is probably the oldest Yoeme mask to have been preserved in a museum. Since he tried, where possible, to purchase groups of objects relating to a single theme, he also bought other dance objects, such as two of the drums that were beaten by the tampaleos (drummers) and a set of ankle rattles used by one of the dancers. From bystanders he bought an ironwood war club, a painted leather tobacco pouch with fringes, a woven wicker basket, and a set of silver earrings.

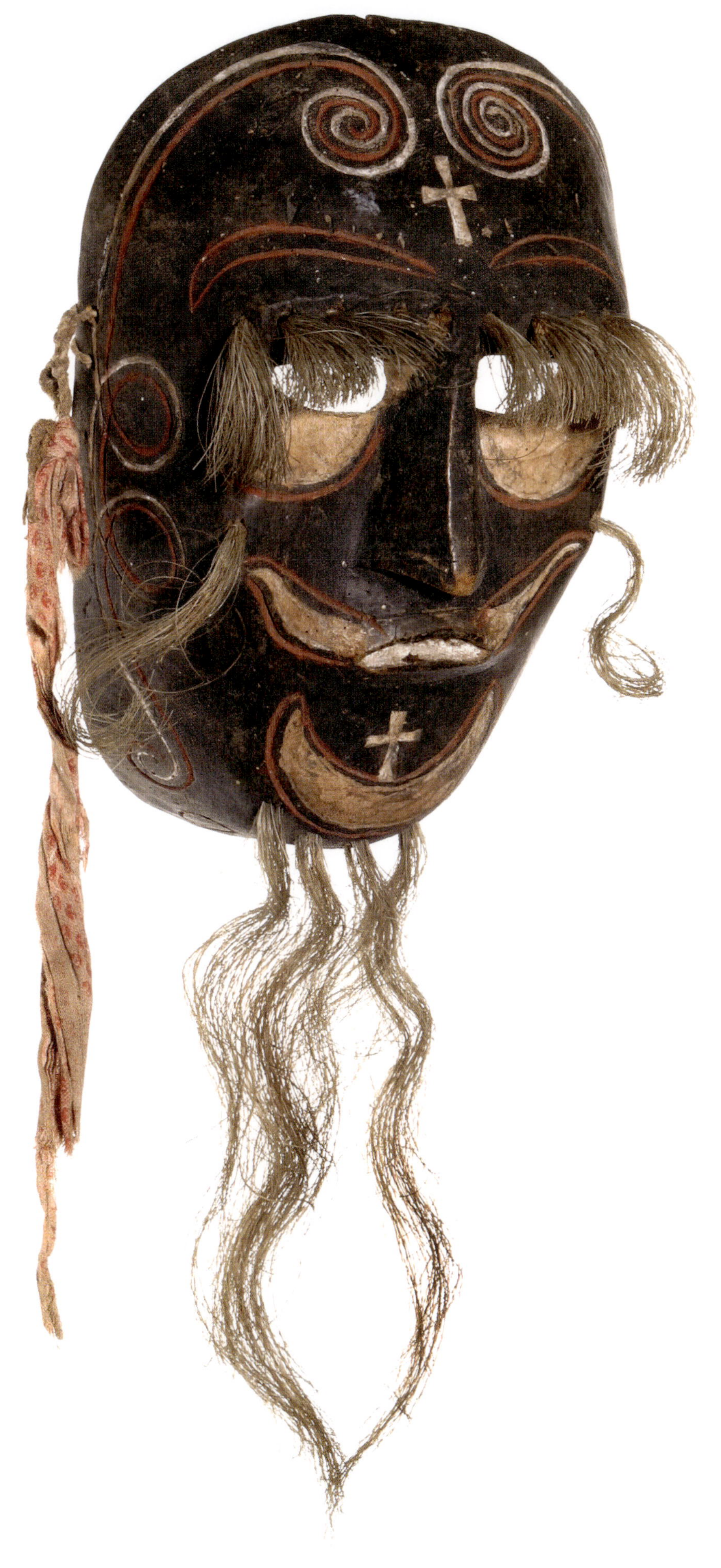

Three bronze Buddhas

Edo period, Japan
1648
right: h. 99.5 cm, w. 82 cm, d. 72.5 cm; centre: h. 113 cm, w. 81 cm, d. 73 cm; left: h. 100 cm, w. 82, d. 73 cm
bronze, cast work

RMV 418-5 (right), RMV 418-4 (centre), RMV 418-1 (left) (1883)

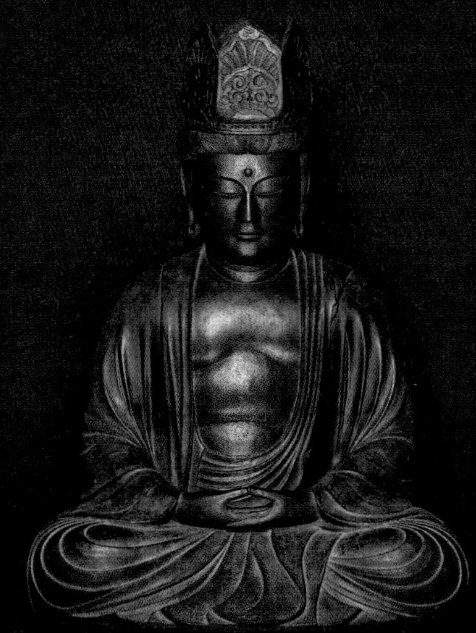

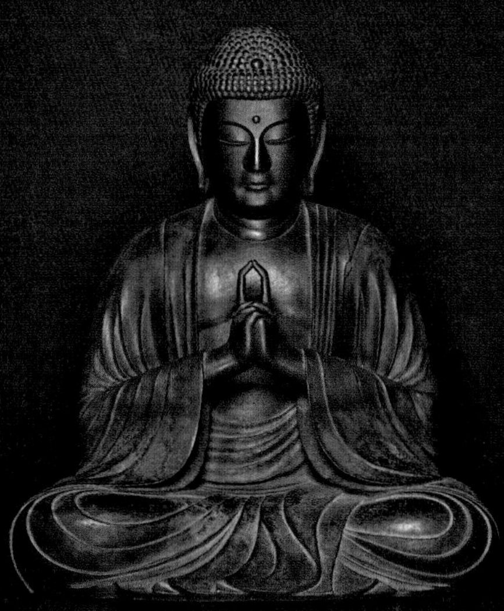

Three bronze Buddhas

Three bronze statues depict three Buddhas: on the right and in the middle Dainichi Nyorai, and on the left Yakushi Nyorai. Dainichi Nyorai or the Cosmic Great Sun Buddha (right detail), seated with the gesture of Holding the Jewel, represents the centre of the world of all phenomena. The Dainichi Nyorai (left detail) in the middle has his hands in the gesture of meditation. He embodies the manifestation of Ichiji Kinrin, the Cosmic Buddha of the Golden Wheel, the personification of supreme virtue, denoted by the crown on his head. Yakushi Nyorai, on the left, with the same hand gesture, is the popular physician Buddha. He watches over people's well-being and protects them from disease and danger. With his thumbs he presses a jar of medicine against his belly, a sign of his healing powers.

The mausoleum of the Tokugawa

These three statues come from the mausoleum of the Tokugawa shōgun. They stood in one of the buildings of the Zōjōji temple, in the south of Edo. Japan's opening its harbours to foreign ships in 1854 led to xenophobia, which culminated in Buddhism being classified as an undesirable foreign religion. When the Tokugawa Dynasty came to an end in 1868, the new government ended its ties with, and support to, the Buddhist temples. Much of the Zōjōji complex was demolished and turned into a public park.

Travelling Buddhas

After the mausoleum's demolition, the statues appeared on the art market and were purchased by Philipp Franz von Siebold's son, Heinrich, who sold them on to Siegfried Bing, a dealer in Japanese and Chinese art in Paris. In 1883, Bing sent the statues to the 1883 Colonial Trade Exhibition in Amsterdam. The sculptures were placed together with two other Japanese Buddhas in the garden of the Museum's Japan and China section, which was then in the building at Rapenburg 67 in Leiden.

New arrangement

In the museum's 1999 renovation, the Buddhas were returned to the permanent exhibition, but the old atmosphere had been lost. Many expressed their disappointment. In the renewed arrangement of 2012, an effort has been made to recreate the original atmosphere. The five bronze Buddhas are now at the centre of a special room, enriched with treasures from the temple that were purchased at the same time as the Buddhas.

The Buddha Room

When the museum moved to its current location on Steenstraat in 1937, the Japan curator C.C. Krieger refused to allow the statues to be exhibited in the open air any more. Defying furious reactions from the population of Leiden, he stuck to his guns and moved the statues into the building, installing them in what is still known today among countless inhabitants of Leiden and the surrounding area as the 'Buddha Room'. Because of the changing play of light from outside, which was reflected onto the Buddhas using an ingenious mirror contraption, many people saw the Buddhas come to life or even move. That experience may possibly have owed more than a little to marijuana: in the 1960s and 1970s, visitors sometimes congregated around the Buddhas to smoke a joint.

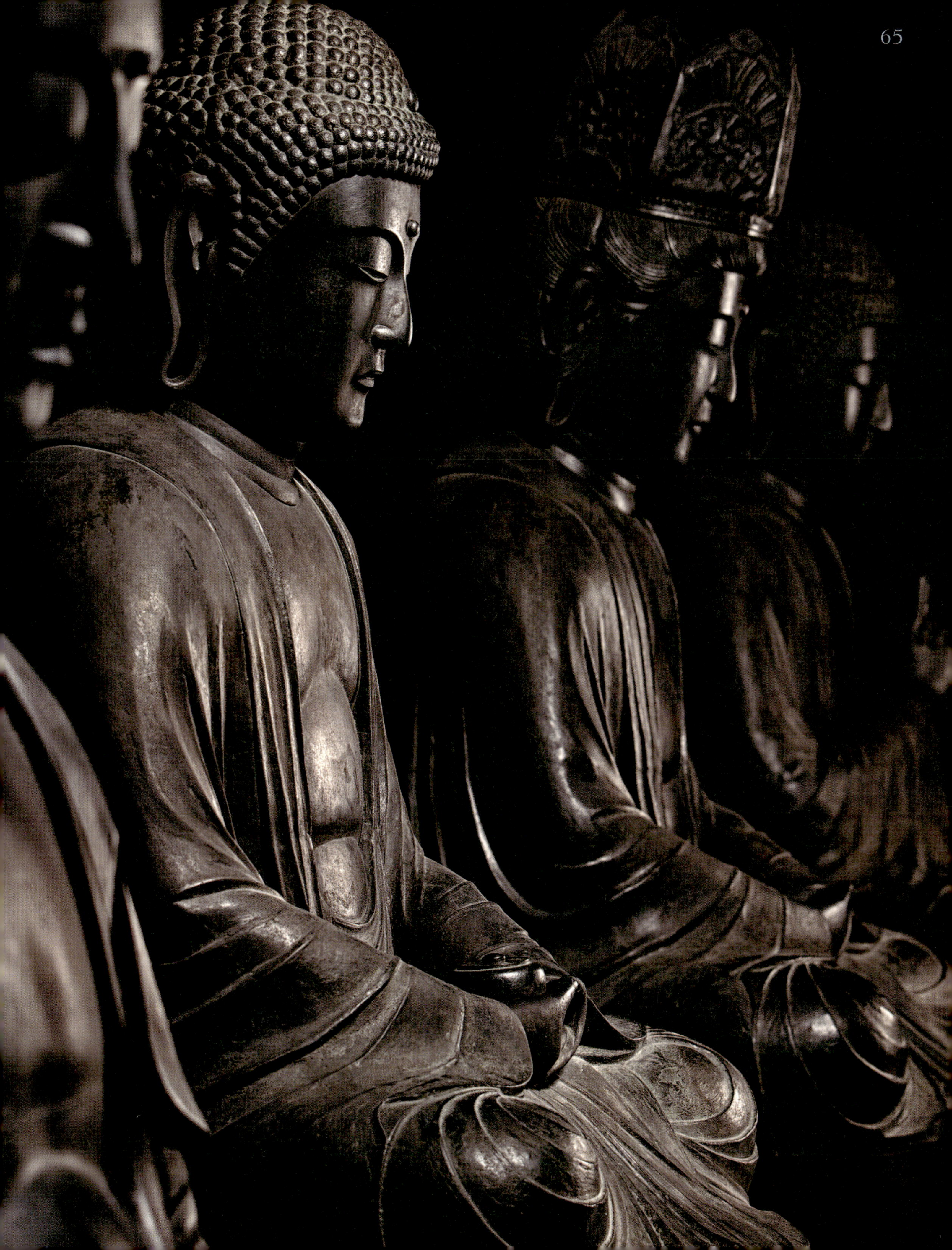

Playing-card money

Colonial period; Suriname (former Dutch Guiana)
1796
51.5 x 79.5 x 24 cm
paper

RMV 490-1 (1883)

Surinamese playing-card money

In 1761, playing-card money was introduced in Suriname. The soaring demand for currency, partly caused by the costs of expeditions to suppress maroon uprisings, prompted the colonial authorities to resort to issuing paper money made from playing cards, as an easy expedient. They issued far too much of this currency and its value plunged, forcing a switch to the Dutch guilder in the colony in 1828.

Jack of hearts

The note illustrated here was made from a jack of hearts. The faded and barely legible date stamp suggests that this superb piece can be dated to 1796, a dating supported by the fact that it bears the signatures of councillors Visscher and Stolkert.

Most important collection

The Rijksmuseum Volkenkunde possesses the largest and most important collection of Surinamese playing-card and paper money in the world. Besides this card, the museum also possesses a number of other similar items dating from the period up to 1844. They were donated to the museum in 1885 by Baron A.J. Schimmelpenninck van der Oye.

'Deplorable introduction'

Not long after the introduction of the playing-card money, the first concerns started to be voiced about forgeries. Many colonialists started to make their own playing-card money for payments to Indians, maroons, slaves and illiterate whites, whose illiteracy made it impossible to judge the notes' authenticity. The colony's Court of Justice therefore issued a ban in 1771 on the 'deplorable introduction [and] fabrication of said small cards and their representation as possessing value as currency.'

Forgeries?

On 25 June 1802, the colony's Court of Justice posted a warning in public places around the colony, notifying people that diverse forgeries had come to light of the ten-guilder cards issued in 1796 and signed by councillors Visscher and Stolkert. This was the first and only such public warning about a specific series of card notes. The forgeries could be identified by various telltale discrepancies: the faulty imitations of Visscher and Stolkert's signatures, the peculiar shapes of the numerals in the year, and a difference in the coat of arms. Unfortunately, most of the card notes in the Rijksmuseum Volkenkunde's collection are so worn that it is impossible to say whether they are originals or forgeries.

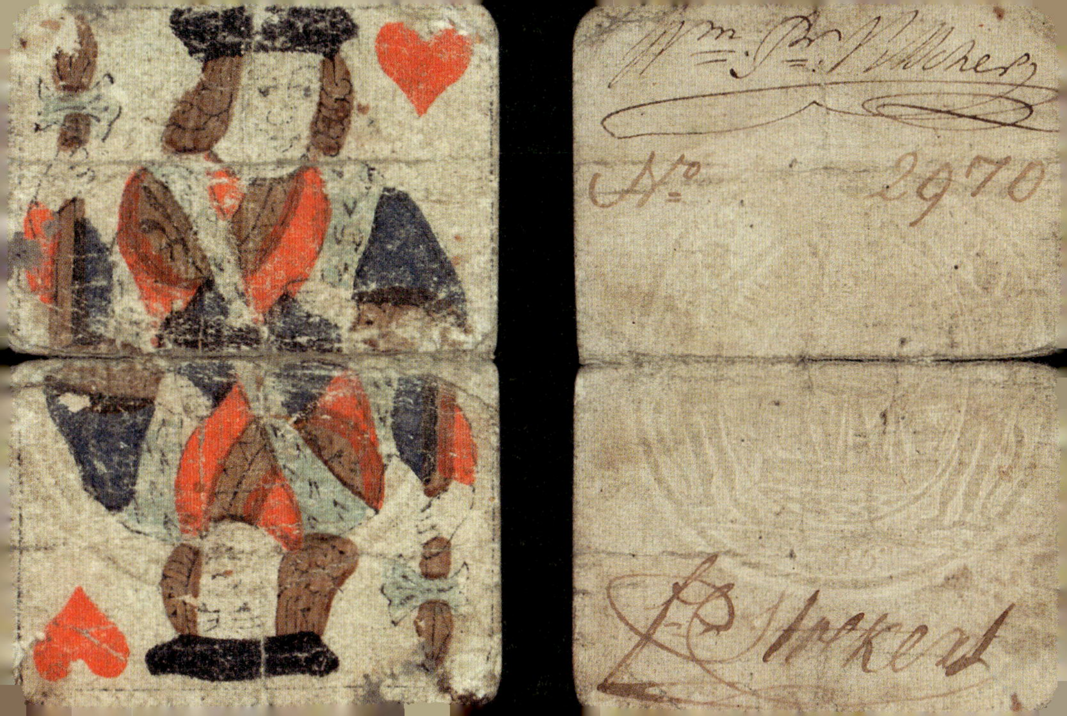

Wm. P. Mulbress
No 2970
P. Mackett

Sufi headdress and staff

headdress: Persia, staff: Saudi Arabia
headdress: 1850-1885, staff: c. 1885
headdress: 27 x 21 cm, staff: l. 90 cm
headdress: wool, cotton; staff: iron, cotton, silk, beads
RMV 503-232 (1883) and RMV 2107-1 (1927)

Cap with inscriptions

The tall, pointed cap or *taj* consists of four triangular pieces of felt sewn together. Each section is decorated identically with two lobed medallions bearing Arabic inscriptions. This type of headgear was part of the standard dress of Islamic mystics or Sufis. The cap's shape and colour identified the particular order of dervishes to which the Sufi belonged. The top of the iron staff and its handle are bound with cotton. Long, colourful strips, iron chains, beads and bells are attached to the handle's hooks. These dangling accessories would whirl along with the Sufis' movements as they performed their ecstatic dances.

Snouck Hurgronje and Hotz

The objects were collected by two Dutchmen who lived in the Islamic cultural region towards the end of the nineteenth century. The staff was donated to the museum in 1927 by the Islamic scholar Christiaan Snouck Hurgronje (1857-1936). He probably bought it in Mecca or Jeddah between 1884 and 1885. The cap comes from Persia and belonged to a collection of weapons, tools, household utensils and garments acquired by the merchant Albertus Hotz (1855-1930). The Rijksmuseum Volkenkunde purchased this collection, which was displayed at the 1883 International Colonial and Export Trade Exhibition in Amsterdam, that same year. Hotz ran the Persian Trading Company of J.C.P. Hotz and Son, a family company operating in Persia.

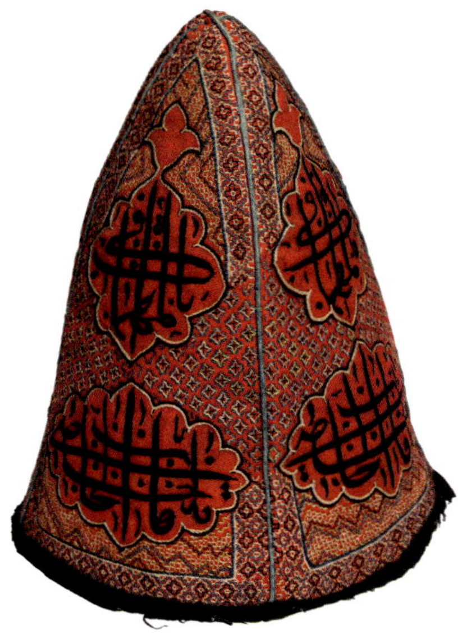

Crown

The standard accessories of itinerant Sufis in nineteenth-century Persia and Turkestan included a simple robe, a pointed *taj* (lit. 'crown'), a dervish staff, a begging bowl, and an instrument such as a flute or tambourine. For Sufis, the *taj* derived mystical power from its association with Muhammad's head-dress. It was worn in combination with a turban. The colour, shape and number of sections sewn together conveyed information about the mystic's order and his status. Thus, the colour red symbolised Ali, and four pieces of fabric (*terk*) alluded *inter alia* to the four caliphs, the four archangels, and Muhammad, his son-in-law Ali and his grandsons Hasan and Husayn.

Sufism

Those who pursue the mystical branch of Islam, Sufism, embark on a spiritual path. Repentance for sins, complete faith in God, patience and acceptance are among the stages that will ultimately lead to the love and knowledge of God and bring one closer to Him. Mystics seek to achieve this through spiritual exercises, abstinence from worldly pleasures and a sober way of life, and also through part-song, *dhikr* (the repetition of the name of Allah or Huwa (He)) and love poetry. Sufis often belong to orders or brotherhoods and are led by a spiritual leader or sheikh. The term *sufi* derives from the word for wool (*suf*), the plain material used to make the robes of early mystics.

Felt

The *taj* consists of four triangular felt sections which are sewn together. The surface is decorated with geometrical and floral patterns of white, beige, blue and black cross-stitching. The black inscriptions in the lobed cartouches are also composed of dense cross-stitching. The simple, cheap material of the dervish staff symbolised the mystic's modest lifestyle. The same simplicity characterises the dangling strips of fabric as well as the metal chains and bells. The metal parts would jangle when Sufis performed their dervish dances.

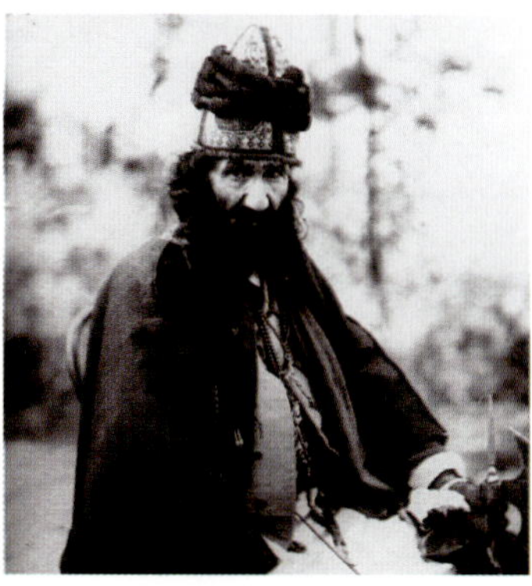

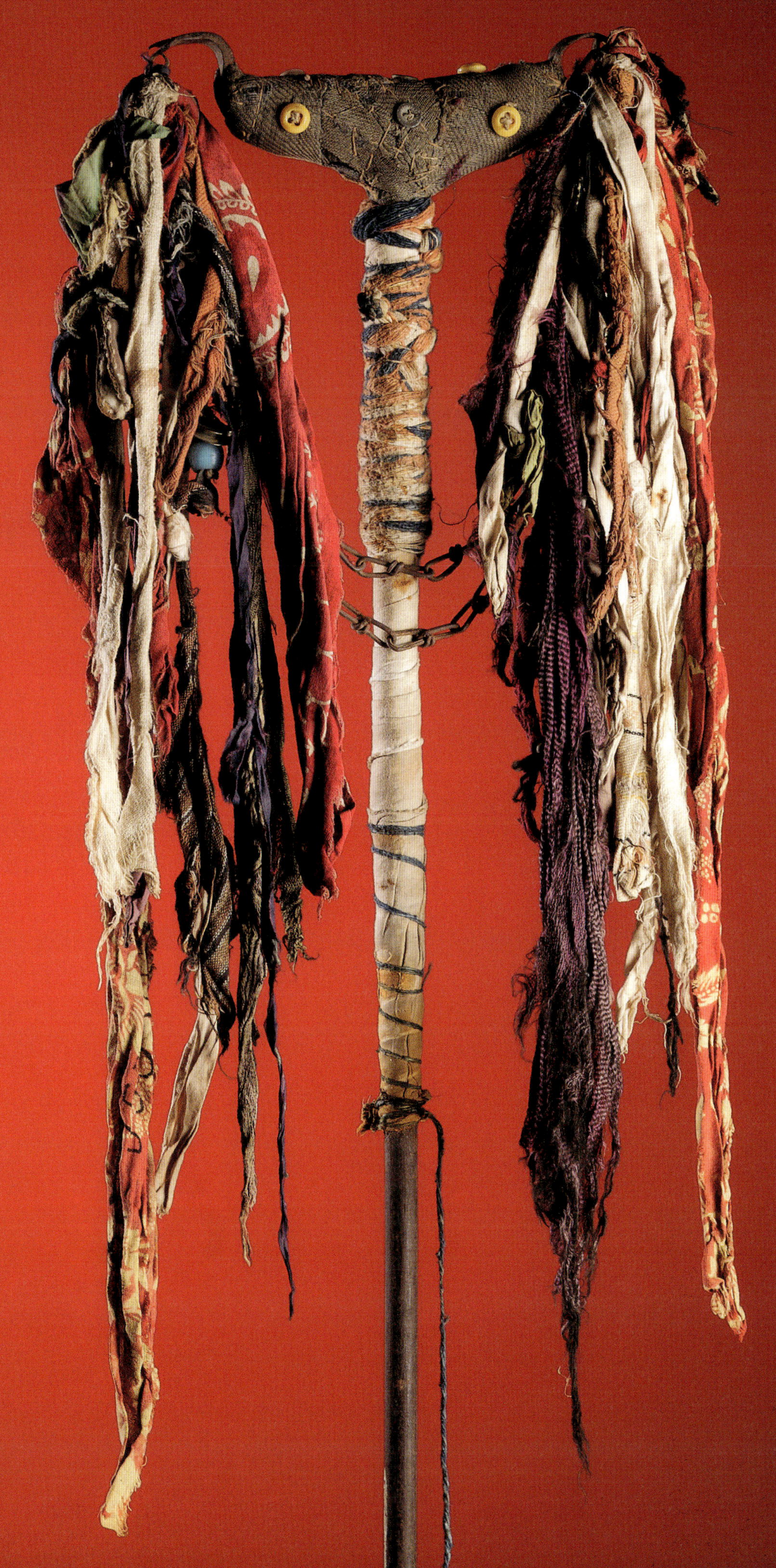

Kayak

Kilaamiut (Inuit), West Greenland
1700-1800
34.4 x 547.4 x 40 cm
hide, wood, bone, whalebone
RMV 349-1b (1883)

A light, silent hunting boat
Kayaks were long, narrow, highly manoeuvrable hunting boats, ideally suited to summer hunting in open water. Hunters rowing in kayaks could cover great distances. When the water was partly covered with ice, the Inuit transported them over the frozen areas on dog sleds. Since the kayak was relatively light, it could be carried upside down on the head, or crosswise on the back, using a special device to lash it in place.

Learning kayaking: The younger the better
Boys were taught kayaking at an early age, and were given their own child-sized kayaks and paddles. Babies would playfully practise keeping their balance and making paddling movements on their mother's lap. Since the 1980s, kayaks have been superseded by motorboats. For a while, the art of kayaking seemed to be in danger of being lost altogether. But a kayaking club in Nuuk has successfully revived the old tradition among young people, who practise kayaking recreationally and as a sport.

Ever present danger

The vulnerability of the hide was one of the main weaknesses that made kayaking dangerous. If a hole developed, for instance when knocking into a jagged piece of ice, the hunter would plug it temporarily with a piece of blubber. Another problem was the sunlight reflected on the water. This could deprive the paddler of his sight and in some cases it could even give rise to dangerous 'kayak dizziness', causing hunters to drown. For this reason, kayakers often wore wooden sunshades, beautifully decorated with inlaid ivory circles to symbolise the sun or the eyes.

Kayaks on the ceiling

In some Dutch coastal regions, it was common to hang model boats from the church ceiling. These were usually European types, but sometimes exotic models were hung up. For instance, in the nineteenth century, in the church in Hallum on the island of Ameland, a Greenland kayak could be admired, possibly as a souvenir or trophy brought back by a whaler. A most intriguing tale is told of a 'mummy' in a kayak that was discovered in Hoorn two hundred years ago (now in the West-Friesch Museum). It was initially claimed that the navigator came from Greenland, and that his kayak had drifted off course and remained afloat for some time. In 2001 DNA research was carried out on the remains, which revealed that the sailor is unlikely to have come from Greenland. The kayak that is depicted here was donated to the museum by the municipality of Brielle in 1883.

One watertight whole

Kayaks were made from a driftwood frame, across which the hides of some six large seals were stretched. The hide was moistened to enable it to be stretched taut over the kayak frame. Women would sew the hide onto the frame with watertight stitching to limit leakage in the joints. Seal oil ensured that the hide itself remained watertight. There was a scupper hole in the point of the kayak, with a wooden plug that could be removed to drain off water as needed. The hunter slipped his legs through the 'manhole' to seat himself in the kayak. He would often wear a special sealskin anorak, which would be seamlessly tied to the ring around the manhole. This made the paddler one with his kayak, and ensured that the boat would not fill with water if it capsized. Skilled kayakers perfected the art of 'rolling', in which the paddler would cause the kayak to roll over and right it again on the other side.

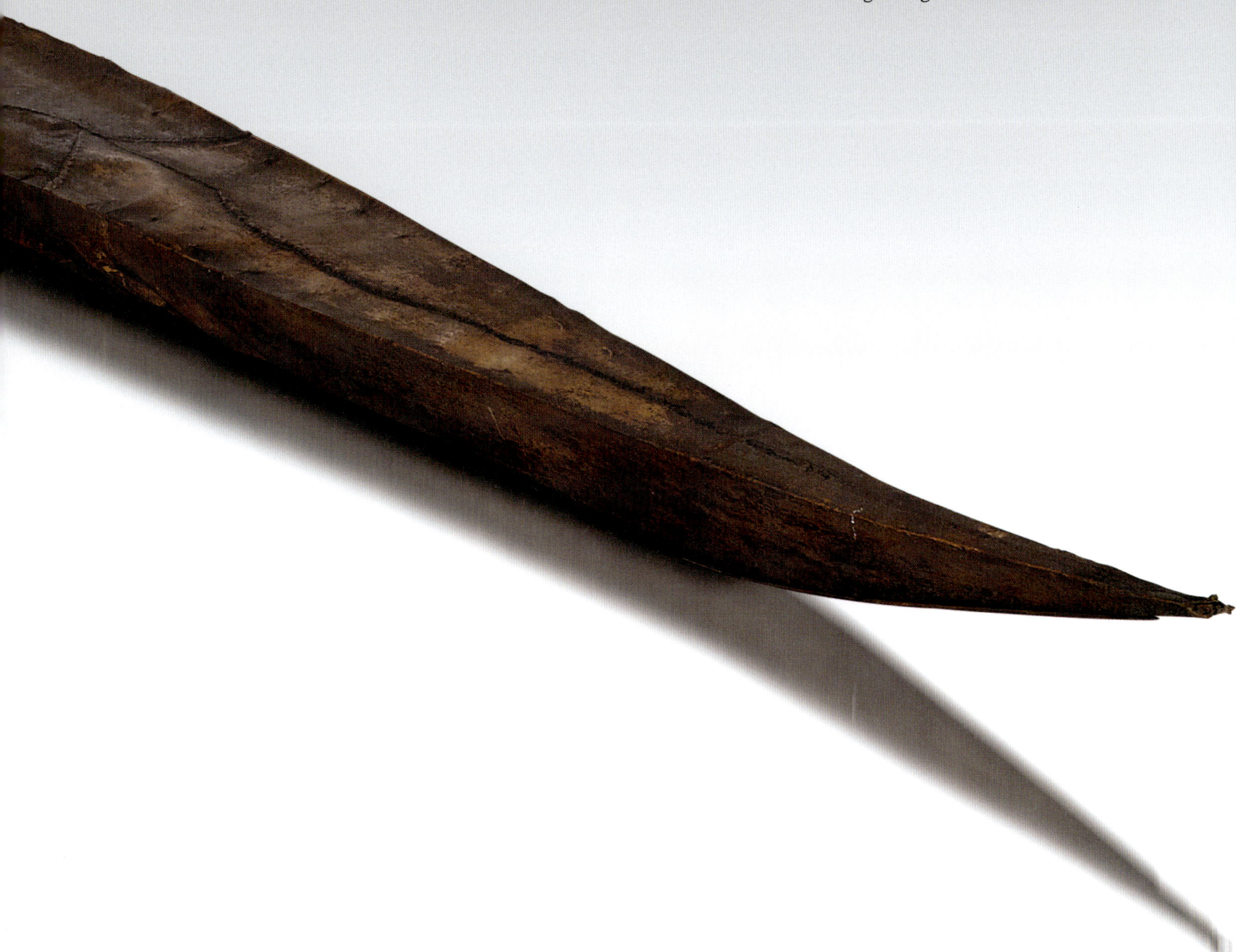

Officer's cloak and helmet

Late Chōson; Seoul, Korea
19th century
132.5 cm
wool, silk, otter fur, metal, iron, leather, horse hair, copper
RMV 666-120 (1888)

Red officer's cloak

This rare woollen officer's cloak was worn with the accompanying iron helmet. The cloak belonged to a high-ranking officer, as is clear from the blue silk lining and the hems trimmed with otter fur. The shoulder decorations of dragons' heads and necks also reflect the wearer's status. Worldwide, only a handful of high-quality Korean cloaks have withstood the ravages of time; in fact this may be the only such uniform in the world. These items were collected in the period in which Korea sought to reform its army along Western lines. Because of the Japanese occupation and the Korean War, no uniforms of this kind can be found in Korea itself.

Lack of development

When the Japanese government forced Korea to open up to foreign trade and imports in 1876, the country had witnessed a long period of technological stagnation, caused by the nationalist politics and economic decline that had followed the Japanese invasions of 1592 and 1597 and the Manchu invasions of 1627-1636. For instance, we know from illustrations in an official fifteenth-century publication *Oryeui: 'The Five Rites'* that armour had been made in much the same way for centuries.

The cloak

It is mainly the materials used for the uniform that give it its aura of splendour. The cloak is made of gloriously bright, red wool; the delicate blue silk and otter fur confer an elegant quality that is enhanced by the fact that the cloak's upper section is covered with wonderfully gleaming metal scales, lacquered alternately in black, red and gold. The bottom section is covered with copper nails and dragons' heads made of gilded bronze.

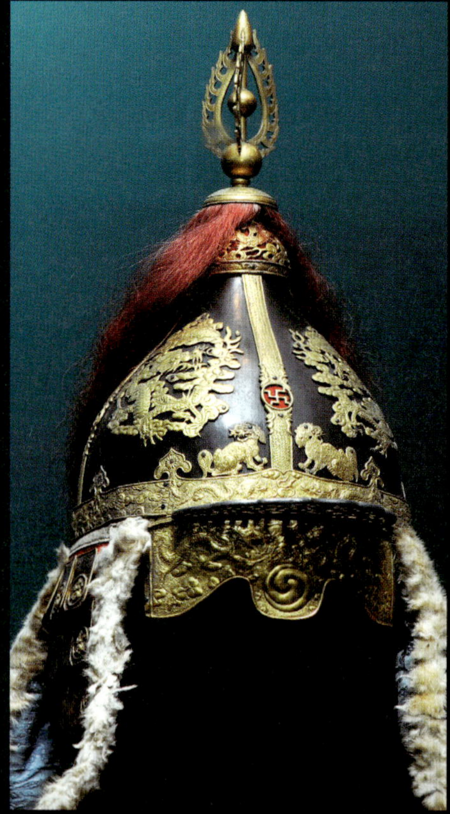

The helmet

This helmet is an enthralling object. It consists, as was customary, of four iron plates riveted together, covered with a thick layer of black lacquer. The inside is lined with leather and padded blue silk. Attached in a hole that has been left in the metal is a separate copper point, to which the elegant red horse hair is attached. The decorations on the helmet are made of openwork and chased copper-gilt and depict a dragon in the clouds, cranes and lions. Other smaller motifs include swastikas and flowers. The helmet also has a fixed visor and a piece to protect the forehead displaying the same recurrent decorations.

Use

Cloaks like this were worn by high-ranking officers for equestrian battles and ceremonial occasions. Under the cloak, which covered only part of the body, they wore their actual armour, which provided far better protection. The cloak was fastened in front with a wide belt denoting rank. In contrast to Chinese and Japanese armour, Korean uniforms consisted only of upper sections.

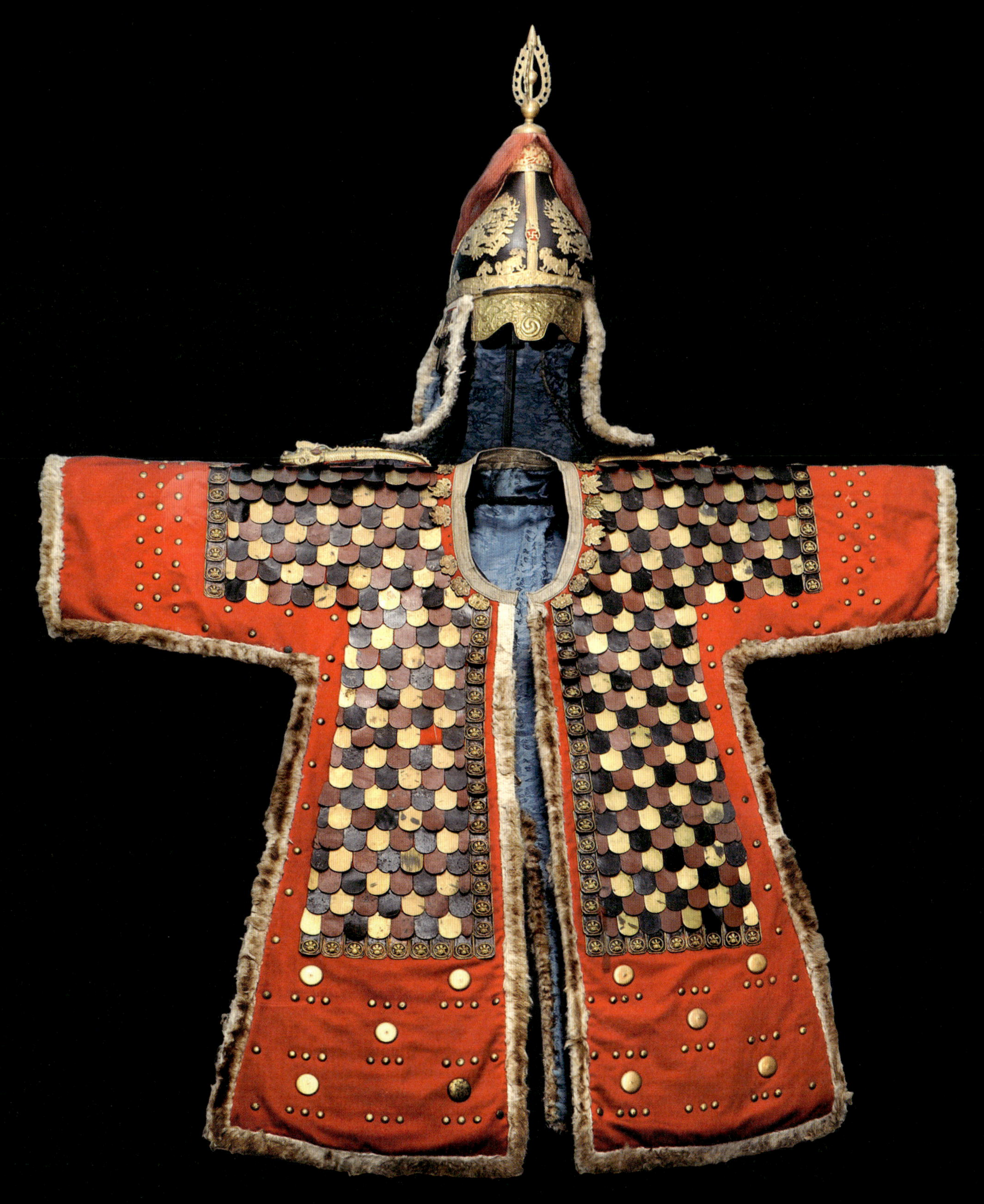

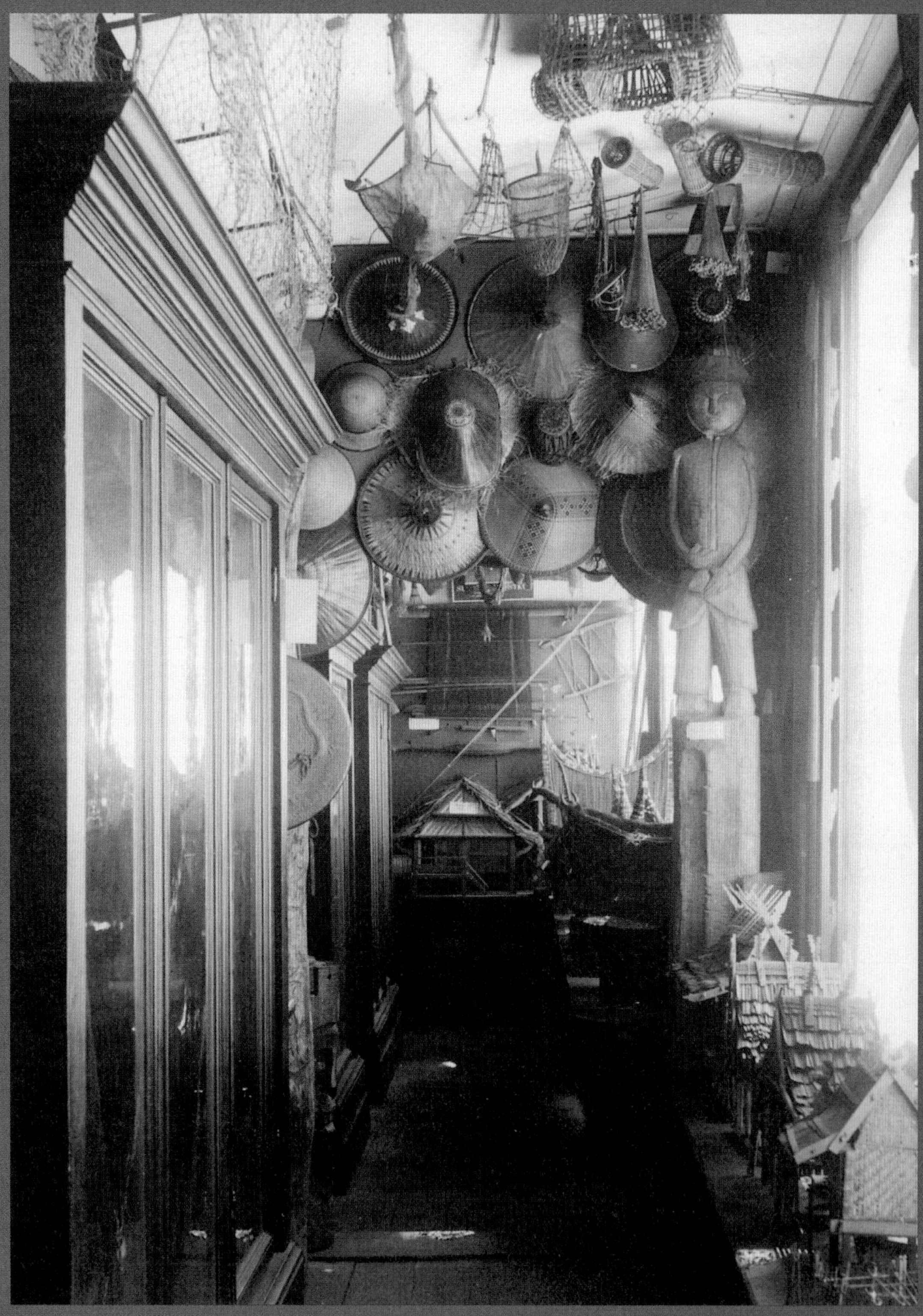

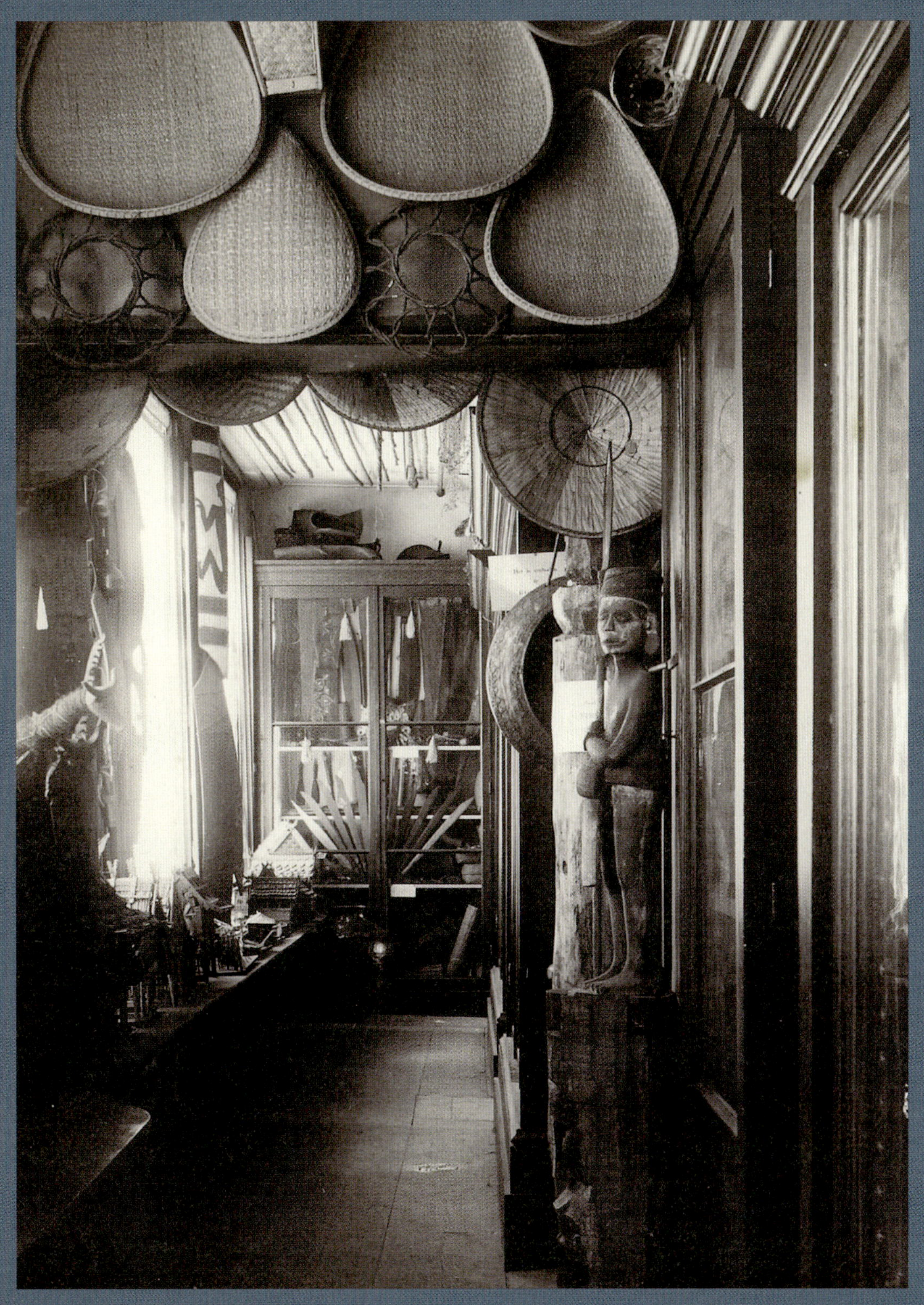

Boomerang

Southeast Australia
1850-1860
58 x 7 x 1 cm
wood, pigment
RMV 680-9 (1888)

Bird boomerang

This highly unusual bird-shaped boomerang, from which an elongated slit has been carved, probably comes from southeast Australia. Both sides of the head are decorated with finely engraved motifs depicting a 'dancing' figure holding a boomerang and the characteristic emu. The surface also displays a number of finely incised strips. Decorations of this kind are frequently seen on spear-throwers from southeast Australia. Although the number of figurative drawings increased in the contact period between 1840 and 1880, the motifs are nonetheless characteristic of the time before European influence. The bird's beak is clearly drawn in, with 'nostrils' carved out on both sides, a highly unusual feature..

Multifunctional

The Aborigines of southeast Australia used two types of boomerangs: a returning and a non-returning kind. Boomerangs could be used as knives, hammers, clubs, digging sticks, sticks rubbed to make fire, percussion instruments, and naturally as weapons and for hunting. Given its shape, this one was probably the returning kind, but it displays a number of unusual features such as a flared tip at one end and a beak shape at the other. Returning boomerangs obey several laws of physics: Bernoulli's principle of differences in air pressure, gyroscopic stability and precession, and Newton's laws of motion.

The call of the hawk

No other boomerangs are known with a carved image of this kind. However, ethnographic sources do report that Aboriginal hunters from the southeast endowed their boomerangs with a whistling noise to imitate the sound of a hawk. When the boomerang was tossed above a group of ducks, the ducks would fly very low along the waterway and become entangled in a net that other hunters had stretched there.

Dreamtime

Like the familiar boomerang, the concept of Dreamtime is also a deeply-ingrained part of Aboriginal culture. Dreamtime links past, present and future. It explains how mythical creatures created the landscape, and provides guidelines and laws indicating how people should act today in order to preserve continuity in the future. Dreamtime stories are extremely diverse, although they often feature returning boomerangs. The stories tell of the magical flight of the boomerang, but they also tell of objects that have vanished from sight and then mysteriously reappear.

The wanderings of a boomerang

This boomerang has a highly unusual provenance. It was acquired around 1860 by the merchant Friedrich August Lühdorf and incorporated into a collection of items from the region of the Amur River in Siberia bordering on the Sea of Okhotsk. It appears from Lühdorf's correspondence from the time when he transferred his collection to the museum in 1882, that he had acquired the boomerang – which was already broken – from an Ainu man on the island of Sakhalin, in exchange for a sack of rice. The boomerang had probably left southern Australia from the harbour of Encounter Bay, South of Adelaide, or from Portland in western Victoria. These major whaling ports were active between 1840 and the early 1860s. It was very common for whalers to sail from southern Australia to the northern Pacific during the whaling season.

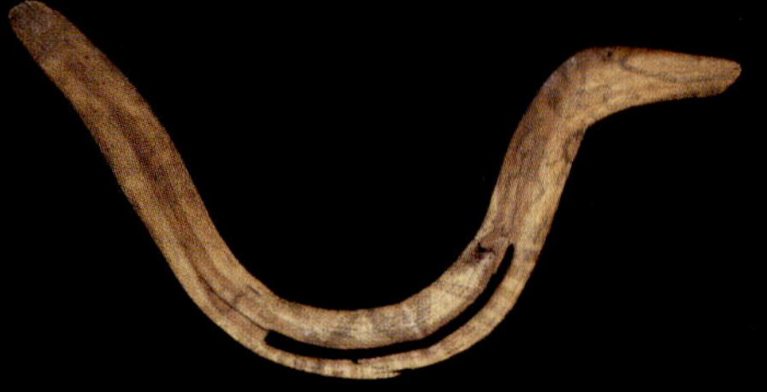

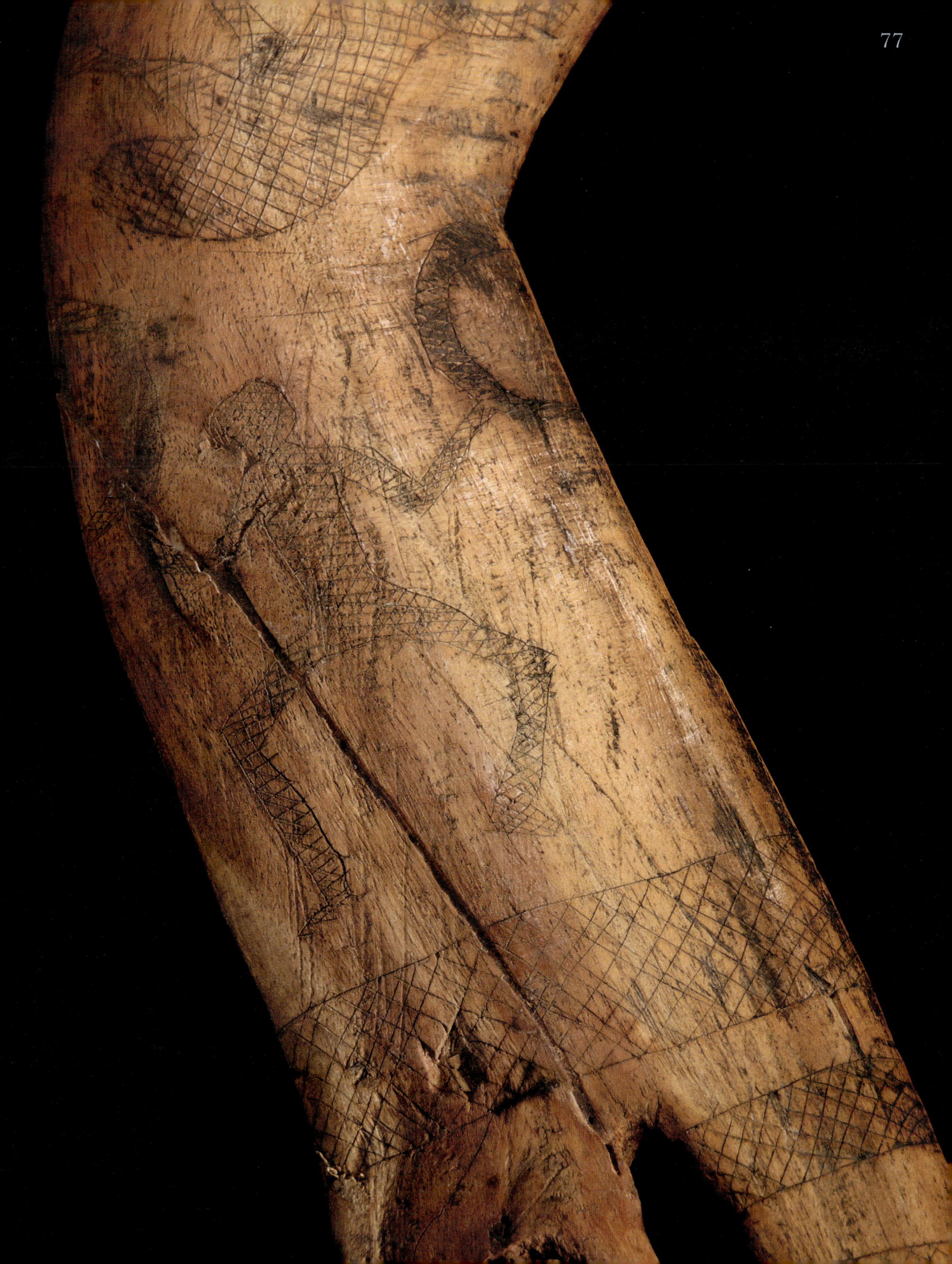

Headdress (*Epaku*)

Enggano, Indonesia
1st half 19th century
h. 17 cm, diam. 10.5 cm
wood, tin foil, Nautilus shell, beads
RMV 712-1 (1888)

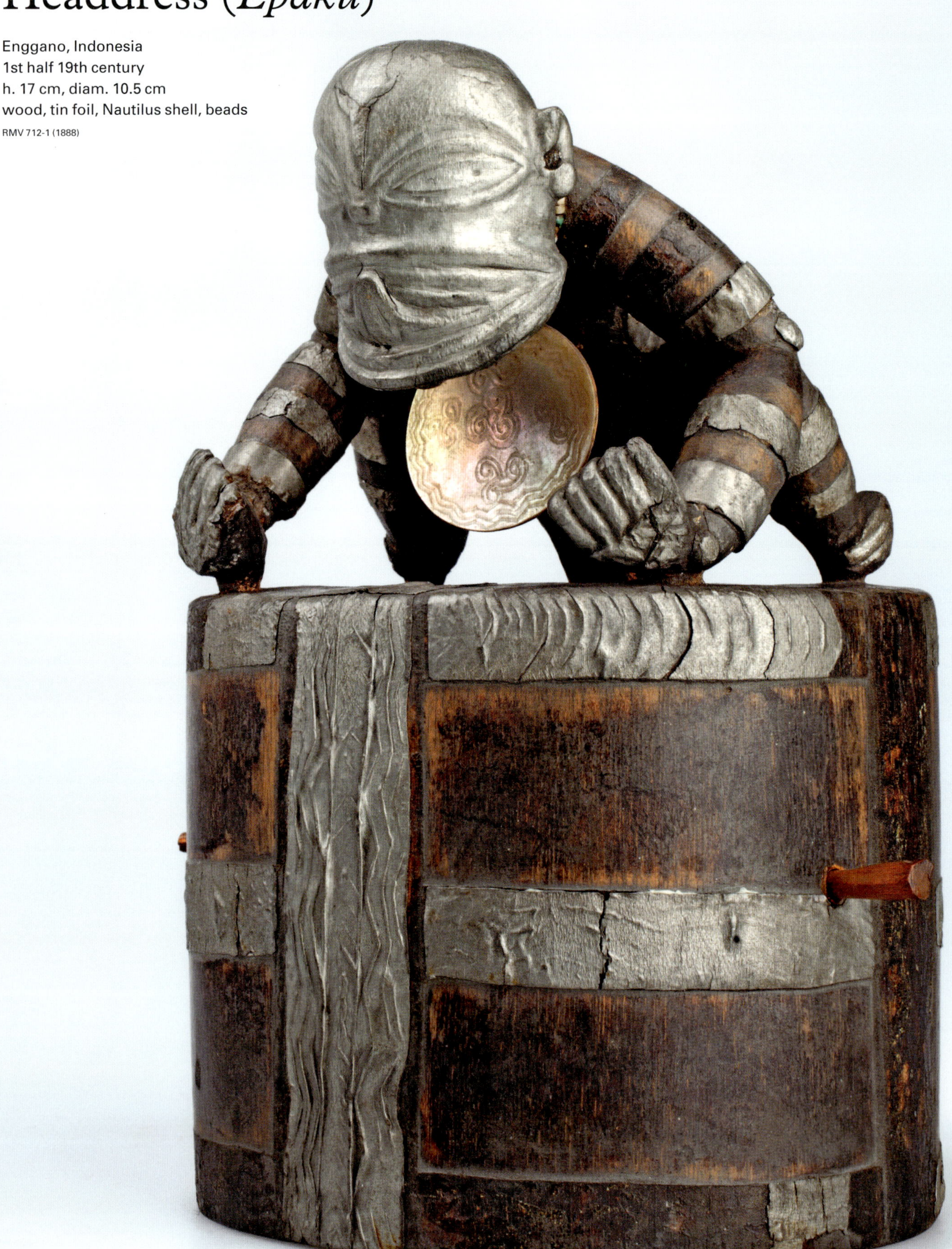

Worn by women

This extraordinary hat or *epaku* consists of a wooden cylinder to which bands of tin foil have been applied, with zigzag decorative lines. The cylinder has holes in which wooden pegs can be inserted. These are used to attach it to the woman's gathered-up hair, over which the cylinder is placed. On the upper surface of the cylinder, which is also overlaid with tin foil, we see a crouching human figure with a strikingly large head, large eyes, and a mouth with a protruding tongue. The figure wears a string of beads, from which hangs an oval pendant made from a Nautilus shell.

Lost culture

Enggano is a small island off the coast of Southwest Sumatra, whose population had their own unique culture and language. In the latter half of the nineteenth century, diseases such as cholera, introduced into the region by foreign travellers, almost wiped out the indigenous population who had not developed any resistance to them. Censuses held in 1866 and 1909 showed their numbers plunging from 6,420 to 372. From the beginning of the twentieth century onwards, migrants from Sumatra and Java settled on the island. They were soon so numerous that aspects of the original Enggano culture were no longer discernible. This history of loss adds unique value to the Enggano collection in the Rijksmuseum Volkenkunde.

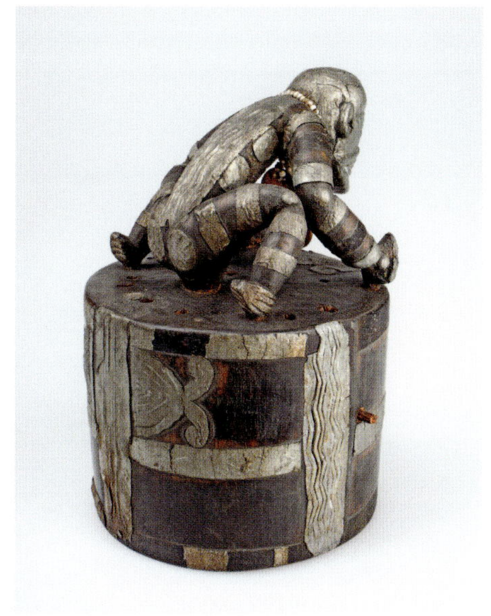

Tin, copra, and slaves

The tin foil with which the hat is overlaid came from the tin mines of the island of Bangka, to the east of Sumatra. Buginese sailors probably bartered it for copra (the dried kernel of the coconut) in the nineteenth century. Coconut palms abounded on Enggano, and provided the island's main products for trade. The VOC did not conduct much trade with Enggano. The crew of the first Dutch ship that passed the island on 5 June 1596, captained by Cornelis de Houtman, did not dare go on land, fearing the population's hostility. In 1645 the Dutch sailed two ships loaded with slaves from Enggano to Batavia.

Harvest feast

Images are known of women wearing *epaku* headdresses while dancing during an important war ritual, *Eakalea*. The hats were generally decorated with long feathers, which swayed back and forth as the women made circular movements with their heads during the dance. At the big harvest feast, celebrated by the whole village community, the rich harvest from the land, the sea and the forests would be gathered together, displayed and redistributed by the women, who owned the land. The men brought their hunting spoils, wild boar from the forests, to the village square, which was called 'the place where heads are chopped off'. Boars' heads were distributed among the most important women in the community.

Defeated foes

It is not known whether Enggano's cultural traditions included headhunting, but wars were certainly frequent there. New life, the fertility of the land and people, was closely related to death, the defeat of enemies. The combination of the spoils of hunting, which the men brought into the village community during the harvest feast, and the ritual in which the women danced around these spoils, related to the continued existence of this people's society. The bowed, crouching figures on the women's hats probably represent war trophies, defeated enemies. Knives from Enggano display the same motif.

Icon

The 'crown' type of headdress, made from eagle feathers, is possibly the most iconic object that is widely associated in the outside world with North American Indians. But headdresses of this type were originally worn only by a limited number of Plains tribes – that is, those who lived in the Great Plains between the Mississippi River and the Rocky Mountains. After the forced settlement on reservations, headdresses of this kind became fashionable among more and more Plains nations, but they were worn almost exclusively at social and ceremonial gatherings, as Herman ten Kate (who bought this headdress for his collection) remarked back in 1883. In the twentieth century, tribes in other parts of North America also adopted this type of headdress for such occasions. Its use was eventually commercialised.

Feather headdresses

Plains Indians used the feathers of eagles, hawks, turkeys, pheasants, and partridges for their headdresses. Those worn by Blackfoot and Cree consisted of a hide headband to which the eagle feathers were attached vertically: the 'straight-up' type. The Sioux, Mandan, Arikara, and Hidatsa nations of the northern Plains favoured the crown type, consisting of a tight hide bonnet with a wreath of eagle feathers radiating outwards and backwards. This shape symbolised the Sun, the source of all life. Sometimes the headdress was furnished with a single or double 'tail', also feathered, as in this case. This 'trailer warbonnet' was mainly worn on horseback.

Eagle feathers

The eagle was believed to possess supernatural powers. This bird was frequently seen as the messenger between the world of human beings and the gods. He also embodied the mythical Thunderbird, who caused thunder by flapping his wings, and who brought forth flashes of lightning by blinking his eyes. Eagle feathers possessed spiritual power and gave supernatural protection. Only those who had proven their courage in battle were entitled to wear them.

Warrior dress

The earliest description of Native Americans' fighting outfits and weapons was written by the French scholar Jean-Louis Berlandier and dates from 1828, when he undertook an expedition to the Southern Plains in the service of the Mexicans: 'Their clothes display much variety. I have seen some dressed elegantly, proud and defiant with a headdress and feather coat, whole others were rigged out horribly with caps made of bison hide with horns, their bodies painted grotesquely [. . .] The edges of their shields are also decorated with flared feathers. On their heads they wear feather headdresses to which they attach a kind of tail of feathers that hangs over their shoulders and floats in the wind behind them when they spur on their horse.'

Status and beauty

Only men who had frequently been distinguished for their courage in battle by being presented with an eagle feather could obtain a large enough number of feathers to make a crown-type head-dress. Wearing such a headdress was an expression of collectively recognised status. This Comanche headdress has fifty feathers. For aesthetic reasons, feathers from other birds were added to the headdresses, along with tufts of painted horse hair, strips of ermine, and coloured beads.

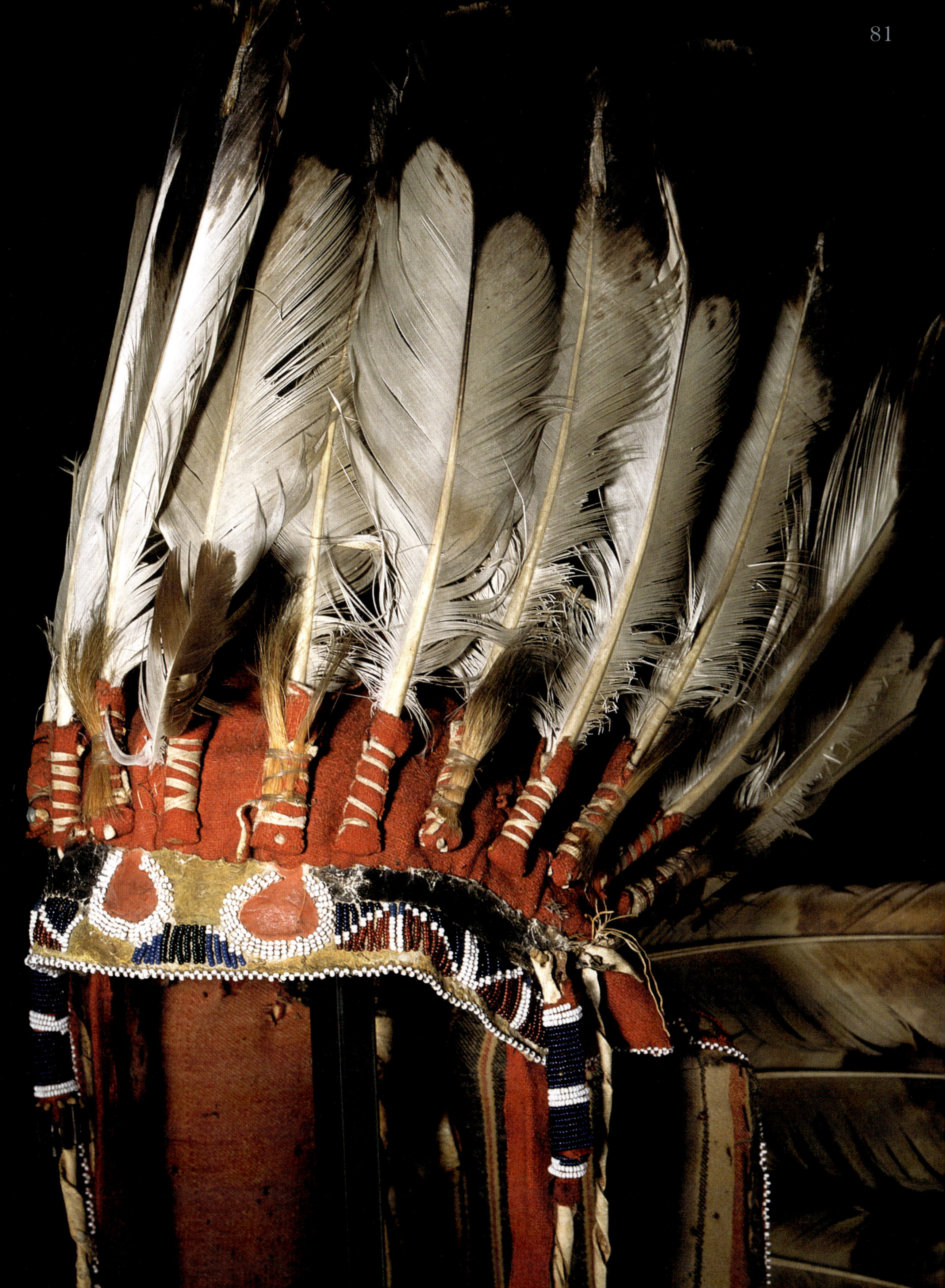

Powder bag

Yanktonai; North Dakota, United States
1850-1870
h. 25.5, w. 18 cm
hide, wool, silk, glass, horn, wood
RMV 710-7 (1889)

Acquisition
Even before the young anthropologist Herman ten Kate embarked on his journey of discovery in the Wild West at the end of 1882, he purchased an important collection of objects originating from the Yanktonai Indians with his own money. The items were offered to him by a merchant at Niagara Falls, an important place of transit for goods to and from the northern Plains. The objects came from the Two Bears group, so named after their leader, who belonged to the Yanktonai Sioux who lived on a reservation in North Dakota.

The Yanktonais and Chief Two Bears
The Yanktonais are a subgroup of the Sioux who left the eastern forests of Minnesota at the end of the seventeenth century and became bison hunters on the northern Plains. Even so, they also absorbed certain influences from the sedentary Mandan, Arikara, and Hidatsa tribes, lived in teepees as well as earth lodges, and made hide bags as well as baskets and pottery. Such external influences have helped to make their artistic style more eclectic than those of other indigenous groups. In the period 1850 to 1870, the Hunkpatinas, a subgroup of the Yanktonais, were led by Chief Matononpah, Two Bears. He signed the Treaty of Fort Pierre of 1856, which regulated trade and relations with the whites. In 1863 he and his people settled at Fort Rice, where he mediated between the military authorities and Sioux leaders who were still hostile to the whites.

Bandoliers
Bandoliers are square or rectangular hip pouches with wide straps to be worn diagonally over the shoulder. These indigenous powder bags were based on the shoulder bags used by Euro-American soldiers and civil militias, who kept lead, flints, tinder and gunpowder in them. Bandoliers started being produced after the introduction of firearms. The bags spread across a very large area. Most were made and used in the Great Lakes region, particularly by the Ojibwas. The Sioux were the first to obtain guns, around 1790, and they started to make powder bags. After the Civil War, there was a shift to modern rifles like Winchesters with bullet magazines, which made the primary function of powder bags obsolete.

Usefulness and decoration
The earliest bags were purely functional, and were used for storing a variety of personal possessions as well as powder. As time went on, however, it became common to decorate them, and they served as expressions of taste, style, and status, eventually losing their primary function altogether. Traditional decorations were made of coloured porcupine quills, but these were rapidly superseded by glass beads imported from Europe.

Ribbons
Another decorative innovation involved appliqués of coloured cotton and silk ribbons obtained from white traders. This technique was found primarily on the southern Plains. Certain geometrical patterns and stylised plant shapes are characteristic of the Indian garments that were decorated with coloured ribbon. On the southern Plains, this kind of decoration almost completely supplanted porcupine quill work. Ribbon appliqués were much used by the southern Siouans (Iowa, Osage, Omaha, Ponka, Oto and Kaw tribes) and Caddoans (Caddo, Pawnee and Wichita tribes). The blue ribbon on the bag from Leiden has become badly discoloured and is partly decomposed.

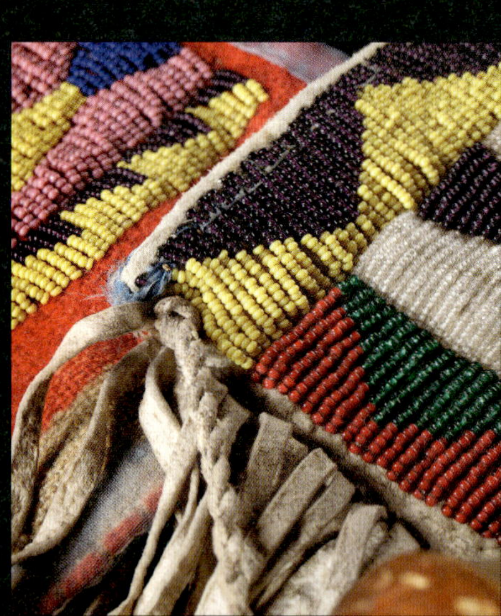

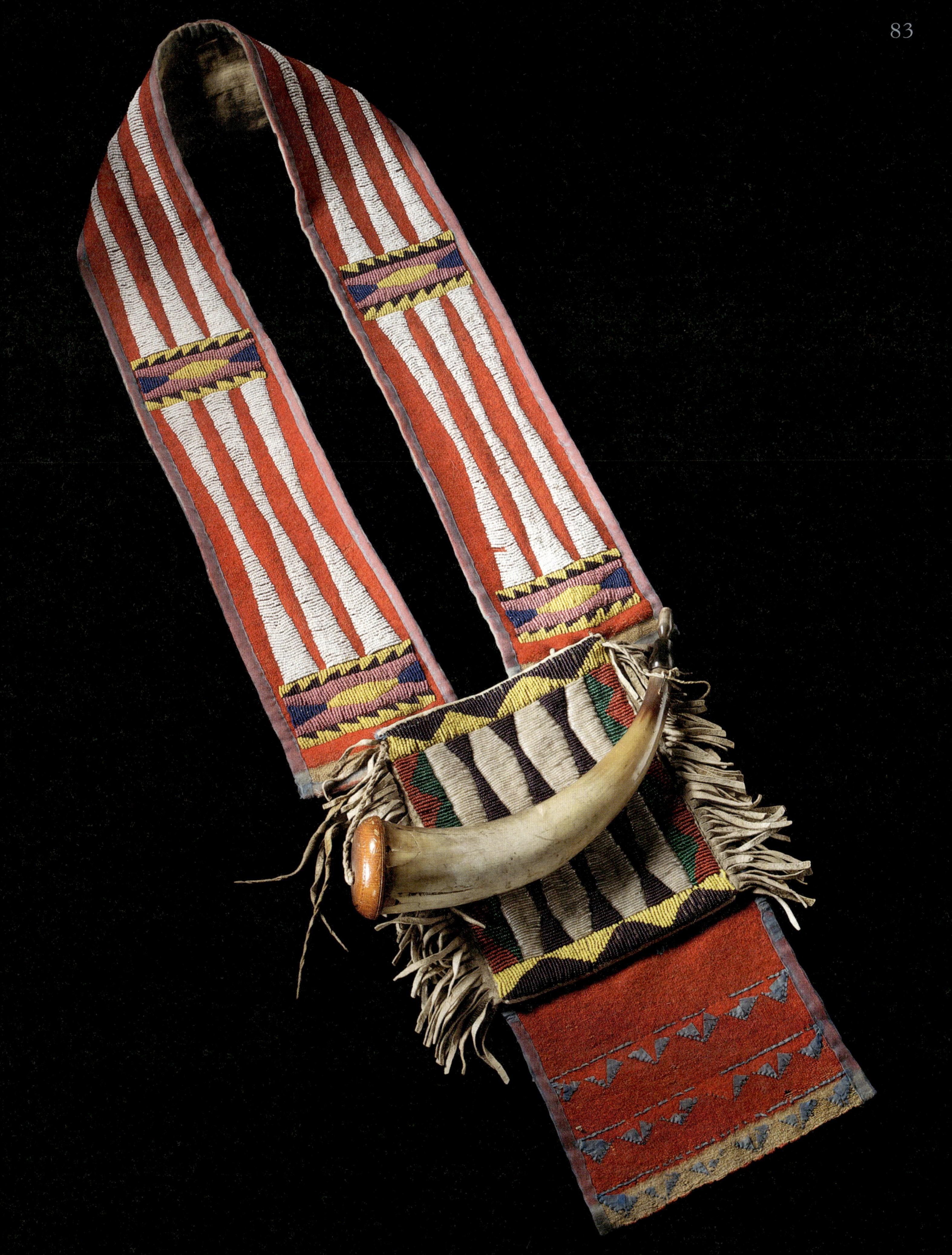

God figure (*Tino*)

Caroline Islands, Nukuoro, Micronesia
before 1891
58 x 7 x 1 cm
wood, pigment
RMV 828-63 (1891)

Simplicity

God figures from Micronesia are in general rare. Worldwide, fewer than twenty statues of the type discussed here have been preserved. The 'Leiden' specimen displays certain idiosyncratic features within this group. For instance, it lacks elementary delineations of eyes, nose, ears and navel, feet, fingers, kneecaps and tattoo motifs, details that are sometimes found on other such statuettes. In short, the general features of this example combine Western Polynesian sculpture with the Micronesian preference for simplicity.

Good and evil times

Tino were placed in temples and dressed with woven fine mats. They were sometimes decorated with flowers and endowed with a form of headdress resembling a crown. These gods would be invoked by priests on important occasions such as births and weddings, divorce or illness, death, natural disasters, and the building of houses and canoes. Sometimes offerings of coconuts and fruit would be placed before the god figures. Some travel journals from the years 1870-80 refer to human sacrifices that allegedly took place around this time on altars erected in front of statues.

Polynesians in Micronesia

Nukuoro belongs to the Polynesian Outliers: a group of islands that, though geographically not located in Polynesia, is nonetheless inhabited by Polynesians. Characteristic Polynesian concepts of hierarchy and rank played an important part in society. Figures of this type are known in general as *tino*, 'bodies, figures'. Each statue bore the name of a specific male or female deity associated with a certain clan. The years 1910-13 were a period of sharp cultural decline, in which the *tino* lost their function. It was probably around this time that the last surviving statue was acquired by a collector.

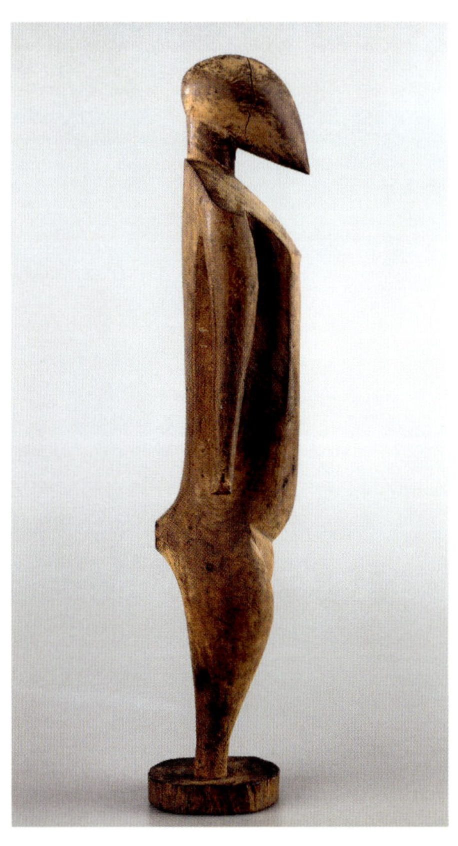
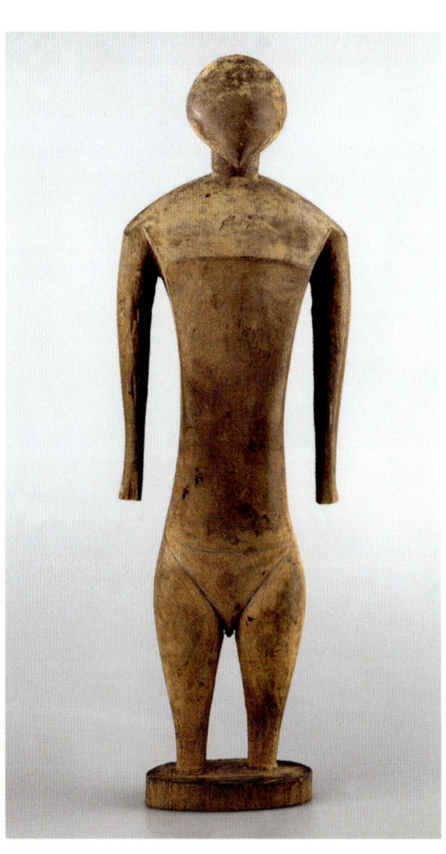
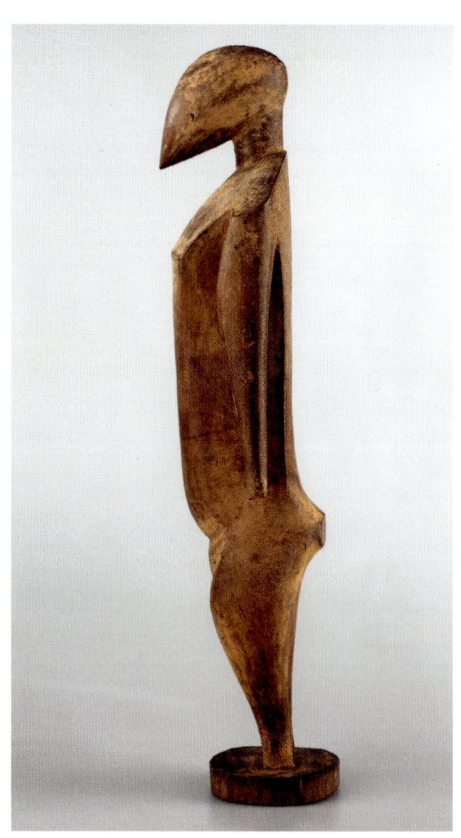

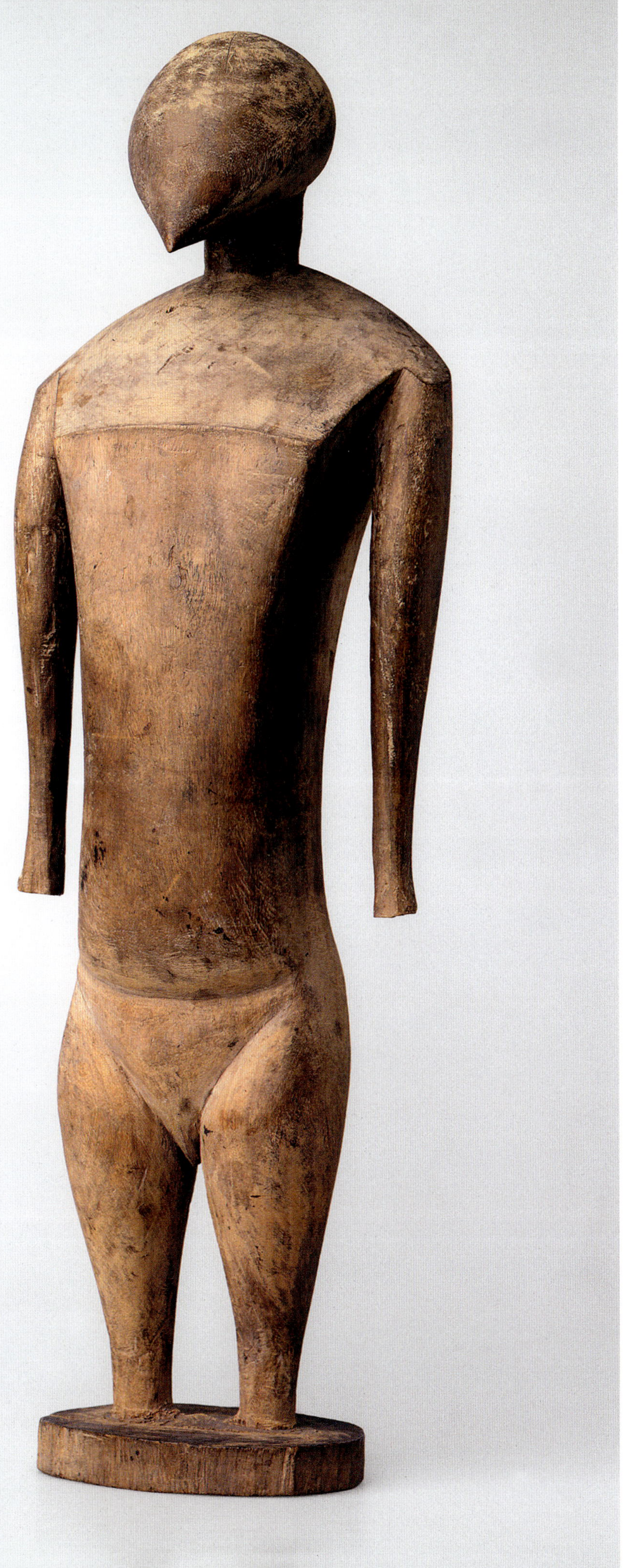

Giacometti and Moore

The Europeans who collected a number of these figures around 1870 thought them coarse and 'cumbersome'. Nowadays, the sculptures are praised for their sober, elegant lines. This highly stylised rendering of the human body attracted the attention of prominent twentieth-century Western artists. For instance, the sculptor Alberto Giacometti made a sketch of a figure of this kind, after an illustration in the journal *Cahiers d'Art*, around 1929. This ultimately led to his famous sculpture *Hands Holding the Void (Invisible Object)*. Henry Moore regarded a Nukuoro statue in the British Museum as a major highlight in the history of sculpture.

Globetrotter

This figure has a rich exhibition history. It was shown in 1949 at the Stedelijk Museum in Amsterdam and the Museum voor Land- en Volkenkunde (nowadays the World Museum) in Rotterdam. More recently, in 2009, it was displayed at the Fondation Beyeler and in the Linden-Museum in Stuttgart.

Statue of a seated couple

Oesba, Geelvink Bay, Northwest New Guinea, Indonesia
before 1893
33 cm
wood, fibre
RMV 929-691 (1893)

Man and woman on a bench

This completely unique statue, made of reddish-brown wood, depicts two figures seated on a bench, the outside of which is decorated in a leaf-edge pattern. The larger figure probably represents a man and the smaller one a woman. Stylistically, the statue differs from the well-known ancestor or *korwar* figures, because it has been carved in a more naturalistic design. Moreover, most *korwar* statues depict only a single figure.

The power of ancestral spirits

If this object was ever used as a *korwar*, offerings would have been brought to the spirit residing in the statue and his help invoked in times of tension and danger. The priest would use a *korwar* to contact the spirit of a dead person. He would take it in his hand and enter into a state of trance: at such moments it was believed that the spirit had taken possession of him.

Colonial times

The statue was acquired by Frederik Sigismund Alexander de Clercq, a Dutch colonial official working for the sultan of Ternate, an island in the Maluku Islands. He must have acquired the object during one of his four journeys to the west and north coasts of New Guinea in the years 1887 and 1888. In the nineteenth century, the Dutch used objects to help them develop an approach to their colonial possessions, but nowadays these objects also prompt critical reflections on the country's colonial past.

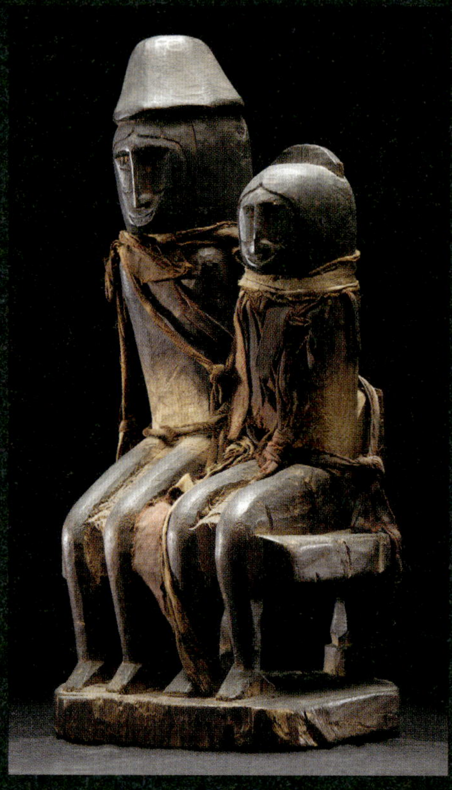

Destruction

Korwars are seldom found in the indigenous communities of Northwest New Guinea today. Conversion to Christianity was usually accompanied by the mass destruction of these 'heathen' statues, a radical act of faith that sadly curtailed the preservation of knowledge of the region's ancient culture and art.

Spirits of the dead?

The significance of this statue is not known. We cannot be sure whether it possessed the same emotional and symbolic value as *korwar* figures. *Korwar* means, first and foremost, the spirit of a dead person. This name derives from the belief that the spirit took up residence in the statue for a short or longer period of time.

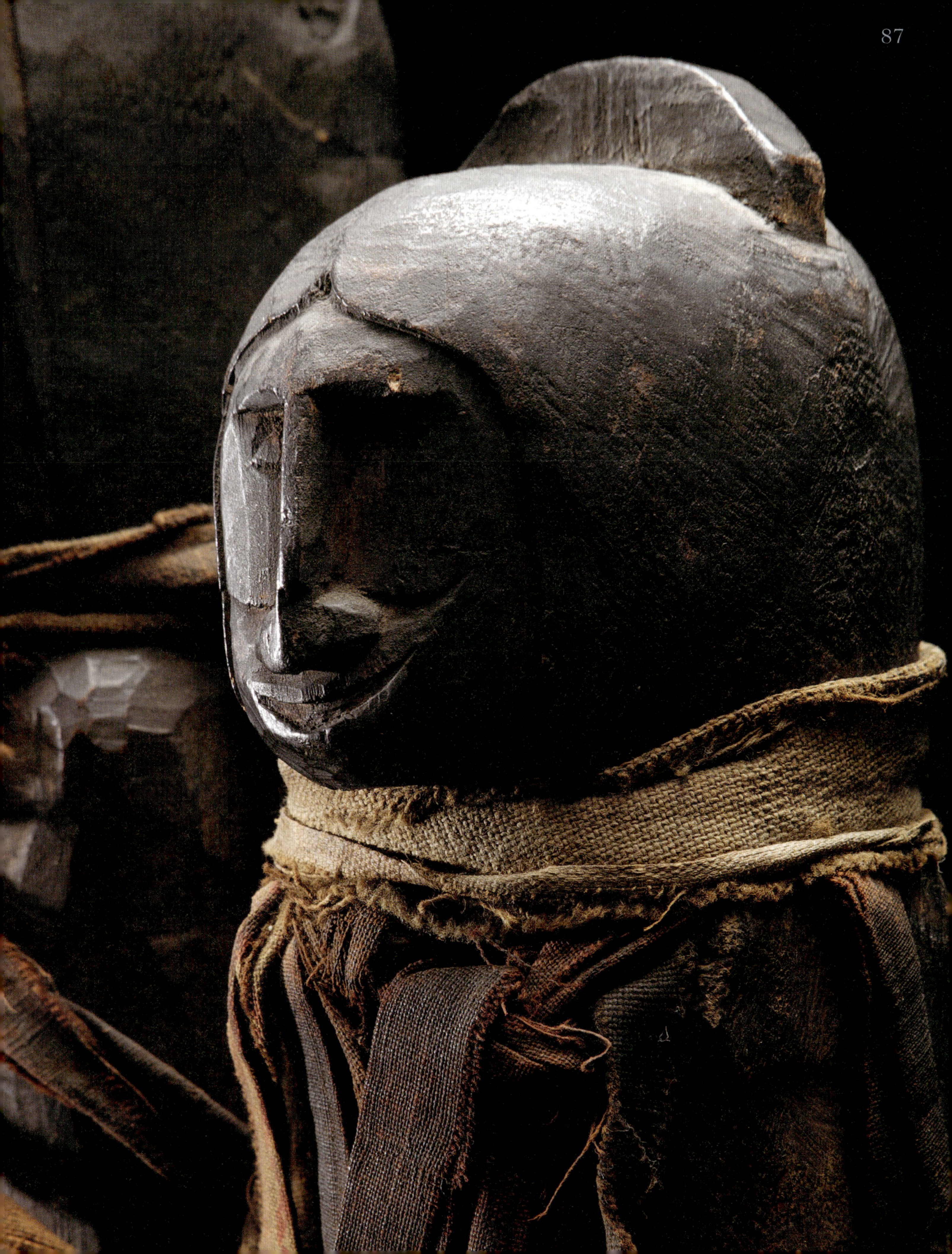

Mask (*Hudoq*)

Kayan Dayak; Upper Mahakam, Kalimantan, Indonesia
1st half of 19th century
82 x 38 x 28 cm
wood, feathers, rattan, copper, vegetable fibres, hide (orangutan)
RMV 1308-155 (1897)

Rhinoceros hornbill and water snake

Kalimantan is the Indonesian part of the vast island of Borneo. In the hinterland, along the banks of the major rivers, live diverse Dayak groups, such as the Kayan and the Kenyah. They live primarily from agriculture. Their traditional world view is based on the equilibrium between the heavens, which are ruled by the rhinoceros hornbill, *burung enggang* (associated with the sun), and the underworld, where the water snake (*naga*) lives. A variety of rituals are performed to preserve this equilibrium and to foster the fertility of the land.

Hudoq mask

The Kayan Dayak call this mask, which was found around the upper reaches of the great Mahakam river in the late nineteenth century, a *hudoq* or spirit mask. In this *hudoq temengang* mask – one of the many different kinds of *hudoq* masks – the powers of the rhinoceros hornbill (in the form of the bill and the copper plate symbolising the sun on the forehead) and the water snake (the large muzzle with teeth) are united, making this mask extremely sacred and highly effective in ritual contexts.

Unique

Kayan men once made their own masks, which explains why each one is unique. This one, carved from wood, is extremely expressive. It has two small round mirrors for eyes, and wears earrings such as those worn by the Dayak themselves. The lower jaw, with its vegetable fibre beard, is attached loosely, so that it can be moved to create a rattling noise. Over the mask is a rattan warrior's cap, the surface of which is covered with orangutan hide. The feathers come from a rhinoceros hornbill and an argus pheasant.

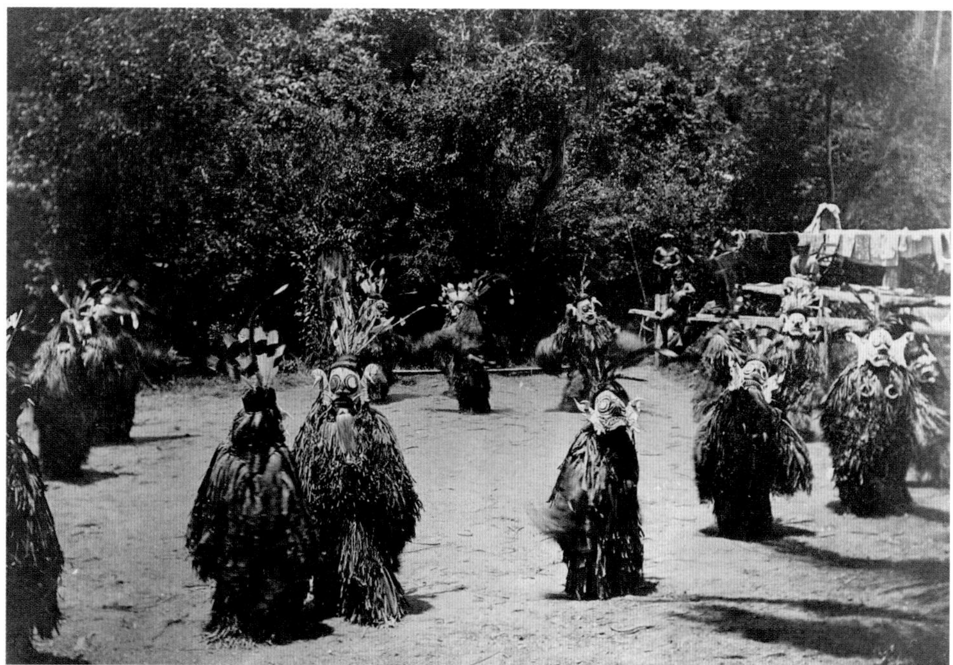

Mask dance and rice cycle

Those who wore *hudoq* masks could communicate with the spirit world. They played a role in agricultural rituals, to ward off evil influences when sowing rice and to achieve a good harvest. This mask comes from the collection of A.W. Nieuwenhuis, who describes the week-long agriculture ceremony. In this week, a group of men, all wearing *hudoq* masks and costumes made from dried banana leaves, performed an impressive dance on the riverbank, accompanied by gong music. The purpose was to protect the rice and to placate the strayed rice spirits with offerings and entice them back to the field.

Anton Willem Nieuwenhuis

Anton Willem Nieuwenhuis (1864-1953) went on three expeditions to map out Kalimantan. On his second journey he procured this *hudoq* mask, along with other ethnographic objects. Nieuwenhuis worked as a medical officer in the Dutch East Indies Army from 1892 onwards. His journeys were academic field trips. Nieuwenhuis himself was a physician and ethnographer, and his companions were a biologist, a botanist, and a geologist. But he also had a political mandate. His third expedition was devised in part to bring peace and stability to Central Borneo, under Dutch rule. In 1904 Nieuwenhuis returned to the Netherlands and took up a chair at the University of Leiden.

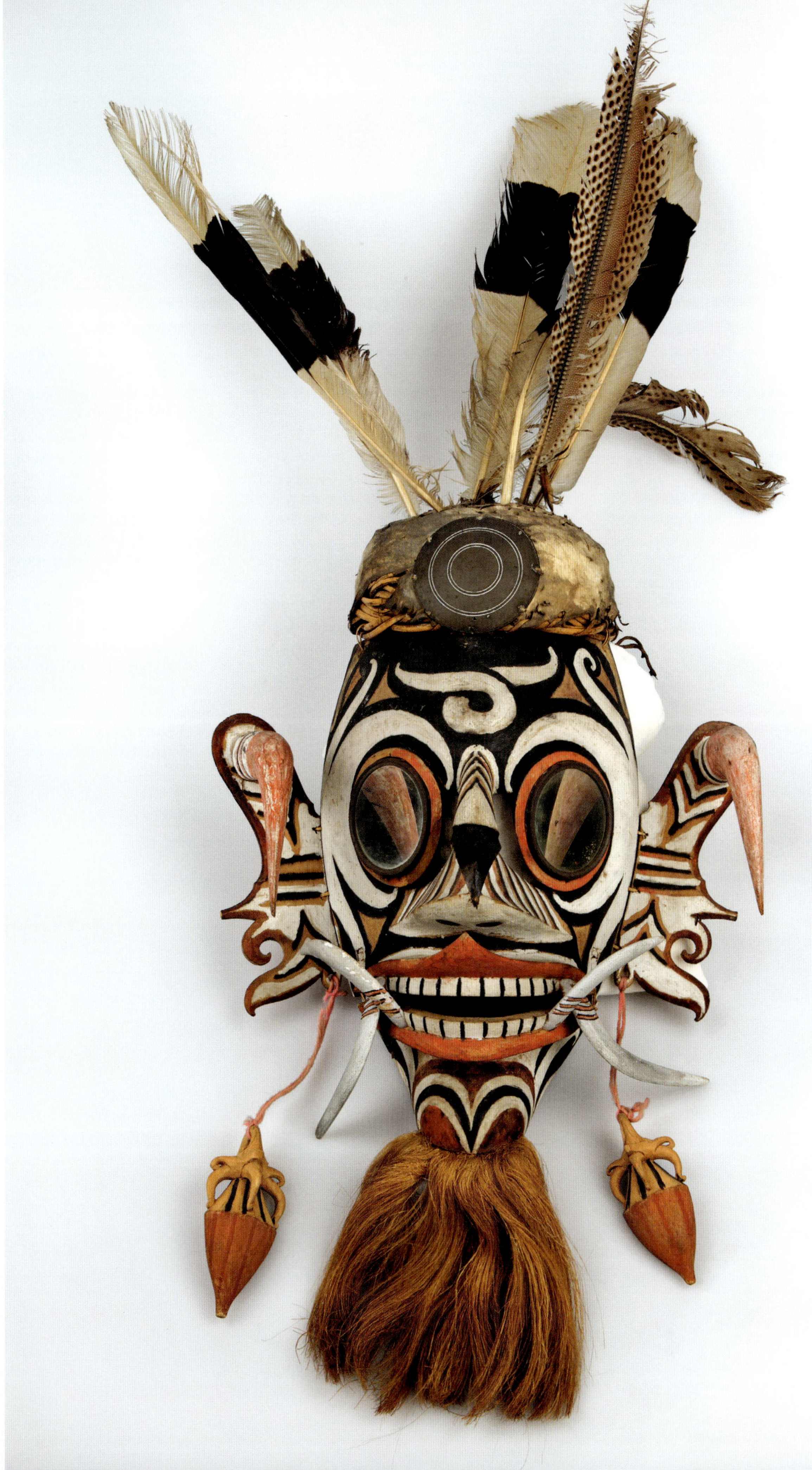

Bronze head

Bini, Nigeria
1600-1750
24.2 x 17.5 cm
brass or bronze
RMV 1164-4 (1898)

The Oba

Such is the technical perfection of the Benin Bronzes that they are among the most famous art objects of the African continent. In the kingdom of Benin, owning these objects was the exclusive privilege of the king, the Oba. When an Oba died, his successor would commission a number of bronze heads, which would be placed on the ancestral altar dedicated to the deceased. The heads are standardised images that cannot be linked to historical figures. Each one has a circular opening on top for the insertion of an elephant tusk with carved decorations. The necklace and headgear represent red coral beads. The three tattoos in the face, above the eyes, are characteristic of Benin style.

Ancestral altars

The Oba was regarded as a living God who mediated between mortals and the supernatural world. Only the king could entreat the gods and spirits to grant his people prosperity. He could not do so directly; the Oba had to direct his supplications to his ancestors, through the mediation of the bronze heads on their altars. Altars were erected in a variety of places inside and outside the palace. Offerings were frequently placed there.

The 'lost-wax' method

Local tradition has it that the bronze casting technique was introduced into Benin in the thirteenth or fourteenth century, from the city of Ife. The earliest Benin bronzes are made from scarce indigenous copper alloys. As more European brass was imported by Portuguese merchant sailors, working in bronze became a popular fashion. A special group of craftsmen specialised in casting bronze objects for the court. The bronze was cast using the 'lost-wax' method. Only one bronze could be made with each cast using this method, since both the model and the cast were lost during the process. The bronze founders mastered this technique to perfection.

Punitive expedition

The British merchants pressured the Oba to give up his monopoly on trade, seeking to engage in free trade with the local population. After British soldiers had been ambushed, the British mounted a punitive expedition. In 1897 they attacked the capital of the Kingdom of Benin and destroyed the king's palace. All precious items (made from bronze or ivory) were shipped to Britain as the spoils of war and sold to pay for the expedition. The objects, which had been used to worship the Oba's ancestors, ended up in museums and private collections around the world.

Determining age

Determining the precise age of the objects is a specialised task. All we know for sure is that these objects were made before 1897. The seventeenth-century travel accounts written by Dutchmen, illustrations depicting Europeans, archaeological and ethnographic research and oral history are all important sources. In addition, the results of chemical analyses of the materials used, advanced techniques such as thermoluminescence and the study of stylistic development make it possible to narrow down the age of specific objects. The Bini still observe many of their ancient traditions, albeit in modified forms. Although regional kings no longer possess institutionalised power in present-day Nigeria, they still occupy a special position in society, and ritual 'bronzes' are still made for the Oba to this day.

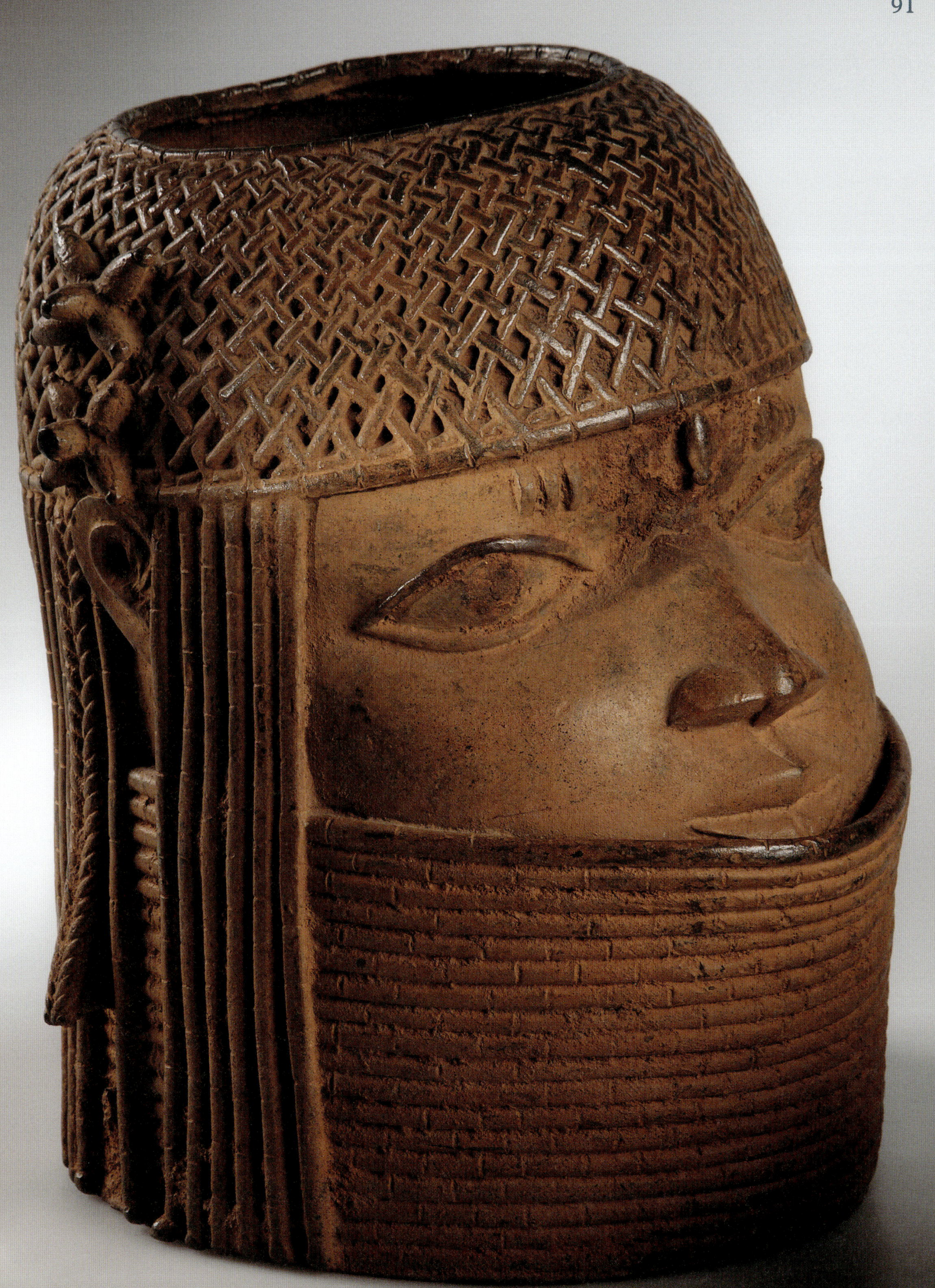

Fish-skin coat

Nivkh, Southeast Siberia, Amur region
1850-1880
95 x 141 cm
fish skin, copper
RMV 1202-267 (1898)

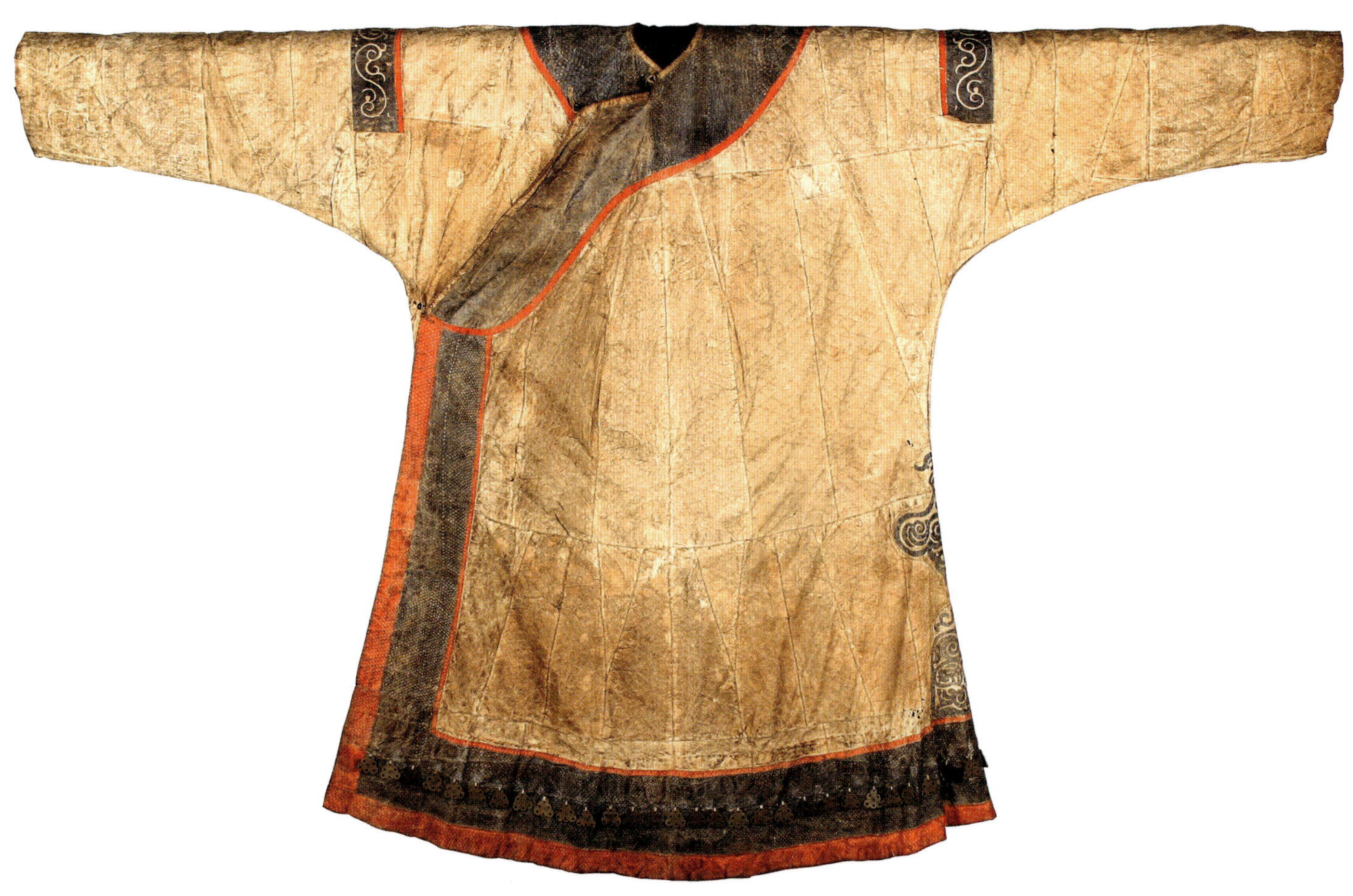

Fish skin

The coat is made from fish skin, probably salmon and carp. Black, porcelain buttons accentuate the diagonal, Manchurian or Mongolian-style fastening, and the back of the coat is decorated with bluish-black arabesques, spirals, birds and fish. The copper disks along the seam, a feminine symbol, were added for decoration and to ward off evil spirits. These disks would have made a jangling noise when the wearer was walking. Making a fish-skin coat of this kind was a highly skilled task. Expert seamstresses had good marriage prospects and were held in great esteem.

The German connection: Adolf Vasil'evich Dattan

This coat was donated to the museum in 1898 by Adolf Vasil'evich Dattan (1854-1924), a merchant in the service of the German firm of Kunst & Albers, which was founded in Vladivostok in 1864. Dattan engaged in barter trade with representatives of indigenous peoples in the Amur region and built up a large collection of art objects and utensils from this region. After the outbreak of the First World War, Dattan was accused of being a German spy and exiled to Kolpashevo, north of Tomsk. The Dattan Collection in the Rijksmuseum Volkenkunde gives a fine picture of the material culture of the Nivkh and Oroch of southeast Siberia at the end of the nineteenth century.

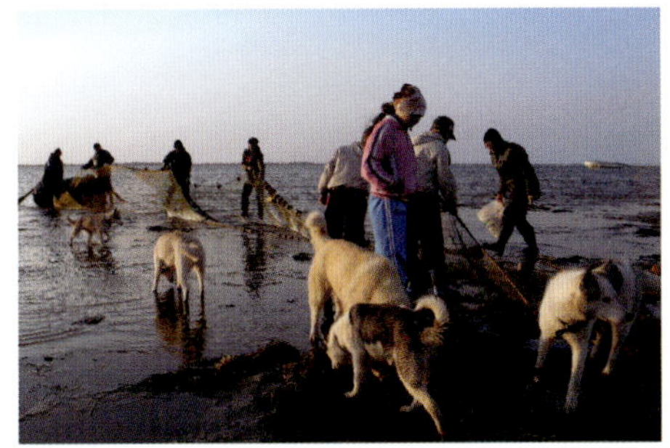

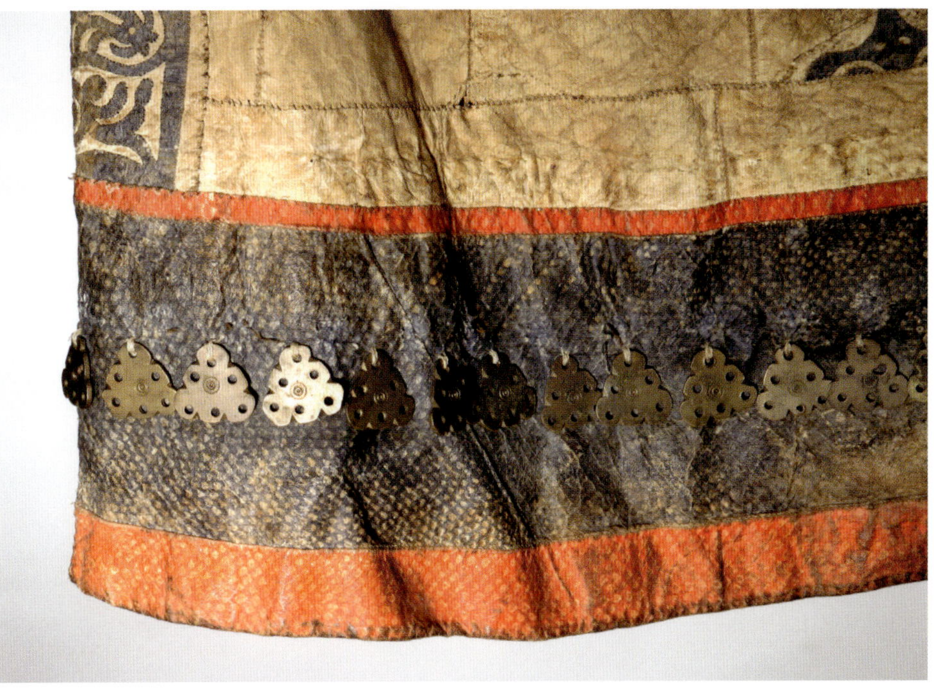

Watertight

One material surpasses all others in its water-repellent qualities. This is, of course, fish skin – how could it be otherwise? Fish skin is light and elastic, easy to model, and yet it is also sufficiently durable. However, it is also very thin, and largely for this reason, fish-skin clothing does not provide good insulation. In the late nineteenth and early twentieth centuries, men tended to wear these garments primarily in the summer months. Women wore fish-skin coats all year round, however, over several layers of cotton dresses. .

Symbols galore

The Nanai woman Nina Beldi, from a nation neighbouring on the Nivkh, states that the upper world is represented by the hems at the top of the garment, the middle world by the decorations in the middle, and the underworld (the world of fish) by the bottom part of the coats. One legend holds that the decorations on the back protect a woman from things she cannot see, for instance when working at the fire with her back to the door. In traditional societies, women were not permitted to look directly at their guests, and compensated for this by ensuring that the backs of their garments they displayed were richly decorated.

An endangered culture?

The Nivkh [pl. *Nivkhgi*, meaning 'people'] from the Amur region inhabit a subarctic wooded region along the Amur River and on the island of Sakhalin. Since Russian culture played a fairly dominant and oppressive role from the first wave of migration around 1580 up to and including the communist era (1917-1987), only a small percentage of the Nivkh still speak their indigenous language. Perestroika, the new political openness of the 1980s, generated a movement of cultural revitalisation. New organisations such as RAIPON helped the indigenous people enforce their rights.

Salt-cellar

Bini-Portuguese, Nigeria
1525-1600
13.7 cm
ivory
RMV 1323-1 (1901)

Tourist art?

Ivory salt-cellars were commissioned from Bini artists in Africa by the Portuguese especially for export. In old African workshops, which undoubtedly existed before the Portuguese arrived, the same artists made items for the local market as well as for their more demanding European clientèle. Worldwide, only fifteen Bini-Portuguese salt cellars are known. Since they are all quite similar, it is assumed that they were probably made in the same workshop.

Arquebus

Afro-Portuguese ivory salt-cellars and ivory spoons circulated in the Netherlands in the sixteenth century. There are only two ivory sculptures that can be assumed to have been taken directly from Benin by Dutchmen: this salt-cellar and the ivory figurine of a kneeling woman (see p. 108-109). The salt-cellar probably belonged to the collection of Stadholder William V. It was transferred to the Rijksmuseum in Amsterdam and in 1901 it was incorporated into the collection of the Rijksmuseum Volkenkunde. The rifle held by one of the horsemen helps us to date the salt-cellar. It is an arquebus, a very common weapon until around 1520-1530, when it was replaced by a more effective firearm. No salt-cellars were made in Africa after the seventeenth century. The objects seized during the British punitive expedition of 1897 (see p. 90-91) included a few extremely old ivory objects, but no salt-cellars.

Bini-Portuguese themes

All Bini-Portuguese salt-cellars contain two chambers and are composed of three parts. In this one, the top part, the lid of the second chamber, is missing. Two themes can be distinguished in the decorations of these salt-cellars: standing Portuguese figures, and Portuguese horsemen accompanied by winged figures. This is a hybrid art form combining African and European iconographic and stylistic elements. The European elements are the characters, costumes and weapons, while the traditional Bini elements are represented by the decorative motifs, some of which display clear similarities to Benin bronzes and ivory.

Horsemen and an angel

This salt-cellar contains several human figures, among them Portuguese horsemen. The model, with a base in the form of a truncated cone, appears to quote European models of salt-cellars from the early sixteenth century. The packed image includes two horsemen, an outlandish figure with a branch of leaves sitting between the forelegs of the horses or mules, and a nude winged figure. The latter may possibly be intended to represent an angel from Christian iconography. If so, its significance was evidently lost on the artist, since he has depicted the figure's genitals quite clearly.

European examples

The angel must have been based on a sketch, since this Biblical figure would probably not have belonged to the maker's frame of reference. Perhaps the client furnished the artists with illustrative drawings. In their own work, Bini artists opt largely for a static, frontal representation of human figures, while in the case of these salt-cellars, the figures are very dynamic, and depicted in profile. It is possible that the Portuguese client or agent was stationed in Benin for several years. The death of this person, or his return to Europe, could explain why the production of these items was halted so abruptly.

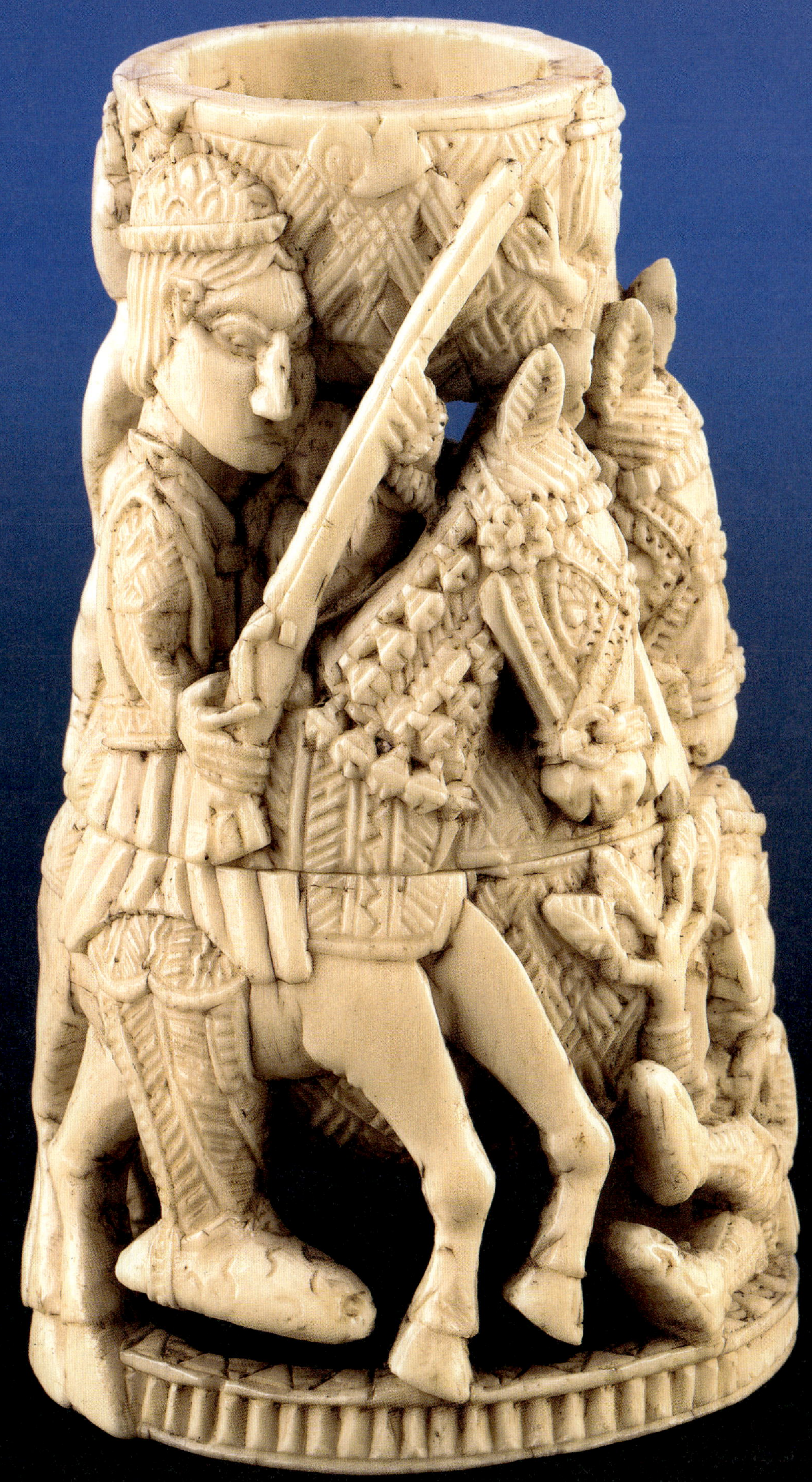

Brahma

Singosari; East Java, Indonesia
late 13th century
174 x 87 x 58 cm
andesite

RMV 1403-1582 (1903)

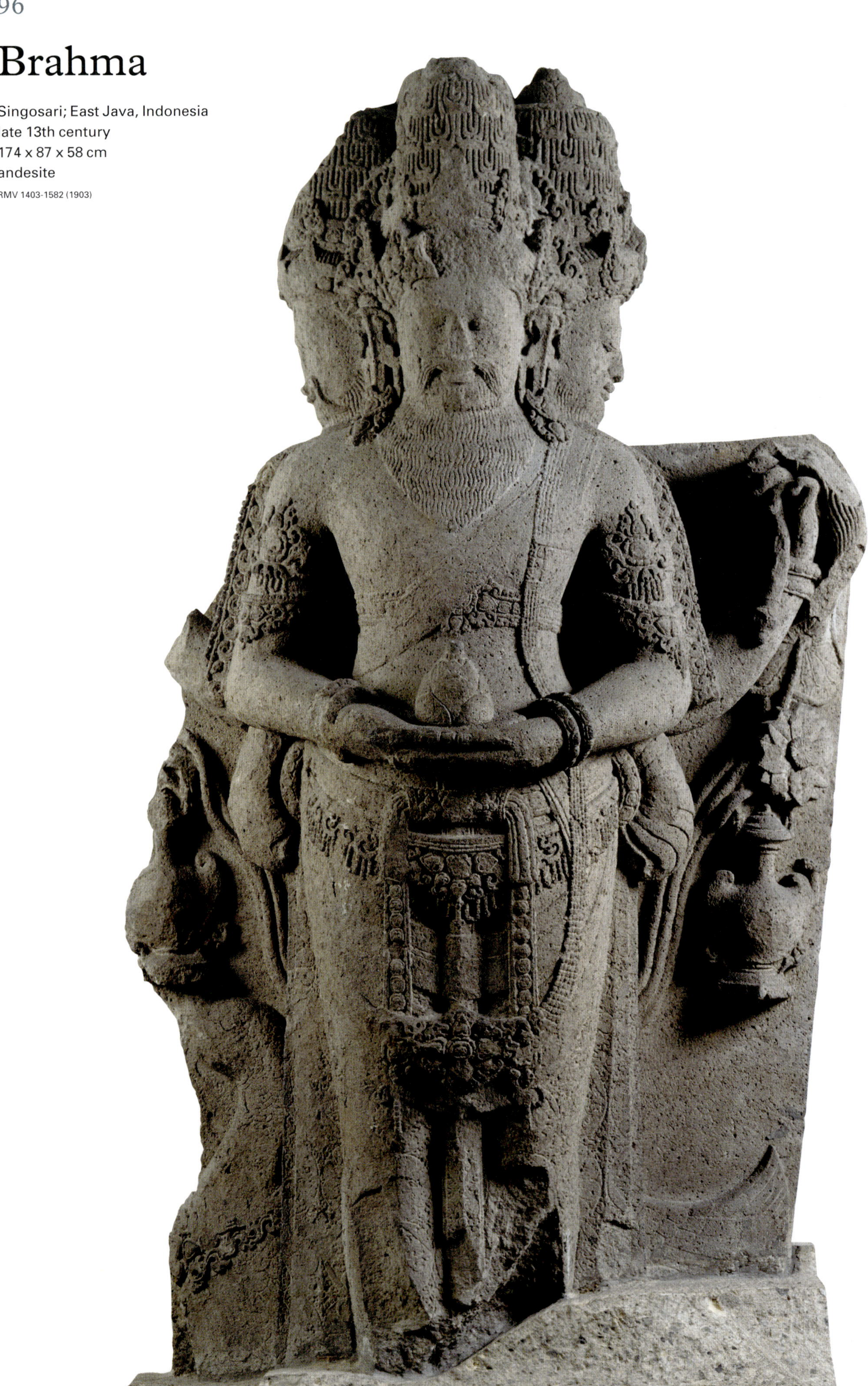

Four heads

Its four heads (one being at the back) make this statue instantly recognisable as Brahma, the Hindu god who created the world. He is depicted as an ascetic, with strands of tangled hair wound around his head schematically like a crown. He has a beard and moustache here, as befits his ascetic nature. His hands make a gesture of meditation. His half-closed eyes similarly denote his absorption in meditation. His mount, the goose, is depicted in relief on the backslab. Lotus plants with two water vessels decorate the sides. The water vessels have an unusual shape, deriving from Chinese examples.

Divine rivalry

Various myths refer to the rivalry that exists between Vishnu and Shiva. One myth states that Brahma is born after Vishnu, from a lotus flower that rises from Vishnu's navel. According to another, Vishnu and Brahma are arguing about who is the supreme god. Amid this debate, a great pillar of fire rises between them. The pillar is so big that neither the top nor the bottom of it can be seen. Vishnu changes into a wild boar and digs his way into the ground to reach the bottom of the pillar of fire. Brahma flies into the air in the form of a goose to try and reach the top. However, neither the top nor the bottom can be found. At this point, Shiva emerges from the pillar, and Brahma and Vishnu are forced to concede that he is greater and more powerful than they are.

Brahma temple

On Java, Shiva was the most important god, but the three gods were also worshipped together, for instance at the temple complex of Prambanan in Central Java. The largest temple in that complex is dedicated to Shiva, but beside it stand temples for Brahma and Vishnu. This large statue comes from the temple grounds of Singosari in East Java, and may have been the primary statue of a separate temple, dedicated to Brahma. Only one temple still stands in Singosari today, but once there were several, as is clear from the oldest surviving map of the complex. It is a map produced by J.T. Bik in 1822, which is preserved in the Rijksmuseum Volkenkunde.

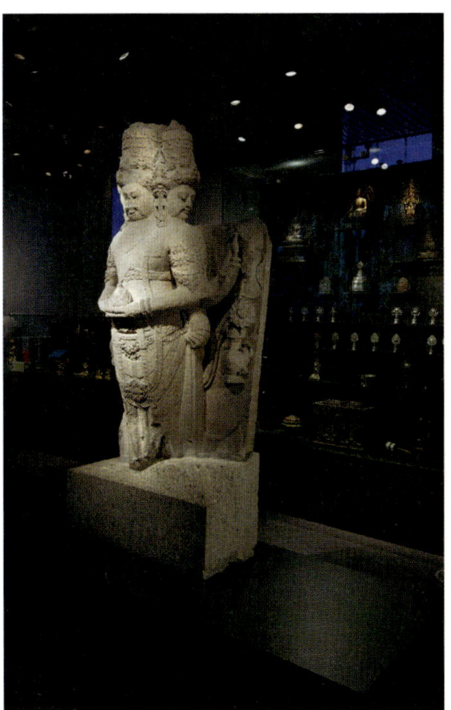

Colonial cultural politics

C.G.C. Reinwardt, professor of botany in Leiden and the founder of the botanical garden in Buitenzorg (Bogor) on Java, was also an enthusiastic collector of Javanese antiquities. He travelled around Java together with the draughtsmen A.J. and J.T. Bik – photography did not yet exist. It was probably Reinwardt himself who took this statue from the ruins of Singosari in 1822. In accordance with a decree issued by the Minister of Colonies, it was added to the archaeology collection of Leiden University along with 'numerous other stone statues'.

World cycle

Together with Vishnu and Shiva, the most important gods of Hinduism, Brahma ensures the world's existence. Brahma creates the world; Vishnu ensures that it is preserved by maintaining the right equilibrium between divine and demonic forces, and Shiva destroys the world when demonic forces become too powerful and the equilibrium can no longer be restored. At that point, Brahma can create the world again and the cycle recommences.

The Leiden Plate

Early Classic Period, Maya; Guatemala
320
21,7 x 8,6 cm
jadeite
RMV 1403-1193 (1903)

Balam-Ahau-Chan

The 'Leiden Plate' is a jadeite pendant. One side bears an image of King Balam-Ahau-Chan of the city of Tikal. The king can be identified by regalia such as the double-headed serpent staff that he holds in his arms. This staff was carried only by kings. His headdress is topped by the face of the Jester god, the symbol of royal power. The ruler stands on a vanquished man whose hands are tied and whose head is turned away. The other side of the pendant bears an inscription explaining why the pendant was made and what the image depicts.

Accession

The text on the Leiden Plate can be rendered as follows: 'After the period composed of 8 baktuns, 14 katuns, 3 tuns, 1 uinal and 12 kins, on the day 1 Eb, when the fifth Lord of the Night ruled and the month Yaxkin commenced, Balam-Ahau-Chan was installed as ruler'. This refers to the date on which Balam-Ahau-Chan ascended the throne, corresponding in the Western calendar to Friday, 17 September, AD 320.

The discovery

The Leiden Plate was discovered in 1864 by the Dutch engineer J.A. van Braam. He was in charge of the digging of a canal in the vicinity of Puerto Barrios in Guatemala, where he chanced to find some extremely important archaeological objects. The Leiden Plate became world-famous, because the date mentioned in the text was for a long time the oldest known Maya date. It bears an English name because, in view of its great importance, the first publications dealing with it appeared in the English language.

Use and re-use

The pendant was a status symbol. There is evidence for this on the Leiden Plate itself: three 'Leiden Plates' dangle from the Balam-Ahau-Chan's belt. One of the king's children probably inherited the pendant after his death. It was discovered together with some small bronze bells. Since bronze was not used in the Maya region until the post-classic period (from AD 900 onwards), it is clear that the pendant continued to be used for a very long time. The Leiden Plate was probably not buried with its original owner, but was passed down by inheritance or given away as a present and only buried centuries later.

The Maya

'The Maya' is an umbrella term for almost thirty different peoples who speak related languages and share a similar cultural background. Most Maya lived – and still live – in Mexico, Guatemala, Belize, El Salvador, and Honduras. It makes as little sense to speak of 'the Maya' as to speak of 'the Europeans'. The first identifiable Maya monuments date from around 500 BC. The Maya became famous largely because of their script, the most complex system of writing ever developed in America, and their intricate calendar, which uses up to thirteen different ways of tracking time simultaneously. After the arrival of the Spaniards, the Maya suffered oppression for centuries and were forced to adapt. Even so, they succeeded in conserving their language, their culture, and much of their knowledge. There are now between seven and nine million Maya living in Mexico, Central America and the United States.

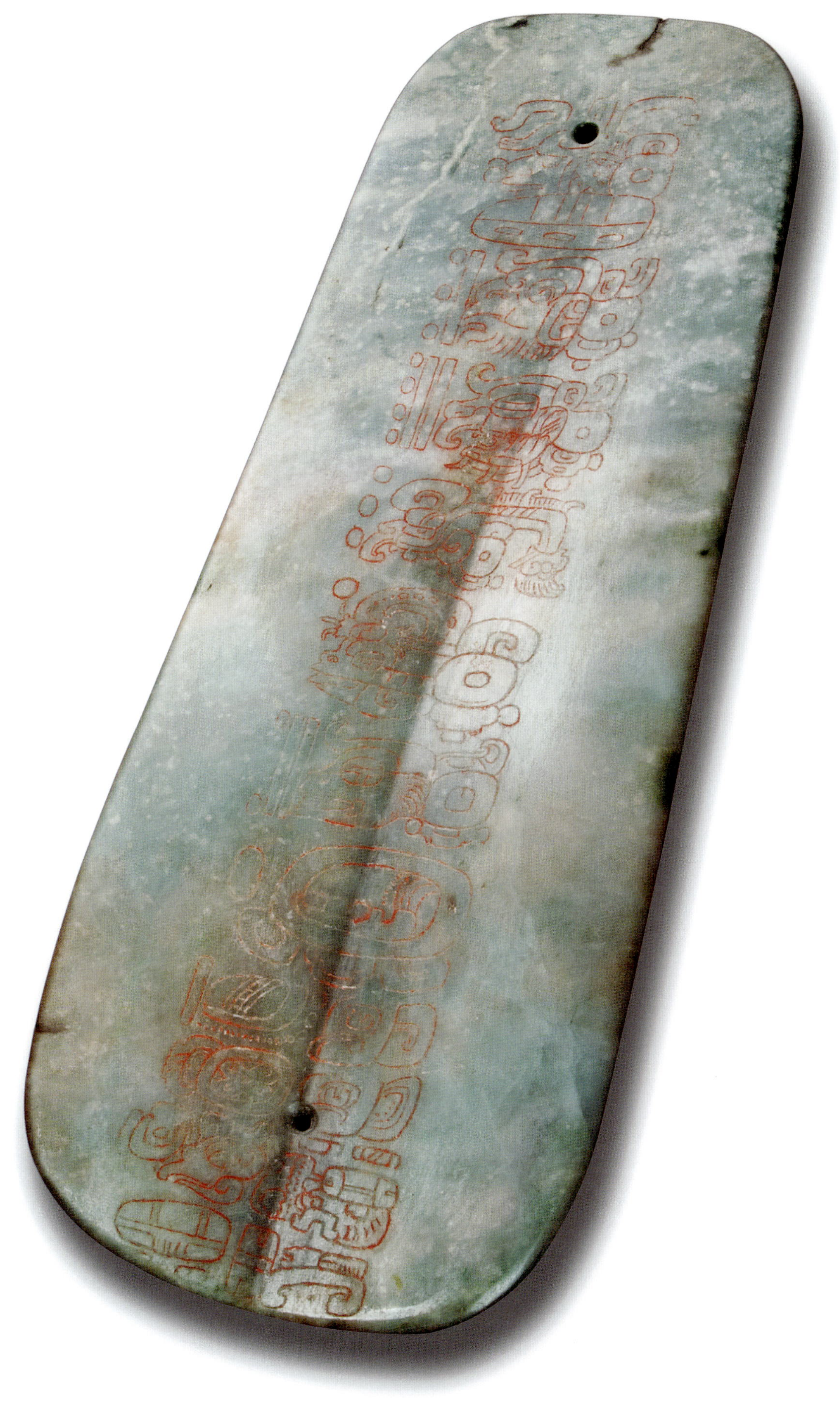

Ganesha

Singosari, East Java, Indonesia
late 13th century
h. 154 cm, 2,500 kg
andesite
RMV 1403-1681 (1903)

Skulls

This image of Ganesha is remarkable because it is full of skulls: his earrings are shaped like skulls, its crown has skulls on it; skull motifs are incorporated into his bracelets and the pattern of his loincloth.. He is also carrying skull-shaped bowls and sitting on a row of skulls. The skulls recall a tantric context such as that familiar in India, in which the symbolism of cremation and charnel grounds (with skulls, demons and prowling jackals) plays an important role. But skulls possessed a different significance in Indonesian cultures than in India: here, they were seen as a source of supernatural power that could confer protection. According to one recent theory, the skulls were adopted from a tantric context, but applied here in order to express Ganesha's protective power as well as possible in a Javanese context.

Back in their country of origin

2005 was a remarkable year. In that year, these marvellous statues briefly returned to Indonesia, after almost 200 years, for the exhibition 'Warisan Budaya Bersama' (Shared Cultural Heritage) which was organised by the National Museum in Jakarta in partnership with the Rijksmuseum Volkenkunde.

Singosari

There were once several temple complexes in Singosari (near Malang, East Java). This statue of Ganesha comes from the eastern niche of the sole remaining temple there. It may be the temple in which Kertanagara, the last ruler of the Singhasari empire (1222-1292), was immortalised and deified after his death as Shiva and Buddha. The Rijksmuseum Volkenkunde possesses three other statues from this temple: two divine gatekeepers, Nandishvara and Mahakala, which stood in the two niches beside the west entrance, and the goddess Durga, who occupied the northern niche.

Elephant head

Ganesha is the god who can remove all the obstacles at the beginning of a new enterprise. He is therefore much loved. India has a wide range of myths that seek to explain his elephant's head. Java had its own tradition in this respect. It is recorded in the Smaradahana, an ancient Javanese text dating from the thirteenth century. According to this story, Parvati, wife of the god Shiva, was so shocked by the sight of the elephant Airavata, the mount of the god Indra, that her unborn son came into the world with the head of an elephant.

New contexts

When Java's Hindu-Buddhist culture died out, around 1500, the abandoned temples became overgrown. In 1804, Nicolaus Engelhard, governor of Java's Northeast Coast, discovered the temple of Singosari. He had it cleaned and found the most beautiful statues. He decided to leave the damaged Agastya, in the southern niche, where it was. He had the other four statues and two more discovered in the surrounding area (Nandi and Bhairava) removed and placed in his garden in Semarang, with the permission of the colonial government. In 1819 he relinquished them 'to enrich the nation's public collections'; Ganesha, Nandi and Bhairava were the first to be shipped to the Netherlands, where they were placed on display in Amsterdam. The other three statues (Durga, Nandishvara and Mahakala) were kept temporarily at the botanical garden in Buitenzorg (present-day Bogor, Java) and arrived in Leiden several years later, in 1827 and 1828. The three statues from Amsterdam joined them in Leiden in 1841.

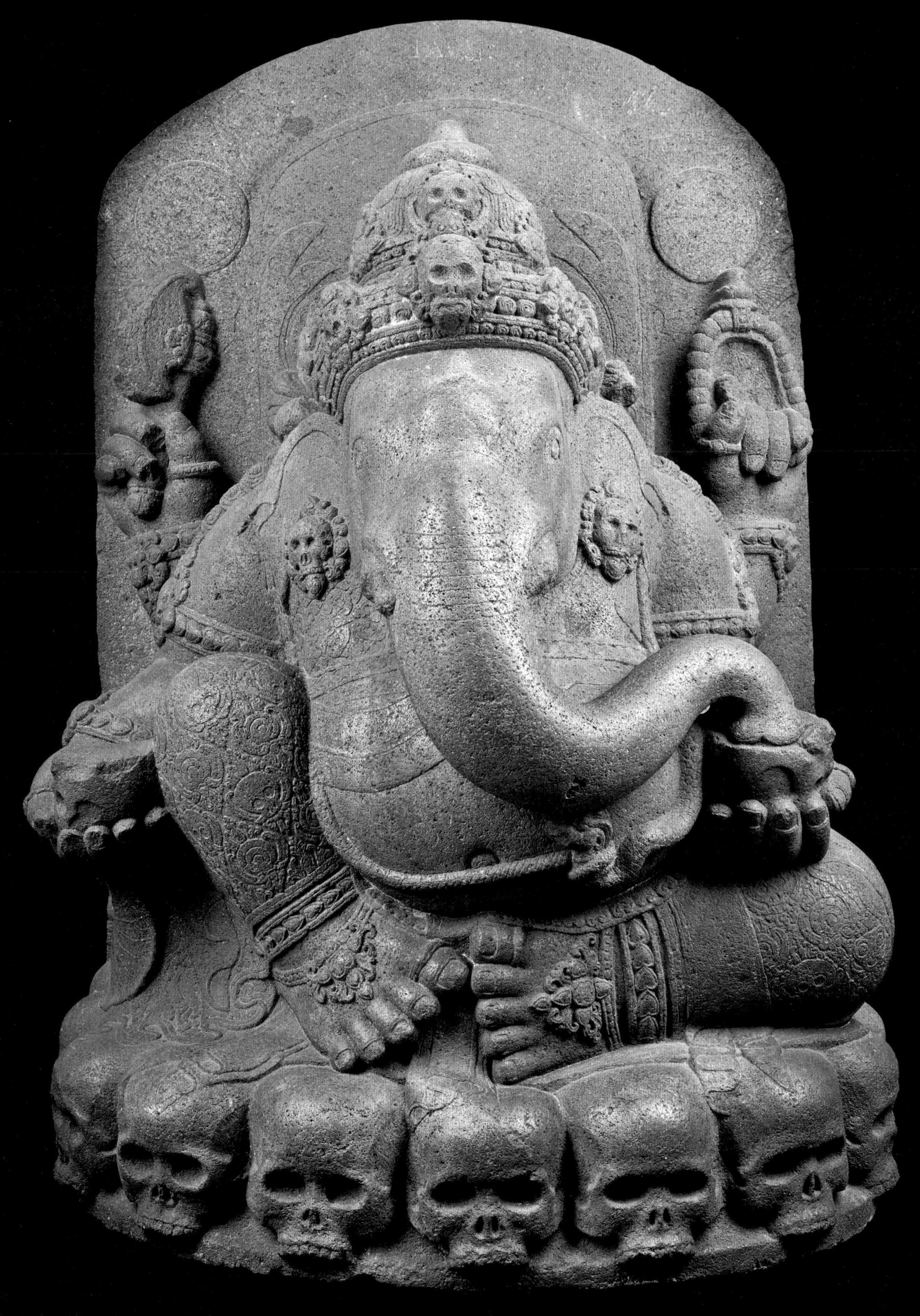

Power figure (nail fetish; *Nkisi*)

Lower-Congo region, Democratic Republic of Congo
1880-1900
113 x 44 x 39 cm
wood, iron, textile, raffia, shell, resin, clay, pigment
RMV 1407-14 (1903)

Power figure

This power figure or *nkisi* comes from the region of the Chiloango River in Lower-Congo. Much of the chest, part of the abdomen and the upper arms are pierced by nails, screws, rings, knife blades, and triangular pieces of iron. The figure also displays two important additions, consisting of a resin-like material filled with a magical substance. One of these is attached around the lower jaw as a fringe beard, while the other is a cylindrical bulge on the abdomen, covered by a shell.

Bilongo

Without its magical ingredients or *bilongo*, a *nkisi* is a dead image. The *nganga* or spiritual healer adds the *bilongo*, enticing a personified spirit from the invisible world of the dead to the figure. Once the spirit resides in the statue, it can be urged into action by the *nganga*. The magical substances are almost always placed on the abdomen, since the belly signifies life, but they may also be placed in hollows or bulges on the head, such as a fringe beard. The head is regarded as the seat of communication with spirits.

Activating the nkisi

To activate the figure, nails are driven into it. This rouses the spirit in the statue, so that it sets off in search of vengeance. The nails are metaphorical elements that refer to the pain that the victims will experience. However, the nails may also be licked by the members of an oath or a treaty before being driven into the statue to make sure that the statue remembers the assignment and is able to identify the participants. For it may be called upon several times on the same day, possibly causing confusion. In some cases, the figure may be activated by cursing it.

Function

This type of n*kisi* was used primarily to make oaths and alliances binding. Such figures were invoked to ratify peace treaties between enemy villages and to lend weight to protestations of innocence. Their public functions included endorsing initiation vows, military agreements, rules of criminal law, and moral or judicial soothsaying. They played a particularly important role in regions lacking institutionalised powerful chiefs, and in places where the legal and political systems were weak. To a large extent, *minkisi* (the plural of *nkisi*), as personified objects, were functionally interchangeable with human beings, who were in turn 'objectified' as a result of a ritual act in which they were possessed by super-natural powers.

Provenance

This figure strongly resembles those that are attributed to the nameless artist known as the Master of the Chiloango River. Like all highly important *minkisi*, this one had its own name: *Mangaaka*. It is often difficult to trace a figure's precise origins, since the *minkisi* entered the museum with relatively little explanatory information, and indeed, little value was attached to detailed descriptions of objects in the past. In addition, recovering information about the *minkisi* tradition is difficult, since the custom had died out by 1900.

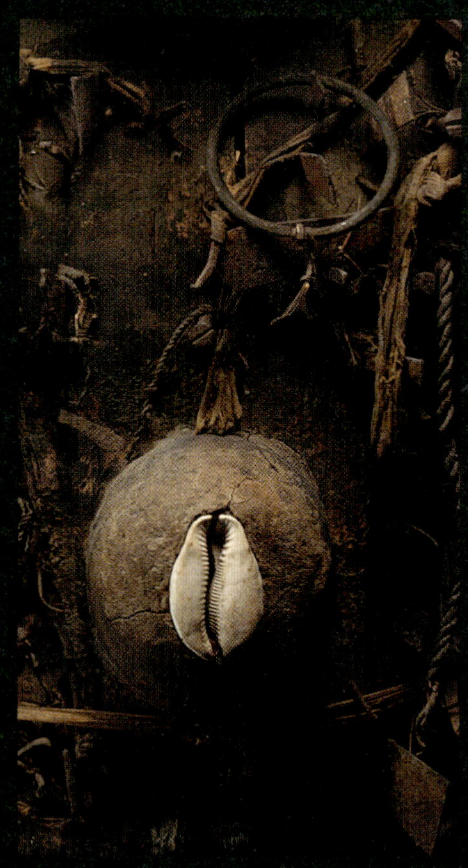

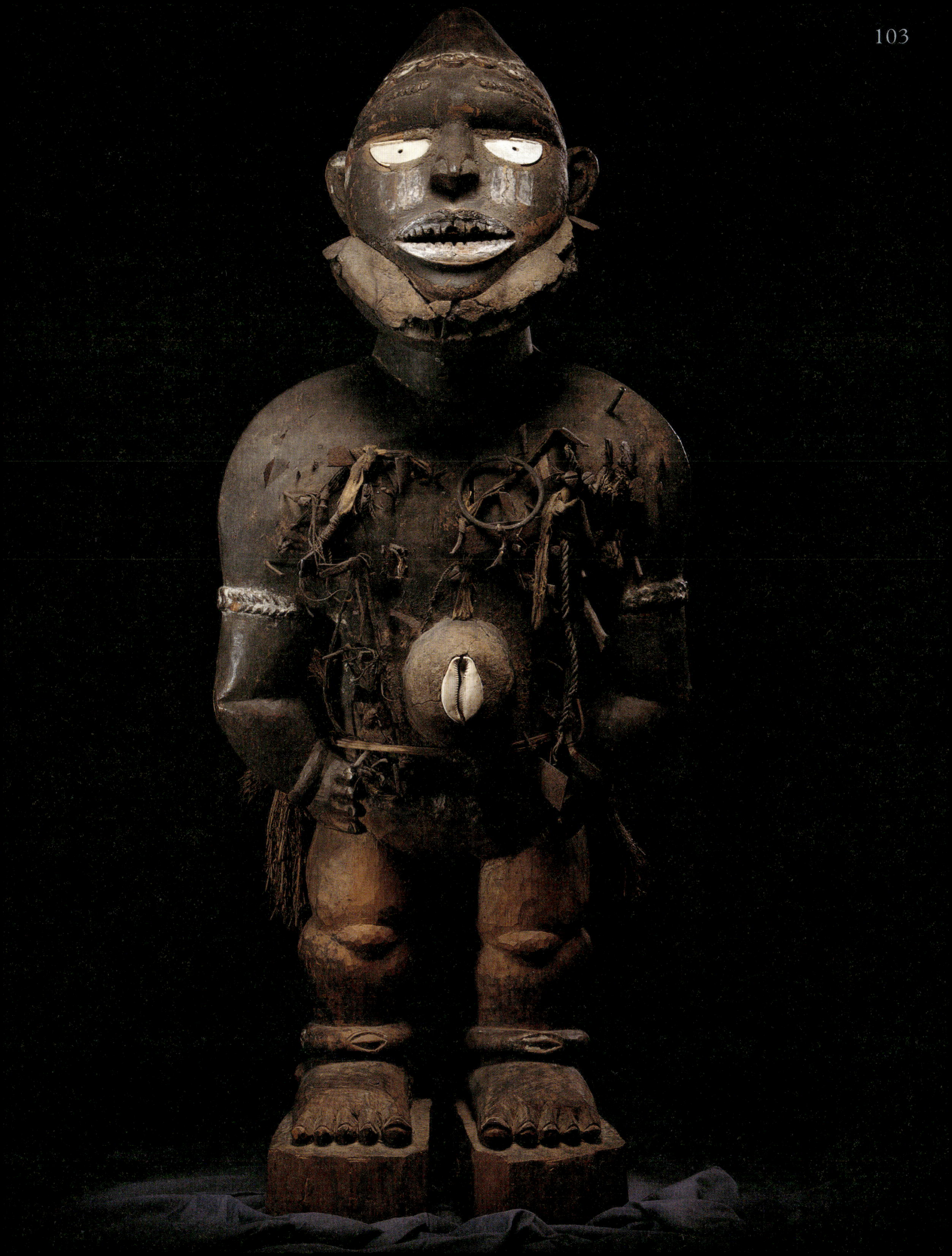

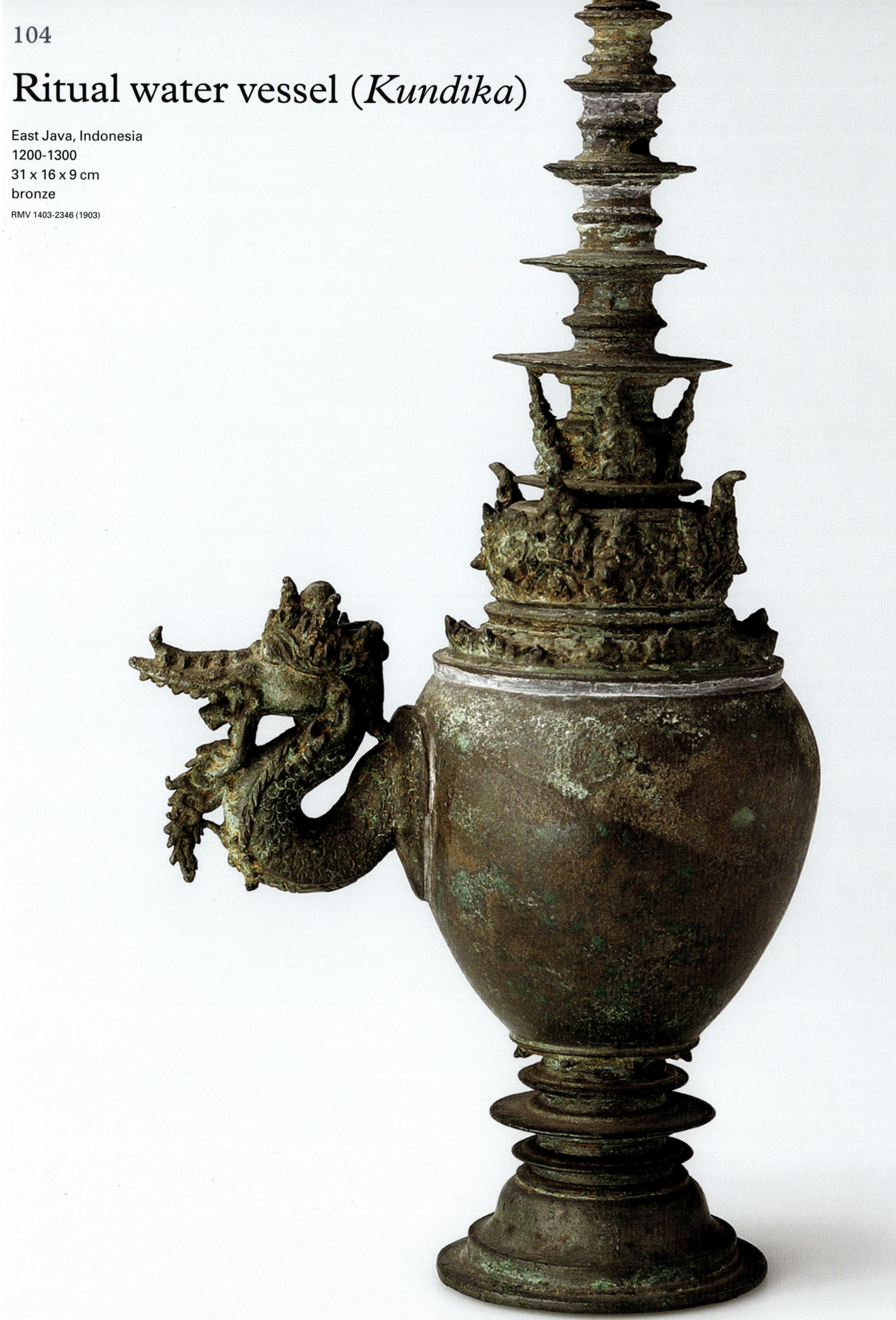

Ritual water vessel (*Kundika*)

East Java, Indonesia
1200-1300
31 x 16 x 9 cm
bronze
RMV 1403-2346 (1903)

Indian origin
In India, an undecorated version of this vessel was popular between the third century BC and the eighth century AD. Ascetics and monks drank water from these vessels, which are known as *kundi(ka) or kamandalu*. The vessel was filled through the spout and the user drank from the neck, but without touching the opening. Buddhist monks in China, Japan, and Korea also drank from the *kundika*. In Java the *kundika* did not come into use until the eighth century, when it was similarly adopted by monks and ascetics.

New shape
From the thirteenth century onwards, a different type of *kundika* came into use on Java. This vessel is an example. Several beautifully carved bronze water vessels of this kind have been found in East Java. They date from the thirteenth to fifteenth centuries. The vessel's four parts (neck, body, foot and spout) were cast separately and then forged together. There are three openings: one at the top of the neck, and two in the spout, which is shaped like a snake (*naga*). The snake's dragon-like appearance reflects Chinese influence. The neck displays stylised parasols and rock-like points.

The churning of the ocean
The pitcher's shape alludes to a myth according to which the gods churn the ocean to obtain the nectar of immortality (*amrta*). They use the mythical Mount Mandara as a churning stick and coil the serpent Vasuki around it as a churning rope. They themselves pull at one end, and ask the demons to pull at the other. In the churning process, all sorts of remarkable things emerge from the ocean: a white horse, a wish-fulfilling cow, a unique jewel, and finally the coveted *amrta*, which makes the gods immortal. The vessel's high neck and rock-like projections refer to the mountain, while the spout refers to the serpent that is coiled around the mountain. The new form of vessel appears to suggest a new function: as a storage container for the elixir of life.

Ritual use
This theory is confirmed by a relief on the wall of Candi Kidal, a temple in the vicinity of Malang, East Java. It shows Garuda carrying a vessel of this kind on his head. This image refers to the story according to which Garuda steals the *amrta* from the gods to ransom his mother, who is being held in prison. The text does not relate how Garuda carries the *amrta*, but the sculptor has produced this specific type of vessel with its *naga*-shaped spout. This type of vessel was evidently deemed apt in the context. Another relief, on the wall of the main temple of Panataran, near Blitar in East Java, shows a priest using a similar vessel to pour water over the bride in a marriage ritual. Strikingly, the water is poured in this case from the spout, not from the neck.

Donation
This water vessel was found in Trenggalek in the southwest region of East Java and donated to the National Museum of Antiquities by A.F.H. van de Poel in 1863. Van de Poel had a long career as an administrative official in the Dutch East Indies. Between 1859 and 1862 he served as Resident of Kediri, to which Trenggalek belonged at the time. In 1903 the National Museum of Antiquities' Indonesian collection, including this bronze vessel, was incorporated into the collection of the Rijksmuseum Volkenkunde.

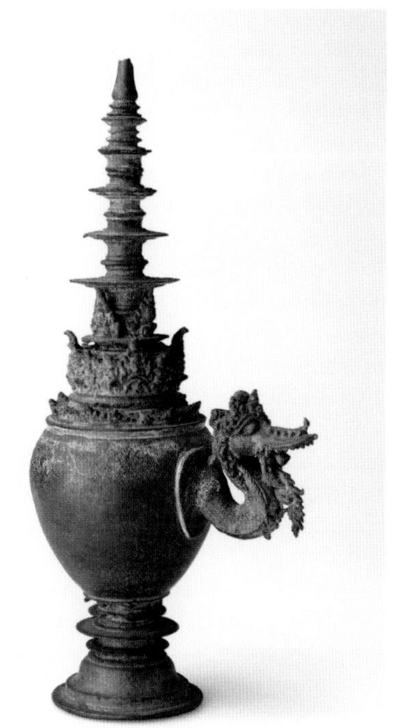

Gold *ushnisha*

East Java, Indonesia
900-950
15.5 x 14.4 cm
gold
RMV 1403-2783 (1903)

Curls turning to the right

The most striking feature of this hollow gold object is its rows of spiral-shaped curls on the outside. They look like the short curls, which are traditionally described as turning to the right, that cover the Buddha's head. One of the thirty-two remarkable features of the Buddha is the protuberance on his head (*ushnisha*). This too is covered with these right-turning curls. Since this gold object does not have a protuberance and is quite small, it represents the protuberance itself. Separate gold *ushnishas* of this kind have only been found on Java.

Gold treasure

This gold *ushnisha* comes from the Muteran treasure, found to the south of Surabaya in East Java. The treasure was discovered in 1881 and contained twenty-seven gold and silver objects, including Buddhist figurines, jewellery, and two gold *ushnishas*, one relatively small, the other larger. Half of the treasure was sent to Batavia and the other half to Leiden. The *ushnishas* were also divided up. The one from Batavia was exhibited at the Paris World Exhibition in 1931, but it perished in a fire that raged through the Dutch pavilion. In 1990 an even greater treasure was found in Wonoboyo, to the southeast of Surakarta in Central Java, totalling over thirty-two kilograms of gold objects. This treasure also included two *ushnishas*: one relatively small, the other larger.

Dating

The *vajra*-shaped top helps us to date the *ushnisha*. Objects that are characteristic of esoteric Buddhism, such as the *vajra*, do not occur in Java until the ninth century. Since gold *ushnishas* of this kind are rare, and they have been found both in Central and East Java, it seems very likely that they date from the brief period (between 900 and 928) when Central and East Java were united, or shortly afterwards. Later Javanese *vajras* have flared points that do not touch.

Enigma

The use of the gold *ushnishas* is still an enigma. Possibly they were intended to be placed over the *ushnisha* of a stone or bronze Buddha. This would explain why some of the items of jewellery from the Wonoboyo treasure are too large for any human wearer. In that case, it is curious that the *ushnishas* were found in pairs. No pairs of Buddhas are known in which one is smaller than the other. The literature does refer to monks who take the Bodhisattva vows during meditation and who then see themselves in a vision as if they were Buddha, with his unique features such as the *ushnisha*. The gold *ushnishas* may possibly have been worn by a royal or priestly couple who were taking these vows. But this theory too raises new questions.

Vajra-shaped top

On top of the *ushnisha* is a lotus flower on which are four curved prongs that touch in the middle. They resemble the tip of a *vajra*, the ritual sceptre that an esoteric Buddhist priest holds in his right hand during rituals. The *vajra* has a fifth, straight point in the middle, which is absent here. Since a photograph of the *ushnisha* that was lost in Paris shows that a crystal ball was attached there, we can assume that in this case too, the curved prongs originally enclosed a crystal ball.

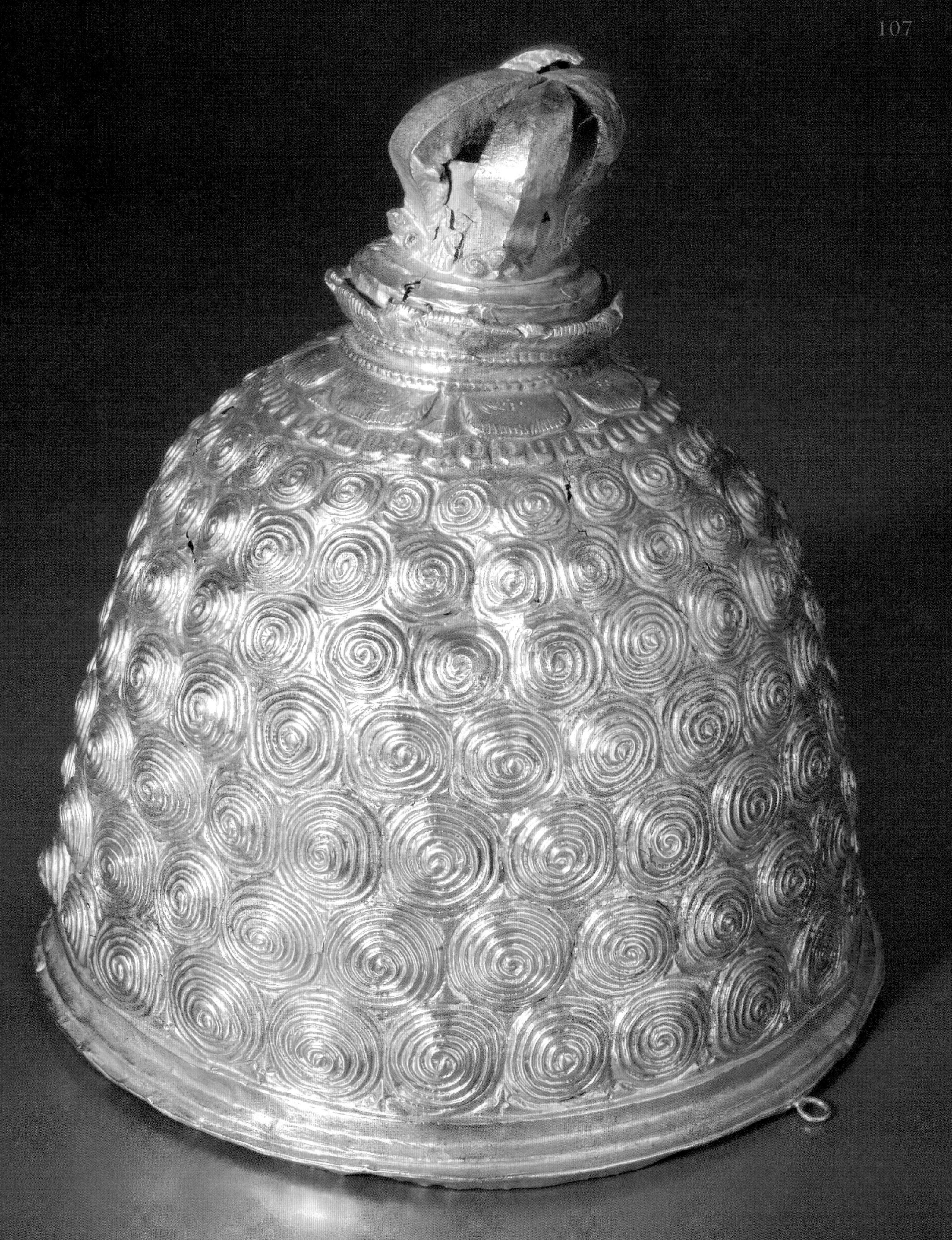

Woman with dish

Owo, Nigeria
before 1700
25 x 10 cm
ivory
RMV 1415-1 (1903)

Historical reconstruction

One of the former directors of the Rijksmuseum Volkenkunde, Dr J.D.E. Schmeltz, purchased this figure in 1903 from J.G. Roering Warmolts (1867-1949), a baker from Groningen. He thought that it had been made quite recently and based on a European model. It languished in the storage facility for a long time. Not until 1992, when research on the collection linked the figure to the publication *Selecta Sacra*, did the remarkable collection history of this figure, and its important place in the history of the Owo, become clear.

A single dated piece

Judging by the style, this figure comes from Owo, one of the Yoruba kingdoms in West Africa. Owo ivory figures are extremely rare and almost impossible to date. Only five others are known that bear some similarity to this one. The one shown here was described by Johannes Braun (1628-1708), professor of theology in Groningen, in the Groningen Chamber of the Dutch West India Company. In his book *Selecta Sacra* (from 1700) he mistakenly identified the figure as the Egyptian goddess Isis. Nonetheless, his description is very valuable. Thanks to Braun, the Leiden specimen is the only ivory Owo figure in the world that can be furnished with a *terminus ante quem*, a date before which it was certainly made, namely of 1700.

The West India Company

The West India Company, founded in 1621, traded merchandise including gold, ivory, timber, pepper and slaves along the coast of West Africa. Most of this trade took place in coastal settlements, such as the modest-sized trading post near Arbo or the small coastal town of Ardra. The Netherlands did not have any direct contact with the Owo. Dutch sailors working for the WIC probably took this figure as a curiosity from Benin, which did maintain trading relations with Owo. The Europeans took little interest in indigenous objects and these had little commercial value. This probably helps to explain why so few African objects were taken to the Netherlands (see p. 94-95).

For the local market

This figure was probably made for the local market, not for export to Europe like the Bini-Portuguese salt-cellars (p. 94-95). Although one must be careful comparing present-day traditions to historical objects made several centuries ago, this figure none-theless displays striking similarities to present-day Ifa oracle bowls. The Yoruba and related peoples use these bowls when predicting the future. Most are made of wood. The fact that this one was carved from ivory may mean that it was made for a high priest or to be used exclusively at the court of a king..

Stylistic features

Although the figure displays stylistic similarities to objects from Ife and Benin, it also possesses a number of striking characteristics that are suggestive of an Owo provenance. The strength and vitality of the figure, its decorative scars, the facial expressions such as the 'Yoruba mouth' and the representation of the hair are all indicative of an Owo origin. Oral tradition records that Benin and Owo maintained good relations. It is even possible that famous Owo carvers worked at the Oba's court in Benin.

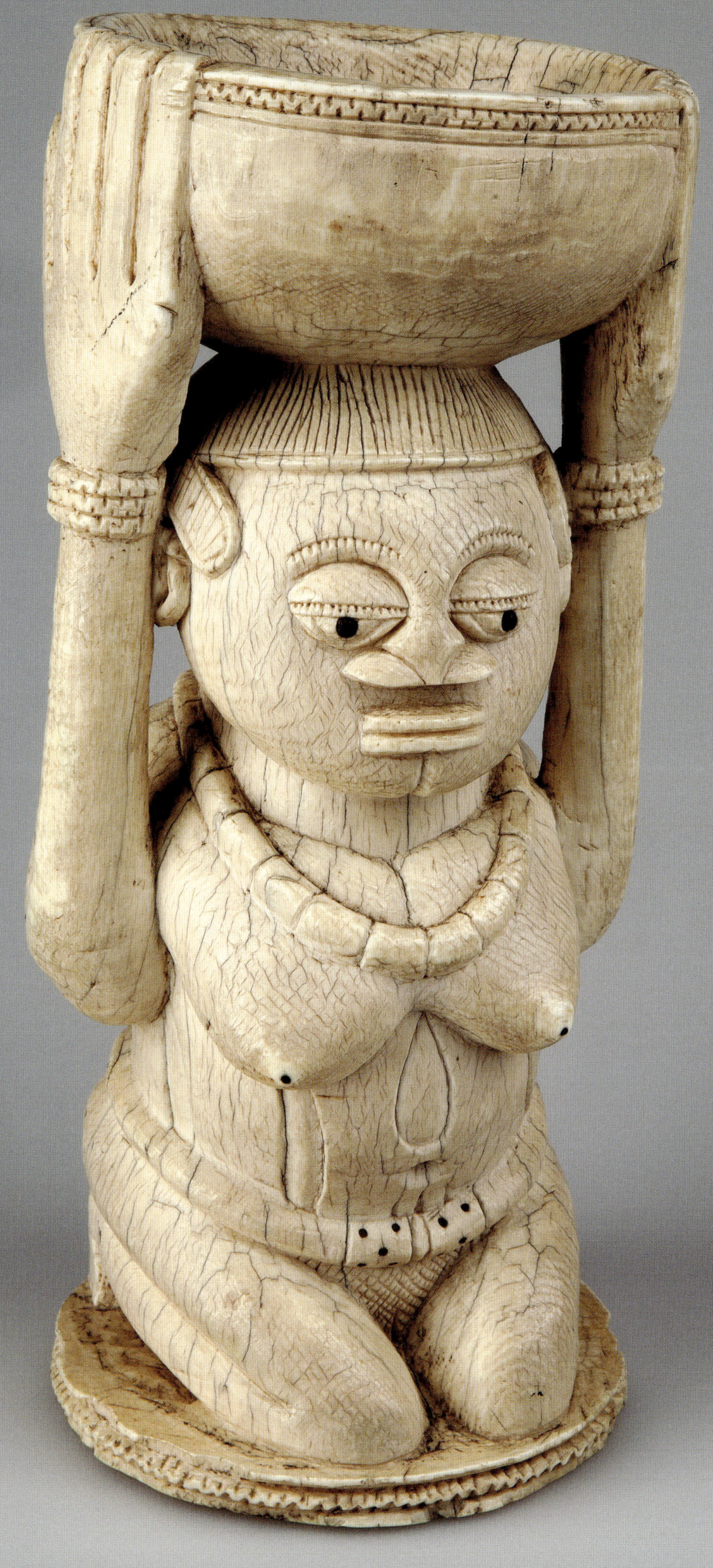

Preaching Buddha

Central Java, Indonesia
c. 800
h. 37.2 cm
bronze
RMV 1403-2844 (1903)

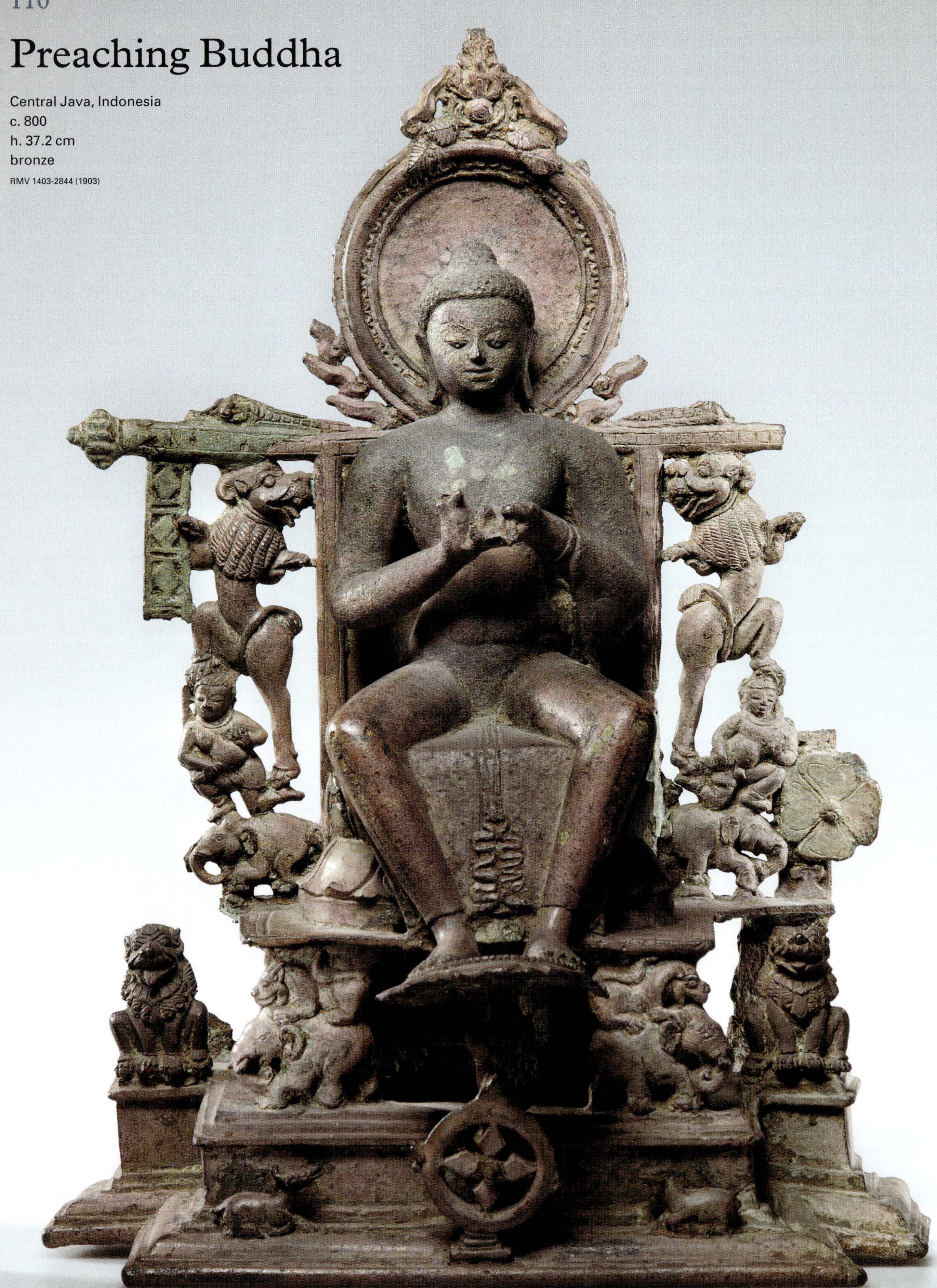

Royal symbolism

This bronze statue shows the Buddha as a sovereign seated on a throne with his legs hanging down (*bhadrasana*). His feet rest on a lotus flower. His throne is richly decorated with royal symbols, such as lions and elephants. The Buddha is making the hand gesture of *dharmachakra* mudra, which denotes setting in motion of the wheel (*chakra*) of Buddhist doctrine (*dharma*). This too is royal symbolism. Just as a sovereign causes the wheels of his carriage to roll to the four corners of the earth in order to vanquish the world as a true conqueror, the Buddha causes the wheel of Buddhist doctrine to roll to the four corners of the earth to ensure that the doctrine is disseminated around the world.

First sermon

On the pedestal, we see a wheel and two recumbent deer. Together with the *dharmachakra mudra*, they refer to the Buddha's first sermon, in the deer park at Sarnath, near Varanasi (Benares). According to tradition, this was where the Buddha expounded the basic tenets of Buddhism: 1. The truth of suffering; 2. The truth of the cause of suffering; 3. The truth of the cessation of suffering; and 4. The truth of the path to the cessation of suffering. This was the first time after his 'awakening' that he shared these truths with others, namely his first five pupils.

Cultural exchange

Like Bodhgaya, where the Buddha experienced his awakening, Sarnath has become a major place of pilgrimage. Besides Buddhists from India, it also receives pilgrims from Sri Lanka, Burma, Thailand, Tibet, and Japan. This was probably the case many centuries ago, if not on the same scale as today. Then too, Buddhist monks travelled back and forth. The Chinese monk Xuanzang, who visited Sarnath in the seventh century AD, wrote that there were thirty monasteries and 3,000 monks there. The *dharmachakra mudra* is mainly associated with Sarnath, but it spread throughout the Buddhist world. This Buddha statue shows that Java also took part in this traffic. Similar bronze specimens have been found in Northeast India and Bangladesh.

Mendut temple

Closer to home, we find a similar statue in the Mendut Temple, not far from Borobudur in Central Java. It is an impressive stone statue, flanked by two Bodhisattvas: Avalokiteshvara on the left, and another Bodhisattva, probably Vajrapani, on the right. Here too, the Buddha is seated on a richly carved throne, his legs hanging down and his hands in the *dharmachakra mudra* gesture. The pedestal of this statue also displays an image of a wheel between two deer. Since the bronze statue is quite similar to the Mendut statue, which dates from about AD 800, it is dated to the same rough period.

Royal Cabinet of Rarities

Early on, the bronze Buddha entered the Royal Cabinet of Rarities in The Hague, which had been founded in 1816 by King William I and was the first step towards the establishment of a national museum. After the Cabinet attracted harsh criticism in *De Gids* in 1873, in a piece describing it as a 'bizarre junk store', it was closed down in 1883. Its objects were distributed among a number of museums; this statue was allocated to the National Museum of Antiquities in Leiden. In 1903 the entire collection of classical Indonesian objects was transferred to the Rijksmuseum Volkenkunde.

Palace doors

Tabanan; South Bali, Indonesia
before 1906
260 x 50/47 x 9 cm
wood, paint, gold leaf
RMV 1586-32 (1907)

Balinese courtly art

This pair of wooden doors from the former palace of the raja of Tabanan (West Bali) is a splendid example of refined Balinese courtly art. The delicately carved reliefs have been gilded. The decorations include animal motifs among tendrils abounding in leaves. On the left-hand door are images of the following animals, from top to bottom: a tiger, a rat or mouse opposite a parrot, a buffalo, a deer opposite a bird, and a winged lion (*singa*). Depicted on the right-hand door are a goat, a bird facing a deer, a *singa*, a dog opposite a horse, and an elephant.

'Vagando acquiro'

As a multi-faceted artist, the well-known painter and graphic artist Wijnand Otto Jan Nieuwenkamp (1874 – 1950) took a great interest in the art and culture of Bali. He admired the craftsmanship with which many of the objects were made. His motto was 'Vagando acquiro', 'While wandering, I acquire [knowledge, ideas, objects]'. On his trips to Bali he acquired items for his own private collection and for museums. He incorporated his drawings and diaries into travel accounts, books and articles, including the invaluable book Bali and Lombok. In 1906-1907 W.O.J. Nieuwenkamp undertook a second journey to Bali, to build up a collection for the Rijksmuseum Volkenkunde. It was a period of military conflict in South Bali.

The conquest of Tabanan

In September 1906 the small kingdom of Badung was attacked by the Dutch East Indies army. A dramatic 'fight to the end' (*puputan*) left two rulers along with hundreds of their followers dead. A week later the army advanced on the small neighbouring state of Tabanan. The old raja I Gusti Ngurah Agung and his son I Gusti Ngurah Anom were imprisoned in Denpasar, where they took their own lives. In January 1907 the precious contents of the palace were sold at auction in Tabanan, after which the palace was demolished. The proceeds of the auction were given to the relatives of the deceased raja, who had been banished to Lombok.

The ruler's bedroom doors

Nieuwenkamp, who had witnessed the military clashes in South Bali, purchased valuable treasures from the palace for the museum in Leiden at the Tabanan auction, including these handsome doors. On Bali, a palace consists not of a single building, but of a walled complex of buildings and courtyards separated by internal walls. These have stone gateways with wooden doors decorated with woodcarvings giving access from one area to the next. The entrance doors to the different buildings are generally rather smaller than those in the gateways. Perhaps these doors belonged to the ruler's bedroom, since Nieuwenkamp purchased two painted bed panels at the same auction.

Animals and their significance

The animals that are depicted on the palace doors together reflect the animal world over which a monarch rules. Birds and four-footed creatures, animals from the forest (tigers and deer) and around the house (dog), animals that are considered pests (rats), or that perform useful labour (horses), animals to eat or to use in sacrifices (goats, buffalo), all are depicted realistically. Other animals, such as the winged lion (*singa*) and the elephant, are known only from stories and myths from India. These powerful animals are associated with kingship.

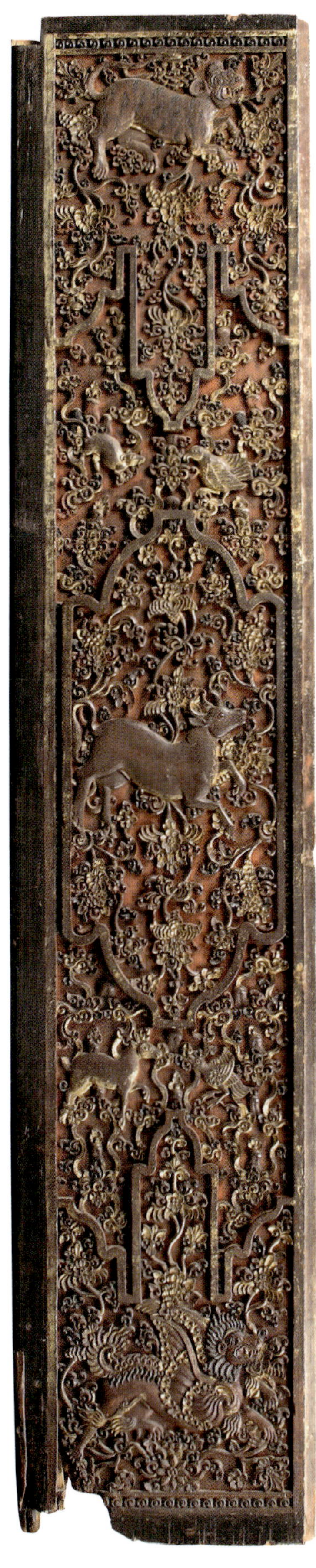 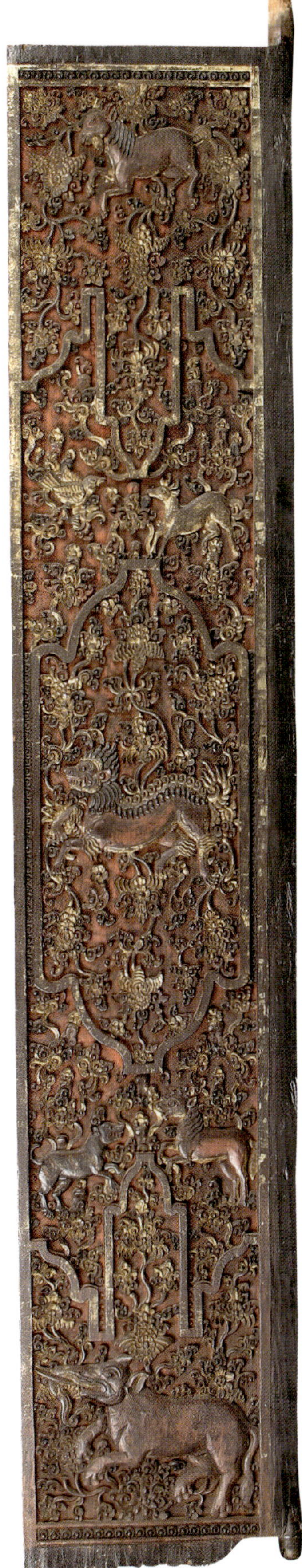

Porcelain dish

Edo period, Japan
1675-1700
diam. 21.3 cm, h. 4.9 cm
porcelain, glaze
RMV 1645-1 (1908)

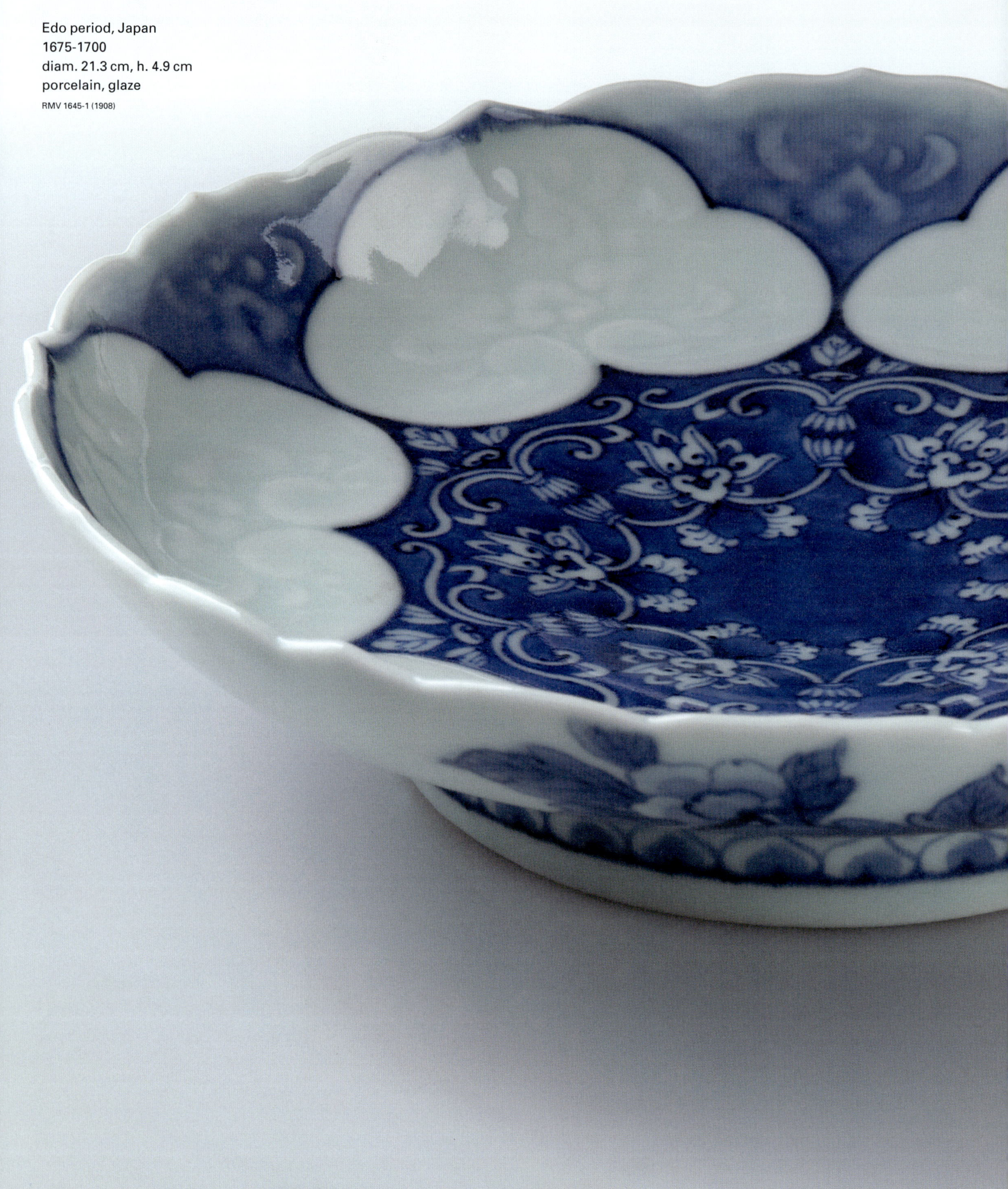

Recognisability

The dish is decorated with stylised lotus flowers and peonies. But the heart pattern on the base is one of the most characteristic decorations of Nabeshima porcelain. The logical, almost natural division of the surface and the restrained finishing of the edges in the form of leaves are particularly striking. The dish has a diameter of 7 *sun* (1 *sun*=3.03 cm), one of the formal standard sizes of early, circular Nabeshima dishes that were rigidly maintained and help to make them instantly recognisable.

Acquisitions and sales

In the early collecting history of virtually all European museums, we find an enormous number of exchanges and acquisitions from other museums. But the Museum für Kunst und Gewerbe in Hamburg, founded in 1874 and modelled on the Victoria and Albert Museum in London (founded in 1852) and its derivatives, the Museum für Angewandte Kunst in Vienna (founded in 1863) and the Kunstgewerbemuseum in Berlin (founded in 1868), did little in this area. In contrast, some museums appear almost to have adopted a policy of acquiring large collections, only to subsequently sell off parts of them to other museums.

Exchanges and acquisitions

Hamburg museums were particularly active in this regard: Museum Godeffroy (1861-85), a museum that went so far as to publish sales catalogues, and the Museum für Völkerkunde (from 1879), which was run by the merchant Carl Lüders until 1896. Museum Godeffroy sold 415 objects to the Rijksmuseum Volkenkunde in 1881 and another 20 in 1882. In the same period, the Leiden Museum acquired a further 221 objects from Lüders. Although the Museum für Kunst und Gewerbe was involved in few such transactions, it did sell the Leiden museum three absolute masterpieces of Nabeshima porcelain, including the piece displayed here.

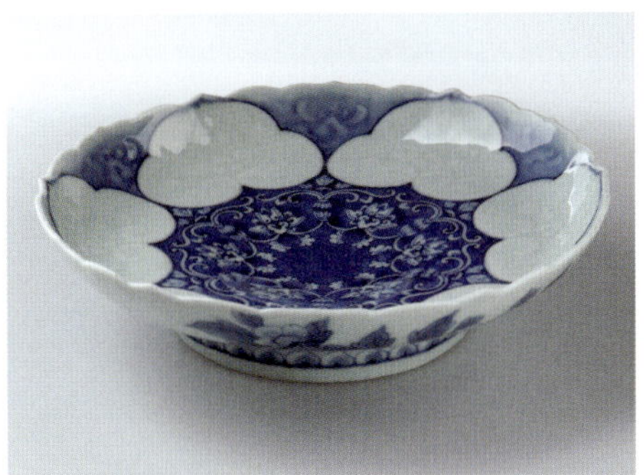

The Nabeshima mystery

Not so long ago, even though the fame of Nabeshima porcelain as the most refined porcelain ever produced by Japan, no one knew precisely how it was made. For centuries it remained a well-guarded secret of the Nabeshima clan that ruled over the Saga Domain and that would never accept anything but the best. The kilns were hidden away deep in the mountains and the entire production process was solely for the clan's private use. There was no trade or commercial production, as existed around many other kilns. It was not until around 1950 that the kilns in the Okawachiyama mountains near Arita were discovered and a start was made on systematic excavations, eventually shedding light on this remarkable production process.

Nabeshima porcelain

Nabeshima porcelain was ordered by the feudal lords of the Saga Domain in the province of Hizen and was exclusively intended for use at their court. Exclusivity and outstanding quality were its primary features. This dish is the only known example with motifs in monochrome relief from the heyday of Nabeshima porcelain, namely the late seventeenth to mid-eighteenth century. Relatively early Nabeshima pieces are characterised by a deep cobalt blue against the light greenish-white of the reliefs of Chinese floral motifs. Blue and white on porcelain is always underglaze. The shape of this dish, like that of many Nabeshima dishes, derives from that of wooden offering dishes or *mokuhai*.

Dragon

Meji period, Japan
before 1908
l. 88 cm, w. 32 cm, h. 15 cm
iron
RMV 1675-31 (1908)

A realistic dragon
This wholly articulated dragon consists of over one thousand iron components, all carefully fitted together. The body can twist in all directions and the legs can bend in any way. The disadvantage of all this flexibility is that the creature is unable to stand without support. But that was not the craftsman's concern; what he wanted was to demonstrate his consummate skill.

Looking for jobs
With the abolition of the class system in the Meiji period, metalworkers and goldsmiths who had for centuries served the samurai and *daimyō* found themselves having to find new sources of income. And because Buddhism was regarded as a foreign religion in this period, the patronage of temples had evaporated too. Craftsmen had to go in search of new markets where they could demonstrate their expertise and skill. Some found jobs at the world exhibitions that made their entrance in this period.

The world exhibition
Whether this dragon was exhibited at one of the world exhibitions is not certain, but it was common enough for articulated metal creatures like this, along with other large metal objects, to be displayed as works of art to the European public. Take the gigantic bronze censers produced by the artists Suzuki Chōkichi and Hayashi Harusada, for instance. These censers were four metres high, and decorated with exotic scenes from Japanese and Chinese mythology.

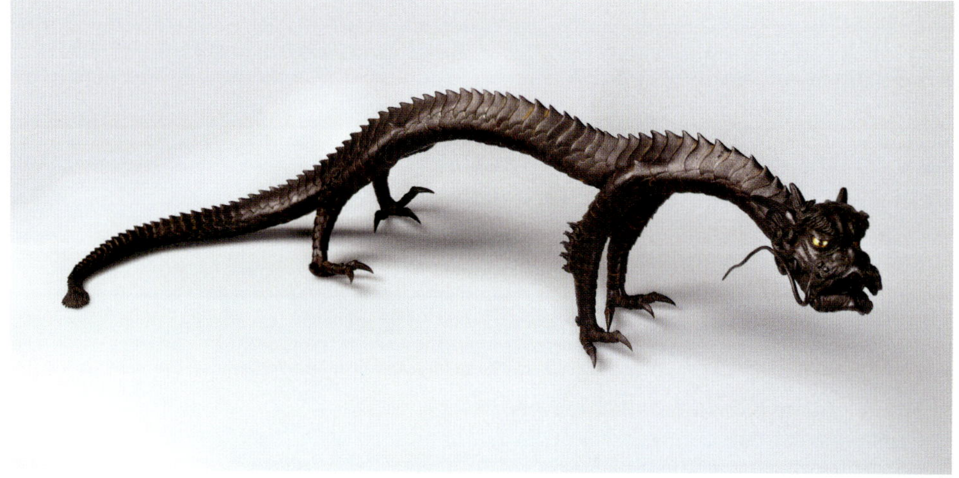

Japanese metalworking
The choice of material here is striking, since iron is certainly not a precious metal. A British designer named Christopher Dresser, who travelled to Japan in 1877, believed that Japan's metalworkers were 'the only people who do not think of the material, and regard the effect produced as of far greater moment than the material employed.'

Mythical dragons
Both Japanese and Chinese mythology have a great variety of dragons. There are four primary types: Celestial Dragons, protectors of the gods, Spiritual Dragons, which bring rain, Earth Dragons, which determine the course of the rivers, and Treasure Guarding Dragons, which protect the treasures of the earth. Not everyone could choose which dragon to forge a bond with. There was a hierarchy, based on the number of claws: five-clawed dragons were assigned exclusively to the emperor and four-clawed dragons to the nobles, while ordinary commoners had to make do with three-clawed dragons.

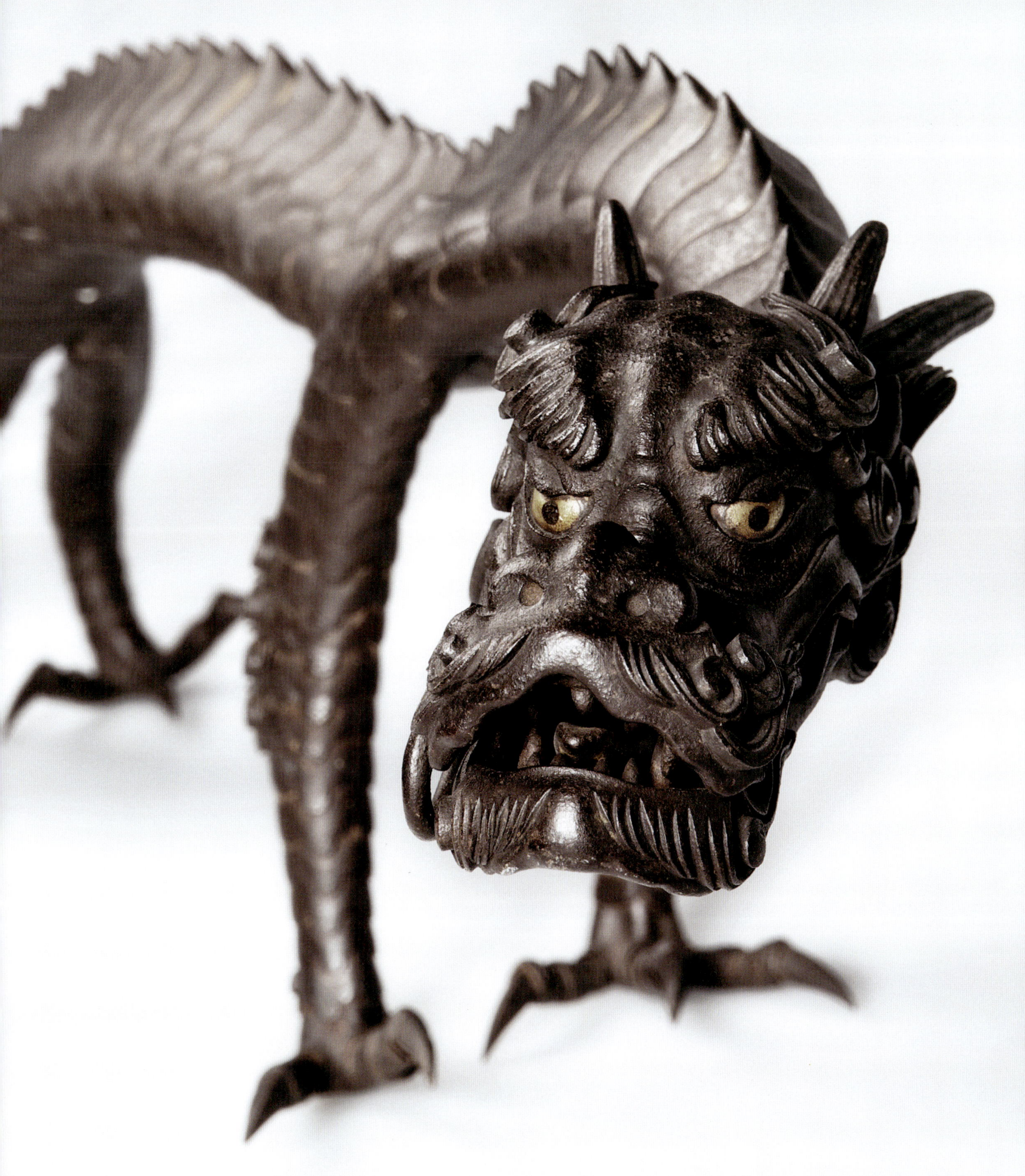

Tsongkhapa

Eastern Tibet
1800-1900
39 x 31 x 19 cm
wood
RMV 1840-1 (1913)

Gelugpa Order

This statue represents the monk Tsongkhapa (1347-1419). He was born into a nomadic family in northeast Tibet and recognised at an early age as an incarnation of the Bodhisattva Manjushri. According to legend, at the age of seventeen he journeyed to central Tibet, where he became a prominent scholar and a respected philosopher, and founded Ganden Monastery in 1409. His followers are called Gelugs or Gelugpas. Because of their typical yellow headdress they are also known in the West as the 'Yellow Hat' sect, to distinguish them from other monastic orders, who wear red hats. The Dalai Lama is associated with the Gelugpa Order.

Ganden Monastery

Ganden is one of the three great monasteries of the Gelugpa Order in the vicinity of Lhasa. The other two are the Drepung and Sera monasteries. All three are large complexes with different buildings, located at an altitude of approximately 4,000 metres, against the slopes of the Himalayas. Ganden Monastery consists of more than fifty buildings. In one of them, the body of Tsonghkapa lies in state in a tomb of silver and gold. Once a year, a huge scroll painting (*thangka*) with an image of the Buddha is taken out into the open air and unfurled so that everyone can see it.

Tsongkhapa

Tsongkhapa touches thumbs and index fingers in circles in the hand gesture known as *dharmachakra mudra* (see p. 110-111). He is dressed as a Tibetan monk. This differs somewhat from the clothes worn by Buddhist monks elsewhere, since the inner garment consists of two parts: a wrap shirt with cap sleeves and a skirt wound around the waist and reaching to the ankles. The outer robe is draped over this. Here, we see that the outer robe is draped only over the left shoulder, leaving most of the right arm bare. In contrast to other regions, where monks wear garments in a single colour, Tibetan monks wear a combination of yellow and deep, dark red.

Lotus flowers

Tsongkhapa usually carries a lotus stem in each hand, on which lie a sword and a book at shoulder level. These are the attributes of Manjushri, thus signifying that Tsongkhapa is a manifestation of this Bodhisattva. There is no sword or book here. Possibly they were lost at some time in the past. The lotus flower is a very common motif in Buddhist art. The motif would sometimes be embellished and adapted to suit local taste. We can see this here: the decorative leaves are not in fact lotus leaves at all. On the other hand, we do see the lotus's characteristic seedbox on the right-hand side.

Varnish

Most nineteenth-century Tibetan sculptures in Western collections are made of bronze or another metal. Wooden sculptures are rare. Even rarer are wooden sculptures on which the layer of varnish has survived for such a long period of time. The fine condition of the varnish on this impressive statue of Tsongkhapa is extremely unusual. The gilded layer of varnish and the delicate carving of the fingers and face, for instance, give the statue the appearance of a metal sculpture.

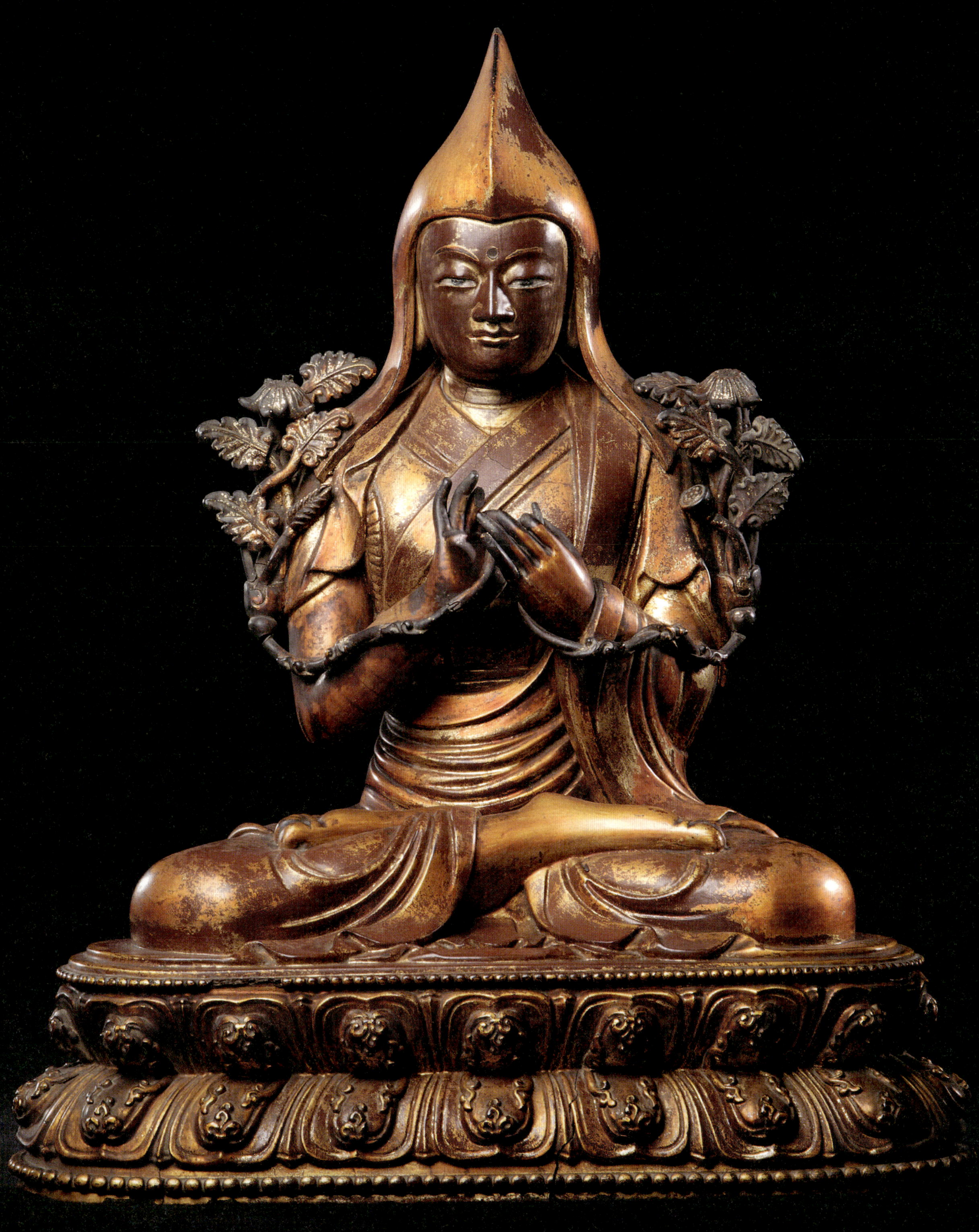

Scene with mountain god and human sacrifices

Moche, Peru
c. 350
21 cm
pottery
1872-125 (1913)

Moche

The Moche civilisation of northern Peru flourished from AD 100 to 800. The majority of the population lived from farming and fishing. Moche is particularly well known for the many vessels that have been preserved, thanks to the extremely arid climate of the Peruvian coastal deserts. These vessels are decorated with images of sacrifices, portraits, war, hunting and fishing scenes, and complicated rituals. They were mould-made, and the moulds too have survived in large numbers and have been found at archaeological sites.

Craggy mountain peak

This vessel depicts a large, craggy mountain peak, with a number of smaller peaks on the way up. Right at the top lies the figure of a human sacrifice, his hair hanging down along the incline. On the left stands the mountain god. He wears a hair band representing a bat and holds a battle club. His belt ends in a serpent that coils around beneath his feet. A fox stands below, looking round. On the right stands an iguana in part-human form. Before the god sits a human being holding a bag. Lying in front of this figure is the decapitated body of another human sacrifice, whose head lies to the left of the vessel.

The treasure digger

This item was excavated in Peru between 1890 and 1895 by Thomas Hewitt Myring, who worked for a British company in Bolivia. When he fell seriously ill, Myring accepted a friend's invitation to travel to a sugar plantation in the Chicama Valley, for his convalescence. During his stay there, he heard a legend told by the local population, according to which the gold treasure of Atahualpa, the last Inca emperor, lay buried in the valley. Once Myring had recuperated, he decided to set off in search of this treasure. Two months later he started excavating in a burial mound and retrieved over 600 pieces from the soil. He did not find a gold treasure.

The collector

On his return to London in 1909, Myring sold the fruits of his excavations to Henry van den Bergh (1853-1937), a Dutchman who lived in London. Van den Bergh worked for the company Margarine Unie, which merged with Lever Brothers to form Unilever in 1929, under the leadership of Henry's brother Samuel. After the purchase, Van den Bergh donated 250 pieces to the British Museum. He later donated another 216 items to the Museum of the American Indian in New York, and finally, in 1913, he donated 150 pieces to what was then the Rijks Etnografisch Museum, now the Rijksmuseum Volkenkunde. The size of the collection, combined with the fact that the site from which it originates is known, makes the Van den Bergh Collection one of the most important Moche collections in the world.

The significance of mountain sacrifices

Archaeologists disagree about the significance of sacrifices in Moche society. According to one influential theory, sacrifices were offered in the mountains at the beginning of the rainy season, to guarantee the land's fertility and a good harvest. The images of young foxes and snails that frequently occur in such scenes are said to allude to the beginning of the rainy season.

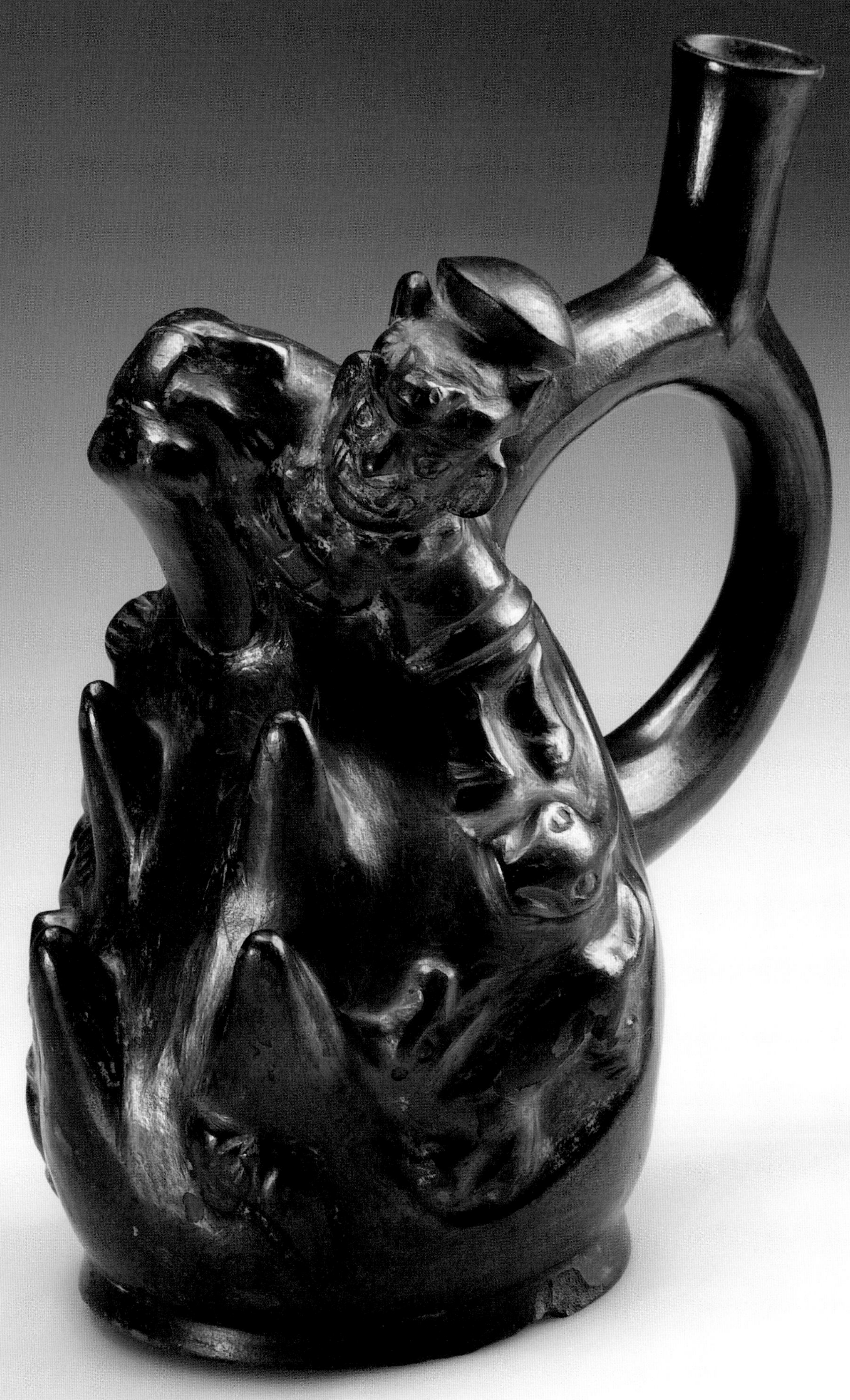

Statue of a pregnant woman

Kamoro; Southwest New Guinea, Indonesia
before 1913
296 x 30 cm
wood, charcoal pigment, lime and burnt ochre

RMV 1971-591 (1919)

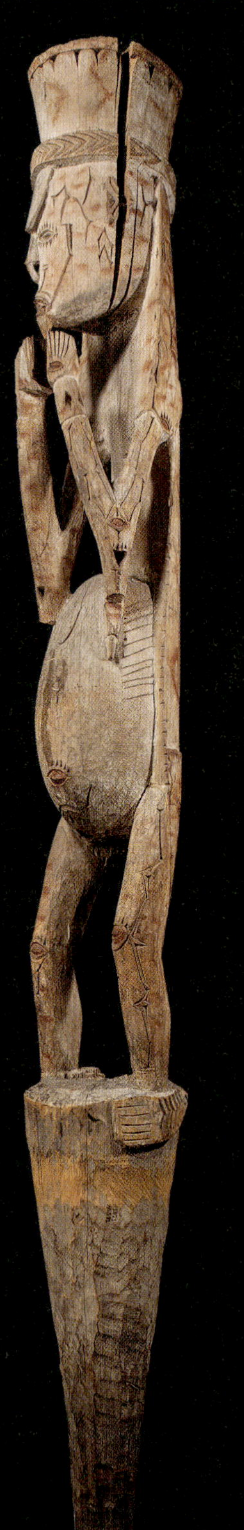

Pregnant woman

This statue of a woman is one of the oldest objects in the Kamoro collection. It is unique. The woman is depicted standing, her legs bent, belly swollen, arms bent, and hands raised towards her projecting chin. A band, with scored decorations, distinguishes the high, cylindrical headdress. The ears and genitals are depicted clearly. The hair is decorated with *mopere* motifs. Similar motifs are used to depict the eyes, mouth and navel. The legs display engraved decorations on the outside and the feet are part of the pedestal. The eyes are embellished with black dye and the navel with red.

Military expedition

Statues of this kind were collected around 1907 as curiosities by A.J. Gooszen during the first of the three expeditions to South New Guinea (1907-1913), the aim of which was to reach the 'eternal snow' of the peaks of the Central Highlands and to conduct research on the way. On the first of these expeditions in 1907, Gooszen was instructed to chart a region measuring 180,000 square kilometres. Interestingly, though he was a soldier, Gooszen did not see the use of topographical studies. In his view, he could serve the Dutch East Indies Army far better by conducting ethnological studies and collecting objects.

Navel

The literal meaning of *mopere* is 'navel', referring to the mother's navel, the essence of life. The motif is also used here to depict moving parts of the body such as hands, shoulders, hips and feet. For movement was one of the essential aspects of life. The abundant use of this motif on this female statue shows that the figure is associated with fertility and the renewal of life.

Child spirits

According to Kamoro beliefs, the mother brings forth life, but pregnancy can only come about if child spirits (*ipu-ajru*) enter the woman's womb at night. Pregnancy can also be caused when a man scatters a fertilising substance, without his wife's knowledge, during the celebration of the *emakame* or *kaware* ritual. The woman is the bearer of new life; the spiritual origins of life, the underworld, is the domain of the man. It is also the man's task to ensure that the formless foetus undergoes further development. For each part of the body, sexual intercourse must take place. Men and women play complementary roles in their relationship.

Creation and fertility

Few facts have been gathered concerning the statue's meaning and function. It comes from the eastern Kamoro region where it was used in the *kiawa* festivities, a local variant of the *emakame* ceremony that took place throughout the Kamoro region. During the main ceremony, which revolved around the creation of human beings and the renewal of life, four of these statues would be placed side-by-side in the ceremonial house. One of the key objectives of this ritual was to increase fertility.

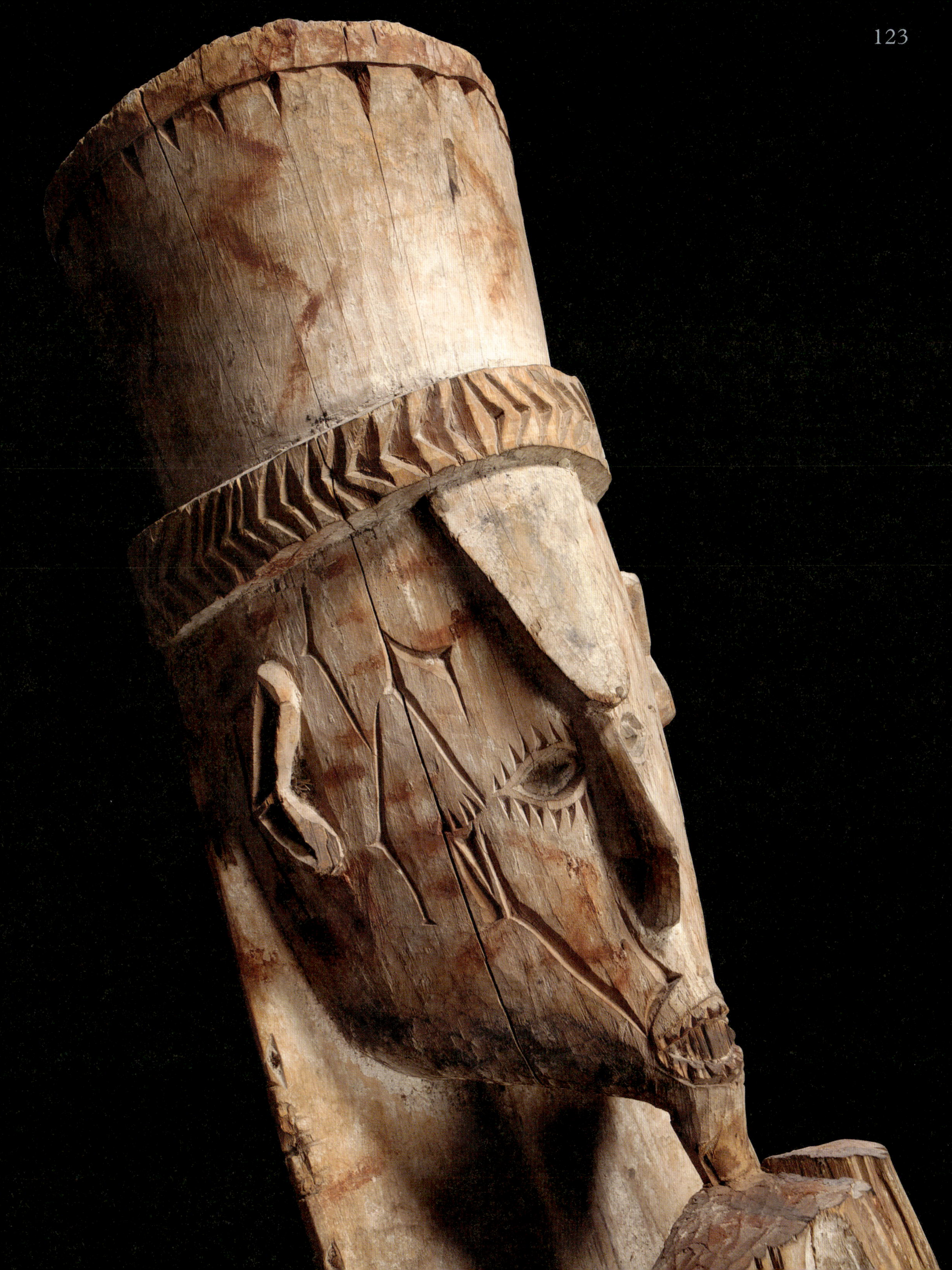

Lute (*Qanbūs*)

Western Arabia
before 1884
99 x 22.8 x 13 cm
wood, animal hide, gut, paint
RMV 1973-25 (1919)

Qanbūs

Men and women playing the lute were depicted in ancient Egypt as early as 1500 BC. Their music enlivened court banquets and ceremonies. The body of the instrument was originally made of hide, but in the sixth century, the preference shifted to wood (Arabic al-'ud, 'wood'), from which the name 'lute' derives. This six-string lute, or *qanbūs*, was made from a single piece of wood. In this model, the instrument's soundboard consists of both the egg-shaped belly – with hide stretched over it – and the hollow neck. There is no combined bridge-tailpiece, as in classical lutes. Instead, the six strings pass over a separate bridge, and there is a separate tailpiece that serves as a support for the right arm.

Rich musical tradition

Although religious authorities some-times adopted a negative attitude to music, the Arab world has a rich musical tradition. Western Arabia, where this lute was played, was full of secular and religious, urban and Bedouin music. Cosmopolitan Mecca had musicians and instruments from all parts of the world. Indeed, this was already the case in the seventh century, when Mecca's elite invited musicians from Persia and the Byzantine Empire to their city. This rich musical life encouraged the development of new styles. Arab music does not have chords; singer and musicians perform the same melody, with subtle variations.

Hide and gut

Spruce was the timber most favoured for lutes in Western Arabia. Ideally, the length of each lute was attuned to the length of the musician's arm, which varied from ninety to a hundred centimetres. Lamb's hide would be stretched across the belly, and gut was used for the strings. Here, floral decorations have been carved into the wood of the back and the S-shaped top of the neck and on the bridge. The belly and the top of the neck display meander-ing floral patterns and rosettes, applied in gold paint.

Everyday life in Western Arabia

This type of lute comes from Western Arabia and belongs to a group of eighteen instruments donated to the museum in 1919 by the famous Orientalist and Islamic scholar Christiaan Snouck Hurgronje (1857-1936). During his long stay in Jeddah and Mecca in 1884-1885, Snouck Hurgronje closely observed and photographed everyday life. He published an account of his observations in the two-volume work Mecca in the latter part of the 19th century (originally published in German as *Mekka. Aus dem heutigen Leben* in 1889), richly illustrated with photographs and lithographs of objects. His own collection consisted mainly of everyday objects, and he encouraged friends and acquaintances to purchase objects in Mecca during and after his stay. The musical instruments were offered to him by a friend from Jeddah.

Festive sounds

This type of short-necked, egg-shaped lute was played in regions including Western Arabia and Yemen. Yemeni musicians played with a plectrum made from the hollow spine of a crow's feather. In his book about Mecca, Snouck Hurgronje describes the playing of the four-stringed *qanbūs* to accompany singing for relaxation and enjoyment in the annual festivities honouring Sittana Meymuna, one of the wives of the Prophet Muhammad. Fortunately, thanks to Snouck Hurgronje's persistent requests, sound recordings were made at the Dutch Consulate in Jeddah between 1906 and 1909. As a result, we can still listen to songs sung in Arabic and accompanied by the lute in the early twentieth century.

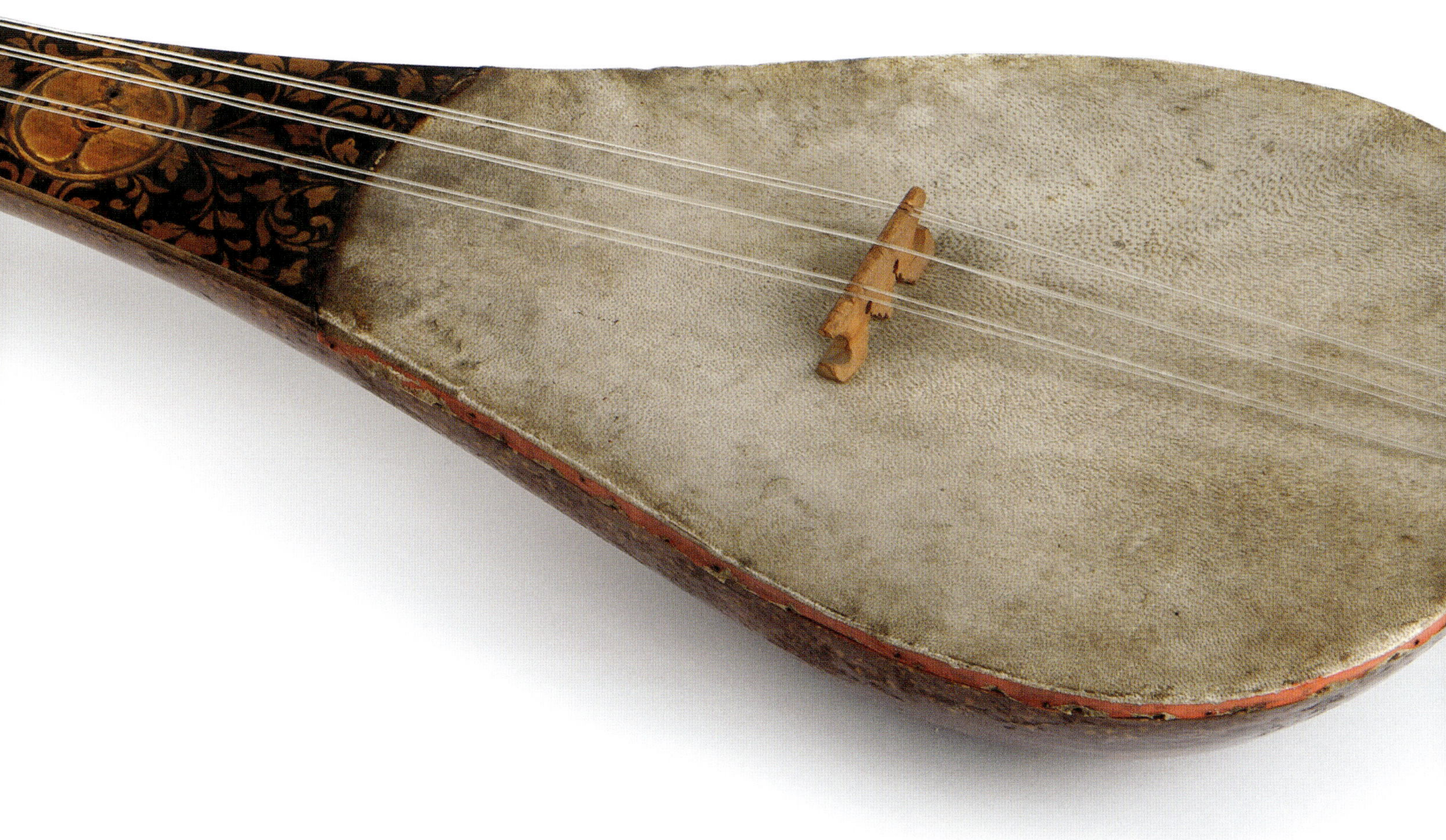

Shield

Northwest Asmat; Southwest New Guinea, Indonesia
before 1893
58 x 7 x 1 cm
wood, red ochre, charcoal, lime, varnish
RMV 1971-976 (1919)

Old shield
This is one of the earliest collected and oldest preserved Asmat shields. Its general shape and decoration, with its M, W and C-shaped motifs, is characteristic of shields from the northwest Asmat region. A human or animal head is represented at the top.

Shield festivals
Asmat shields were made for a shield festival that would serve as the prelude to a headhunting raid, undertaken to avenge the death of those after whom the shields were named. The shield bearer was believed to derive extraordinary power and courage from the dead person associated with the shield. According to another belief, certain motifs on the shield would strike such terror into the enemy that he would drop his weapons and could be taken captive. Men also used shields to drive off evil spirits in the event of sudden or unforeseen death.

Flying foxes and nose decorations
The dominant motifs at the top and bottom, which are M-shaped and W-shaped, respectively, probably represent flying foxes (a kind of bat), identifiable by the tiny claws on the pointed ends. The flying fox motif is often associated with male ancestors. The C-shapes at the heart of the motif section represent bipanew, a piece of shell jewellery that is inserted through the pierced nasal septum on festive occasions. The *bipanew* is a symbol used to denote a headhunter.

Emotional and artistic value
In the northwest Asmat region, shields were not destroyed after the owner's death, because of their symbolic and emotional value. In this region, shields were passed on from father to son, the village war chief being responsible for such ceremonial transfers. This shield was probably several centuries old at the time of its acquisition at the end of the nineteenth century. Its history has died along with its former owners, however. We can only respect the emotional significance of this object and admire the artistic expressiveness that the maker breathed into it.

Master woodcarverr
All Asmat men are capable of carving everyday utensils, but certain master woodcarvers or wowipitsj are esteemed for their great craftsmanship. This reputation is reflected in a wealth of carving commissions. Shields are carved from the fairly hard, flat prop roots of the mangrove tree. The general shape of this shield was hacked out with a stone axe, after which the finer elements were carved with animal-bone chisels and shell knives. The white paint is made from burnt and pulverised shells, mixed with water. Red is obtained from the ochre clay found in coastal riverbanks, while charcoal is mixed with water to obtain black.

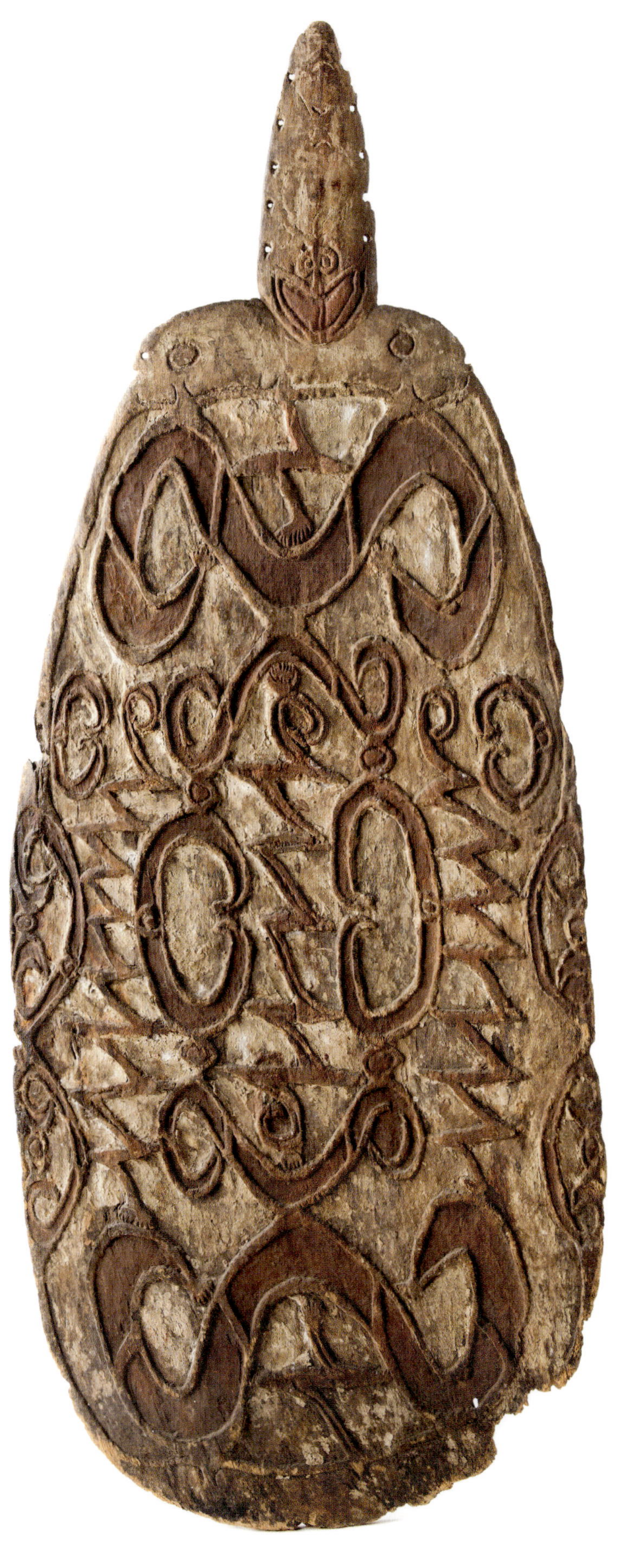

Tomb model

China
6th or 7th century
h. 24 cm
terracotta, colour pigments
RMV 1997-2 (1920)

Female rider

A female rider is posed beating a drum, her feet supported by stirrups. She wears a garment that fastens across her body, and a red head covering commonly associated with the roaming, equestrian economy – or its fashionable affectation – of life in the northern steppes. The horse is hollow above its open underside. The ears, forelock and tail have suffered damage, and bright colouring on both horse and rider has long since perished. The object was probably made in the century before the reunification of China in 581 and the following Tang period (618-907).

Terracotta figures

The history of placing human and animal models near – and inside – tombs extends beyond even the famous terracotta army guarding the First Emperor of Qin (r. 221-210). The Qin established an emphasis on realistic figures engaged in some form of practical engagement, but the elites of later periods preferred to make models on a smaller scale. Through their detailed modeling and painting these objects symbolized the social, economic, military and ceremonial pursuits of their owner's past life, and they materialized the aspiration that the appearances and resources of that life would characterize a new existence after death.

Magic statues

Although destined for an eternal existence underground, tomb models often appeared first at lavish displays and entertainments in the programmes that families arranged during the days ahead of the body's final interment. The enthusiasm for sealing large numbers of models in the tomb waned after the tenth century, but their presence remained undiminished in the popular imagination long afterwards. Hundreds of surviving medieval stories feature tomb models that come magically to life and affect human outcomes both benignly and malevolently.

Glaze or paint?

Terracotta was a common material, and so too was stoneware (fired at a higher temperature). Wood and lacquer models have also survived, as well as a few rare examples of stone, which required unusual and expensive skills. Stoneware could be glazed, a decorative process that made the object's surface more durable. However, glazing was a technique that its users could less easily control to guarantee the details of a model's appearance. This unglazed model of a female musician belongs to a tradition of surface painting, whose slower work embodied greater accuracy in various codes of representational realism.

Cavalry

Horses and riders often appear among the large sets of tomb models created for members of the elite in North China. Their social life was emphatically equestrian: military organisation employed cavalry (rarely if ever seen in South China); sports included hunting on horseback and games of polo; grand social events featured thoroughbred animals, often named after their exotic Central Asian origins. Even musical performance, which was a major feature of medieval court life, was sometimes adapted to a military-athletic expression when the players managed to operate their instruments on horseback – or mounted on camels. The creator of this model did not omit the essential technology of stirrups, which only in the last two or three centuries had facilitated so many innovations in equestrian performance.

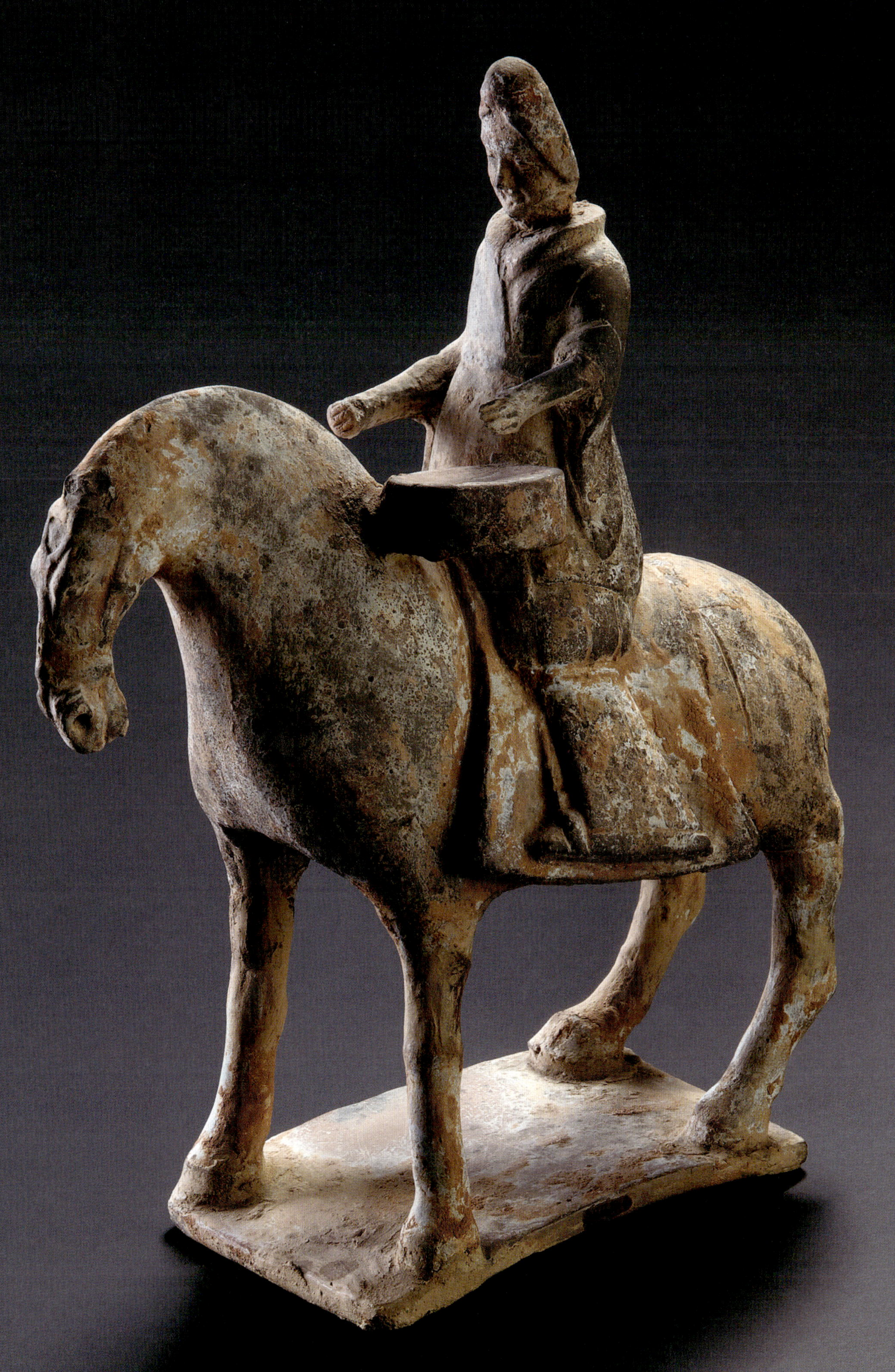

Dish

Maria Martinez; San Ildefonso Pueblo, New Mexico, United States
before 1922
d. 23 cm, h. 6.5 cm
pottery, pigments
RMV 2043-37 (1922)

Missing: wanted
In November 1922, the Rijksmuseum
Volkenkunde acquired a collection of
94 Indian objects, most of them
originating from the states of Arizona
and New Mexico. Among them were
55 painted earthenware pots, including
these ones, made by leading women
potters. According to the inventory
books and the museum's annual
report, the collection was a gift from
Dr H. Postma of Zeist. The museum's
archives contained no details what-
soever about the collector or the provenance of these items, an omission that
sparked a quest for information.

A 'Love' Story
What emerged from the annals was a
love story. For it was the American
woman Lura May Love whose charms
had lured Postma to America. Hessel
Postma (born in 1868) was a serious
student. After training as a primary
school teacher, he studied medicine at
the University of Groningen. He
specialised in psychiatry in Paris and
Amsterdam, and in 1905 he was
appointed as a psychiatrist at the girls'
state reform school in Zeist, an
institution operated by the criminal
justice system. Lura May Love was
travelling around Europe at this time.
She too was highly talented. A striking,
artistic woman, she taught languages,
published poetry, and gave concerts of
classical music. The two were married,
and in 1919-1920 they went on a
journey around the United States,
driving across the deserts of Arizona and
New Mexico, and visiting reservations,
where they purchased products of
Indian craftsmanship.

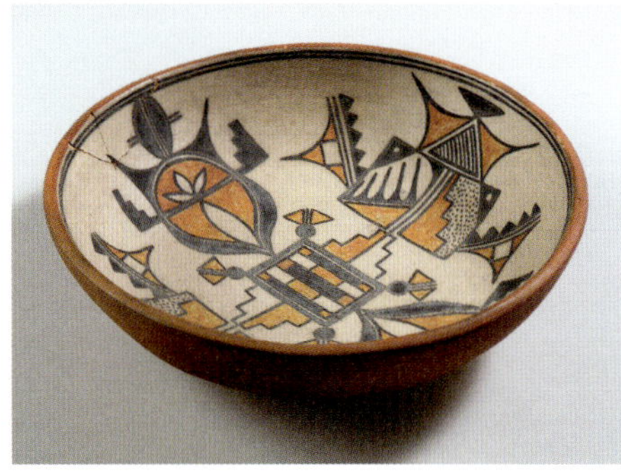

Quest
On a trip to the Center of Southwest
Research in Albuquerque, in 1992, the
Leiden curator of the North American
department discovered Postma's name
and his address in Zeist, in the accounts
of the Babbitt and Roberts Trading Post
of Jeddito, Arizona. The index
(compiled in 1919) revealed that the
Dutchman had visited the Navajo
reservation. After fruitless telephone
calls to all the Postmas listed in Zeist's
telephone book, municipal archivist
Pierre Rhoen found Postma's personal
details in the old index card system of
the population register. He also found
an obituary notice in the Zeister Post
newspaper and a brief report about
Postma's funeral in 1948.

Maria and Julian Martinez
The best-known potter of San Ildefonso
Pueblo is Maria Montoya Martinez
(1887-1980). She worked together with
her husband Julian (1885-1943). She
demonstrated her gift for pottery in
1904 at the Louisiana Purchase
Exposition and in 1915 at the Panama-
California Exposition in San Diego. She
and her husband worked primarily for
the Fred Harvey Company that owned
the hotels, restaurants and souvenir
shops along the railroad. The demand
for their pottery increased still further in
1919, when they developed a new
decorative technique consisting of matt
black decorations on a shiny black
background. The Leiden dish is an
example of their polychrome earthenware. Their work is exhibited in many
museums in North America, Europe,
Australia, and Japan.

Pueblo pottery
Because of the proximity of the city of
Santa Fe, seat of the state government,
an artists' centre, and a popular desti-
nation among wealthy tourists, the
surrounding Indian pueblo villages
attracted a constant stream of white
visitors. Few visitors left without buying
a souvenir, frequently some item of
pottery. The growing demand led to the
production of inferior earthenware.
Still, the people also produced fine,
beautifully painted kitchenware for their
own use, which was sometimes offered
for sale. The demand among affluent
tourists and collectors, as well as the
encouragement of high-quality pottery
by Director Hewett of the Museum of
New Mexico, led several Indian potters
to develop their craftsmanship to great
heights.

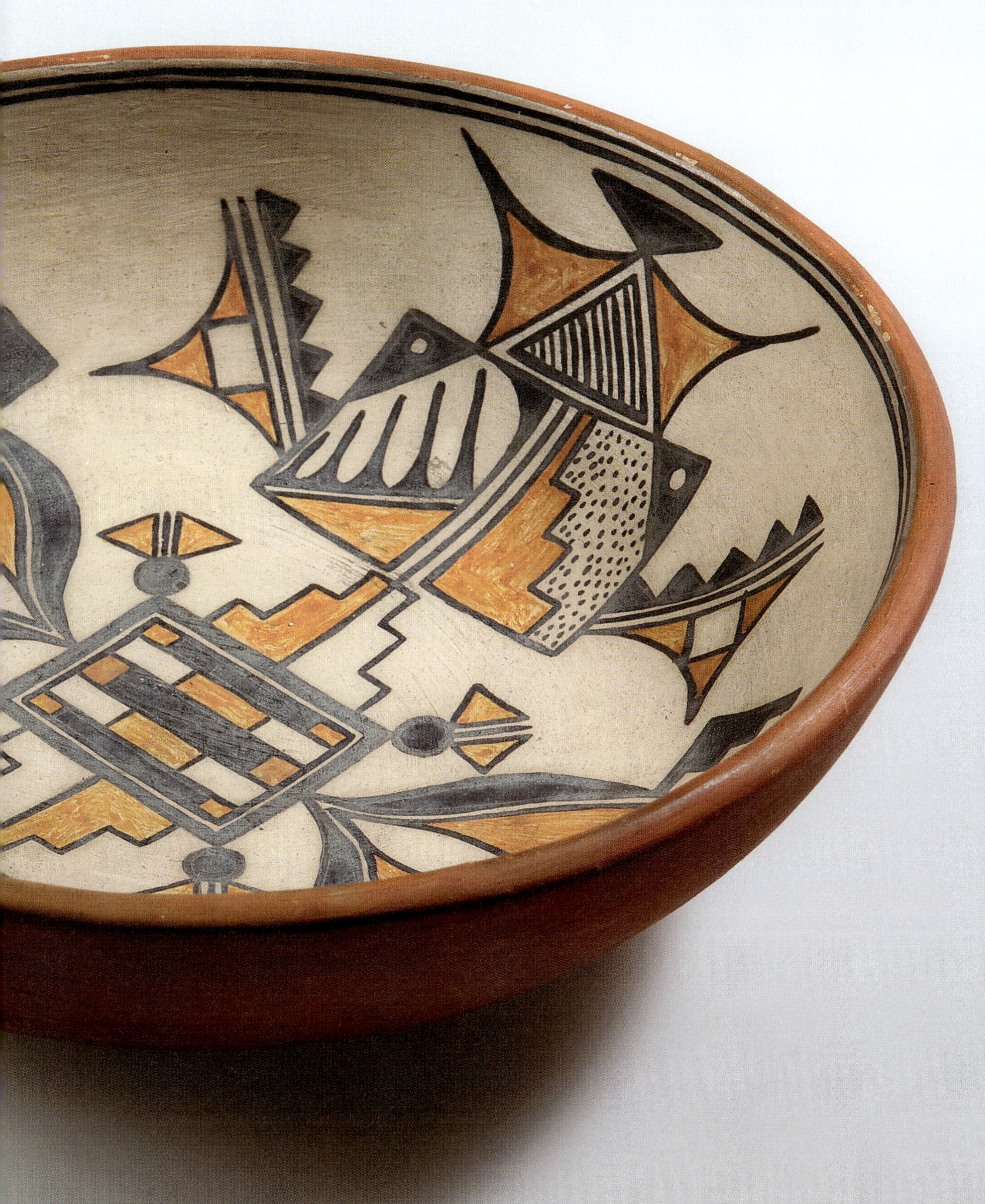

Two miniatures from the *Shahnameh*

Persia
c. 1600
36 x 23 cm
paper, paint
RMV 2103-1 and RMV 2103-2 (1926)

The story of Zal

These separate paintings depict scenes from the famous Persian epic *Shahnameh* (Book of Kings). In the miniature on the right, Princess Manizheh stokes a huge bonfire to guide the hero Rostam to the pit where her beloved Bizhan lies confined in chains, on her father's orders. The miniature on the left depicts the story of Zal, who is aban-doned in the mountains as an infant because of his white hair and his 'old man's' appearance. When a *simurgh*, a mythical bird, comes to grab Zal to feed to her hatchlings in the nest, she takes pity on him and decides to allow him to live, raising him as one of her own.

Book of Kings

The Persian heroic epic *Shahnameh* (Book of Kings) describes the long history of Persia and its people, from the beginning of time until the Arab conquests of the seventh century AD. The poet Abolqasem Ferdowsi (AD 940–c.1020) compiled this epic tale from oral and written sources in the late tenth and early eleventh centuries. Legends and historical facts are inter-mingled in over 50,000 long lines of verse. Many handwritten manuscripts, and later printed copies, followed. In addition, scenes from the epic were depicted on the walls of Persian palaces, in coffeehouses, and on mediaeval pottery.

Copyists

Large numbers of copies were made of the popular epic. Expensive, hand-written ones were furnished with miniatures depicting important scenes. These two paintings were probably made as separate images. It seems likely that they were intended for albums in which the élite collected diverse works of art on paper to fire the imagination, in their small circle, with tales of kings and heroes, their struggles and their loyalty. The common people heard the tales from itinerant storytellers, who would bring to life scenes from the *Shahnameh*, illustrated in narrative paintings

Squirrel-tail brushes

From the end of the sixteenth century onwards, Persian miniature painters discarded egg white in favour of glue and gum arabic as binding agents for pigments. The pigments themselves were obtained from plants and minerals such as gold, silver, and lapis lazuli. Brushes were made from cat hairs or from the hairs of squirrel-tails. The spaces above and below the painting and the margins are spotted with gold, which was applied to the wet paper. Once the paper had dried, the painter would smooth out the surface using glass or a hard stone, after which he applied a sketch of the image.

Ancient Persian civilisation

In the age of the poet Ferdowsi, Northwest Persia was ruled by the Samanid dynasty (r. 819-1005). The rulers took a keen interest in the ancient, pre-Islamic Persian culture. They propagated New Persian, rather than Arabic, as the language of the court. New Persian literature flourished. The cultural climate they created proved ideal for the development of a monu-mental narrative on the glorious ancient Persian civilisation. The *Shahnameh* follows chronologically the rule of fifty kings and queens, from their ascent to the throne, by way of the wars they waged, to their abdication or death. The morality and sense of justice governing the deeds of heroes and the court loom large in these tales.

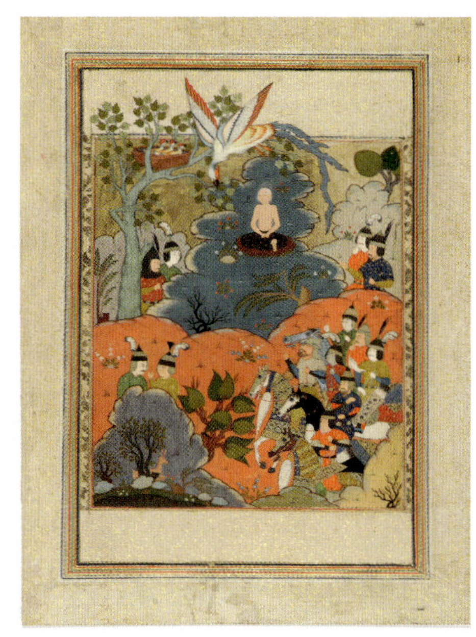

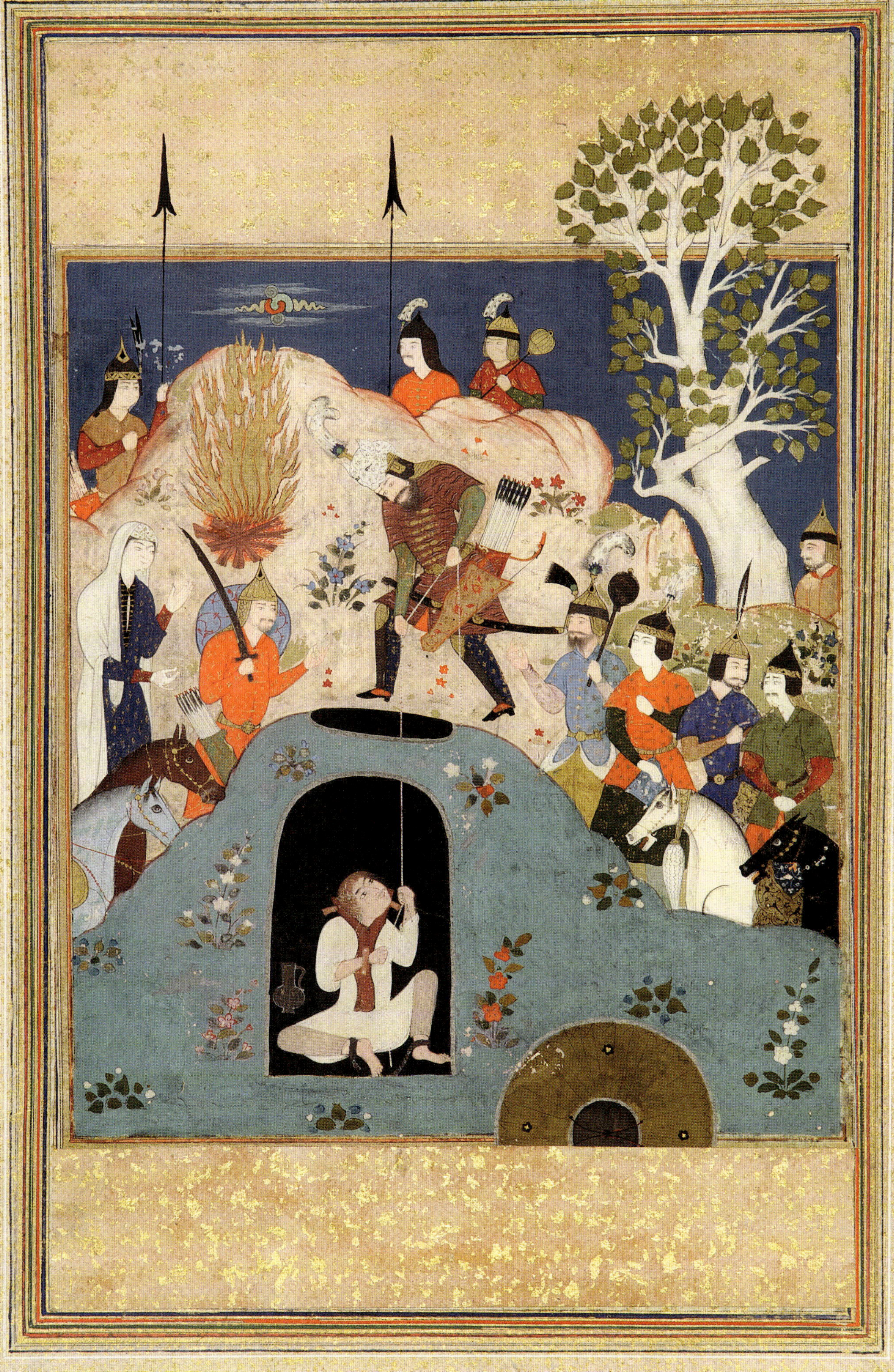

Standing Buddha

Gandhara, Northwest Pakistan
3rd to 5th century
43 x 16 x 8 cm
grey slate
RMV 2207-3 (1930)

Monk's robe with folds

The Buddha is dressed as a monk, in accordance with tradition. There are a variety of ways to depict this robe: draped with folds or clinging to the body; thrown over both shoulders, or worn such as to leave one shoulder bare. This statue has a robe with articulated folds, as is customary in the art of Gandhara (Pakistan and Afghanistan), Amaravati (Southern India), and Sri Lanka. The robe covers both shoulders, something seen more frequently in northern than warmer, southern regions, where there is a preference for leaving the right shoulder bare. Even today, Buddhist monks will pull their orange or reddish-brown robes over both shoulders when the temperature drops.

Gandhara

Gandhara is the ancient name for a plain in Northwest Pakistan, present-day Peshawar. It is traversed by several tributaries of the Indus River. From the west, it could only be reached by crossing the Khyber Pass in the Hindu Kush mountains. This was a major transit route from West to East, from the Mediterranean region to India and China. Because of its strategic location, Gandhara grew into a major centre of commerce along the Silk Road, and early on it developed a sophisticated, multicultural ambience in which Buddhism played an important role.

Growing prosperity

This culture extended from ancient Gandhara to Afghanistan and the Swat Valley, further north in Pakistan. This entire region is known as 'Greater Gandhara', and the Buddhist art produced there is known as Gandhara art. This developed most notably among the nomadic Kushan people of Central Asia, who gained control of Greater Gandhara and northern India from the first century AD onwards and established political stability there. This led to growing prosperity, enormously boosting the patronage of monasteries, stupas and other sacred places. The two largest Buddhas – some 36 and 53 metres in height, respectively –were built into a rock face of a monastery in Bamiyan. They were blown up by the Taliban in 2001.

Cultural encounters

The art that was produced at this cultural crossroads is a fascinating melting-pot of styles, from Iran, Central Asia, India and the Hellenistic world, into which Gandhara had been incorporated after Alexander the Great's conquest of the region in the fourth century BC. This statue displays elements that recall Hellenistic art: on the pedestal we see a pilaster with a Corinthian-type capital, with acanthus leaves, and in the middle is a honeysuckle motif, although both are shaped in innovative ways. The wavy hair and the way the robe is draped also have their roots in Hellenistic art.

New discoveries

For many years only one Buddhist manuscript from this region was known, but recently over a hundred fragments of texts were found. These have now been incorporated into European, Japanese and American collections. The texts are written on birch bark or palm leaves, with the oldest dating from the second century. They greatly illuminate the Buddhism of their day. Most are Mahayana Buddhist texts, which were highly influential at an early stage in Central Asia and China. Gandhara was probably more important for the development of Buddhism than was previously thought, because of the lack of sources.

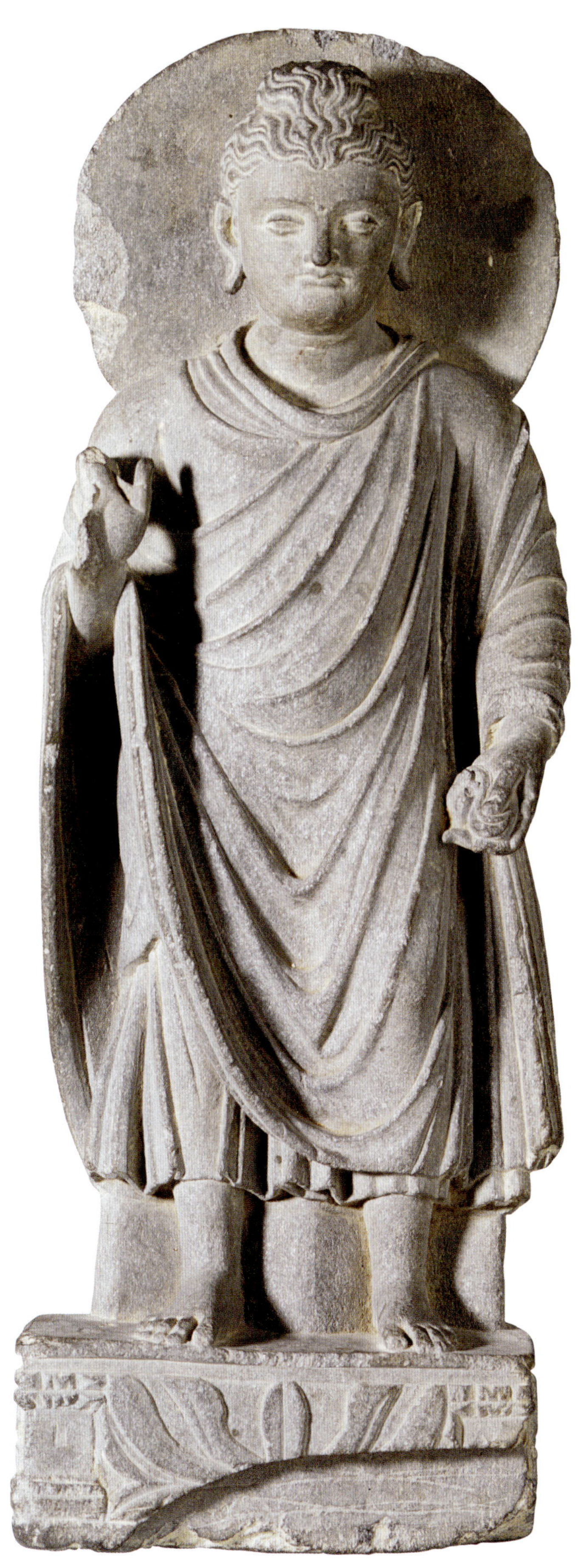

Skull cup

Tibetan, Himalayan region
1800-1930
5 x 18 x 13 cm
bone, turquoise, blood coral

RMV 2220-1 (1930)

Kapala

This skull cup, or *kapala*, was probably made from a male human skull. It is a remarkable item, because it is decorated with death's-heads, a conch shell (left), two crossed ritual sceptres or *vajras* (right), two fish (centre), and floral and foliate motifs. The four-flower heart is inlaid with blood coral or turquoise stones. The conch shell and two fish are among the ashtamangala, the eight motifs that bring happiness. Such skull cups are generally placed on a bronze base and furnished with a lid with a *vajra*-shaped knob (see p. 106-107). The interior of such cups is generally inlaid with silver leaf or bronze, though the piece displayed here does not have this feature.

Symbolic cooking

The *kapala* can be used in diverse Tibetan rituals, for instance to make offerings of wine (symbolising blood), meat, or biscuits in the shape of human eyes or ears to propitiate wrathful, terrifying deities. Sometimes offerings are made only through visualisation. In such cases, the person who is performing the ritual visualises placing the offerings in the skull cup. Together, the skull cup, the lid, and the base represent the symbolic cooking of the offerings in a pot over the fire. The power of the visualisation eradicates impurities from the offerings and transforms them into 'nectar', which keeps replenishing itself.

Tantric Buddhism

Tantric Buddhism is also known as Tantrayana, Vajrayana, or esoteric Buddhism. It evolved through a complex interaction between doctrines, rituals and philosophies that were institutionalised in Buddhist monasteries, and magical texts and practices that developed in the practices of individual saints or *Siddhas*. These *Siddhas* lived on the fringes of society and went in search of extremes that were not accepted in normal social life. Because of this marginal position, extraordinary supernatural powers (*siddhi*) were imputed to them, as a result of which they were held in high esteem and many of their ideas and practices were adopted in the monasteries.

The charnel ground

In the tantric Buddhist literature, the charnel ground (*shmashana*) is the ideal location where *siddhas* can find special supernatural, magical powers. It is the place where people brought their dead who were not to be cremated: a sinister, frightening place outside the inhabited world, where body parts lie around in different stages of decomposition, along with skulls and bones. In the charnel ground, dogs, jackals, crows and vultures feast on the remaining scraps of flesh. Nowhere is the confrontation with the obstacles that give rise to human suffering starker than here. Many of the terrifying deities in Tibetan Buddhism are associated with the charnel ground. They frequently carry a skull cup and are sometimes decked out with bone ornaments.

The best skulls

Certain texts describe in detail the criteria that make a human skull suitable for use as a skull cup. The decisive features include the number of lines on the skull, its colour and shape, and the number of holes. Some descriptions reject a woman's skull as unsuitable, while others claim, on the contrary, that a woman's skull is the most suitable if the skull cup is to be used for more than one purpose. A ritual skull cup may also be made from different materials, such as gold or silver.

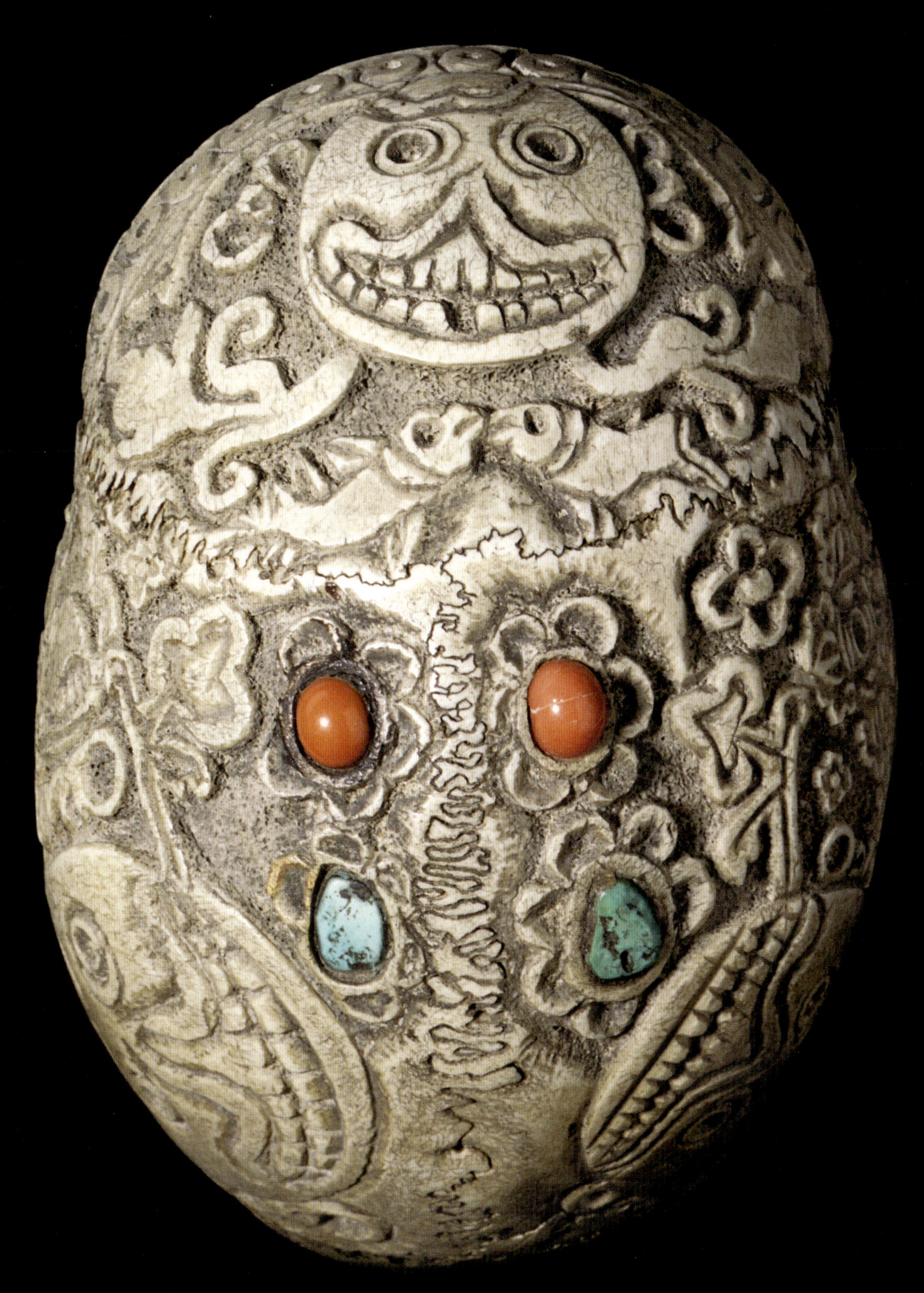

Snake statue

Alor, Nusa Tenggara Timur (Eastern Lesser Sunda Islands), Indonesia
2nd half 19th century
114 x 237 x 32 cm
wood, paint, shell, palm fibres
RMV 2271-2 (1933)

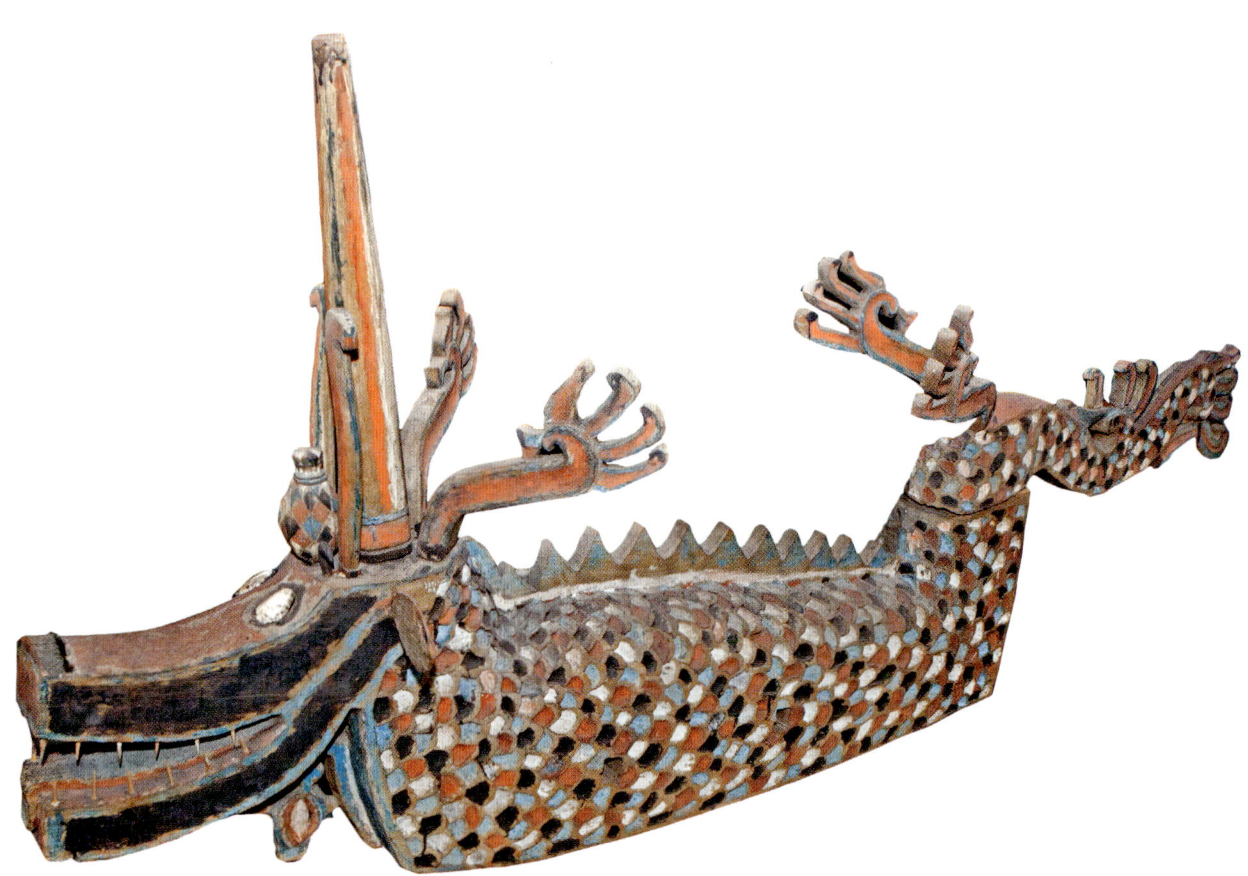

Powerful presence

This painted wooden statue represents the *Naga*, a mythical snake that plays an important role on the Alor Islands. It has open jaws displaying teeth and tongue, and a moustache and beard made of palm fibres. A flame-like decoration is carved into the back of the head and the front of the tail. The flames on the head point backwards while those on the tail point forwards. Numerous scales are carved into the snake's body, and a long pointed crest runs along the middle of its back.

Fertility and protection

Statues like this once stood on Alor (East Indonesia) in village squares and on posts outside houses. Boiled rice and chicken were offered to them here, in the expectation that they would protect people from disaster and disease, as well as bringing fertility, rich harvests, and success in hunting and war. The statues were not 'animated' until they had received the first offering.

The myth of Naga

The myth about the origins of the wealth-giving Naga was recorded by A. Boeken Kruger, the donor of this statue, when he was on Alor in 1933. Once upon a time, there was a man who chanced to arrive in heaven while he was out hunting. There he saw a great snake, named Naga, who lived in the mud. The man took Naga back home with him, along with two pieces of bamboo full of heavenly water. When Naga asked the man to worship him with offerings, the man dragged Naga away and tossed him into the sea. Years later, all sorts of treasures suddenly floated to the surface of one of the rivers: bronze kettledrums and gongs, rice and fruit. People flocked to the river and took the riches home with them. Two men arrived too late. The water moved, and a large, friendly snake came towards them. Naga had come back down the river to present gifts to the people. 'Worship me', said Naga, 'then you too will receive your share.' The men recoiled in fright. That night, an old man came to them in a dream and told them to set a trap. Naga was caught, but the men feared Naga's power and did not dare take him home with them. Instead, they drew images of the snake on the scabbards of their machetes, and hung them up at home.

Influence from China and India

Votive images of Alor are variations on, and mixtures of, snakes, crocodiles and monitor lizards, all of which are found in the neighbourhood of the island. The snake plays a part in other parts of Indonesia too; in myths and rituals it is associated with fertility and the earth or the underworld. *Naga* is the Sanskrit word for snake, and the image of the mythical snake that supports the world and helps human beings is also important in India. Dragons have the same meaning in China. Both these cultures have influenced the indigenous cultures of Indonesia, as a result of centuries of commercial ties.

Headdress (*Olok*)

Wayana, Suriname
c. 1930
105 x 100 x 30 cm
wickerwork, feathers, beetle shields
RMV 2352-1 (1938)

Olok
This *olok* was made by the Wayana
Indians. The feather headdress is used
during the marakè ritual. It consists of a
twined framework that is decorated
with chicken down along the bottom.
Above this are toucan and parrot
feathers. At the top of the headdress are
macaw feathers. The Wayana did not kill
a great many birds in order to make
feather headdresses such as an *olok*.
They kept certain birds as 'pets' in the
village from an early age, plucking a few
feathers at a time from them, after which
the birds would grow new ones.

'Lowland' and 'Upland' groups
The indigenous population of Suriname
is often divided into two broad groups.
The coastal regions are inhabited by
so-called 'Lowland' (*Benedenlandse*)
Indians: the Lokono (or Arawaks)
and the Karina (Caribs). The inland
territory is inhabited by diverse
'Upland' (*Bovenlandse*) groups, the
biggest of which are the Tareno (Trio)
and Wayana. The total Indian population amounts to several thousand,
some of whom now live in cities.

Claudius Henricus de Goeje
This object was collected by Claudius
Henricus de Goeje (1879-1955), who
took part in expeditions with a view to
charting Suriname in the early
twentieth century. In 1907 he led the
Toemoekhoemak expedition, the first to
reach the colony's southern frontier.
Local inhabitants played a crucial role
in the expedition's success, serving as
guides and furnishing the expedition
members with food and shelter.
De Goeje took a great interest in the
Indians' language, utensils and customs.
He engaged the villagers in conver-
sation, made notes, and collected
objects. He also drew up vocabulary lists
of the Wayana and Trio languages.

Marakè
For boys aged between ten and twelve,
the *marakè* is an initiation ritual.
The boys dance all night with the *olok*
on their heads, and they are plied with
large quantities of *kasiri*, an alcoholic
drink brewed from cassava. The main
highlight of the event is the wasp-
stinging ritual. As dawn breaks, a little
mat with stinging wasps or ants is
pressed against their chest and back.
Adult men also undergo the *marakè*
ritual to renew their strength.

Consultations
In 2010, Captain Samé of the village
of Apetina visited the Rijksmuseum
Volkenkunde, for consultations that the
museum was holding with Surinamese
Indians about their heritage. Together
with other Surinamese visitors, Captain
Samé made a libation to the spirit of the
olok. Pe explained: 'The *olok* is a spirit.
When I speak to him, I am also speaking
to my ancestors [. . .] I have spoken to
him, and given him water, since he was
thirsty [. . .] The *olok* likes people to come
and talk to him and drink with him.'
The *olok* therefore needs to be given
food and drink regularly, and to be
celebrated with singing and dancing.

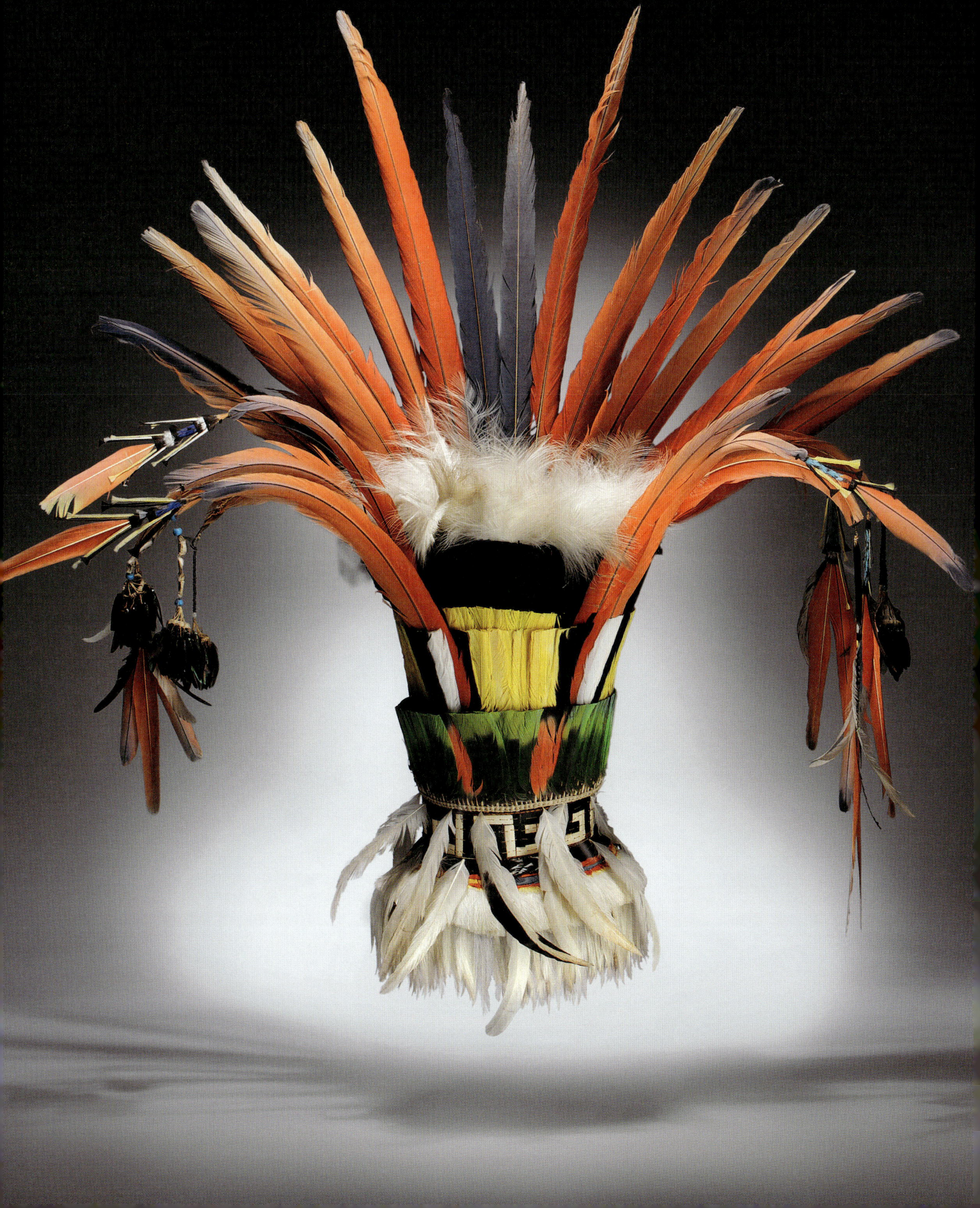

Lombok treasure

Cakranegara, West Lombok, Indonesia
2nd half of 19th century (before 1894)
brooch: 2.5 x 4 x 5 cm, diamond 21 x 19.3 mm; tobacco box: 4.5 x 8.7 x 6.4 cm; ring: 3.2 x 3 x 2 cm
gold, precious stones
RMV 4905-129 (1977), 4905-75 (1977), 2364-0-15 (1938)

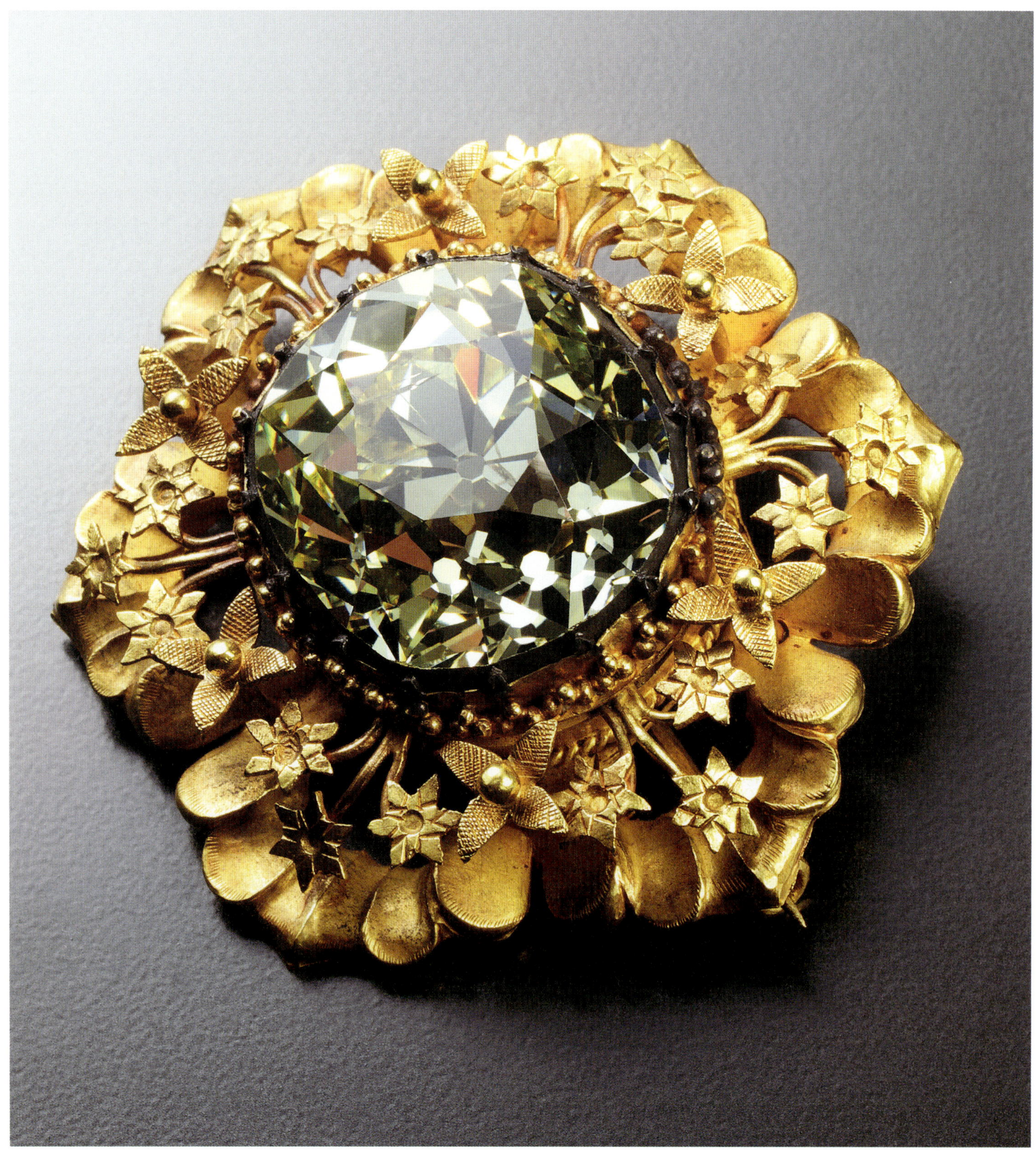

The treasures of the raja of Lombok

In Cakranegara, West Lombok, stood the palace of the raja of Mataram, which was related to the kingdom of Karangasem on East Bali. The last raja to rule here was Anak Agung Gde Ngurah Karangasem (1872-1894). Like other rajas and sultans in the Indonesian archipelago, he displayed his power and wealth by ostentatiously flaunting his possessions: numerous gold objects, decorative weapons, and jewellery set with precious gems. His family and courtiers also wore precious items of jewellery. Goldsmiths employed by the court used the most refined techniques. They acquired gold from Sumatra or Sulawesi, while diamonds came from Kalimantan.

Brooch, ring and tobacco box

The brooch, ring and tobacco box displayed here are specimens from the famous treasure of Lombok. The hexagonal brooch is made of gold and diamond. It is complex in structure and testifies to outstanding craftsmanship. Thus, the gold rim around the diamond is composed of a myriad of tiny spheres, around which are clustered little groups of three flowers on three stems. Amid this delicate, superbly crafted openwork, the goldsmith has placed larger flowers, with leaves below them. The 75-carat diamond weighs 15 grams and is cut into numerous facets. The gold tobacco box is set with rubies and chased with floral motifs. The gold ring has a large, oval, pale green gem in the middle, flanked by two bright pink gems. The setting is granulated.

Spoils of war

Ostensibly in response to a conflict that erupted between the ruler and the local population, the Sasak, but actually in a bid to maintain its monopoly on the opium trade, the colonial authorities of the Dutch East Indies launched a military expedition to West Lombok in 1894. They attacked the raja's palace and after a long battle, Mataram fell to the Dutch. The victors plundered the palace treasury, and robbed many of their fallen foes of their jewellery and weapons. In total, they seized treasure amounting to 230 kilos of gold, 7,000 kilos of silver, and three chests full of precious jewels, gems, decorative weapons, and other objects. The raja was sent into exile in Batavia.

Restitution

In 1970, as part of the drive to restore political and cultural relations with the Netherlands, the Indonesian government asked for objects of national and historic importance to be returned. This included the part of the Lombok treasure that had been sent to the Netherlands. In 1978 most of these objects were transferred to Indonesia and reunited with the rest of the treasure in the Museum Nasional in Jakarta, which had been preserved there since 1894. The Rijksmuseum Volkenkunde retained 200 objects

Batavian Society of Arts and Sciences

The entire Lombok treasure was entrusted to the Batavian Society of Arts and Sciences in Batavia, which selected the most valuable and unique objects and placed them in its museum, today the Museum Nasional Indonesia in Jakarta. The rest of the treasure was sent to Amsterdam and distributed to various museums. Voices were raised in the press and parliament in favour of selling the treasure to cover the costs of the military expedition. The minister refused to do so, and the Dutch part of the treasure eventually ended up in Leiden and the Rijksmuseum in Amsterdam.

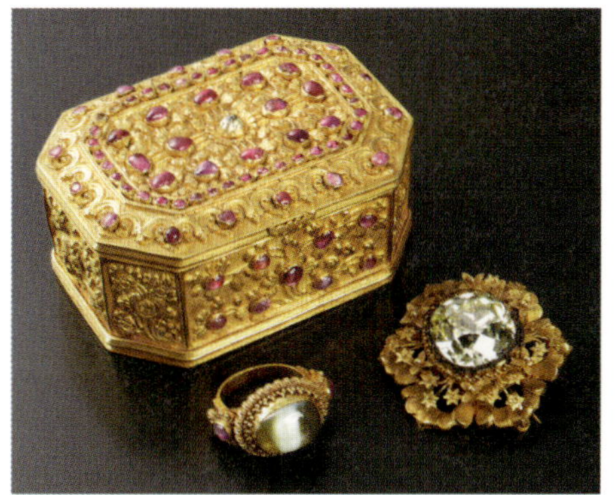

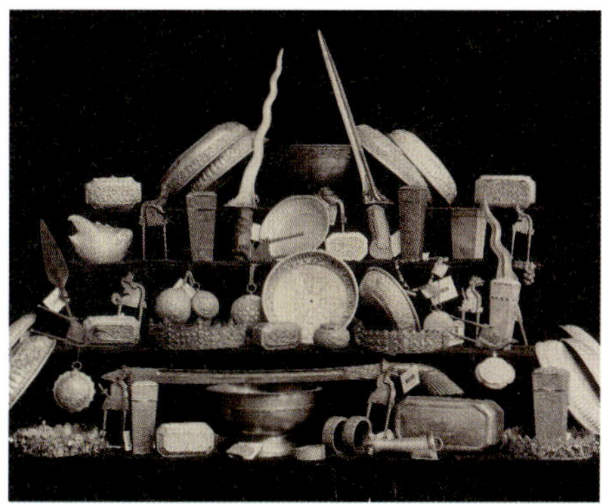

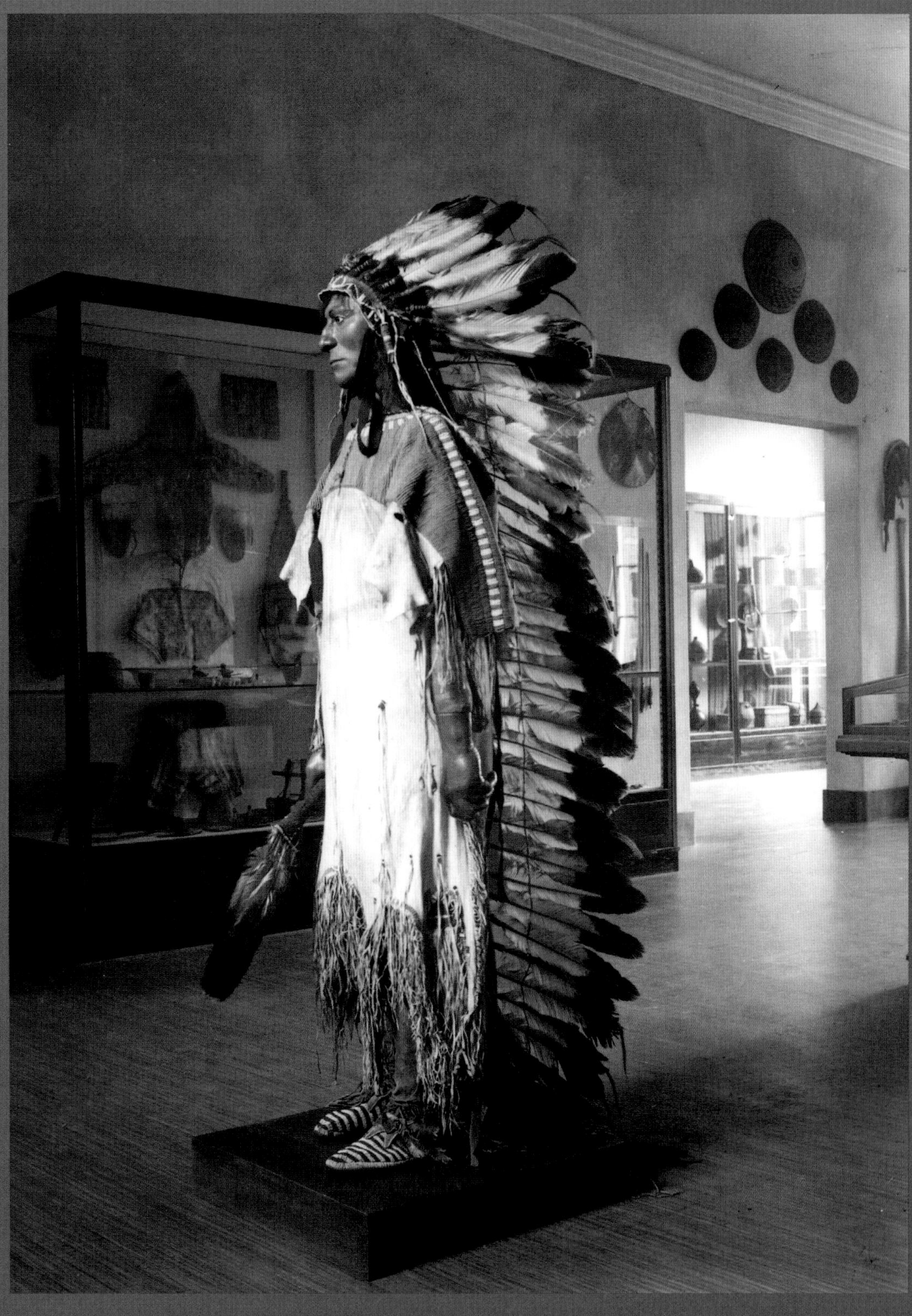

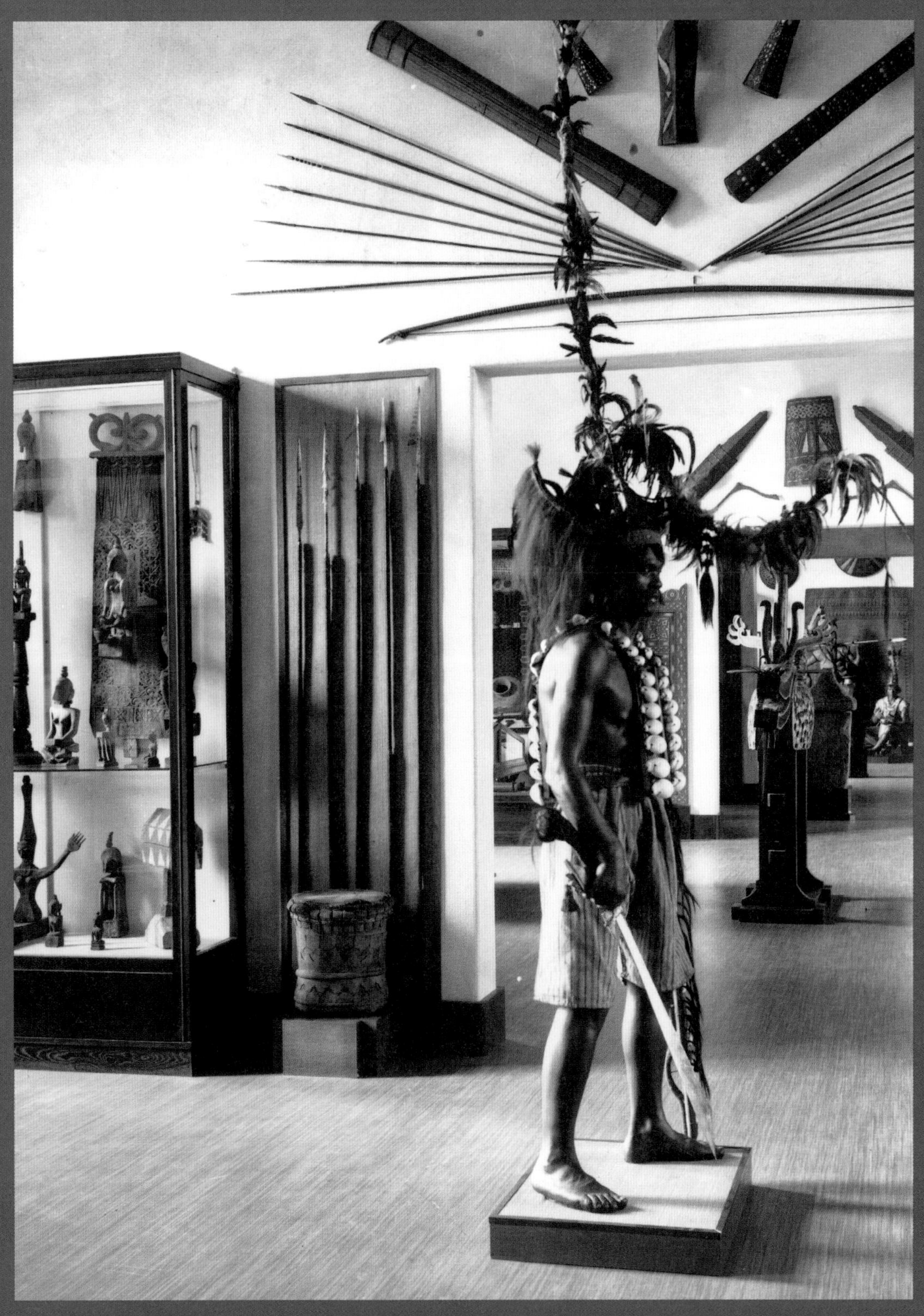

Statue of Garuda with Rama

Northern Bali, Indonesia
late 19th century (before 1912)
95 x 80 cm
wood, paint, gold
RMV 2456-108a (1940)

Garuda as mount

This impressive bird, beautifully carved and painted, is the royal sun eagle, Garuda, an important mythical bird within the Balinese Hindu tradition. The Garudeya, part of the *Adiparwa* (the first book of the Indian epic *Mahabharata*) tells that Garuda set his mother free from her sister's curse by stealing the elixir of life, amrita, from the gods. The honourable bird later returned the elixir to the gods without having drunk from it, and was rewarded by being appointed mount of the god Vishnu, preserver of life.

Courtly art for tourists

This enormous statue, which was carved from a single piece of wood and displays superb craftsmanship, probably came from a palace. Before the colonial era most woodcarvers worked anonymously in the service of the royal courts. They made sculptures that were used, for instance, as kris stands, pedestals, or merely as decorative pieces. From the latter half of the 19th century onwards, Northern Bali was under colonial administration, and woodcarvers also took commissions from Dutch clients, for instance for the great colonial exhibitions and world fairs of that period. In addition, the first tourists went to Bali at the end of the nineteenth century, and more and more sculptures were produced for the tourist market.

Governors as collectors

Beautiful statues of this kind were sometimes presented as gifts to Dutch dignitaries, such as high-ranking administrative officials who visited Bali. This statue may have been a gift of this kind. It was donated to the museum in 1940 by O.L. Helfrich, then eighty years old. The museum was already in possession of several of Helfrich's collections by this time. Helfrich had made a successful career in the department of Internal Administration from 1883 to 1912, primarily on Sumatra. He may well have visited Bali in this period and acquired this statue of Garuda with Rama at that time.

Vishnu and King Rama

On Garuda's back, grasped by his powerful arms, sits the god Vishnu, in the guise of King Rama, wearing a superb royal crown and holding a bow and arrow. To save humankind, Vishnu occasionally appears in an earthly reincarnation (*avatar*). One of the best-known of these reincarnations is King Rama, the protagonist in the Ramayana epic. At the beginning of this story he acquires his beautiful wife Sita by winning an archery contest. Rama is seen on Bali as the ideal ruler, and images of him are therefore often displayed in palaces.

Animals as mounts

Bali is the only island in Indonesia where Hinduism is the primary religion. Its traditional sculpture is dominated by themes and figures from classical epics such as the Ramayana. Animals play important roles in these stories. Vishnu is not the only god to have his own mount. Other Hindu and local deities are also depicted with their mounts, many of which have wings, like Garuda, to enable their masters to travel between heaven and earth. Other animals reflecting Indian influences, such as the winged lion (*singa*), also function as helpers and mediators between the heavens and the world of human beings.

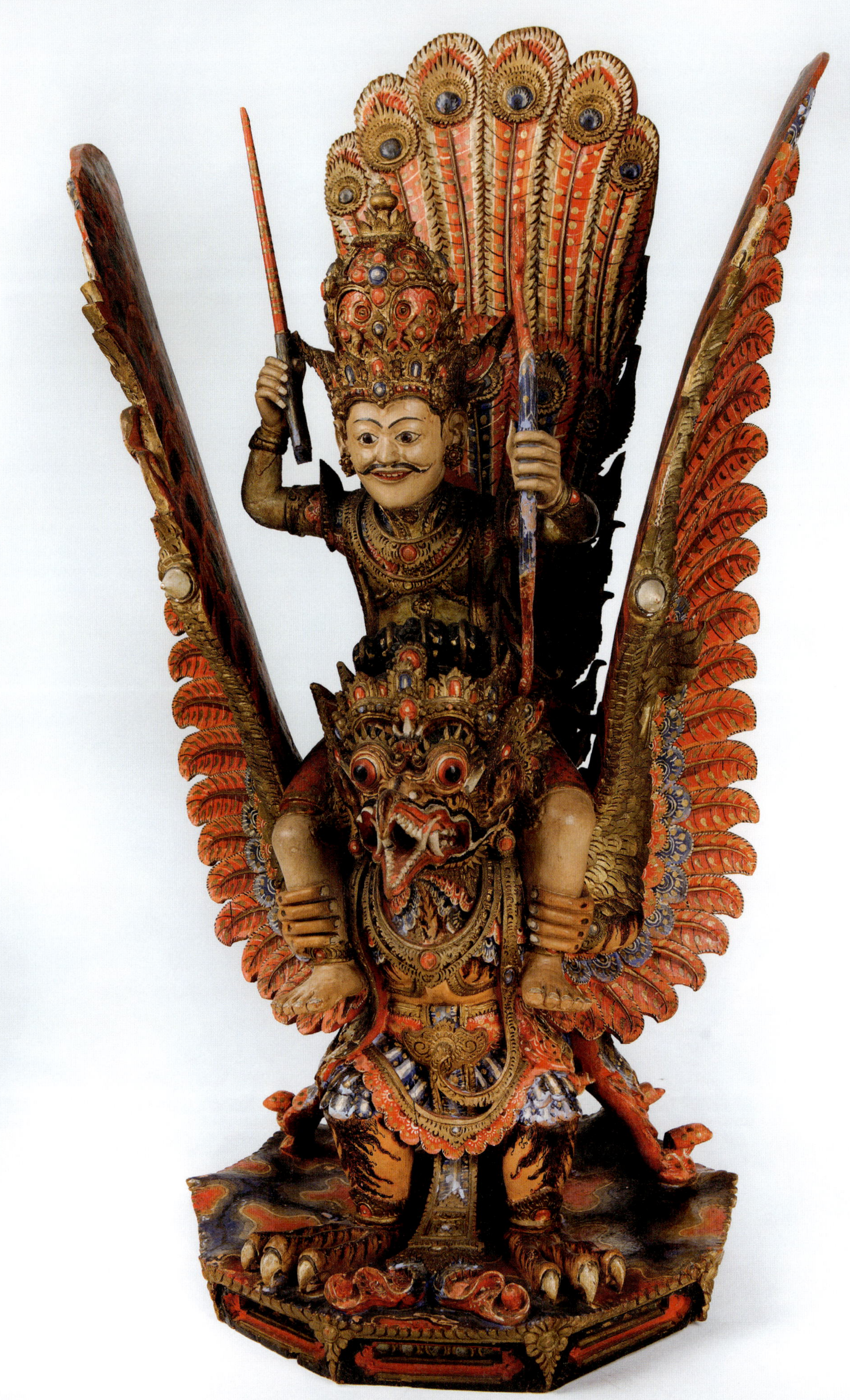

Figure of mother and child (*Phemba*)

Vili; Lower-Congo region, Democratic Republic of Congo
1850-1885
37.5 cm
wood, cotton, glass, resin, brass
RMV 2668-2101 (1947)

Matrilineal descent
According to the information supplied with this figure, its indigenous name is *casi mabialla*, which has been interpreted as meaning 'large fetish (*mabialla*) woman (*casi*)'. In the Lower-Congo region, sculptures representing female figures – often depicted with children in their arms or on their laps – are generally ancestral figures. They are made in memory of the founder of a lineage, since in the Lower-Congo region, lineage is by matrilineal descent.

Mother and child
That this figure also possessed magical significance can be inferred from the hollows in the back, the abdomen and the head of the female figure. A magical substance was inserted into these indentations (see p. 102-103). Two strips of cotton hang from a cylindrical hollow on the head. The eyes of both mother and child are inlaid with reflecting glass. The mother figure wears a brass earring in her right ear and a necklace composed of four strings of red glass beads. In this figure, the woman carries the child on her left hip. The child's hand rests on mother's left breast, and the mother has her left arm around the child. Finally, the mother figure wears a cotton loincloth, and both mother and child wear cotton necklaces.

Well groomed
The mother's attention focuses not on her child but on someone in her field of vision. Her lips are parted, revealing her filed upper teeth. The tattoo on her arm probably reflects her ethnic background. Both mother and child have neatly coiffed hair. The mother's jewellery, such as her bracelets, necklace and earring, enhance her well-groomed appearance.

A 'real' couple?
This figure of a married woman formed a pair with a very powerful nail fetish named *Mangaaka* (p. 102-103). Placing the two figures together was believed to create equilibrium by juxtaposing the man's destructive forces with the creative forces of the woman. The combination of the two figures was also intended to prevent the *nkisi's* rage from being directed against the *nganga* himself, the owner and specialist in ritual practices.

Function
These mother-and-child statuettes are regarded as fertility or ancestral figures, or as objects of veneration. This range of functions reflects their symbolic complexity: the figures are poly-interpretable, and are therefore difficult to 'read'. The mother-and-child figures were probably used in relation to 'women's matters' such as fertility and pregnancy. As mother of the clan, or female chief, the mother figure may focus on resolving conflict and on peacemaking. As an ancestor, she is worshipped as a fertility symbol, since she has produced numerous descendants. Ideas about life and death, fertility and motherhood, peace and war are therefore all interconnected in these objects.

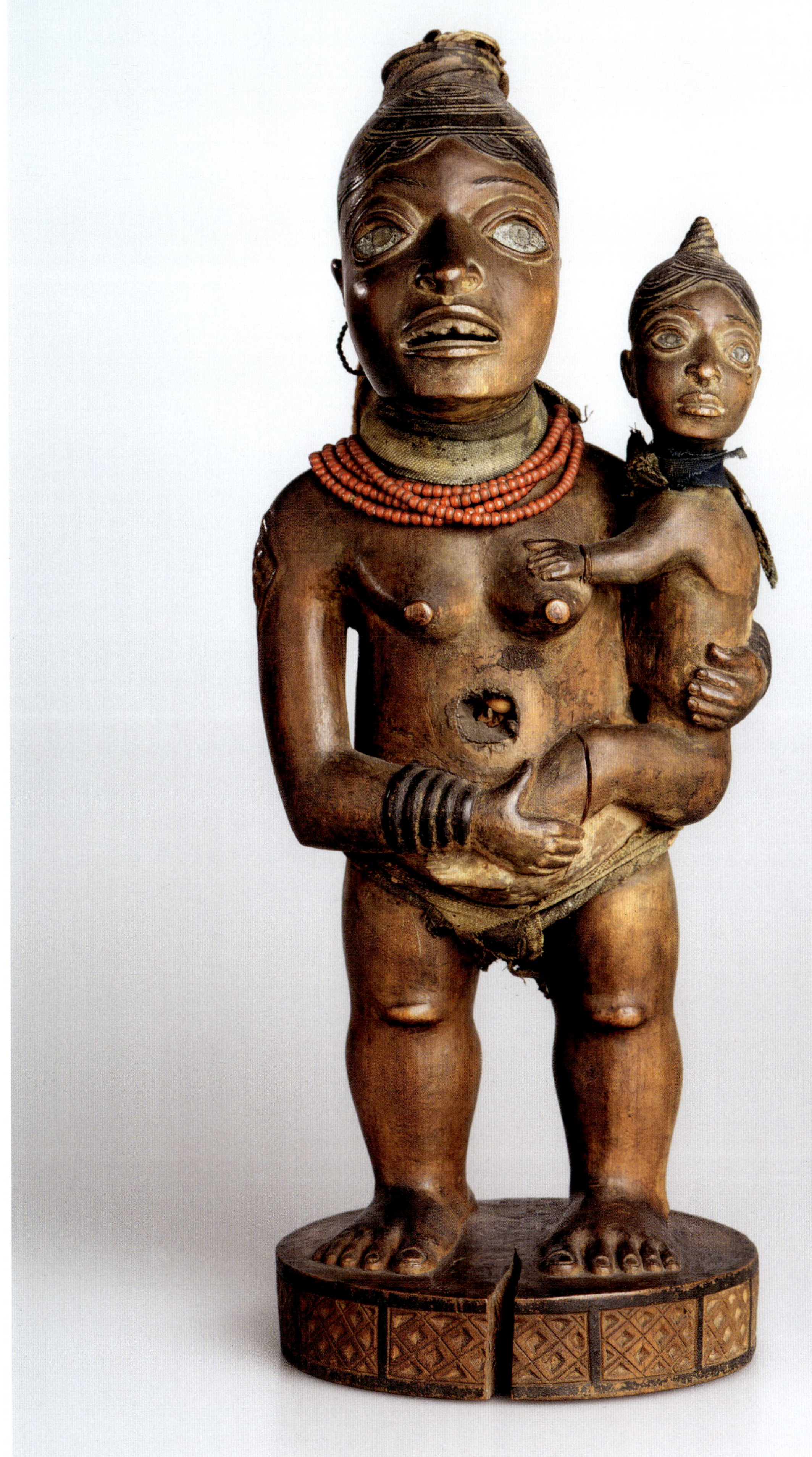

Amoghapasha Lokeshvara and his retinue

East Java, Indonesia
1268-1292
22.2 x 14.5 x 5 cm
bronze
RMV 2630-1 (1947)

Full of compassion

This bronze relief displays a group of Buddhist deities. The large central figure is Amoghapasha Lokeshvara, an eight-armed manifestation of the Bodhisattva Avalokiteshvara, who can be identified by the small figure of the Buddha Amitabha in his crown. His character-istic quality is his great compassion with humanity. In Java, as elsewhere in the Buddhist world, he was the most popular Bodhisattva. Many figurines of this deity have been found, especially bronze ones, in many different manifestations. As Amoghapasha Lokeshvara he rescues the dead from hell, using the infallible noose (*amoghapasha*) that he carries in one hand.

Buddhist group

Amoghapasha Lokeshvara has been depicted in India since the sixth century, but only since the twelfth century is he shown with his retinue, Hayagriva and Bhrkuti (right) and Sudhanakumara and Shyamatara (left), as here. According to a Tibetan tradition, this specific group of deities was revealed in Bodhgaya, India, to the 'Great Teacher from Kashmir', Shakyashri Bhadra (1127-1225). Shakyashri Bhadra fled to Tibet because of Muslim violence in India. The *sadhana* text, describing this group of deities for the purposes of meditation, is attributed to him. This text spread rapidly to other parts of Asia, and probably also to Java.

Identical reliefs

Another four identical reliefs are known, one of which is in the Tropenmuseum and another in the Museum für Asiatische Kunst in Berlin. That is in itself remarkable, since a bronze figurine is usually cast in a mould of baked clay that has to be broken open to extract it. This means that a new mould has to be made for each new figurine. In this case, however, the mould consisted of two parts, and the front, with the relief, remained whole. Only the back was destroyed and had to be remade each time. That explains why the reliefs are of different thicknesses.

Religious gifts

The inscriptions on the back are also different: although the texts are more or less the same, the sentences are divided up differently among the lines. The inscription tells us that Kertanagara, the last ruler of the Singhasari dynasty, who reigned between 1268 and 1292, had these bronze reliefs made as religious gifts. The inscription states that the religious merit (*punya*) obtained through this precious gift would be advantageous to his teachers, his mother, his father, and the whole of humanity, and give them supreme knowledge.

Candi Jago

Two of the five reliefs were found in Tumpang (near Malang, East Java). There is also a temple there, named Candi Jago. The reliefs and the temple are connected, since the same group was venerated in the temple, in the form of separate statues. The primary statue, depicting Amoghapasha Lokeshvara, still stands there today. Its head is unfortunately badly damaged. It was once accompanied by statues of Hayagriva, Bhrkuti, Sudhanakumara, and Shyamatara, as well as statues of Jina Buddhas and their female companions (Prajnas). Most of the statues are now in the National Museum of Indonesia, in Jakarta. One of them, depicting Mamaki, ended up in the British Museum. We also find four Jina Buddhas on the bronze relief, next to the head of Amoghapasha Lokeshvara. Their consorts appear below, beside his arms.

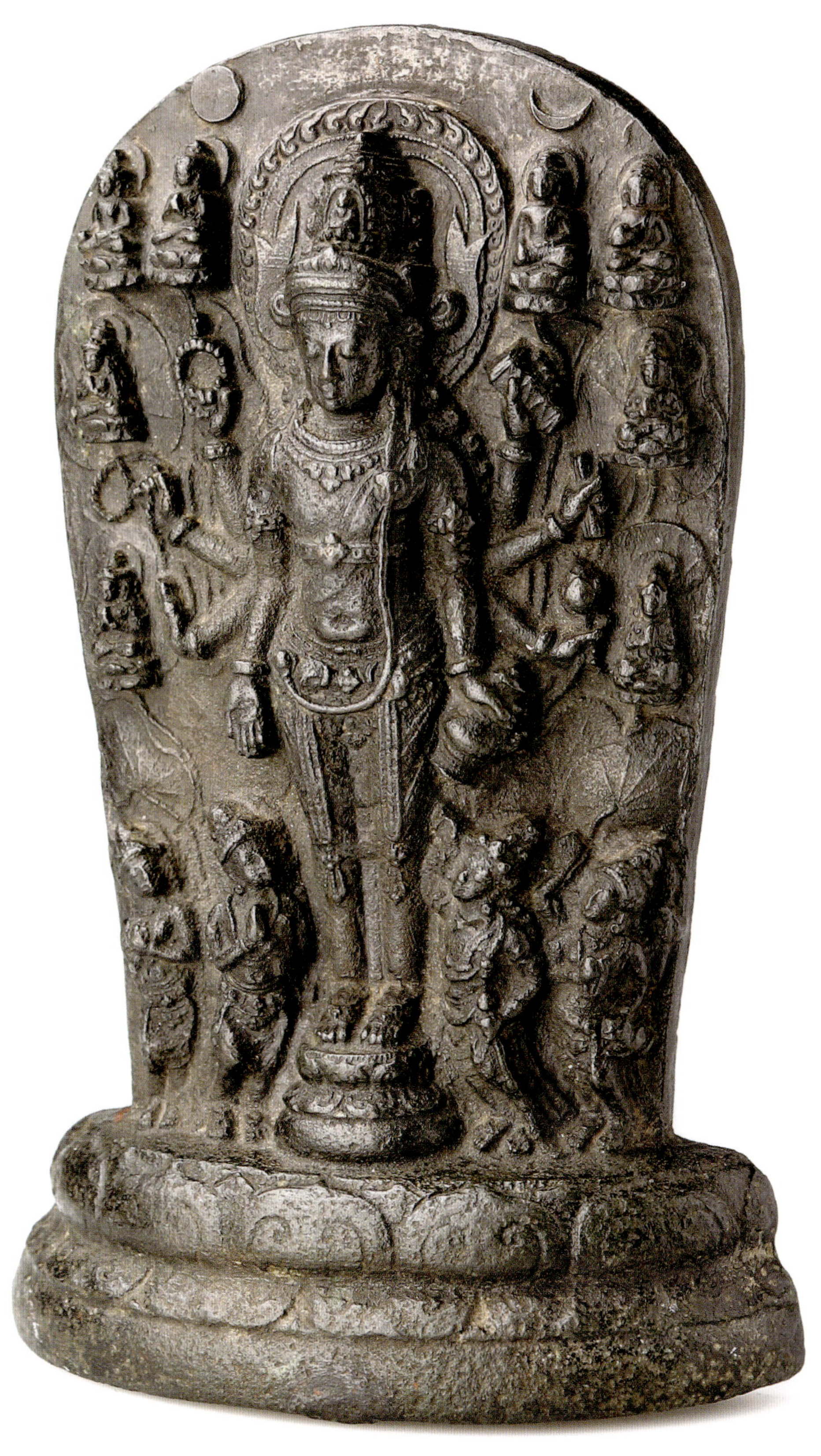

Throwing knife

Zande, Central Africa
1881-1883
48 x 41.5 cm
iron, fibre
RMV 2668-2414 (1947)

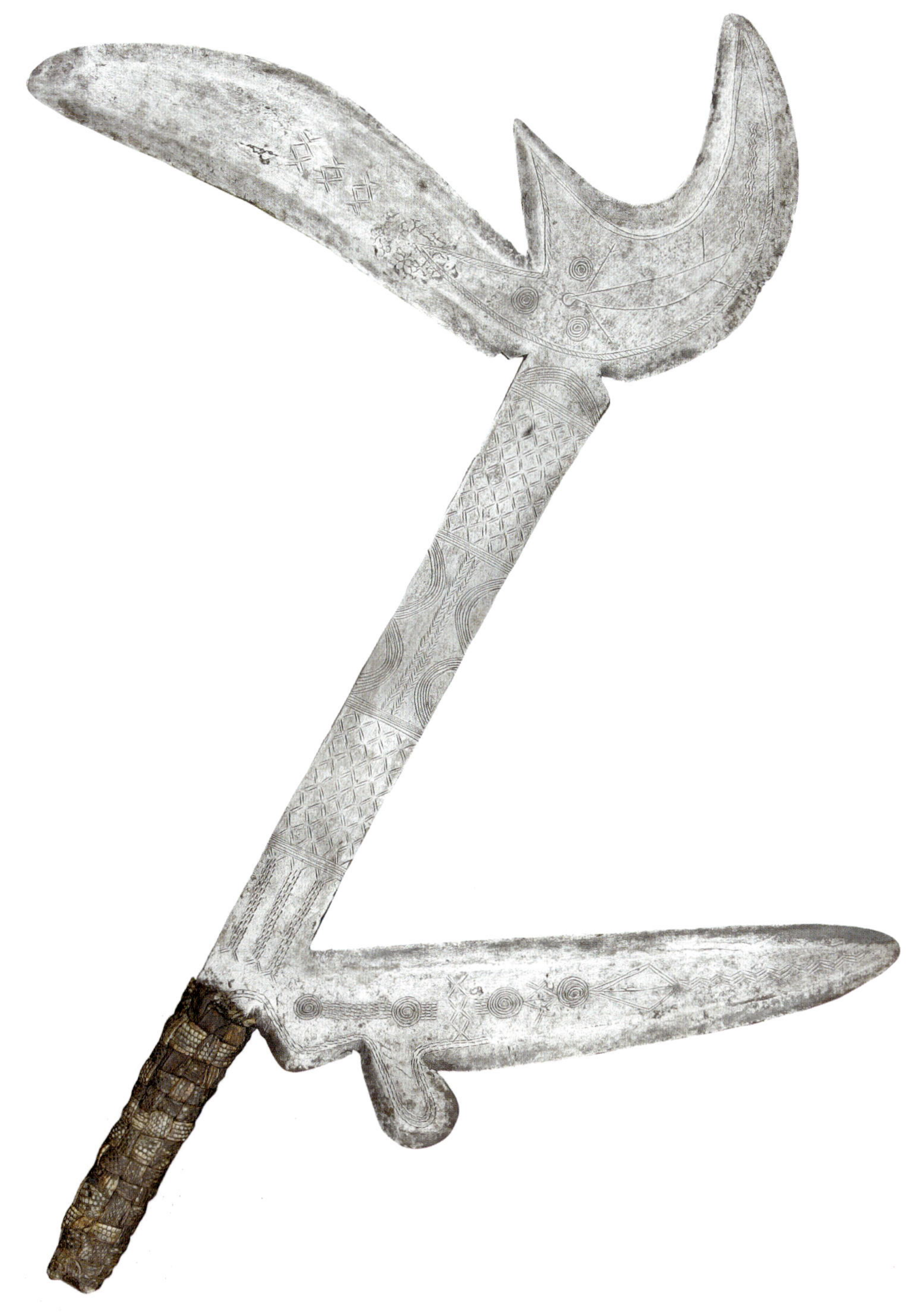

Unique African weapon

Throwing knives are a category of weapons unique to Central Africa. They are very popular as collectors' items. The knife has several cutting surfaces and a loosely-attached handle. Throwing knives are asymmetrical and generally have several blades branching out from the central one. They were used for hunting or as hand weapons. Experienced warriors could wield them to hit their target from a great distance. The knives could be thrown with either an underhand or overarm motion. In the early twentieth century, throwing knives ceased to be used as weapons, but they still possess a ceremonial function and sometimes serve as status symbols.

Flight capacity

The making of African throwing knives, which are forged from iron extracted from local mines, is a craft requiring great skill. Precisely the right balance must be struck between form and weight if the knife is to be an effective weapon. For it has to possess both a fine flight capacity and maximum accuracy. The sharp surfaces on all sides of the blades enhance the weapon's effectiveness. The knife's form, weight and decorations often reflect its cultural origins.

Smiths

In Congo, smiths established family or village guilds. Their position varied enormously from one community to the next: some enjoyed high status while others were regarded as common villagers. Most of the smiths in Central Africa had only a limited amount of time to devote to this special skill, since they were obliged to work on the land for long periods. Diggers, smelters, coarse and fine metal workers all had their particular area of expertise. Together they were responsible for creating the end product.

Johannes Maria Schuver (1852-1883)

Johannes Maria Schuver, who added this object to his collection, came from a prosperous merchant family. His father's inheritance enabled him to fulfil his ambition of making a scientific voyage of discovery. He wanted to sail up the Blue Nile to explore the uncharted regions of East Africa. On 1 January 1881 Schuver set off with a small caravan for a long journey towards Sudan. In 1883 he decided to take an alternative route along the White Nile. This was the period in which the Dinka and Nuer were in revolt, but in spite of the precarious conditions, Schuver obtained permission to continue his journey with his Zande guide. Since Zande soldiers also worked for slave dealers, his movements were followed with suspicion. Schuver became involved in a skirmish, and was killed by a Dinka.

Schuver Collection

Schuver had sent the ethnographic and botanical specimens and samples he had collected to his uncle in Amsterdam before his death, but nothing is known of the circumstances in which he acquired them. He may have purchased the throwing knife from his Zande guide, or bought it at a market. Another possibility is that Carlo Piaggia, the Italian explorer he met in Africa, may have given or sold it to him. Schuver's collection initially belonged to the collection of Amsterdam's zoological gardens (Natura Artis Magistra), which was transferred to the Indisch Instituut (now Royal Tropical Institute) in 1920 and sold to the Rijksmuseum Volkenkunde in 1947. Schuver's heirs donated his original diaries to the museum in 1998.

Ritual bone apron

Southern Tibet
1800-1900
80 x 62 cm
bone
RMV 2851-1 (1950)

Bone beads
This apron is extremely rare. It is no longer completely intact, and therefore appears to have been used. The separate parts of such aprons can easily come loose and fall off. Whatever is left is then reattached. This may explain why this apron is not entirely rectangular, but slopes down at an angle towards the sides. Even so, this apron is still fairly complete compared to other old specimens. The great number of nine oblong bone plates and fifty lozenge-shaped and square elements are all linked with chains made of round beads. Beneath the little openwork carved monster heads hang chains with tiny bells.

Uniformity
Since the different types of bone aprons preserved in museums display a large measure of uniformity in their form and elaboration, P.H. Pott (former director of the Rijksmuseum Volkenkunde and an expert on Tibet) suggested that they all came from the same workshop. Making ritual aprons of this kind may possibly have been the speciality of a specific monastery in the south of Tibet. High-ranking monks still wear aprons of this kind today, along with the other bone embellishments, during certain ritual dances.

Products of the charnel ground
According to certain tantric texts, such as the Hevajra Tantra, six types of ornaments originate from the charnel ground: a crown consisting of five skulls and five types of bone ornaments (a chain, earrings, bracelets, an apron, and anklets). Numerous statues and paintings of wrathful, terrifying gods and goddesses are endowed with bone jewellery. Many carried a skull cup, sometimes also a drum or trumpet made of bone. Besides playing a role in the iconography of gods, these items of jewellery and objects – such as this apron – were also actually worn during specific rituals.

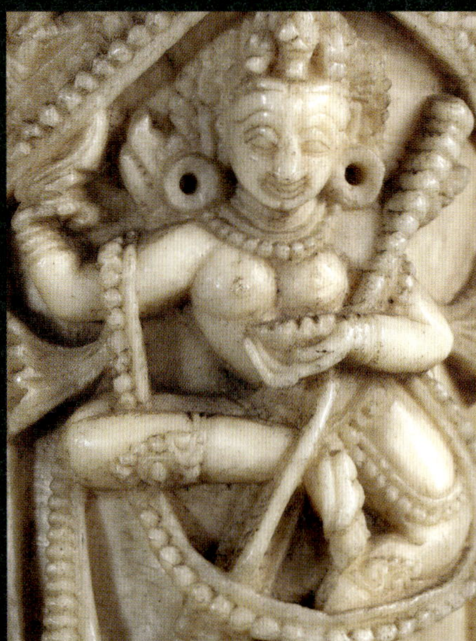

Dancing goddess
The larger elements are furnished with very delicate carvings. Thus, the central bone piece at the top represents Vajravarahi, a tantric Buddhist goddess. She is the most important of the Dakinis, a group of wrathful goddesses, and is identifiable by her attributes – a flaying knife, a skull cup, and a long staff – and by the boar's head (*varaha*, from which she derives her name) on her own head. She also wears a long chain of severed heads around her neck, and like other demonic deities, she dances on a human figure, which symbolises ignorance. Over her head can be seen the five Jina Buddhas, and above them a bird, Garuda, crowned by a parasol.

Jina Buddhas
The five Jina Buddhas (Vairocana, Akshobhya, Amitabha, Ratnasambhava and Amoghasiddhi) are frequently depicted in Tibetan art. An extensive system developed, embracing all their characteristics and correlations. Thus, each one is associated with a specific cardinality (compass point), colour, hand gesture, seed syllable, sense, Bodhisattva, consort, and mount. Garuda is chiefly known in the West as the mount of the Hindu god Vishnu, but in Tibetan Buddhism this mythical bird carries Amoghasiddhi, the Jina Buddha of the north. In Tibetan art one sometimes finds a group of five Garudas depicted as protectors above the heads of the five Jina Buddhas, symbolising diverse aspects of these Buddhas.

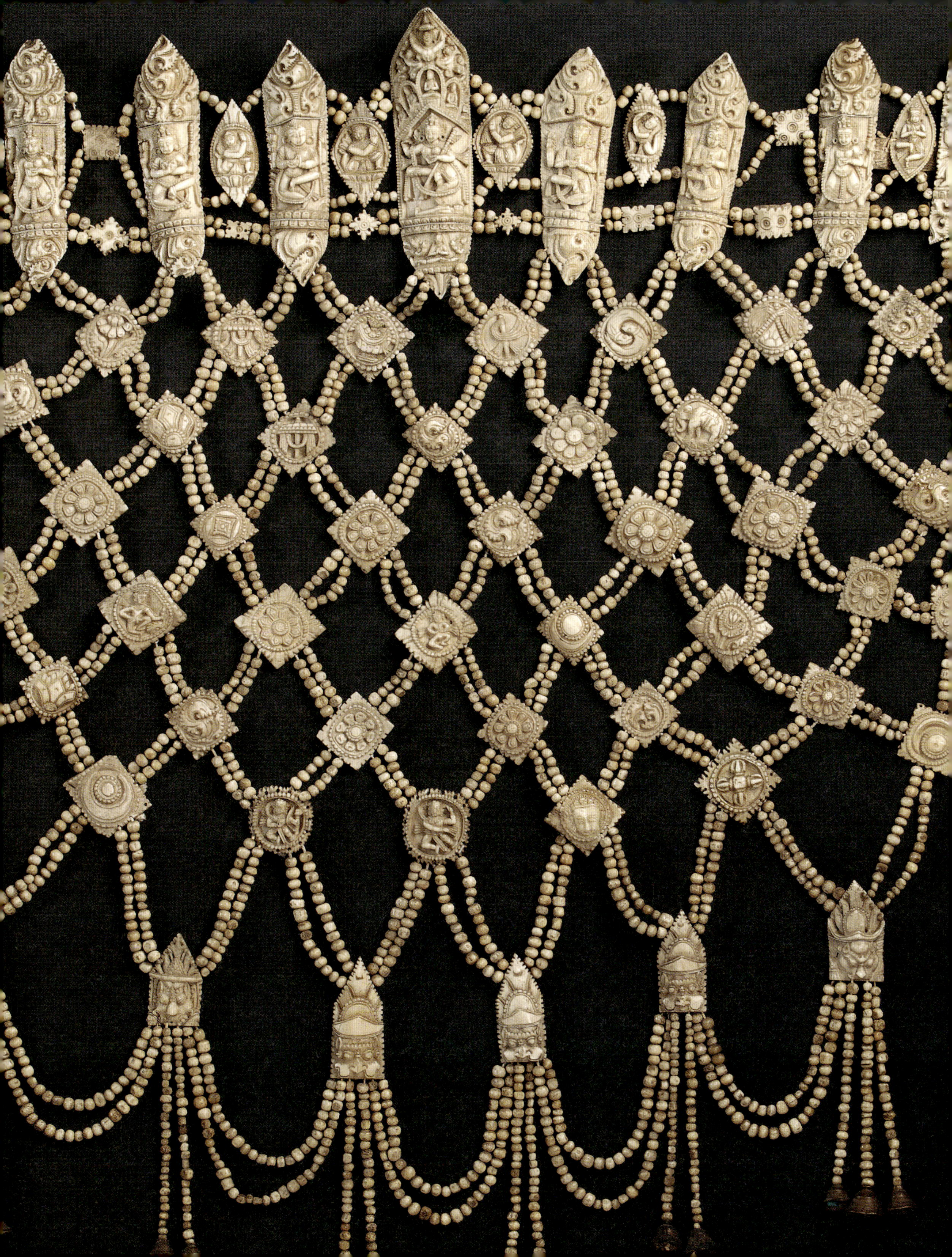

Bodhisattva Manjushri

Western Himalayas
900-1000
17 x 11 x 9 cm
bronze with traces of painting
RMV 2939-1 (1951)

Manifestations

Manjushri and Avalokiteshvara are the two most popular Bodhisattvas in Tibet. While Avalokiteshvara is primarily characterised by his compassion for humanity, Manjushri is the Bodhisattva who is most closely associated with transcendental wisdom. Like many other Bodhisattvas and gods, he can assume a variety of manifestations. His sitting posture, number of arms and attributes may all vary. Sometimes he is depicted with one leg over the other, holding a flaming sword (to cut through ignorance) in his right hand and the book of transcendental wisdom (Prajnaparamita Sutra) in his left. This is one of the commonest manifestations of Manjushri in Tibet.

Youth

Manjushri may also be depicted as a youth (*kumara*), as here, with simple round earrings, five locks of hair and a necklace with tiger claws, all characteristics of youths, exactly as described in the texts. In these images he sits in a relaxed pose on a lotus throne, one leg pulled up under his body and the other dangling down. In this manifestation, Manjushri makes the gift-giving gesture (varada mudra) with his right hand, a hand gesture that is customary for Bodhisattvas and denotes their generosity. His attribute is the book of wisdom, depicted as an oblong Tibetan manuscript.

'Lost wax' method

Bronze figurines like this one are made using the 'lost wax' method. The figurine is first moulded in wax, after which it is covered with a layer of clay. When the clay is baked, the wax melts, draining away through channels constructed for the purpose. This means that the original wax figurine is lost. However, it has left its contours in the layer of clay that surrounded it, which can then be used as a mould. Bronze, which is heated until fluid, is then poured into the mould. Once the bronze has cooled, the mould of baked clay can be hammered open, and the bronze figurine emerges.

Kashmiri influence

The art of Tibet reveals stylistic influences from diverse neighbouring territories: China, Central Asia, Northwest India and Nepal, and Kashmir. This statue is rare and truly remarkable, not only because of its early date, but also because of its successful, elegant merging of styles. Thus, the lotus cushion is characteristic of the early Kashmir style, while the upper torso and eyes reflect a Tibetan tradition. The Tibetan inscription on the base suggests that it was made by a craftsman from Ladakh in western Tibet. Unfortunately the inscription is almost illegible.

Lily and lotus

Here, the book was placed on a blue lily (*nilotpala*; Nymphaea caerulea), which rises up beside the Bodhisattva. Although the lily actually belongs to a different family of plants, nilotpala is often translated as 'blue lotus'. The lotus (Nelumbo nucifera) has a characteristic conical seedbox and the leaves and flowers do not float like the water lily, but rise out of the water. The lotus has several names in Sanskrit, according to its colour. The pink lotus is known as *Padma*. The blue lily is usually shown in Buddhist art with pointed petals, half open and depicted from the side.

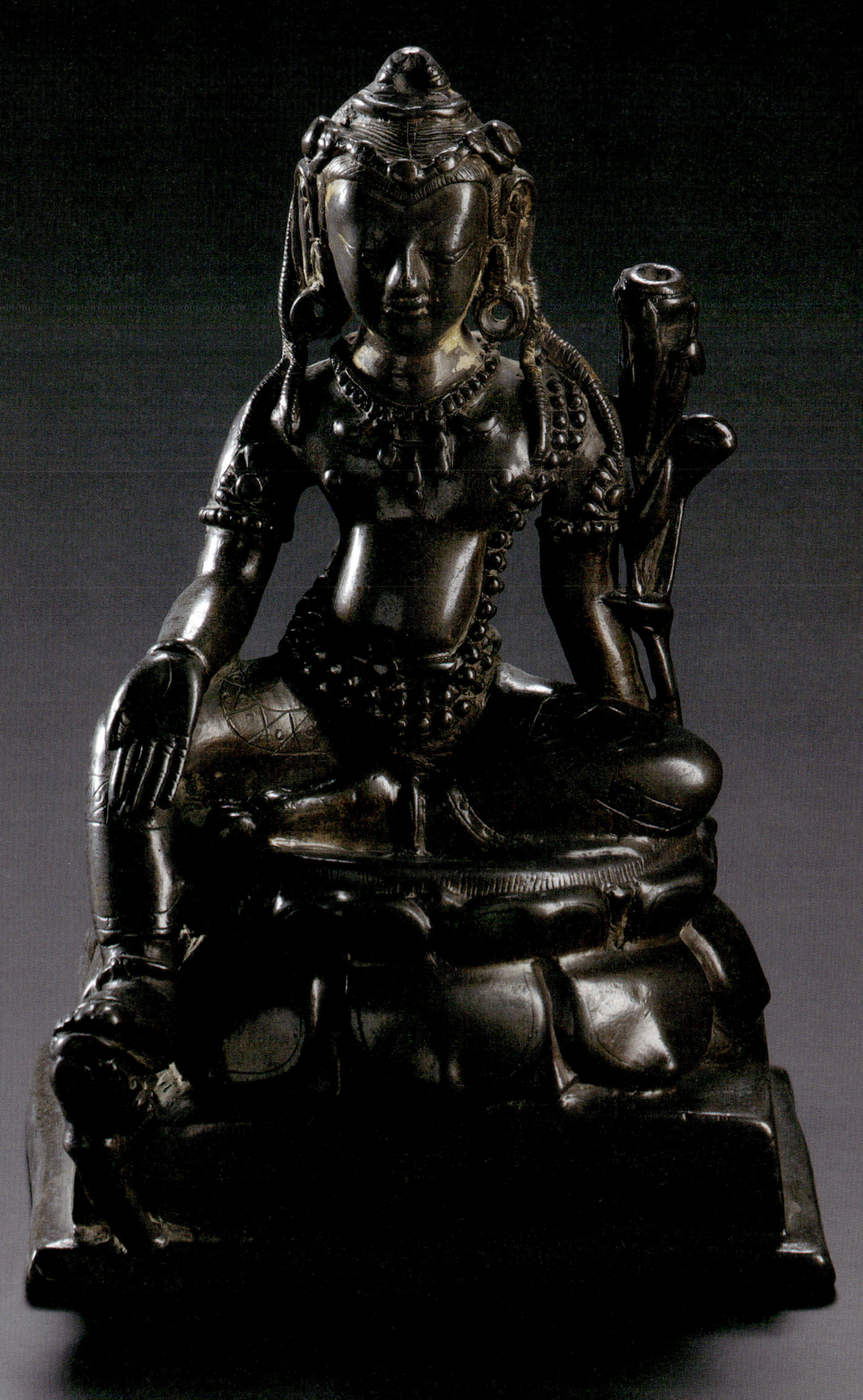

Bodhisattva

China
13th century
h. 160 cm
wood, gesso, rests of gold and paint
RMV 2990-1 (1952)

Transformation

The appearance of Guanyin (Japanese: Kannon; Sanskrit: Avalokiteshvara) is borrowed ultimately from an Indian iconography, hence the references of the figure's clothing, hairstyle and jewellery to archaic forms of Indian court fashion. Representation of Guanyin in China underwent a gradual yet fundamental change, which corresponded to a shift in the conception of Guanyin from male to female. This image, which dates probably to the 13th century, shows a male manifestation, but this need not rule out that it was created in a period when the art of a female Guanyin had become common.

Effectiveness

This figure functions to represent one of the most popular Buddhist manifestations, Guanyin, the enlightened being who, rather than achieve complete release from the cycles of rebirth, elects to remain as a compassionate force among humankind. Widespread devotion to Guanyin determined a high demand for all forms of skilled artistry in depicting this particular bodhisattva. A convincing appearance enhanced by the aura of a temple setting and the use of valuable materials (e.g. gold) convinced believers that the image would be all the more effective in responding to prayers and offerings.

Fine details

The carvers of this figures used perhaps only one piece of timber for the head and body. They made the arms and feet (now lost) separately and inserted them into mortises under the shoulders and ankles. Worn areas show the wood grain, revealing how the carvers expertly converted their material's organic composition into a representational form still determined by natural strength and consistency. The same craftsmen or others layered the wood with gesso, and applied to this the final layers of coloured lacquer and gold. Some of the details, e.g. the lips, are actually the work of moulding or pressing.

Double-edged

Before its purchase from the Berkeley Galleries in London in 1952, this figure belonged to Yamanaka Tejiro, whose art business emphatically shaped European and American taste for Chinese art from the 1890s onwards. Yamanaka even sold Chinese art to the deposed Qing-Manchu ruling family. Yamanaka's London branch opened in 1919. Yamanaka's agents must have removed the figure from its temple setting at a location probably in North China. This common but unethical collecting practice caused damage that few modern museums now condone. Paradoxically, however, Yamanaka's control of this figure ensured its prominent position within Western approaches to art in China.

With arms and legs

The figure was on view in Yamanaka's London gallery when Osvald Siren included it in a short historical survey of Chinese carving. The arms and feet shown in Siren's photograph were repairs perhaps executed during the object's later history. By 1952 a restorer had removed them. This aesthetic intervention reveals a Western antagonism to repairs that detract from the pristine authenticity of a 13th-century object. Today, research on the history and sociology of Buddhism helps to re-imagine the whole figure as integral to an entire temple iconography, itself located within a geography of temple networks.

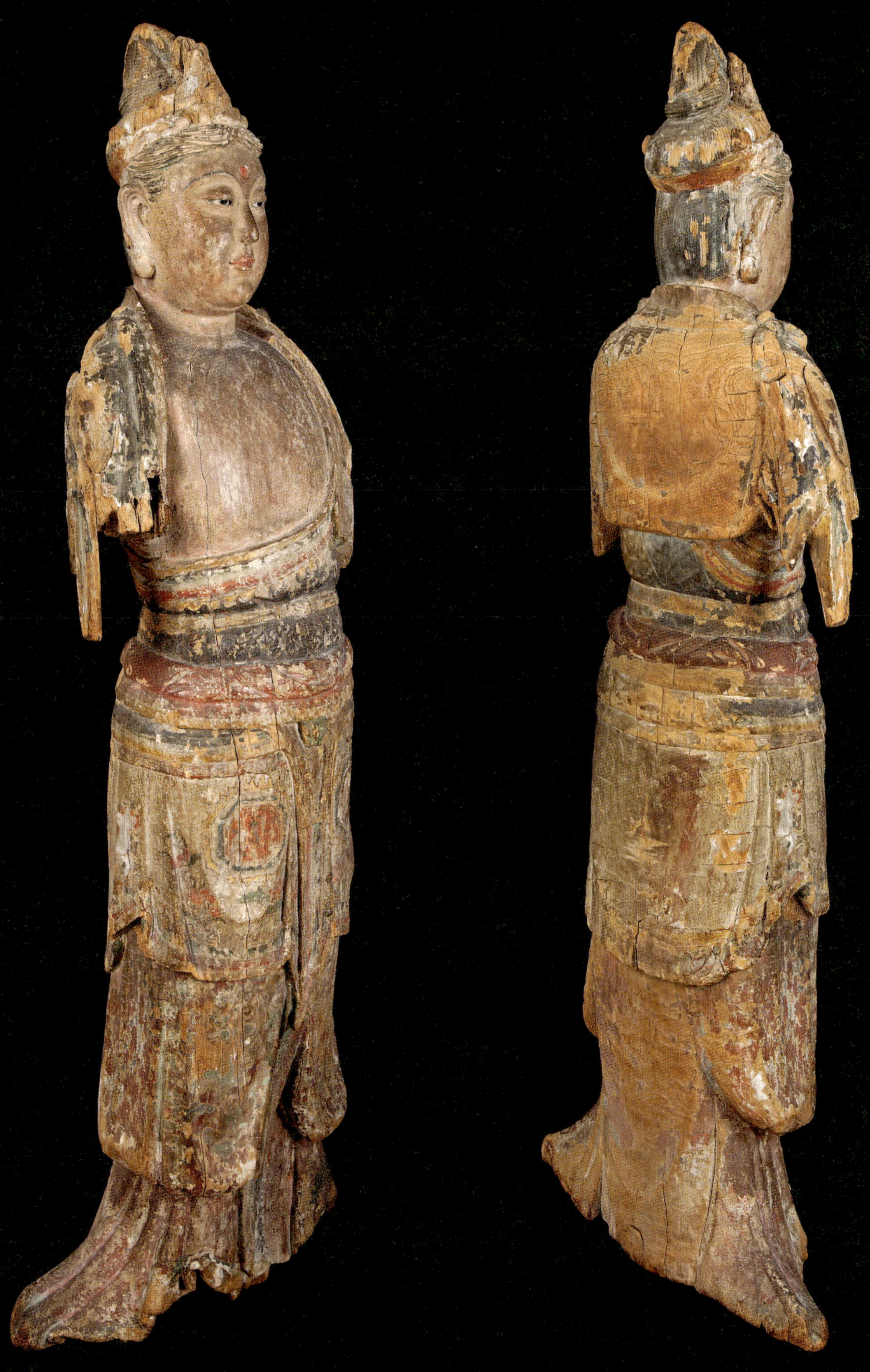

Indian miniature drawing with elephant

Pahari or Kangra style, Northern India
1785-1800
24.5 x 18.5 cm
drawing on paper, watercolour
RMV 3025-65 (1952)

Elephant in forestry

This splendid, realistic drawing depicts an elephant uprooting a tree. Elephants were valuable resources for carrying out work that required force in forestry and construction. They were also deployed in the battlefield. It was common to urge the creatures on with an elephant hook or *ankusha*, seen here in the hands of the man riding the elephant. The other two men are goading the elephant by sticking their lances in its rear end. The back of this miniature shows a toilet scene with maidservants waiting on a lady. Women are holding up a sheet behind the lady to shield her from prying eyes.

Art-loving emperors

From the thirteenth century onwards, Indian courts took great interest in painting. Since wealthy rulers had Persian as well as Indian painters in their service, many remarkable fusions of techniques and styles ensued. Under the patronage of the art-loving Mughal emperors, Indian painting developed to unprecedented heights of refinement: Mughal painting won universal admiration, from China to Rembrandt's living room. Within the Indian Empire, rulers – especially in the Rajput and Deccan territories – strove to outdo each other by tracking down and recruiting the best painters for their studios.

Pahari style

The drawing comes from the city of Guler in the Pahari hills, in the district of Kangra. Pahari or Kangra style is a mix of the refined, realistic, Mughal style and the more schematic, colourful Rajput styles. At the peak of its refinement, Pahari painting displays a melody of fluid lines and colours and exudes spaciousness and tranquillity. Even the unfinished drawings unfold their own charms, especially through a looseness achieved with lines sketched freehand. These features are exemplified by this drawing, with its bold and graceful realism. Thin layers of watercolour impart the desired volume to the elephant and the tree.

Birds for Vogel

The drawing was purchased by the Leiden professor Jean Philippe Vogel (1871-1958), when he worked for the Archaeological Survey of India. In 1914 he returned to Leiden to take up the chair in Sanskrit and Indian archaeology. Vogel always adhered to the principle that objects with great cultural significance must remain in their country of origin. Consequently, his private collection consisted primarily of objects that were of personal significance to him but that did not possess any great commercial value. He found unfinished drawings interesting, because they shed light on the process of creation. Since his name means 'bird', Vogel also enjoyed collecting paintings of birds.

Paper

The paper that was used for Pahari miniatures was handmade, pressed and polished with care. First came the underdrawing: a rough sketch in red or yellow ochre, after which bold black contours would be applied. After the paper had been primed with a thin white coat of paint, the painter would reproduce the contours and apply the colours. Monochrome drawings are really unfinished paintings or exploratory sketches, by pupils or the masters themselves. The end product is frequently the work of more than one person.

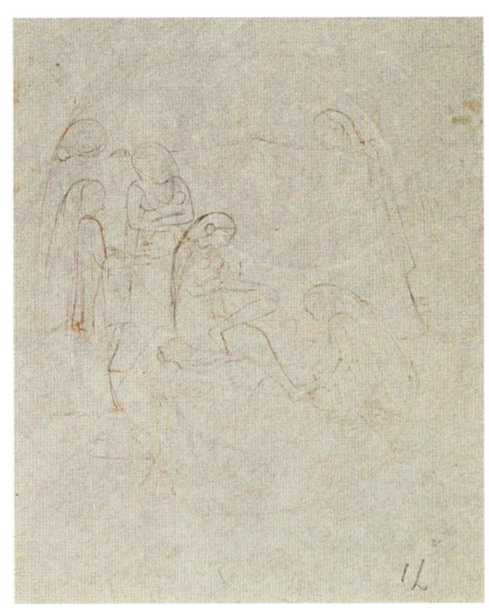

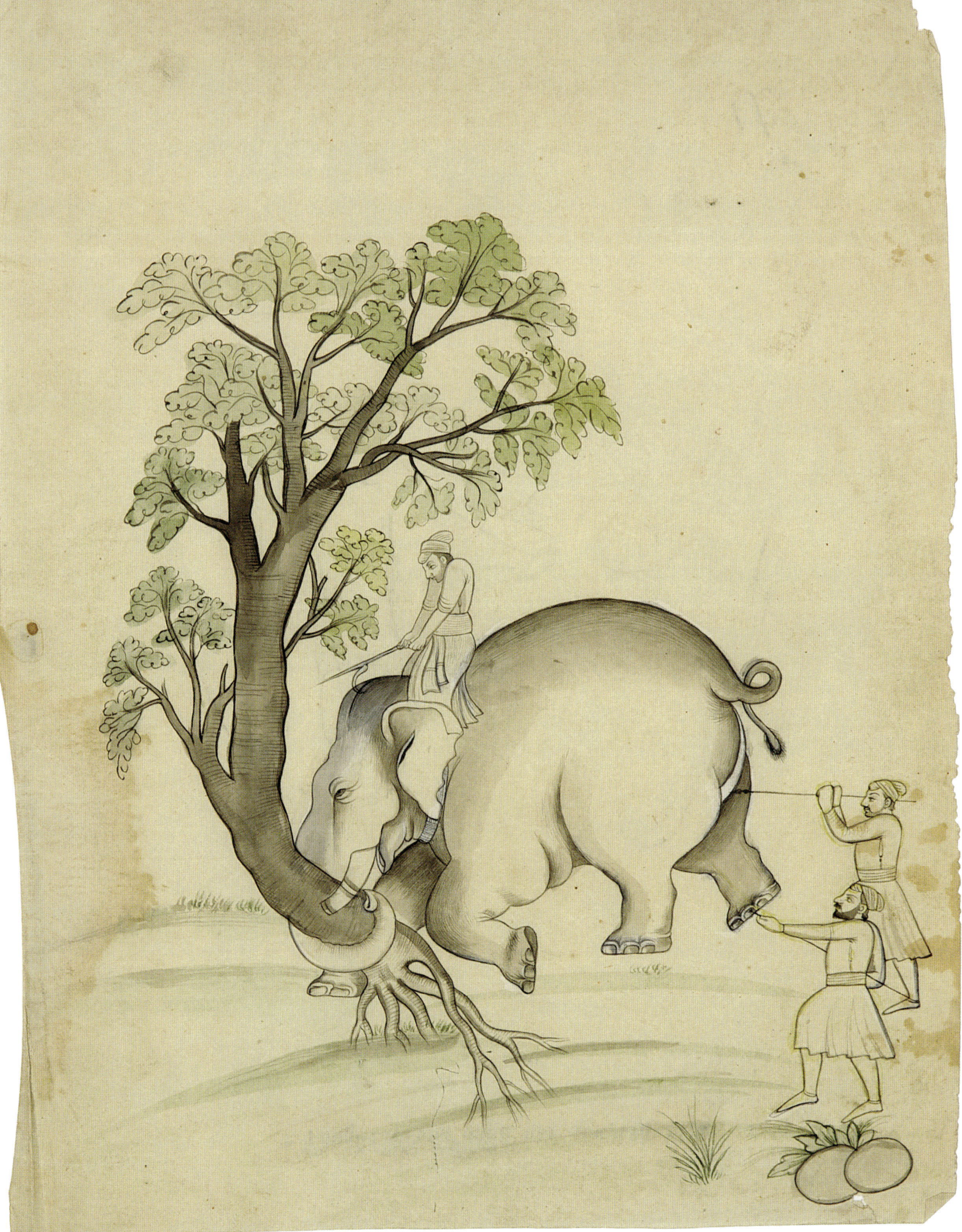

Jar (*Guan*)

Yangshao culture, China
3000-2000 B.C.
30 x 43 cm
pottery
RMV 3041-1 (1953)

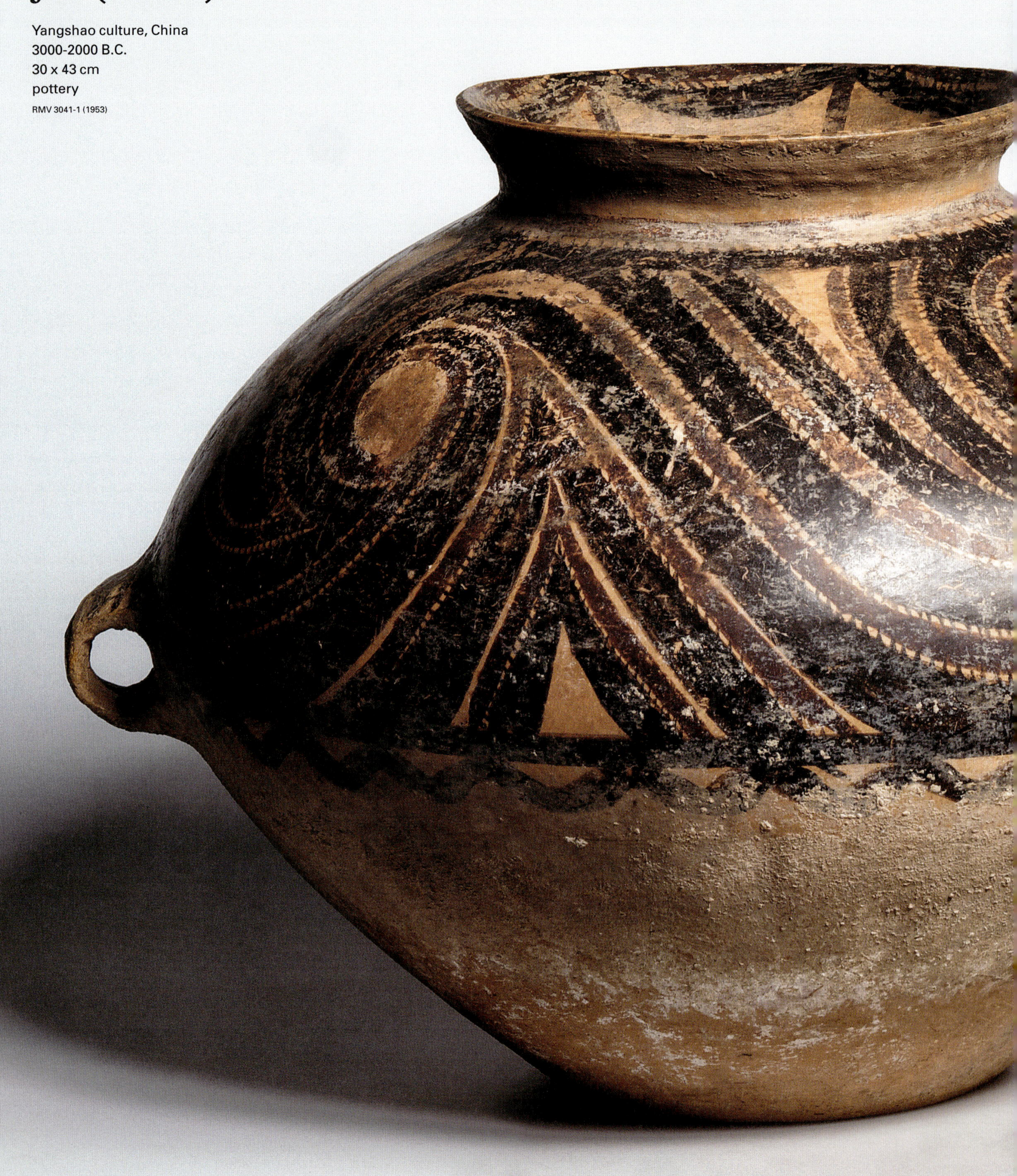

Guan

This wide jar is made of red fired clay, only the top half of which has been painted in purple-brown and black designs. The painted surface was also polished to give it an extra vibrancy. The Chinese name guan today refers to a storage jar, but, since nothing is known of Neolithic language, any form of its name as well as any conception of its appearance 4000 years ago elude us. Visual anthropology will explain this object much better than art history.

Yangshao cultuur

The jar is a typical product of the Yangshao culture, so named after a small town in Henan province. John Gunnar Andersen, the Swedish pioneer of prehistoric archaeology in China, excavated a site near Yangshao in 1921, and established it as the type site for the Yangshao culture extending through a broad zone of north China. Artifacts (and rubbish) at these sites characterize common patterns of social life and expressions of material culture, in which pottery is often the best evidence of this prehistoric population's art.

Finds

One major division within China's vast geography of Neolithic material finds is defined by painted pottery from the Western interior and monochrome black pottery from sites along the Eastern (Pacific) coast. Pottery from Western sites usually reiterates this jar's colours in similar repetitive and kinetic patterns. Eastern pottery demonstrates more complex vessel profiles – perhaps first exploiting the technology of the potter's wheel. The potter of this jar achieved a wide bulge by raising its walls out- and then inwards with coiled "ropes" of clay. The jar's broad upper surface is consequently a virtue that its painters could exploit to good effect.

Jars in pits

Jars like this are found in tombs where they probably functioned to hold food and drink that the living believed necessary to provide for the dead. They appear also as the remnants of less high-quality jars abandoned on the Neolithic living surface where they were used in daily life. Excavated Yangshao settlements often show evidence of how the users of wide storage jars stabilized them in pits dug exactly to the depth of the jar's waist. Clearly, therefore, jar painters did not waste effort and materials painting the lower half of the vessel's body.

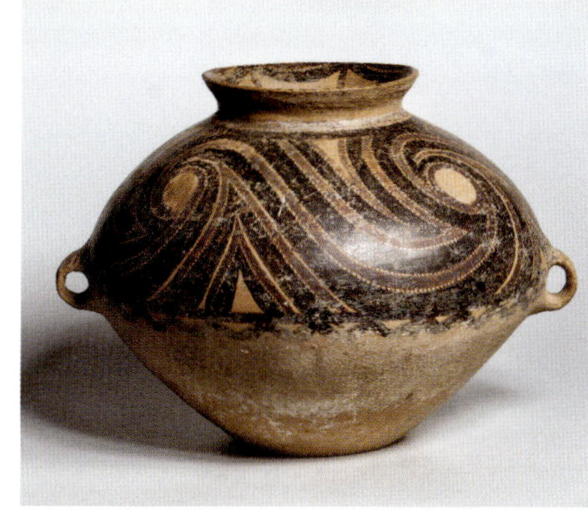

From above

The limits of the painter's labour fitted also within a Neolithic visual economy whose inhabitants looked at decorative pottery from above. East coast pottery, which was placed on raised structures within the tomb settings where it has been found, depended on quite different angles of vision to perceive variations of shape and profile. That the makers and users of this jar treated it as an object of high aesthetic priority suggests also how they visualized the concept of storage to correspond with a wider social ambition for the advantages of a sedentary life, itself an obvious precondition for the accumulation of resources and wealth.

Ancestral figurine

Leti, Maluku Tenggara (Southeast Moluccas), Indonesia
1st half of 19th century
h. 13 cm
wood
RMV 3109-1 (1954)

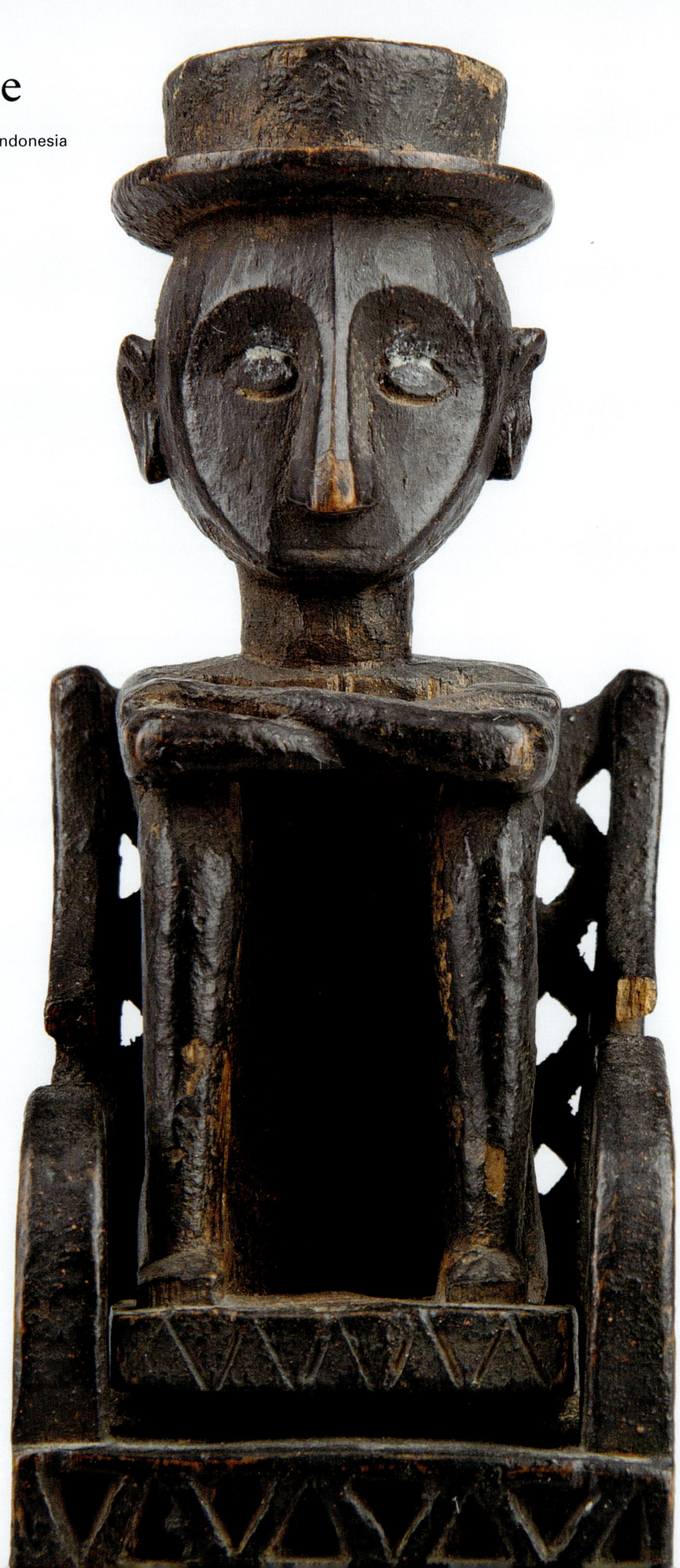

Protective shadow

On the islands of the Southeast Moluccas, including Leti, human beings were seen as combinations of two elements: vitality (associated with the body) and identity, a person's 'individuality', frequently compared to the soul or spirit and known on many of the islands as a person's 'shadow'. It was believed that while the body perishes with death, since vitality has abandoned it, the deceased's 'shadow' continues to exist and can still exert considerable influence on the earthly lives of his or her descendants. This did not apply merely on a personal level; these ancestral figures could also influence the lives of entire families, or their clan or village.

Temporary dwelling

Until the early twentieth century, the surviving relatives would have a small wooden figurine or *yene* carved with the deceased's identity, so as to be able to communicate with his or her 'shadow'. The deceased person's status would be indicated by their ear jewellery and headdress, for instance. The relatives would place these figurines, which served as temporary dwellings, in a high place in the house, together with family heirlooms. Here, the surviving relatives could present offerings to their ancestors and seek their advice. Since the figurines were only temporary dwellings, some island-dwellers were willing to exchange them for tobacco or cloth, after which they would have a new figurine carved. This gave rise to an early form of tourist art.

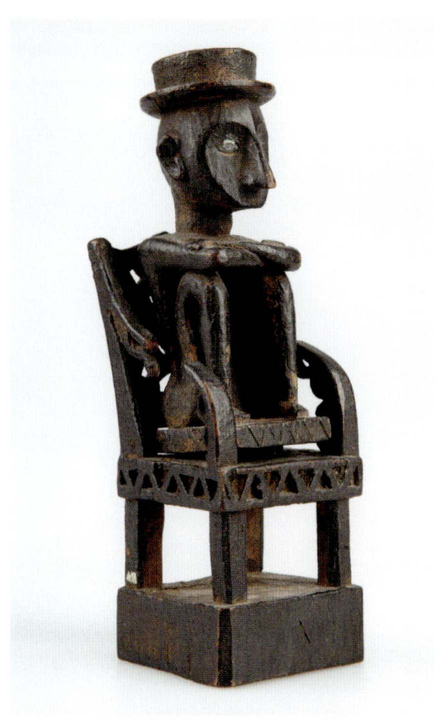

Christian ancestors

Not all statues were destroyed or removed. Especially during the transition to Christianity, in the mid-nineteenth century, ancestral figurines were carved on Leti, which were precisely intended to depict the deceased's Christian identity. In such cases, traditional ancestral beliefs and the Christian faith went hand in hand. Dutch items such as a hat and chair as seen here refer to Christianity. But typical stylistic features of a traditional ancestral figurine from Leti, such as a very long nose and raised legs to denote a man – female ancestors sat with crossed legs – arms resting on the knees, were retained.

Squatting posture

The typical squatting posture of this ancestral figure recurs not only on other islands of the Moluccas but also on Timor, Kalimantan, and Papua, for instance, and among the Batak and Toraja peoples. Outside Indonesia too, in Taiwan, the Philippines, and Vietnam, sculpted figures frequently have raised legs, with the elbows resting on the knees. This might suggest a cultural affinity among these peoples, all of whom speak Austronesian languages. Prehistoric remains show that Austronesian-speaking groups spread out from Taiwan via the Philippines to cover wide tracts of Southeast Asia about five thousand years ago.

Convert and collect

Christian clerics from Ambon first started proselytizing among the population of Leti in 1835. The colonial authorities encouraged missionary activities, fearful of the growing influence of Islam in the Moluccas. Protestant missionaries (unlike Catholics) sometimes acted in draconian ways, forcing people to burn in public ancestral figurines and other objects tied to the traditional religious practices, in affirmation of their conversion. Yet these same missionaries 'rescued' the finest pieces from the bonfires and spirited them away to museums.

Thangka with Mahakala

Tibet
1750-1800
89.1 x 62.2 cm
painting in colour on linen

RMV 3329-2 (1956)

Mahakala

This impressive Mahakala is one of the
eight Dharmapalas, protectors of the
Tibetan-Buddhist doctrine. He com-
municates a forceful reminder of the
principle of mortality and the illusion of
the material world. He comes forward in
a frenzied rush of energy, holding in his
four hands a human heart, a sword with
vajra-shaped pommel, a skull cup full of
steaming blood, and a trident decorated
with human heads. He wears a crown of
five human skulls (see p. 154-155).
In his dance he tramples on three nude
human figures, who symbolise three
major impediments to enlightenment:
greed, hatred, and ignorance.

Thangka

A *thangka* is a scroll painting intended
to serve as an aid to meditative
visualisation. A *thangka* may emphasise
a single central deity, portrayed in large
format, or alternatively it may show
circles of deities, hierarchically arranged
in a cosmic diagram or *mandala*. The
purpose of visualisation is to arrive at a
supernatural state of consciousness in
which one experiences a mystical
unification with the central deity, which
may include wrathful gods, such as
Mahakala, as well as Buddhas and
Bodhisattvas. The mystical unification
with the terrifying god offers the person
concerned a chance to triumph over the
evil within himself and hence to improve
his chances of being released from the
eternal cycle of suffering.

Wrathful deities

The wrathful deities assume demonic,
terrifying forms out of compassion with
human beings. They are divided into
three categories: the deities who
primarily help to foster good health,
wealth, and happiness; those who are
one step higher and are mainly known as
the protectors of Buddhist doctrine in
general or of specific texts, rituals or
meditation practices; and right at the
top, the wrathful Buddhas whose
function is to conquer and suppress the
most obstinate and deeply-entrenched
demonic powers. They trample on
Shiva, the model of selfishness, and his
wife.

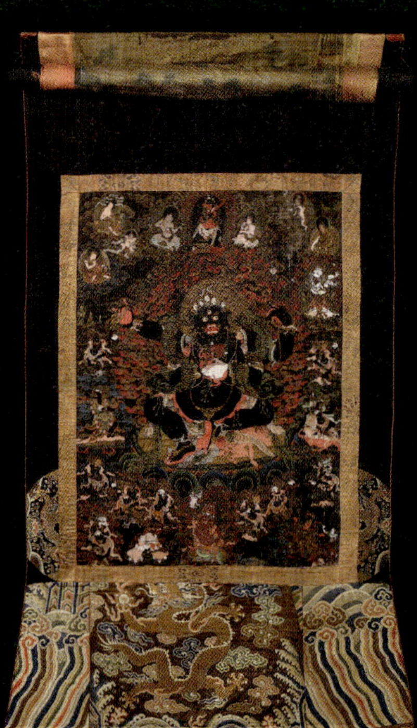

Who is who?

Sometimes, as here, gods belonging to
all three categories are depicted together
in a single painting. At the bottom, in
the middle, the terrifying Rahu, one of
the wrathful deities of the lowest
category, is dancing, surrounded by
goddesses with animal heads. Mahakala,
in the centre, as one of the Dharmapalas,
belongs to the second category. He is
supported on the left and right by four
Tibetan tutelary deities, including his
wife Palden Llamo. Right at the top, in
the middle, Chakrasamvara, a deity of
the highest category, dances in an
intimate embrace with his female
companion Vajravarahi (see p. 154-155).
Important masters and great figures
from Tibetan history are depicted on
either side.

Technical perfection

The technical perfection of this
painting, combined with a remarkable
use of colour, helps to ensure that the
figures stand out from their black
background. The refined painting and
expressiveness of the central figure, in
particular, is all the more impressive
because of the extremely good condition
in which this *thangka* has been
conserved. The scroll painting is
furnished with a frame of blue brocade
with a fine 'door' (embroidered square).
The back of this frame, against the
wooden support, bears an inscription
woven in silk, which indicates that this
thangka was one in a series of paintings
of all eight Dharmapalas.

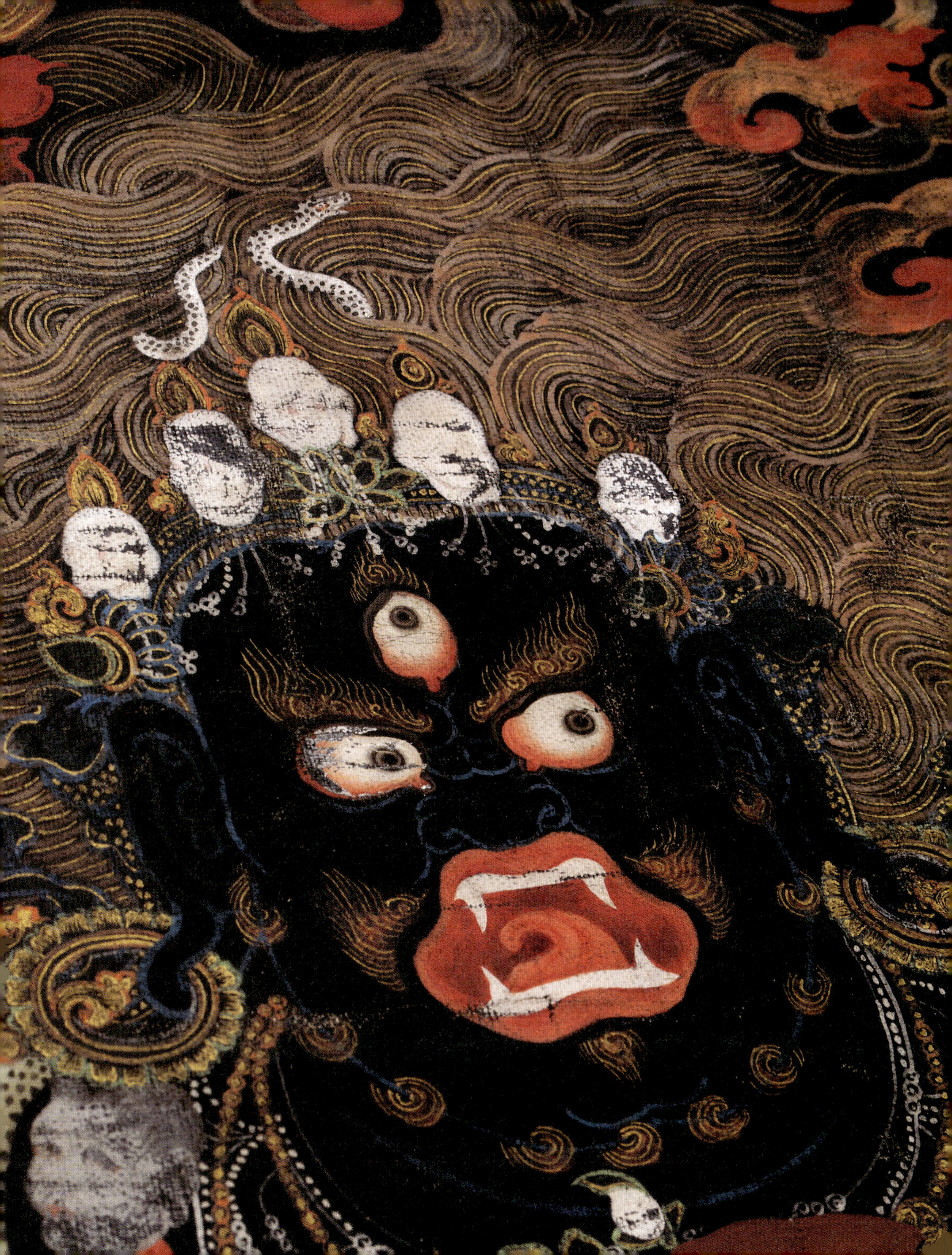

Knotted cord (*Khipu*)

Inca, Peru
1250-1532
53 x 40 cm
cotton
RMV 3344-1 (1956)

The Incas

From 1438 onwards, the Incas con-
quered large swathes of western South
America in less than a hundred years.
What started as a relatively small state
surrounding the city of Qusqu (Cuzco)
in the south of Peru grew into a vast
empire, which at its height extended
from present-day Colombia to
Santiago de Chile, over 3,000 miles to
the south. The Incas called their realm
Tawantinsuyu, 'the empire of the four
winds' and they divided it into four parts
accordingly. An extensive bureaucracy
had to be created to administer this
enormous empire.

Bureaucracy

Inca officials kept a close eye on the
territories under their control. Messages
were sent and received on a daily basis,
with instructions to ensure the empire's
good governance. A great variety of
information was exchanged: details of
storage places and goods that were
needed or available, the output from
mines, and taxes that were due. Tax was
levied in the Inca empire in the form of
labour. Every 'taxpayer' was obliged to
work for the state a set number of days
each year. *Khipus* were used, among
other things, to keep track of the amount
of tax to be paid and to allocate tasks.

Khipu

A *khipu* (meaning 'knot' in Quechua,
the Inca language) is essentially an
assemblage of coloured, knotted, cotton
cords. Its characteristics – the colours of
the cords, the way in which the knots
were tied, and the placing of the cords
and knots – combined to form a
decimal system of numerical
codification, in which the positions of
the knots in each cord denoted the
decimal position. The knots at the
bottom of the cords were the numbers
from 1 to 10, then came the tens,
followed by the hundreds and at the top
the thousands. This system made it
possible to exchange information using
khipus and to use them as a form of
documentation within the Incas' official
apparatus.

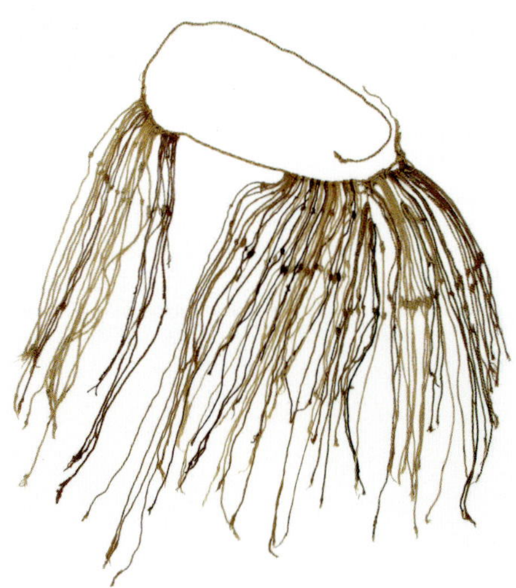

Different types of information

Khipus were not only used for purely
administrative purposes. Of the
600-odd *khipus* that are still known in
museums and private collections
worldwide, about two-thirds of them
are administrative. The other known
examples relate to historiography,
astrology, information about the
calendar, and rituals associated with
the calendar and agriculture. *Khipus* of
that kind used a different codification
system and were made by specialist
khipukamayuq.

Khipuqamayuqkuna

Messages in *khipus* were carried by
chaskis, messengers who travelled at
great speed around the extensive, well-
maintained and safe network of roads
that covered the entire Inca empire.
At least twenty languages were spoken
within the empire. Each message had to
be clear, compact and portable. The
khipu makers (*khipuqamayuqkuna*) were
responsible for coding and decoding the
information. Interpreting a *khipu* always
required the intervention of a specialist,
a *khipukamayuq*. Every settlement had
at least four *khipukamayuqkuna*, to
ensure that information was correctly
coded and decoded.

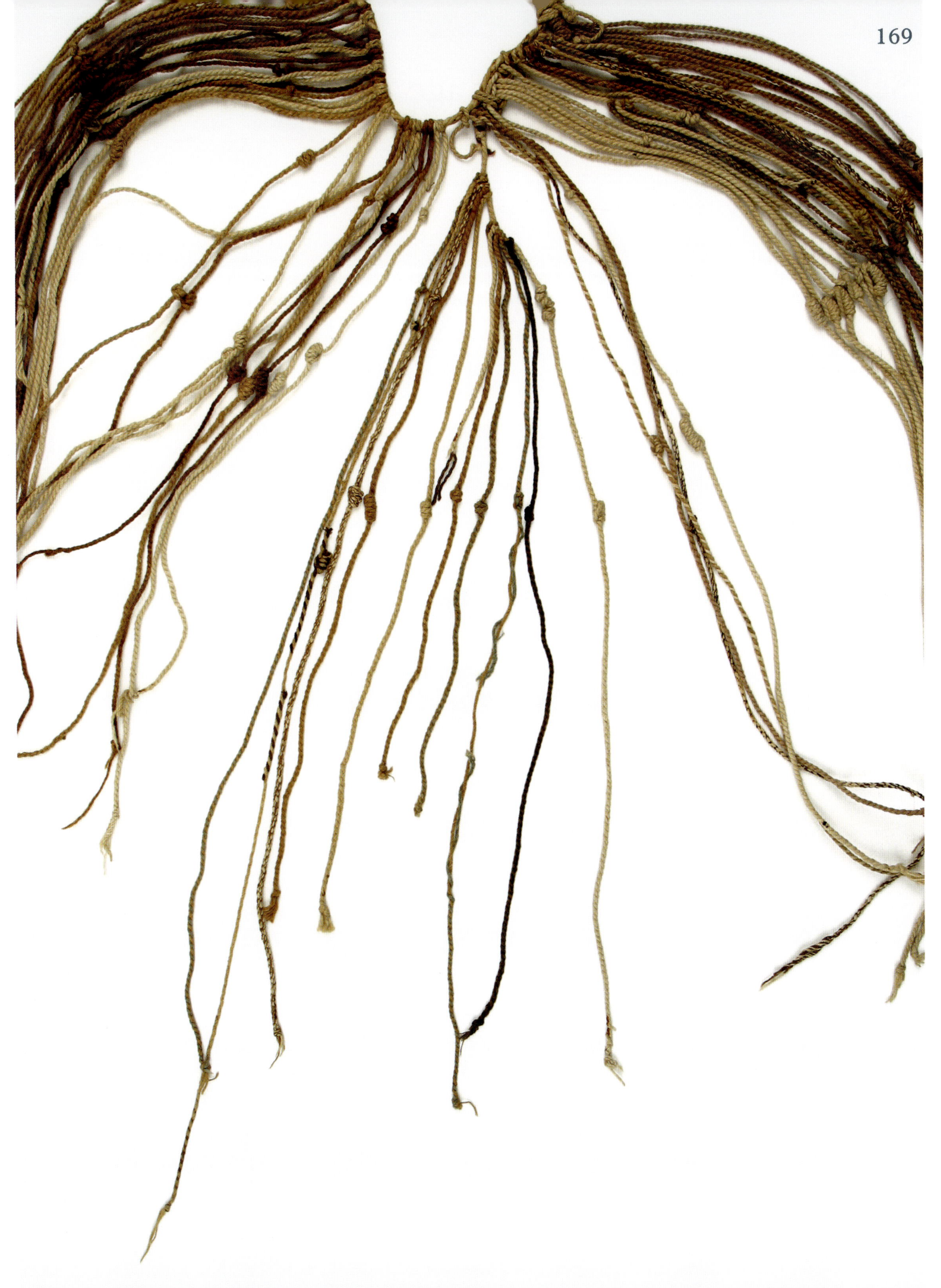

Self-portrait at 83 years of age

Katsushika Hokusai, Edo period, Japan
1842
26.9 x 16.9 cm
paper, ink *(sumi)*, drawing, writing
RMV 3513-1496 (1958)

Letter with self-portrait

In this self-portrait we see the artist
to whom we owe the iconic print
Great *Wave* (see also p. 14-15). He has
depicted himself as an old man, grin-
ning, with his right hand pointing left,
to the space that originally contained
the addressee's name. It is a letter which
was evidently addressed, as the writing
on the right makes clear, to one of
Hokusai's publishers. The message
reads: 'Now the sketches in this section
date from the time when I was about
forty-one or forty-two years old.
A number of them are duplicates.
Some could be improved today, after all
those years. The rest can be dismissed as
immature work from a bygone age and
you are free to laugh at it. Yours with the
greatest of esteem, the eighty-three-
year-old *hachijūsansai*, Hachiemon,
[seal] Manji'.

Trade with a flavour

The provenance of this self-portrait – it
comes from the Japanese collector Fusui
Kaneko –caused it to be approached for
many years with certain reservations,
since Kaneko had been associated with
a number of suspect paintings. Once the
accusation of forgery was made public,
all the objects he had sold were tarred
with the brush of suspicion. This
portrait ended up by way of the Berlin
dealer Tikotin in the collection of
Ferdinand Lieftinck, a Groningen
collector of Japanese prints and
drawings. When he offered his collection
to the Dutch state in 1956, his print
collection was purchased as art by the
Print Room of the Rijksmuseum, while
the drawings were classified as
'ethnographic items' and were acquired
by the Rijksmuseum Volkenkunde.

Katsushika Hokusai

Katsushika Hokusai (1760-1849) was
one of the most versatile and productive
artists of his day. In the West he became
famous primarily as the designer of the
series *Thirty-six views of Mount Fuji*.
Aside from a group of drawings of
fabulous lions, which Hokusai drew
every day for over a year to ward off evil,
few of his drawings have become as
famous as this self-portrait. Interestingly,
the fabulous lions, known as *Nisshin*
joma, were produced in roughly the
same period as this self-portrait, that is,
around 1842.

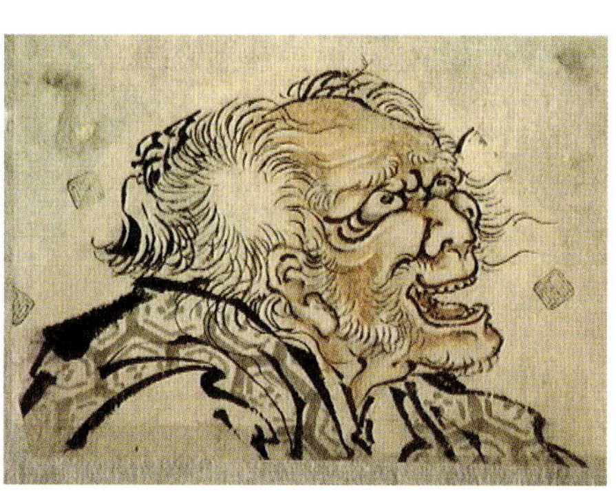

Hokusai self-portraits

On the basis of this self-portrait,
scholars have studied Hokusai's other
drawings and paintings to see if the
artist depicted himself elsewhere.
Virtually identical features are
recognisable in one portrait of an old
man (above), and even more marked is
the resemblance in a painting of the god
of thunder, Raijin, in the collection of
the Freer Gallery of Art (Smithsonian
Institute), painted when the artist was
eighty-eight years old. Hokusai is also
known to have incor-porated small self-
portraits into his letters at times, but
these are drawn so sketchily that the
likeness is very tenuous.

The recipient

It is naturally tempting to speculate
concerning the identity of the recipient.
Was it, perhaps, Eirakuya Tōshirō,
the publisher of the *Hokusai manga*
(12 vols., 1814-34), or Kikuya
Kōsaburō, who published several
albums with miscellaneous illustrations
by Hokusai in 1843? The latter seems
the likeliest possibility. Kikuya's editions
display a wide range of subjects and are
of variable quality.

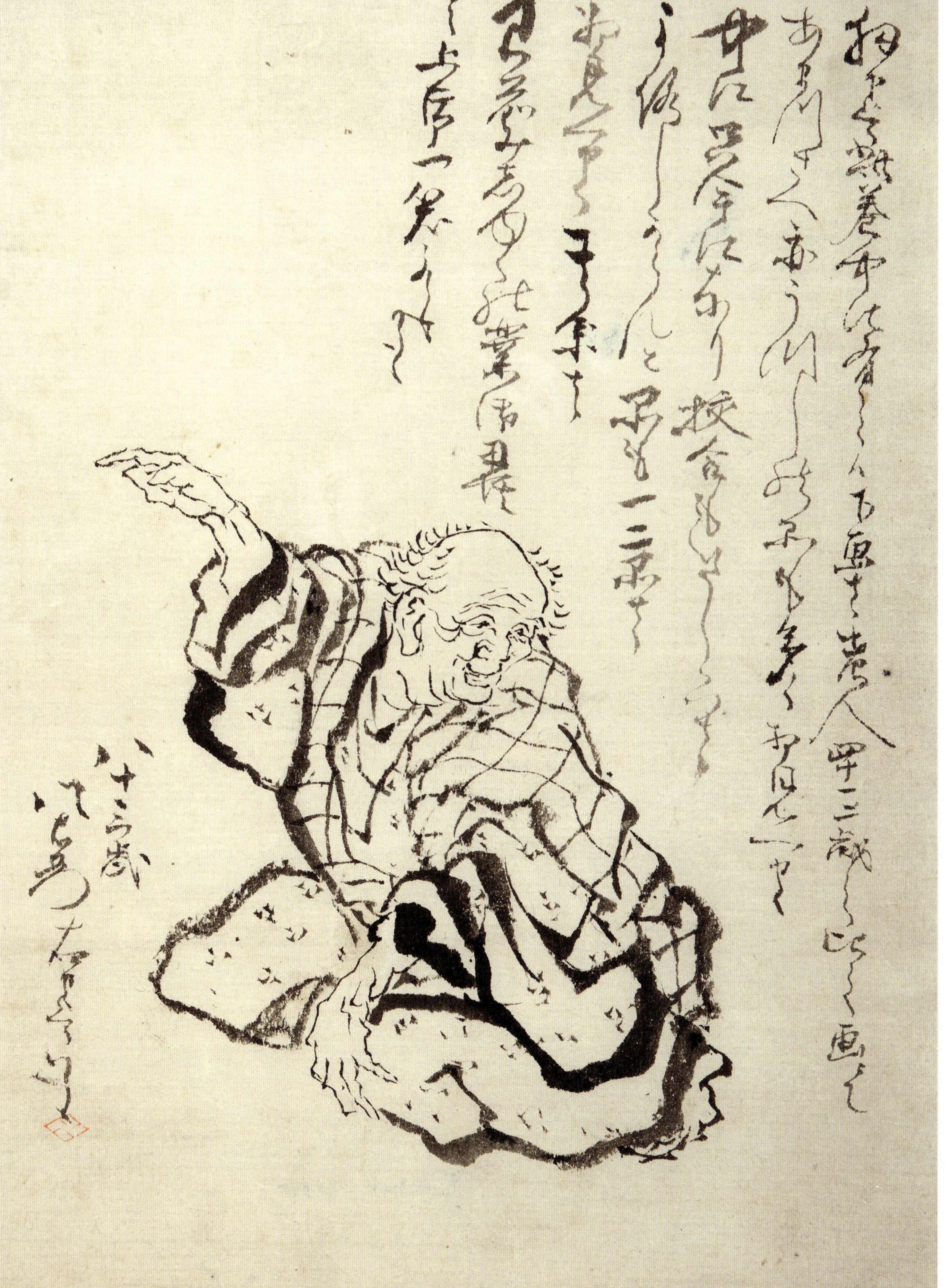

Barkcloth

Lake Sentani, Northwest New Guinea, Indonesia
c. 1930
130.3 x 80.5 cm
tree bark, pigment
RMV 3600-7499 (1958)

Sentani cloth

This painted barkcloth belongs to a small group of Sentani cloths that amazed Western art circles in the 1920s and 1930s. Two sawfish in particular attract our attention, besides which we see smaller fish and snakelike creatures as well as a number of unidentifiable elements.

'Primitive art' in the West

This cloth from Melanesia played a crucial role in bridging the gap between Western and non-Western art. Interest expressed from within the Paris art world culminated in 1929 in Jacques Viot's collecting expedition to Lake Sentani. Not long afterwards, Sentani cloths started appearing in sales exhibitions of 'primitive art'. The artists Max Ernst and Henri Matisse possessed Sentani cloths. A catalogue accompanying an exhibition at the Museum of Modern Art in New York pointed out the similarities between these cloths and certain designs by Matisse – one of which is named after Oceania – as well as paintings by Joan Miró.

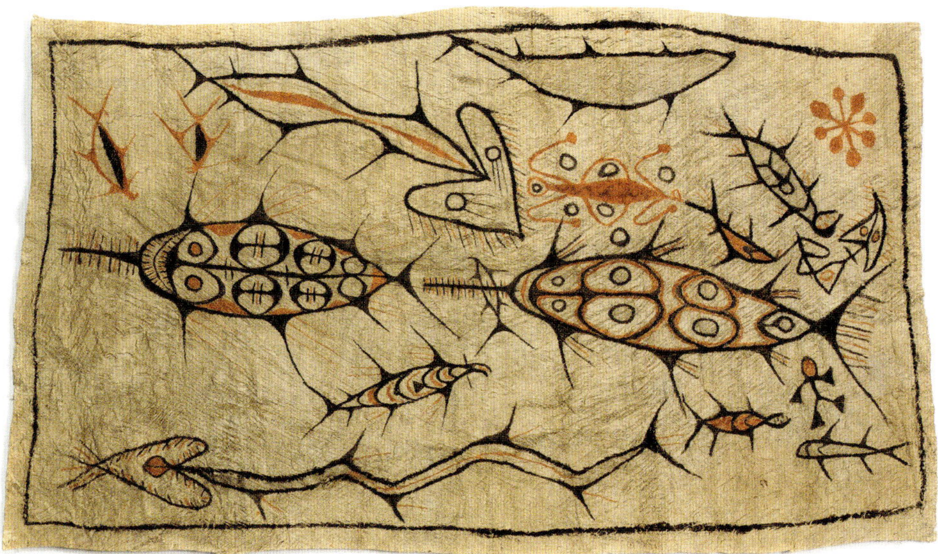

Clan symbols

This decoration with totem animals recalls the motifs of clan symbols painted on the ceremonial cooking pots used in Humboldt Bay, which is close to Lake Sentani, and the carved animal figures in wooden roof decorations of men's houses and grave huts. Fish motifs are closely linked to women, since most fishing was done by women.

Rites of passage

Tree barkcloths played an important role in the life of the Sentani. They were once worn only by married women, while girls went around naked, so that the cloths marked the transition between girlhood and marriage. The cloth was frequently wrapped around the waist with a girdle, reaching down to the knees or over the calves, depending on local custom and the width of the material. Following a woman's death – in particular that of a young woman – a cloth would be hung besides the little hut erected over her grave. Widows wore capes made from barkcloth when they were in mourning, and the dead were buried in barkcloth.

Beating and painting

Women made barkcloths. They started by taking a shell to scrape off the outer layer of bark. The next stage was using beaters to work the inner bark of the paper mulberry, breadfruit, or fig tree. It was probably the men who subsequently added the drawings in free hand, using charcoal, shell lime, and red ochre.

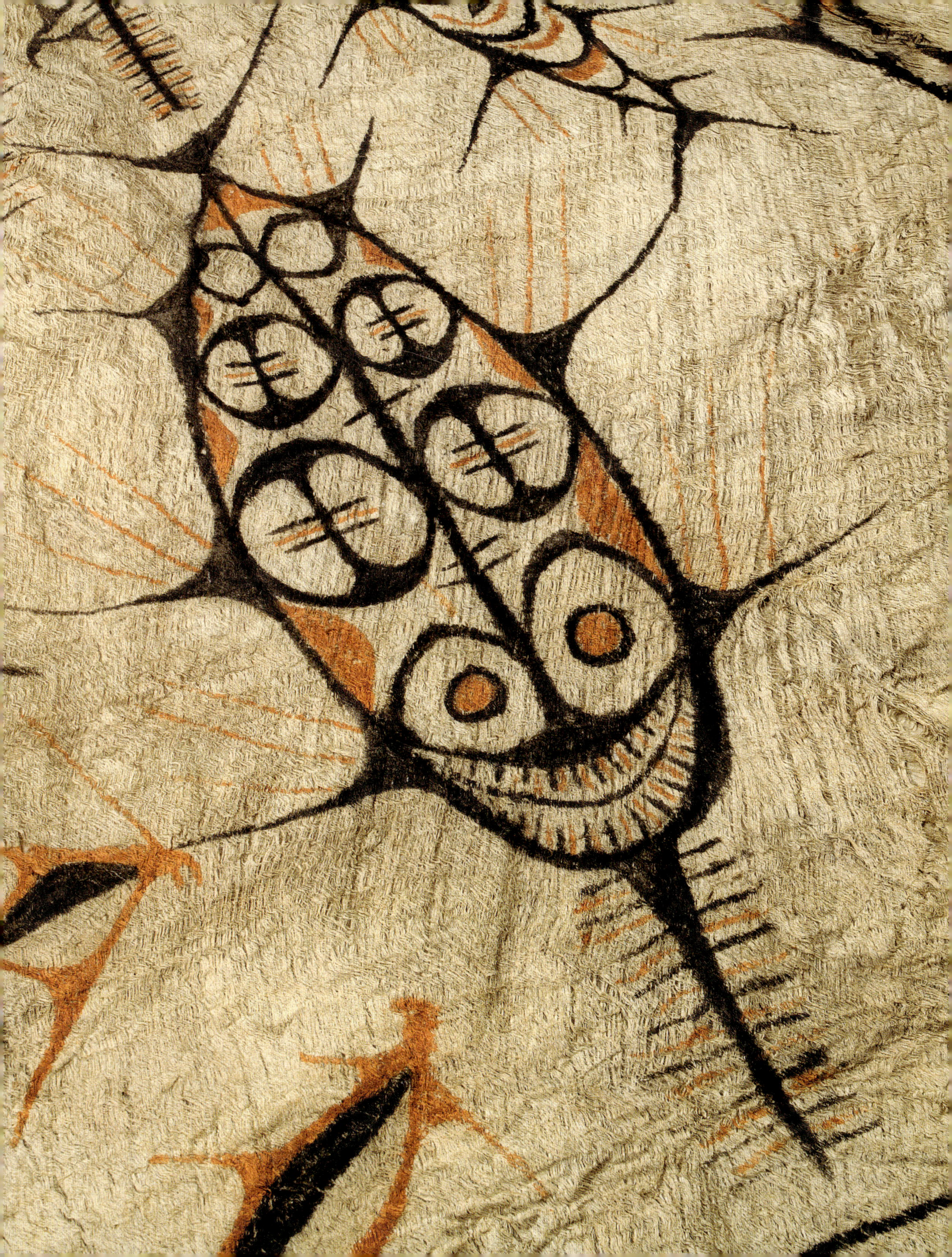

1/30th part of the Qur'an with binding

Persia
mid-16th century
35 x 24 cm
paper, leather, gold paint, ink
RMV 3831-2 (1959)

Verses in gold

The page of this Qur'an is divided into five sections. Three horizontal bands with Qur'an texts in gold, in the monumental *Thuluth* style, alternate with two narrower, rectangular sections with four black lines in the cursive *Naskh* style. The Qur'an verses continue, regardless of colour, format, and calligraphic style. Gold rosettes in the text indicate the end of each verse. The leather binding has borders filled with Arabic text and a central section with a lobed medallion and corner-pieces, decorated with floral patterns in relief. The rest of the surface is full of stylised Chinese clouds. The envelope-shaped flap is a standard part of Oriental bindings.

The Qur'an

Believers see the Qur'an as the literal revelation of God to the Prophet Muhammad through the archangel Gabriel. Although the Qur'an was handed down orally over the centuries, and pupils of Qur'an schools are required to memorise the text, around 650, some twenty years after the death of the Prophet (570-632), the entire Qur'an was written down. Handwritten copies were made of this standard text and sent to diverse garrison cities of the rapidly expanding Islamic empire. Although in early Islamic history, most Qur'ans were written on parchment, the use of paper became customary from the eleventh century onward.

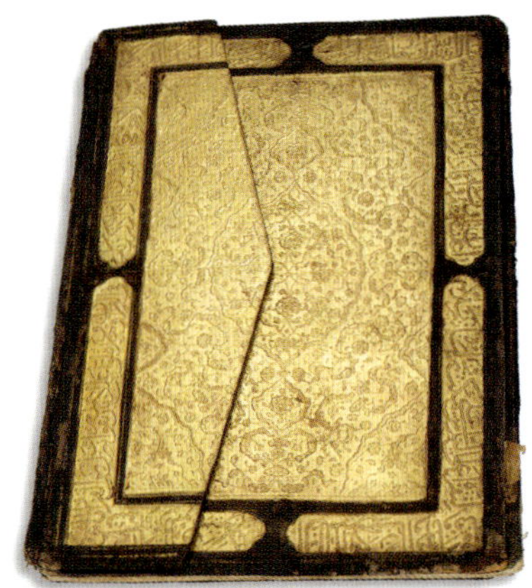

One 30th part

The Qur'an contains 114 chapters or *surahs*, each one consisting of a varying number of verses: from three to 286. The longest *surahs* with the most verses are towards the beginning, while the shortest ones are towards the end of the sacred text. Handwritten copies of the Qur'an were sometimes made in a single volume, but others were divided into two, seven, or thirty parts. Muslims use the thirty parts during Ramadan, the month in which believers fast from dawn to sunset. After sunset, and the breaking of the fast with a meal, one-thirtieth portion of the Qur'an is recited each day. Mosques possess Qur'ans divided into thirty separate volumes for this purpose.

Polished paper

Before the calligrapher could begin, the surface of the paper was polished using a smooth stone, after which a grid of lines was impressed in the paper. The two different styles of calligraphy involved the use of reed pens of different diameters. The binding acquired its sturdy quality from the use of several sheets of paper pasted together and covered with a very thin layer of leather. After that, decorations would be applied in relief, using different stamps for the rectangular central section and the bands of text. This in turn would be covered with a layer of gold paint. The inside of the projecting flap is decorated in the corners with delicate cut-out floral patterns.

Reverence

Muslims treat Qur'ans with great reverence. Qur'ans are placed on specially constructed holders to prevent them from touching the ground, and no book should be placed on top of the sacred text other than another Qur'an. The beautiful calligraphy in ink and gold paint, the floral and geometrical marginal decorations, and the carefully prepared bindings do justice to the divine text and reflect the great esteem in which it is held. The text itself is believed to possess qualities that protect and redeem. It is not uncommon to wear items of jewellery including an engraved verse from the Qur'an.

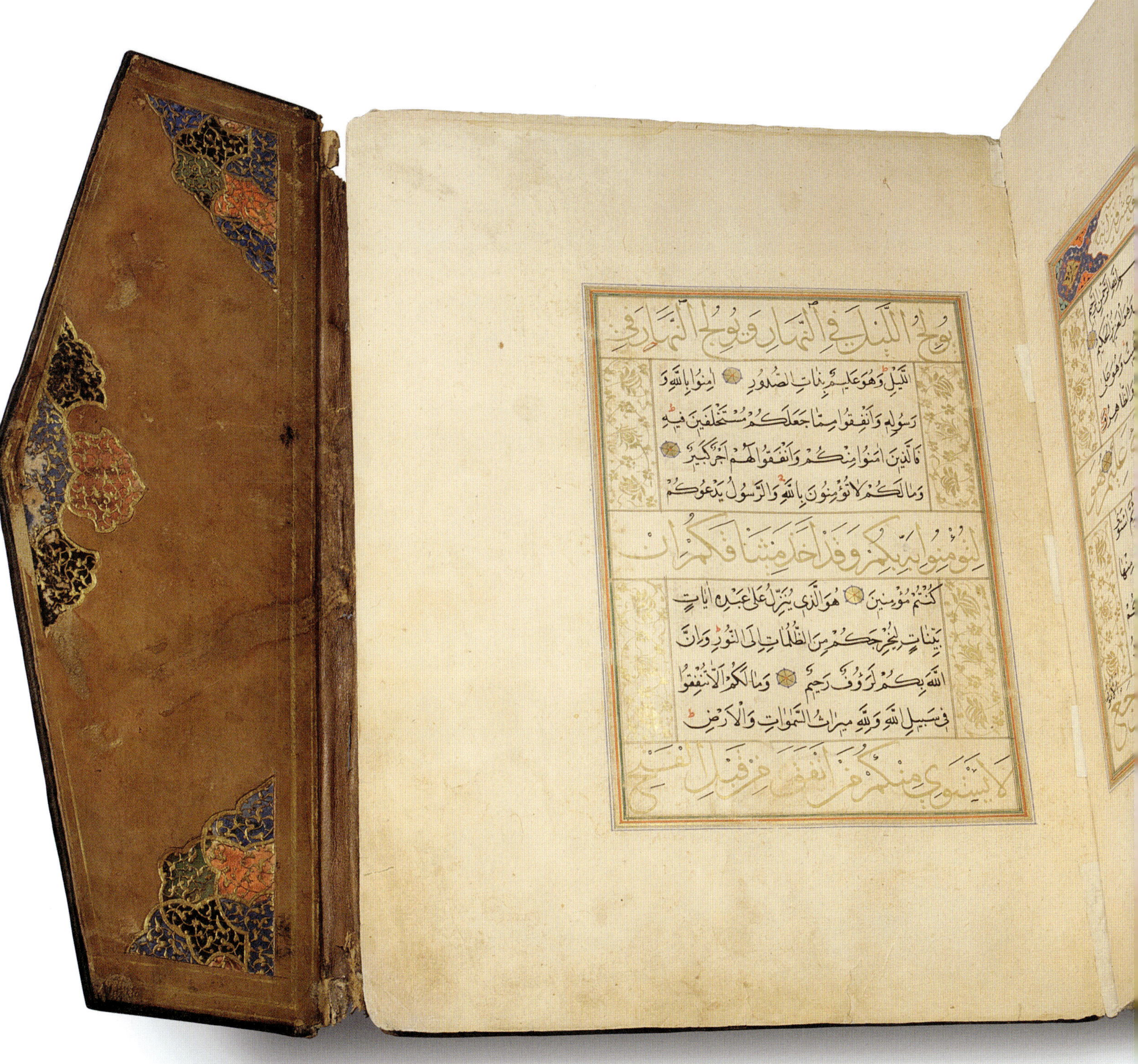

يُولِجُ اللَّيْلَ فِي النَّهَارِ وَيُولِجُ النَّهَارَ فِي
اللَّيْلِ وَهُوَ عَلِيمٌ بِذَاتِ الصُّدُورِ ۞ آمِنُوا بِاللَّهِ وَ
رَسُولِهِ وَأَنْفِقُوا مِمَّا جَعَلَكُمْ مُسْتَخْلَفِينَ فِيهِ
فَالَّذِينَ آمَنُوا مِنْكُمْ وَأَنْفَقُوا لَهُمْ أَجْرٌ كَبِيرٌ
وَمَا لَكُمْ لَا تُؤْمِنُونَ بِاللَّهِ وَالرَّسُولُ يَدْعُوكُمْ
لِتُؤْمِنُوا بِرَبِّكُمْ وَقَدْ أَخَذَ مِيثَاقَكُمْ إِنْ
كُنْتُمْ مُؤْمِنِينَ ۞ هُوَ الَّذِي يُنَزِّلُ عَلَى عَبْدِهِ آيَاتٍ
بَيِّنَاتٍ لِيُخْرِجَكُمْ مِنَ الظُّلُمَاتِ إِلَى النُّورِ وَإِنَّ
اللَّهَ بِكُمْ لَرَؤُوفٌ رَحِيمٌ ۞ وَمَا لَكُمْ أَلَّا تُنْفِقُوا
فِي سَبِيلِ اللَّهِ وَلِلَّهِ مِيرَاثُ السَّمَوَاتِ وَالْأَرْضِ
لَا يَسْتَوِي مِنْكُمْ مَنْ أَنْفَقَ مِنْ قَبْلِ الْفَتْحِ

Fragment of the textile covering the Ka'ba (*Kiswa*)

Mecca, Saudi Arabia; manufactured in Egypt
before 1919
75 x 88.5 cm
silk lampas, gilt silver thread on silk
RMV B118-1 (1959)

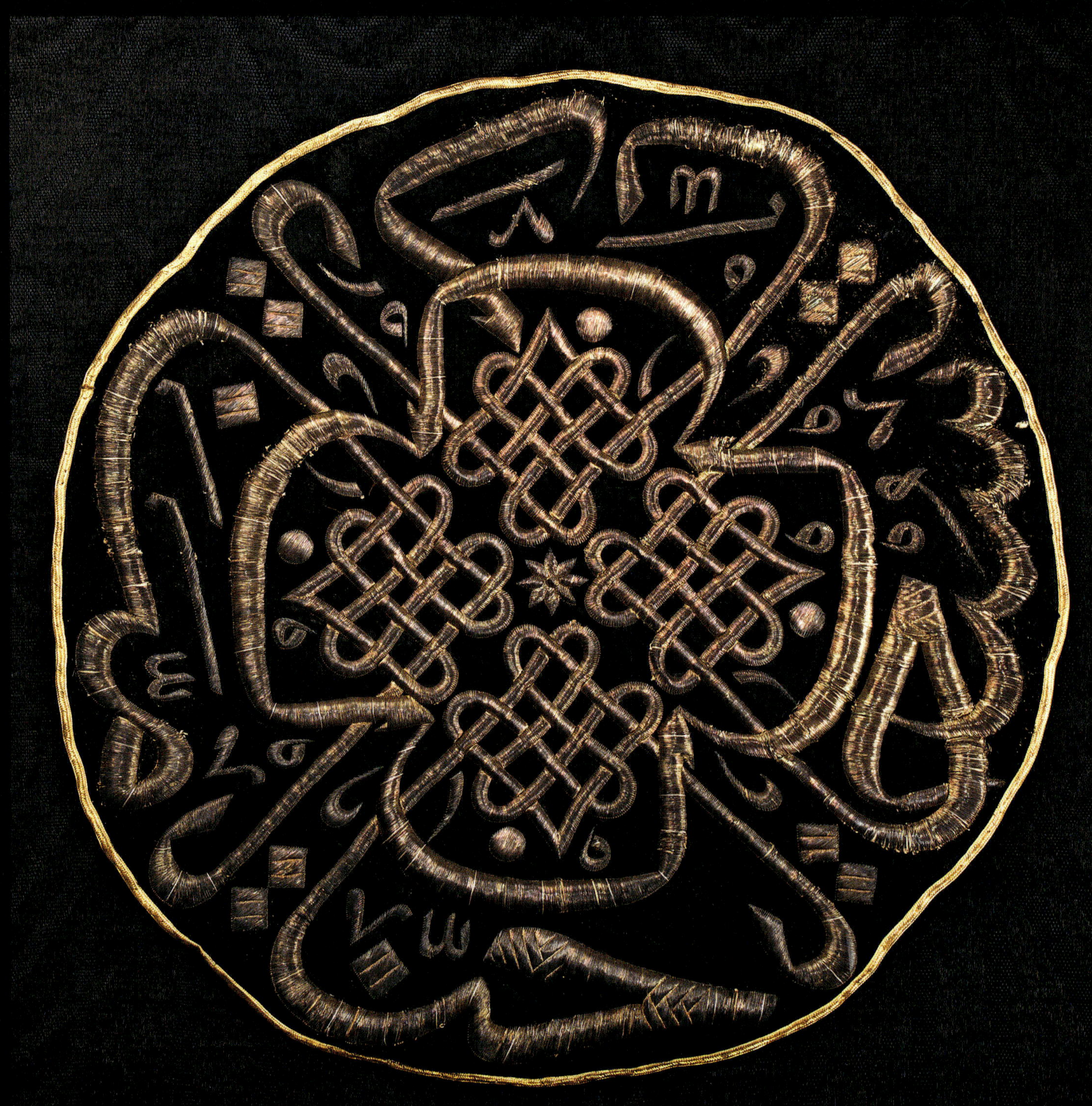

Monumental inscriptions

The medallion of this fragment of the textile covering the Ka'ba (*kiswa*) is embroidered with gilded silver thread on woven silk. Both, the medallion and the ground, are furnished with religious inscriptions in Arabic. The ground contains monumental Arabic texts like 'Oh God' and the profession of faith: 'There is no god but Allah, and Muhammad is His messenger'. In the middle of the medallion are four woven patterns surrounded by a quatrefoil. The quatrefoil consists of four times the Arabic letter equivalent to 'n', the last letter of each of the four names of God that are embroidered along the outer edge of the medallion: *Ya Hannan Ya Mannan Ya Dayyan Ya Subhan*.

Hidden from view

Even before the advent of Islam in 622, it was customary on the Arab Peninsula to hide sacred places out of a sense of respect. This tradition was continued after the advent of Islam with the Ka'ba in Mecca, the cuboid building measuring about 12 x 10.5 metres with a height of 15 metres. Both the inner and outer walls and the inner and outer door were hidden from sight by textiles. The dynasty that ruled the holy cities of Mecca and Medina was responsible for making the cover. Woven or embroidered bands of inscriptions including Qur'an texts and the names of God belonged to the standard decorations from an early stage.

Kiswa

The fragment was part of the *kiswa*, the cloth used to cover the Ka'ba in Mecca. It was in the possession of the colonial official Emile Gobée (1881-1954), who served as consul in the Saudi port of Jeddah from 1917 to 1921. One of his tasks was the logistical operation surrounding the reception of thousands of pilgrims from the Dutch East Indies who undertook the Hajj (the Islamic pilgrimage to Mecca) each year. Whether this fragment was a gift from the authorities in Mecca or a purchased souvenir is unknown. In 1954 the consul's wife, Mrs Gobée-Bosman, provided the fragment to the museum on loan. This medallion fragment (*jamat*) served to divide different verses of the Qu'ran from one another.

Pilgrims' souvenirs

During the annual pilgrimage, the Mecca family of Banu Shayba was responsible for replacing the *kiswa* that concealed the outer walls. Every year, a new cloth, produced in Egypt or Turkey, would be transported to Mecca by caravan. Before the new sacred textile could be put in place, members of the Banu Shayba family first washed and perfumed the Ka'ba. They would cut up the old *kiswa* into little pieces, which would be sold as souvenirs. Some fragments were given to dignitaries such as the Sharif of Mecca. The *kiswa* fragments were in great demand because of their long proximity to the Ka'ba and their devout inscriptions, which were held to possess redemptive power.

Dar al-kiswa

Large quantities of precious materials were needed to make the *kiswa*. In nineteenth-century Egypt, almost 900 metres of silk thread and over 62 kilos of silver-gilt thread were used every year. This thread, for the embroidery of the bands of inscriptions, was applied to raised cotton, so that the calligraphy would stand out in relief. Specialist calligraphers were in charge of producing the model texts. In the nineteenth century, a special workshop was set up in Cairo, the *dar al-kiswa*, for the making of the cloth. Today, the *kiswa* is made in a special workshop designed for the purpose in Mecca. Here, the workers start by impressing the contours of the inscriptions on the cloth, after which the letters are filled in with precious metal thread by hand.

Mitsu tomoe mounted in a cone shell (*Netsuke*)

Edo period, Japan
1800-1850
1 x 3.4 cm
metal alloys, silver, gold, cone shell

RMV 3915 1 (1962)

Unique *netsuke*
As far as can be ascertained, this remark-able *netsuke* is completely unique. Most *netsuke* are figurative, and not only is this one abstract, but it is also made of a most unusual material: a cone shell that has been sawn in two. The tiny disk in the middle is made of *shakudō*, a copper alloy with a small quantity of gold. The motifs are hammered into the pure silver and gold. *Netsuke* were made from a variety of materials, the most common being wood and ivory. *Netsuke* made from shells are extremely rare.

Netsuke for the *inrō*
This *netsuke* enabled the wearer to carry his medicine box or *inrō* by passing the *netsuke*, to which the *inrō* was attached with a cord, under his belt. He could thus have his handsome lacquered *inrō* with him while keeping his hands free – traditional Japanese clothes do not have pockets. That the item to be carried here was a lacquered *inrō* rather than a simple tobacco pouch can be inferred from the *netsuke*'s magnificent finish. In the innermost section of the shell is a small metal plate, furnished with a little eyelet, to which the cord from which the *inrō* hangs could be attached.

Unaffected simplicity
The combination of what at first sight appears to be a simple shell with such refined workmanship in the remarkable metal alloy of *shakudō* conjures up associations with the concepts of *wabi* and *sabi*, which also feature prominently in the tea ceremony. Such natural, unaffected simplicity is recognisable only to the connoisseur who has an eye for it. In addition, the rounded shape, produced by sawing through the shell, immediately conveys a sense of naturalness to anyone who holds this gem in his hand, which is a very important quality for a *netsuke*. It is an object that must have a pleasant feel to it.

Associations with the *bushi* warrior culture
Although the primary component of this *netsuke* is a sawn-off cone shell (not a very common shell, it should be added, in Japanese waters), it is above all the *shakudō* knob that conjures up associations with the *bushi* warrior culture, since *shakudō* is associated almost directly with *menuki* and *fuchi-kashira*, prominent examples of sword decoration.

Imitation *shakudō*
The *shakudō* technique, the superb metal alloy from which the tiny knob in the middle of the cone shell is made, was widely known. Fisscher himself recognised it as an extremely precious metal, and collected an astonishing twenty objects made from this alloy. He also supplemented his collection with thirty well-made *shakudō* imitations, which the Japanese classify as imitation *shakudō*. This involved copying real *shakudō* as well as possible by hammering figures from copper plates; the upper surface would then be coloured and finishing touches added in silver and copper.

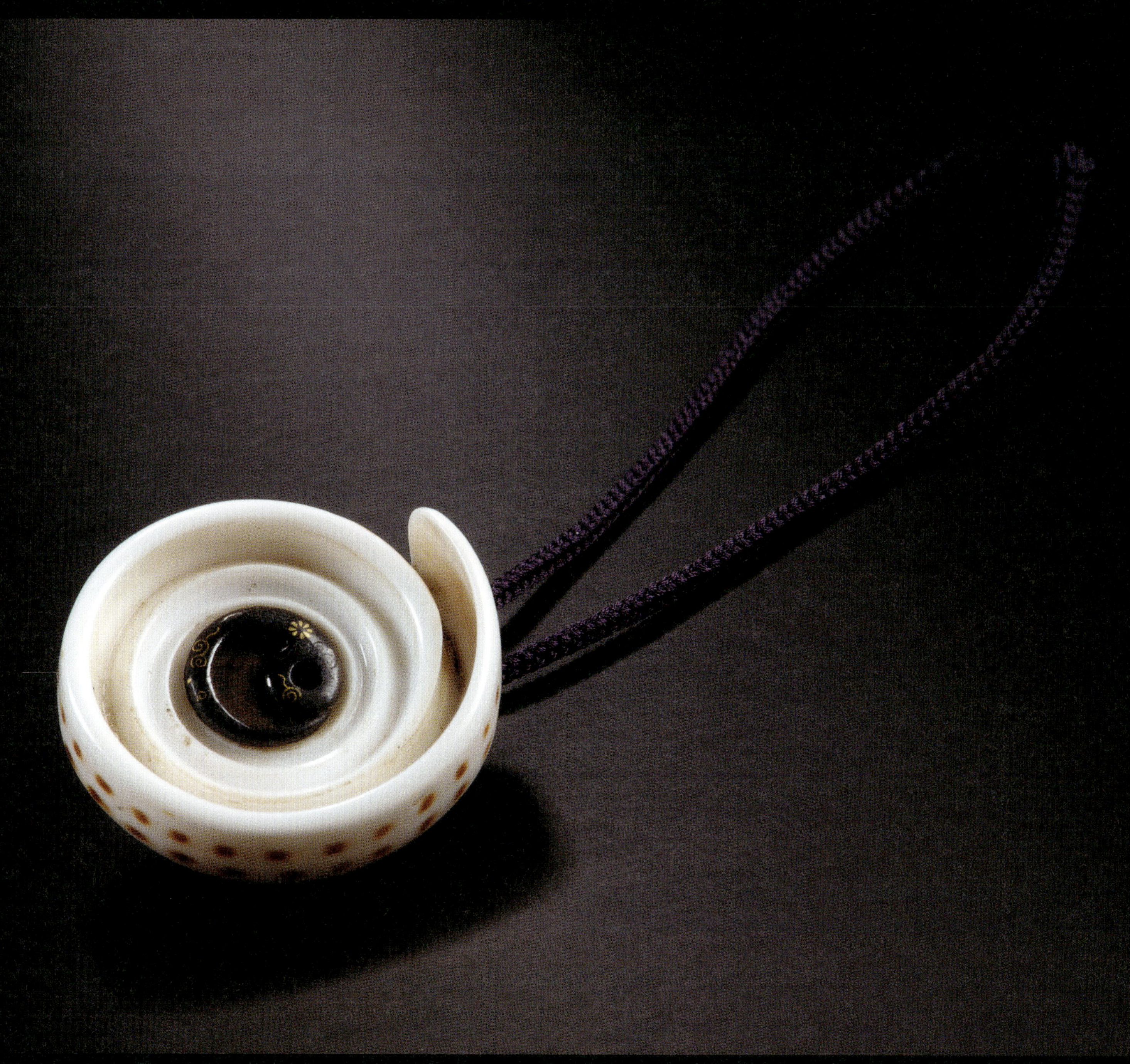

Relief depicting the Bird Jaguar blood sacrifice

Classic period, Maya; Guatemala
19 February 766
117.3 x 90.2 cm
limestone, pigments
RMV 3939-1 (1963)

Lintel

This relief was in 'temple 1' of the archaeological site La Pasadita, a Maya city from the classic period (250-900) on the frontier between Mexico and Guatemala. It once lay as a lintel above the doorway to the temple chamber, in such a way that the priest would have to lean his head back to see the relief. Depicted on the lintel are two men performing a ceremonial act to mark the close of a five-year period or *Hotun*. The image is accompanied by a caption in hieroglyphics, which starts by recording the date, 7 Ahau 18 Pop 9.16.15.0.0, which translates into AD 19 February 766 in the Western calendar.

La Pasadita

The city of La Pasadita lay between two great rival Maya cities, Yaxchilán and Piedras Negras, which waged war against each other for centuries. La Pasadita was founded by King Shield Jaguar, Bird Jaguar's father. The city was probably built at great speed; the entire ceremonial centre was constructed in 25 years. It seems likely that La Pasadita was built as a frontier point (like other nearby cities built in the same period) to protect Yaxchilán's security from attacks launched from Piedras Negras.

Yaxun Bahlam and Tilom

Thanks to the inscription, we know that the figure depicted here is King Yaxun Bahlam ('Bird Jaguar') of the city of Yaxchilán, who, together with his vassal Tilom, governor of La Pasadita, is offering a blood sacrifice. The blood has been obtained from a penis perforation, which can be inferred from the instrument depicted in front of his loincloth. The man on the right is Tilom. This is clear from the title 'Sahal' or governor that is used to denote him.

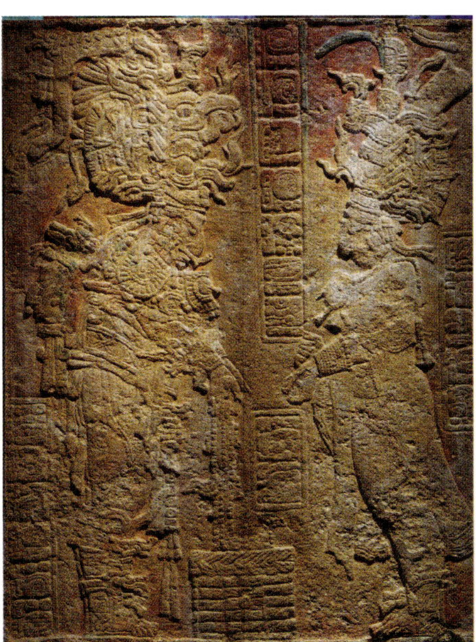

Peace-loving stargazers?

Well into the twentieth century, researchers believed that the Maya had been peace-loving astronomers and scientists who never waged war and were only interested in studying the stars. Popular mythology thus cast them in the role of the opposite of the 'bloodthirsty Aztecs'. However, since the decoding of Mayan script, enabling us to read the numerous Mayan inscriptions on steles and monuments, we now know that the Maya, like every other people in history, had frequent wars between cities, kingdoms and dynasties. They also invested heavily in the development of infrastructure, administrative systems, art, and social cohesion.

Population growth

Yaxchilán and Piedras Negras had waged war frequently since AD 250. These conflicts were probably about the control of trading routes. Finally, in AD 700, Yaxchilán started to build a number of frontier cities like La Pasadita, and long defensive walls to protect the border, possibly prompted by the need for more space and farmland to accommodate the enormous population growth in both cities. After 800, most of the cities in the region, including Yaxchilán and La Pasadita, were abandoned in what is known as the 'Maya Collapse', with people moving away to live in smaller settlements instead.

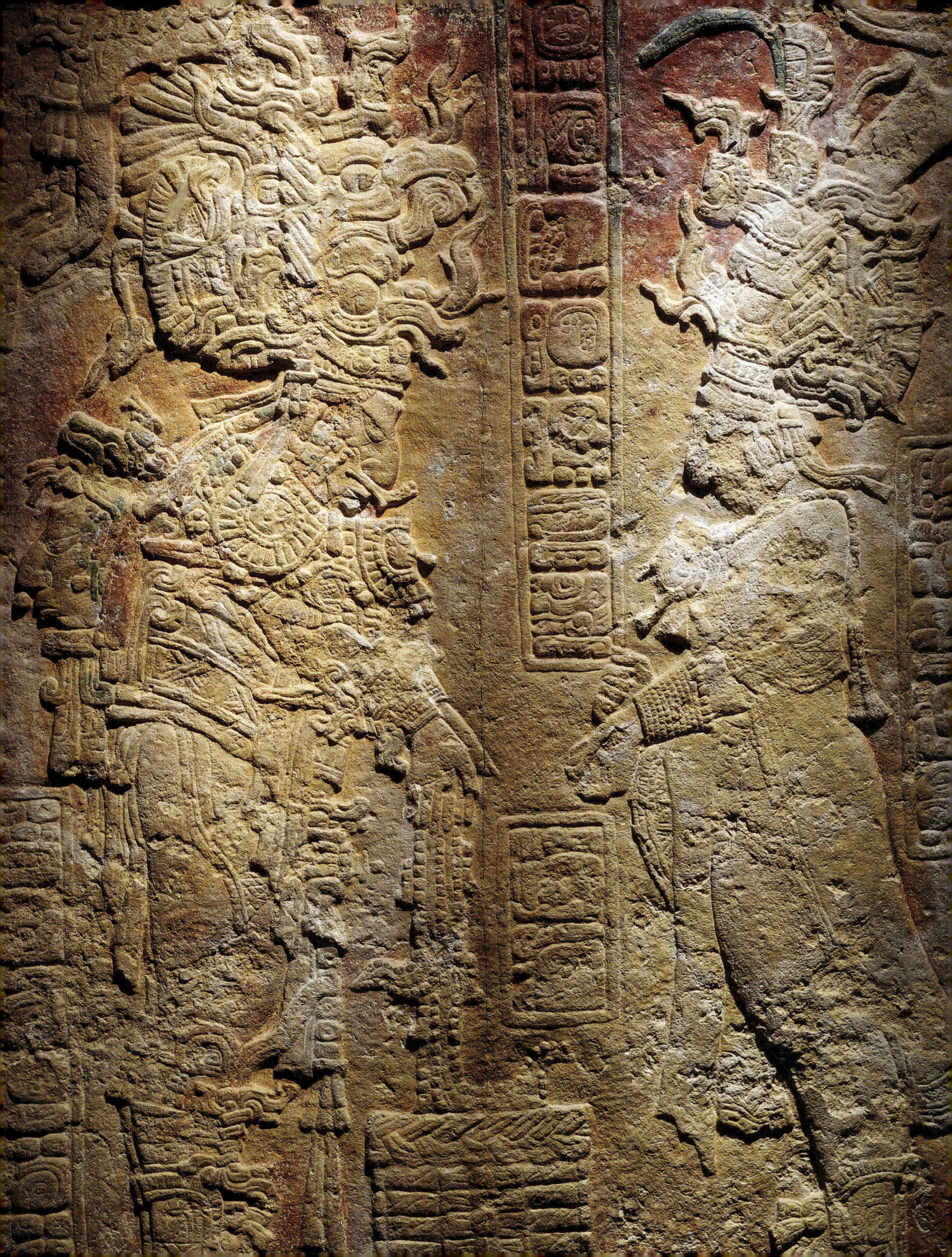

Ancestor skull

Mixteca-Puebla Style, Mexico
1400-1521
22.5 x 14.5 cm
bone (human skull), turquoise, shell, stone, quartz
RMV 4007-1 (1964)

Real, fake or a combination

This skull is inlaid with a mosaic of turquoise and Spondylus shell. The mosaic covers the face as well as the mandible. The skull probably belonged to a male of around 35 years of age, who lived in the highlands of the Mexican states of Oaxaca and Puebla. Research has shown that both the skull and the mosaic are of pre-colonial origin. However, further analysis has also confirmed that the glue, which fixes the mosaic to the skull is of modern origin. As a result, this 'ancestor skull' is probably a spurious combination of authentic elements.

Collecting history

The museum acquired this skull from a foreign art dealer in 1964. The purchase was arranged by the museum's then director, Dr P.H. Pott, who was enormously impressed by it – or 'obsessed' by it, according to one of his colleagues at the time. In a letter to the curators, Pott described the skull as an object of 'such exceptional value that I do not consider myself justified in turning this offer down'. Pott was right about the object's value; worldwide, only nine skulls of this type are known.

Isotope analysis

Unfortunately, since the skull was purchased from an art dealer, little is known about its precise origin. At the time of the sale, the dealer stated that the skull had been excavated at Teotitlan del Camino, a small town on the border of the Mexican states of Oaxaca and Puebla. The museum recently invited researchers from the Faculty of Archaeology of the University of Leiden to subject the skull to isotope analysis – a form of chemical research – to determine its origin. The research showed that the person concerned did indeed live in the region of Oaxaca and Puebla. Since there is a large archaeological site in the vicinity of Teotitlan del Camino, the skull may indeed originate from there.

Mixtecs

Teotitlan del Camino lies on the outskirts of the Mixtec region. The Mixtec people originated from the south of Mexico. Today, there are some 300,000 speakers of the Mixtec language, not only in southern Mexico but also in Mexico City and in the United States, where they have settled as migrant workers. In pre-colonial times, the Mixtecs were known as outstanding craftsmen, who particularly excelled as goldsmiths and in other kinds of metalworking, and made superb jewellery, using materials such as turquoise. They ruled for many years over the ancient city of Monte Albán, now one of Mexico's most famous archaeological sites.

Tomb Seven of Monte Albán

Only one of the nine known mosaic skulls comes from a documented excavation: the mosaic skull from Tomb Seven of Monte Albán. This famous tomb was opened and excavated in 1932 by the famous Mexican archaeologist Alfonso Caso. The tomb was one of the richest burial contexts ever found in Mesoamerica. On a raised platform was found one of the most remarkable objects in the tomb: a skull decorated with a turquoise mosaic. Diverse theories exist concerning the skull's significance, but it is probably related to ancestor worship and the oracular role of ancestors in Mesoamerican culture.

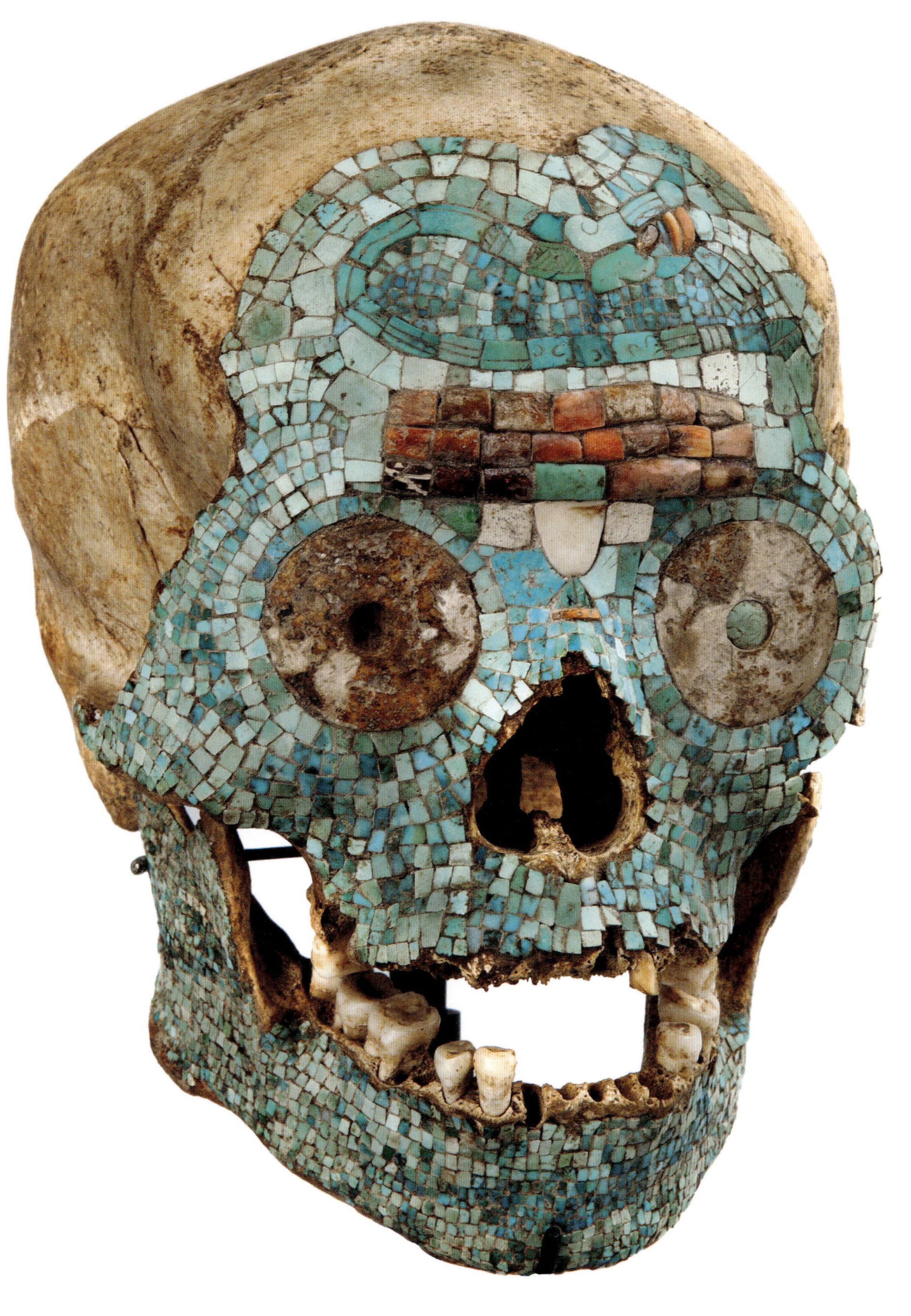

Coat

Cree, western Hudson Bay, Canada
c. 1700-1800
l. 116 cm
caribou skin, porcupine quills, dyes, glass beads, moose hair
RMV 4262-1 (1967)

Acquisition

This coat was donated to the museum in 1967 by the Frans Mortelmans Foundation, which was founded to keep the life and work of this Flemish artist in the public eye. From 1900 onwards, more and more European artists became interested in non-Western art. Among them was Frans Mortelmans, who purchased this painted Indian coat from the Amsterdam art dealer Louis Lemaire, who had bought it at Sotheby's auction house in London – unfortunately without provenance details.

Identification

A more precise determination of provenance was carried out by Sherry Farrell Racette of the University of Manitoba in Winnipeg. She studied painted caribou skin coats of this type, and inventoried sixteen similar items of clothing in European and Canadian museum collections. In some cases, the provenance data had been preserved. The coats proved to originate from the western part of Hudson Bay (the tribal territory of the Cree Indians), where the Hudson Bay Company opened branches from 1684 onwards, to trade with the indigenous population. A large part of this trade was in the hides of fur-bearing animals.

Frans Mortelmans

Frans Mortelmans was born in Antwerp in 1865. His father owned a small publishing and printing company. The liberal and rich cultural atmosphere at home led the young Lodewijk to become a composer and his elder brother Frans to become a painter. Frans studied at the Academy of Art in Antwerp and established a reputation as a painter of floral pieces and still lifes. He taught at the academy of Berchem and served as director there for several years. Frans Mortelmans died in 1936, and the ethnographic items in his estate reflect his interest in objects of non-Western origin.

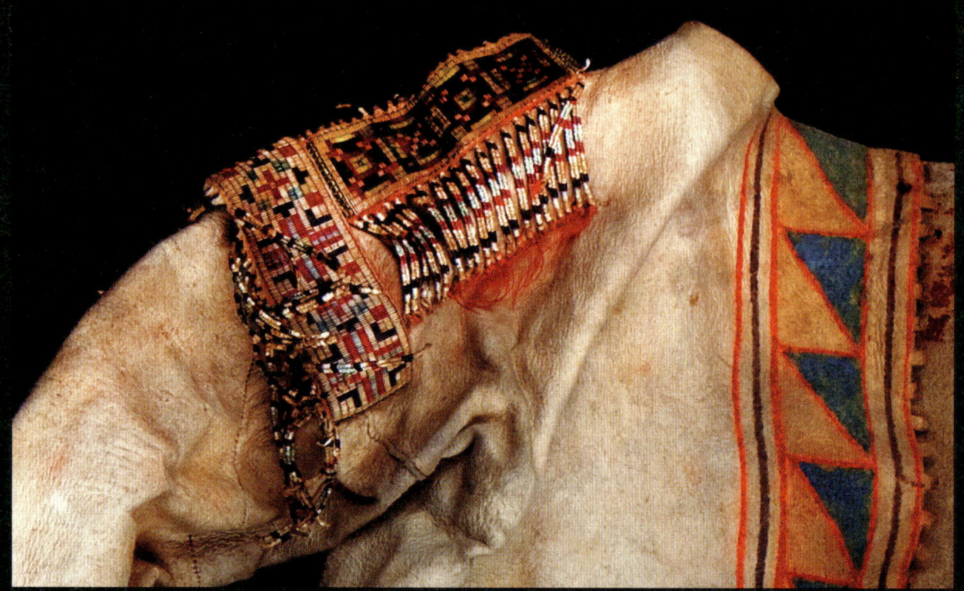

Provenance

The coat is made from a caribou hide. The likeliest place of origin is northern Canada, a theory that is supported by the fact that it was originally purchased in London, long the centre of government for British North America. Western and indigenous clothes were frequently exchanged in Canada. Army coats were distributed as gifts among Indian leaders, who wore them as status symbols. This led to modifications in Indian coats, which started to be cut in styles modelled on French or English ones. It seems likely that the coat displayed here was modelled on an English example and originates from the northern part of the trading territory of the Hudson Bay Company, whose head office was also in London.

Acculturation

The male population of the isolated trading posts in the Canadian wilderness generally married Indian women. This led to intercultural exchanges in clothing and other areas, and produced a mixed Indian-white population known as Métis. Although the coats were cut more and more in European styles, they continued to be painted with characteristic Indian motifs. The typical Western epaulets of gold thread were replaced with similar decorations made of painted porcupine quills that had traditionally been used to decorate Indian garments before the introduction of glass beads. But coats of this type were worn by both Indians and British Canadian men, and the latter in particular valued them for the protection they offered against the fierce cold in the extreme north.

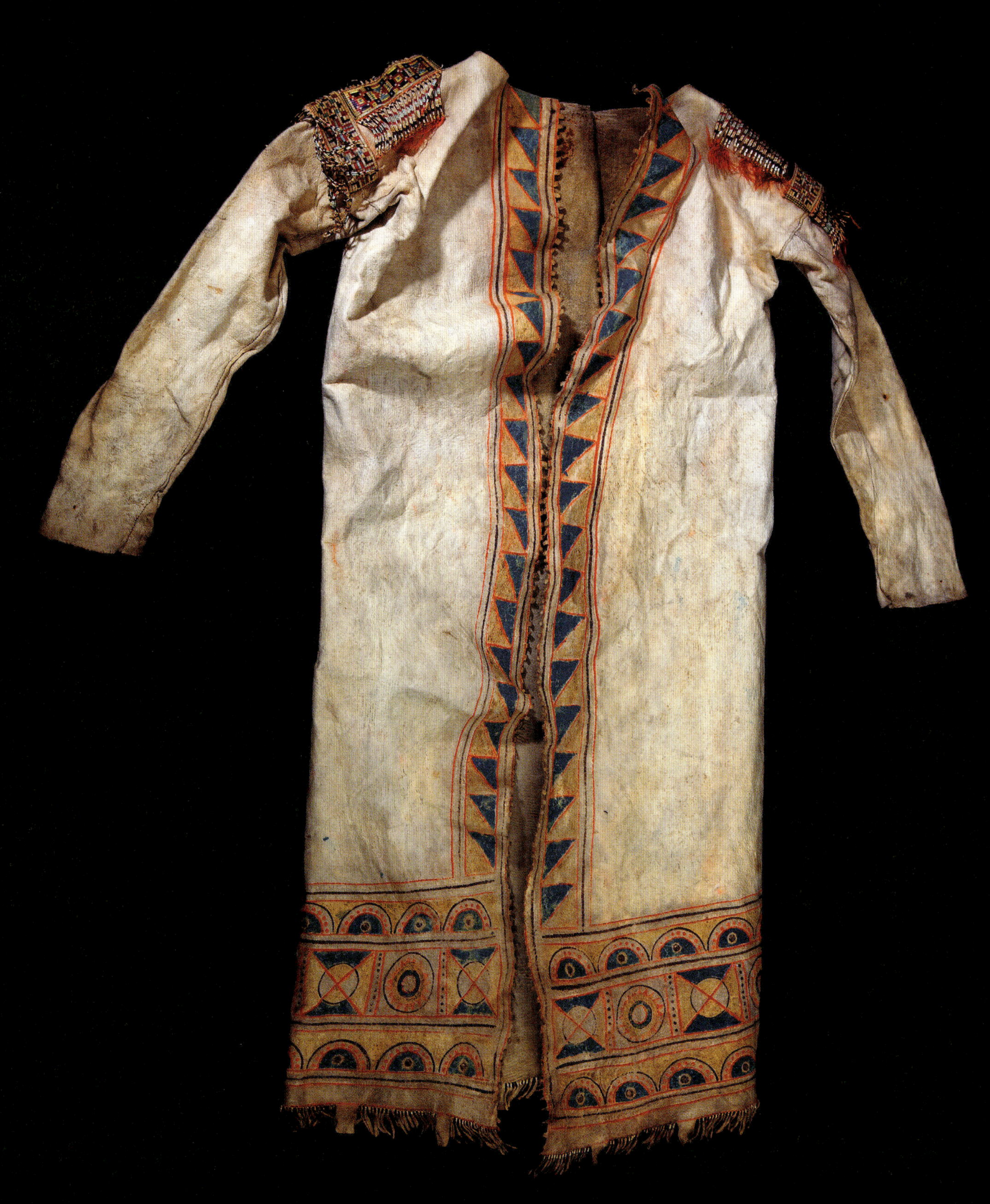

Bamboo tube (*Solep*)

Ngaju Dayak, Central Kalimantan, Indonesia
c. 1910
41.5 x 8 cm
bamboo
RMV 6063-1 (1969)

Expedition

As a missionary doctor in the service
of the Indonesian government, the
donor of this bamboo tube, Dr Arnoud
H. Klokke, travelled deep into the
hinterland around 1950, along the
rivers of Central Kalimantan, visiting
the remote villages of the Ngaju and
Ot Danum. As he toured the countryside by boat and on foot, combating
smallpox and yaws (an infectious
tropical disease), he became fascinated
by the culture of these Dayak tribes,
whose language he spoke. He took
superb photographs on his travels,
collected objects and stories, and
published about them. Thanks to his
scholarship, we have precise details of
the tube's provenance and the images
on it.

Pictorial story

The bamboo tube, solep, was carved
around 1910 by the adat chief Damang
Singa Kenting, in Tumbang Korik on
the tributary Hamputung, in the
upstream region of the Kahayan. In
1952 Klokke acquired the bamboo tube,
along with an explanation of its
significance, from a priest in Kuala
Kuron, who used the decorations to
hand down knowledge of the traditional
Kaharingan religion. Klokke saw an
identical tube in use in Sangal (on the
Rongan), at the wedding of a grandson
of Damang Singa Kenting. It was
displayed beneath a sacrificial altar
along with other sacred objects in the
family's possession.

Fish trap and offering basket

Depicted on one side of the bamboo
tube is a *mihing*. This is a very large fish
trap that is placed in the river, in a
tradition peculiar to the people of the
upper reaches of the Kahayan, towards
the end of the dry season. As the water
rises rapidly with the first heavy rainfall,
it creates eddies that drive the fish into
the trap. The *mihing* was also used in
rituals as a large offering basket. A *mihing*
would be placed in the middle of a
village, filled with gongs and martavan
pots (large earthenware pots), to ward
off disaster. Klokke heard the following
myth of the *mihing* from the village chief
of Tumbang Malahoi.

Myth of the *mihing*

On the upper reaches of the Kahayan
lived a man named Buwak. One day he
was taken to heaven, by a man named
Rawang Tempon Telon, and the two
men competed in trials of strength.
Buwak triumphed in bird hunting and
fishing and spied on his rival when the
latter was making a *mihing*, in which he
collected all sorts of heavenly treasures.
Once back on earth, Buwak too made a
mihing in the middle of the village, and
used it to entice the treasures collected
by Telon from the heavens to the earthly
region below. Telon made Buwak stop
using his basket, but he gave the people
of the upper reaches of the river
permission to use a *mihing* to catch fish.

The *mihing* depicted

According to the priest who once used
this *solep*, diverse episodes from this
myth are depicted on it. The man in the
proa, who is fishing in a river full of sea
creatures, fish, and water snakes from
the underworld, is Buwak. The *mihing* is
partly filled with martavan pots, gongs
and gems, precious treasures from the
heavens. Depicted on the *mihing*, seated,
is Rawing Tempon Telon, wearing a
headdress with two feathers of the
celestial rhinoceros hornbill. The mythological origins of the use of the *mihing* as
a fish trap, its ritual use, for instance as
an offering basket, and the connections
between the heavens, the world of
human beings, and the underworld, are
all beautifully illustrated on this tube.

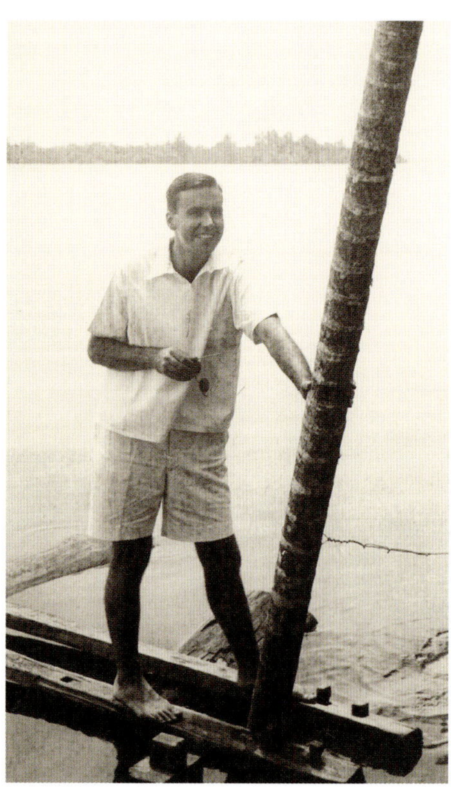

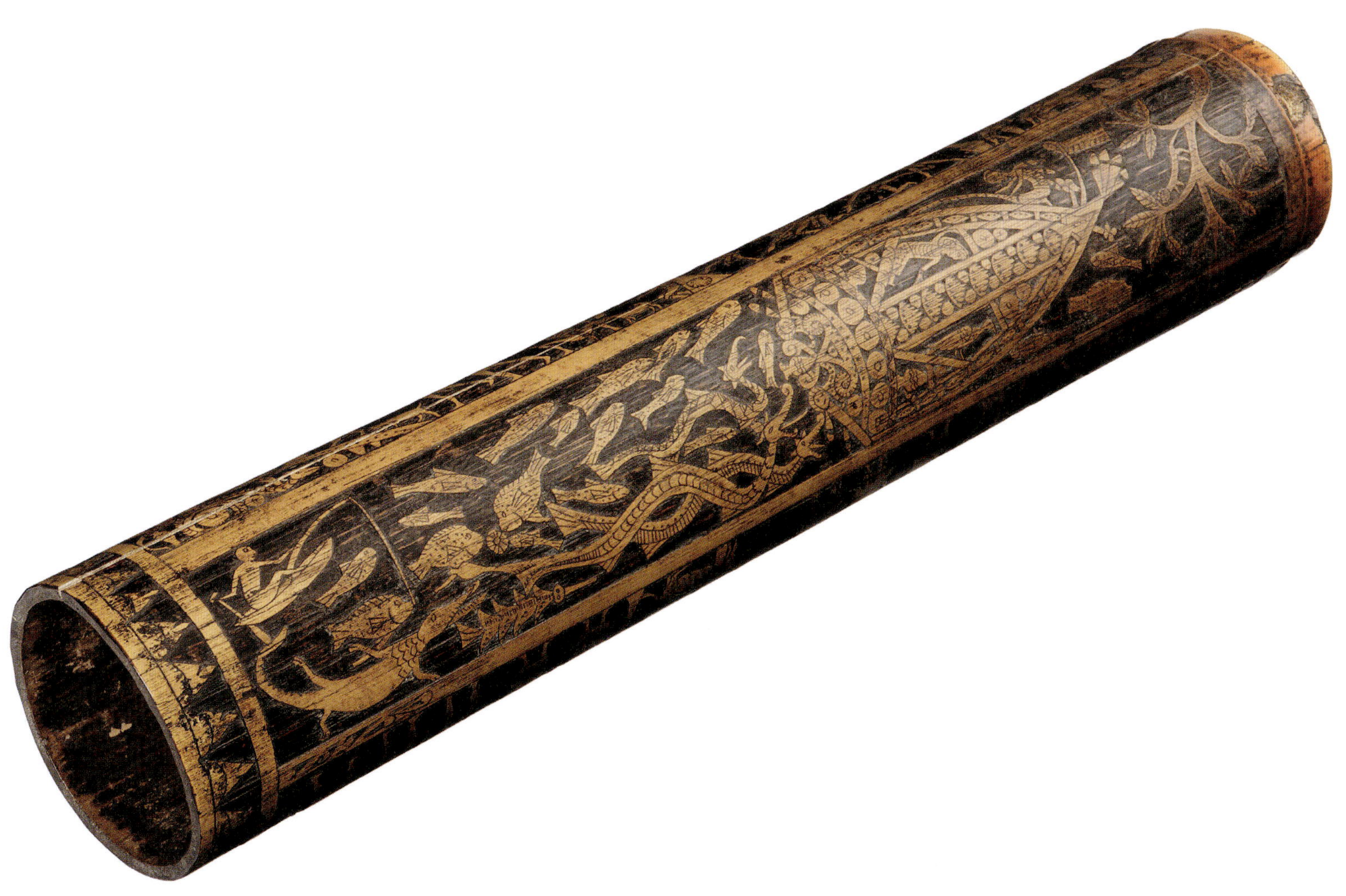

Board game (*Ganjifa*)

Mughal; Rajasthan, India
1700-1900
box: 16 cm x 7.5 cm; cards: diam. 8 cm
wood, material, varnish, paint, possibly paper
RMV 4559-1 (1972)

Board game and lady-in-waiting

There are several ways of playing *Ganjifa*. Roughly speaking, the aim is to collect as many cards as possible by playing those with the highest value, as many as possible in each game. Players sometimes play with more than one set at a time. A set consists of 96 or 120 cards, which are painted in the style of Rajasthan miniatures. The box is usually painted too, as it is here. The lid displays an elegant lady-in-waiting with a deer, while hunting scenes are depicted on the sides.

Popular form of recreation

The *ganjifa* board game was probably introduced into India by way of the court of the Mughal Akbar (reigned 1556-1605). It soon became a popular form of recreation, not only at court but throughout the population. It was often played for money. Other popular games included playing dice (*pachisi*) and chess. The great demand for *ganjifa* sets generated a whole new specialist occupation of *ganjifa* makers, known as *chitrakars*. Apprentices were assigned to making cards, while the more experienced craftsmen added figures, using templates, and the most gifted *chitrakar* painted the details. *Ganjifa* has gone out of fashion as a game, but the beautiful paintings have generated considerable demand for the sets as collector's items.

Emperor leads the pack

Mughal *ganjifa* sets usually consists of eight suits. There are twelve cards in each suit. The symbols used for the suits are variable and may include a crown, gold, silver, a harp, a sword, a slave or servant, generally depicted in an abstract shape. The highest card in each suit is the one depicting the ruler (*shah, mir or raja*) seated on an elephant, on a throne, or surrounded by servants wielding fans or other regal attributes. After the ruler comes the chief minister (*wazir, mantri or pradhan*), generally depicted mounted on a horse or a camel. The rest of the suit consists of numbered cards, the value of which is indicated by the number of symbols.

Dashavatara ganjifa

With the passage of time, a variant developed that was based on Hindu gods: *dashavatara ganjifa*. This game has only ten twelve-card suits, with suits divided up to reflect the incarnations of Vishnu. Other series depict scenes from the life of Krishna or Vishnu. Abstract shapes allude to the stars in the sky and to philosophical concepts. *Dashavatara* was particularly popular among *brahmans* (priests). It was believed to propitiate the gods, besides which it was an ideal way of training philosophical and mythological knowledge.

Luxury sets

Most *ganjifa* cards are cut from textile or paper that has been stiffened (for instance with glue mixed with tamarind seeds). Courtiers, however, favoured luxury sets carved from ivory, tortoise-shell, mother-of-pearl, gold, silver and leather. The game was especially popular in the ladies' rooms of the harem (*zenana*), as a means of combating boredom. The sets are painted in the style of the court concerned, or furnished with images produced with inlaid work.

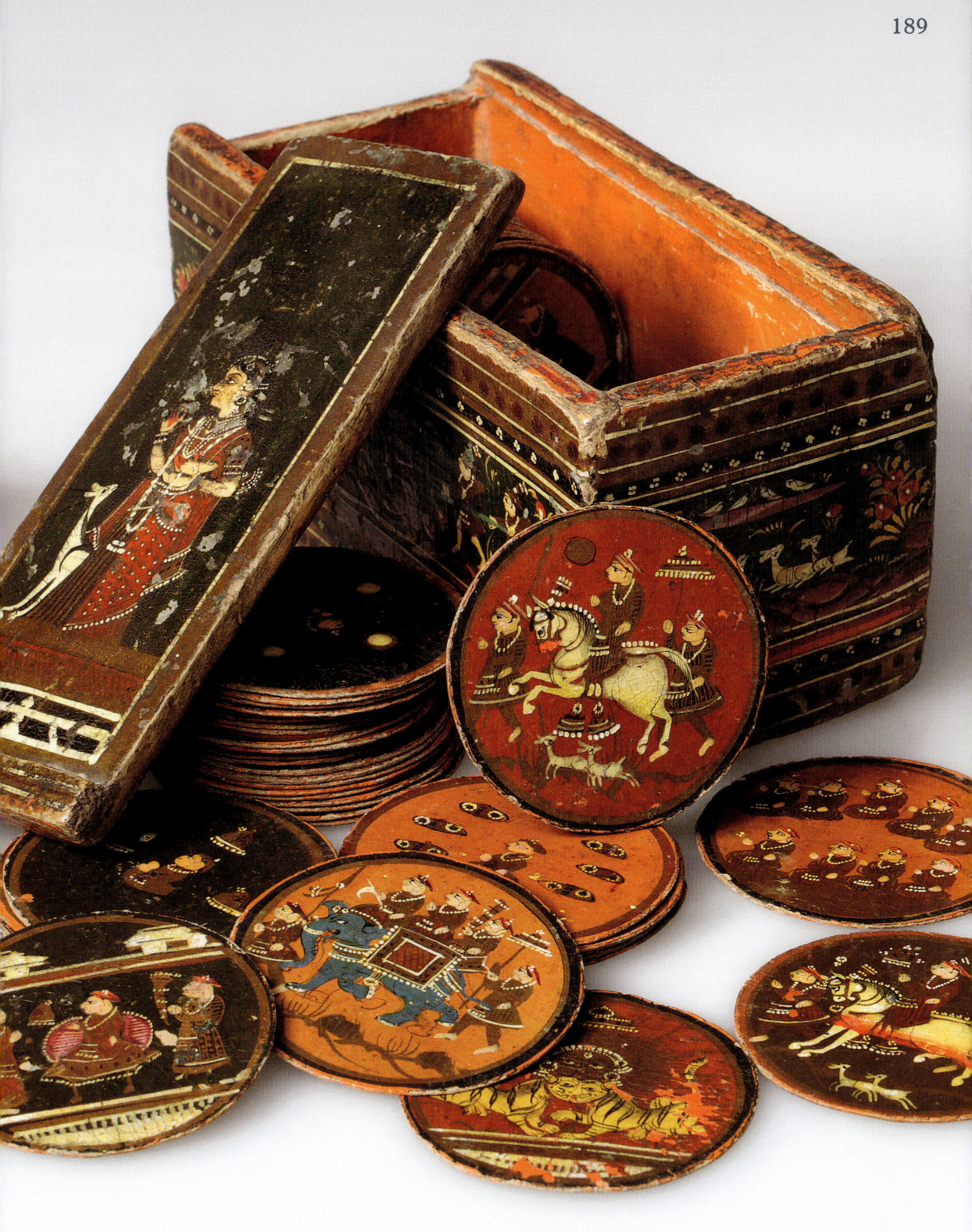

Three porcelain panels

Jingdezhen, China
17th century
23.8 x 37.5 x 1.1 cm
porcelain

RMV 4663-1, RMV 4663-2, RMV 4663-3 (1973)

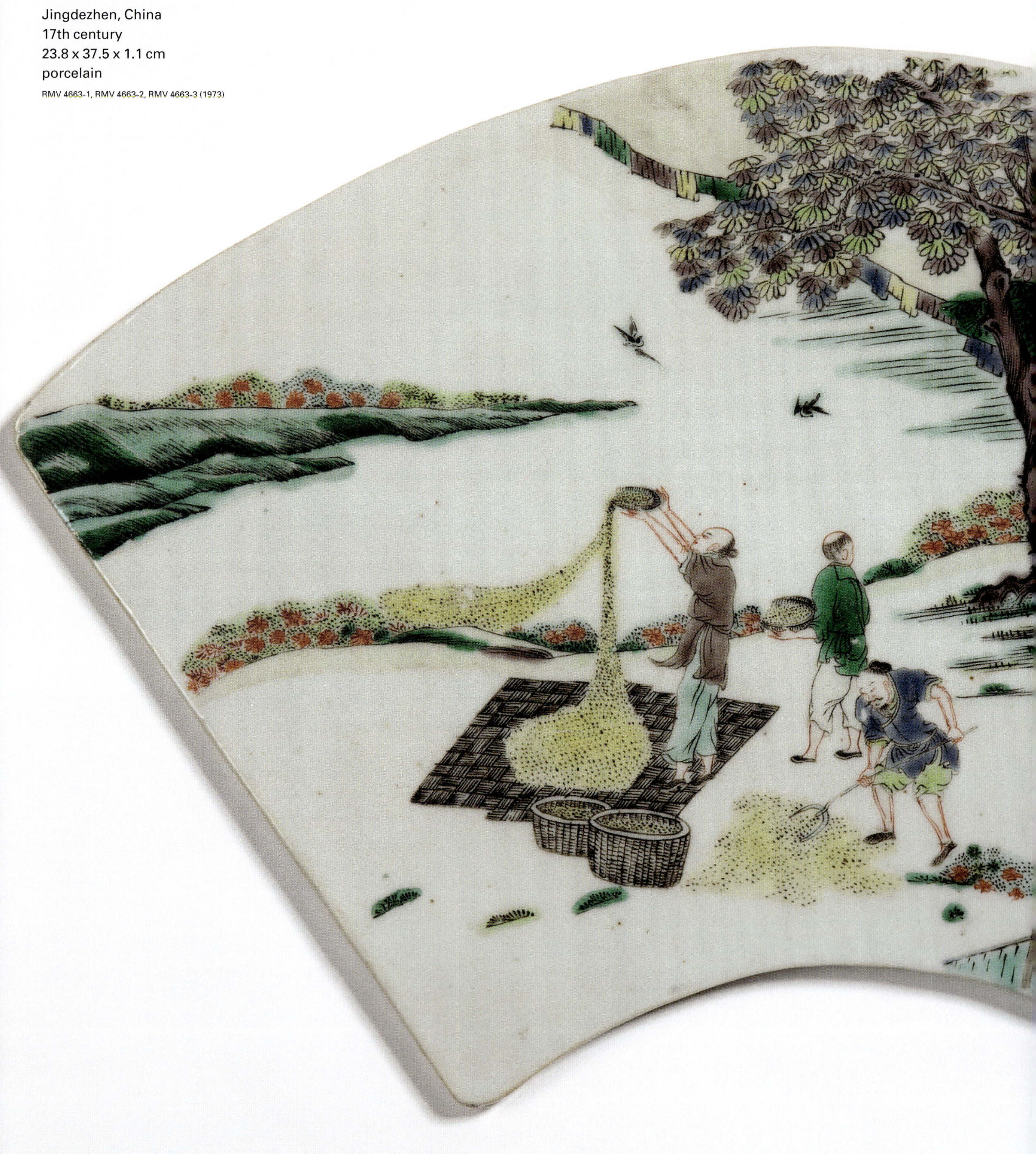

Famille verte

These three robust porcelain plaques are glazed white on one side. Enamelled on these white backgrounds are scenes of people engaged with various farming activities in a clean and somewhat ornate landscape of south China. The enamel colours include green, yellow, black, blue, red and aubergine, but green predominates, hence the categorisation of "green palette", now long established in the French description *famille verte*. The more interesting traditional description in Chinese is "hard colours" (*yingcai*), which refers to the colours' density. Some of the enamel – usually the green – has fallen off.

Jingdezhen

These plaques were made most probably in the late 17th century at Jingdezhen, then – and now – China's premier centre for porcelain production in today's Jiangxi province. This period witnessed a resurgence of Jingdezhen's industry and its product distribution following the disruption of the Ming dynasty's collapse in 1644. The production of items decorated in *famille verte* colours was a highly successful innovation that soon gained huge market affinity in Europe. The first European collectors purchased this type of imported porcelain at brisk auctions in Amsterdam before other Western maritime centres overtook the Dutch lead in East Asian trade.

Chinese poetry

The images on these plaques appear also in hundreds of editions of an illustrated collection of poems entitled *Depictions of Ploughing and Weaving (Gengzhi tu)*. First commissioned in the early 12th century, these benign images of men and women at work – sometimes overseen by their landlords – were frequently reproduced in new paintings, woodblock imprints, stone engravings, and further remediated as images to decorate lacquer and porcelain. The Kangxi emperor's (1662-1722) commission of yet another album edition may have promoted a fashion for this uncontroversial subject matter at the same time that Jingdezhen was making its economic recovery.

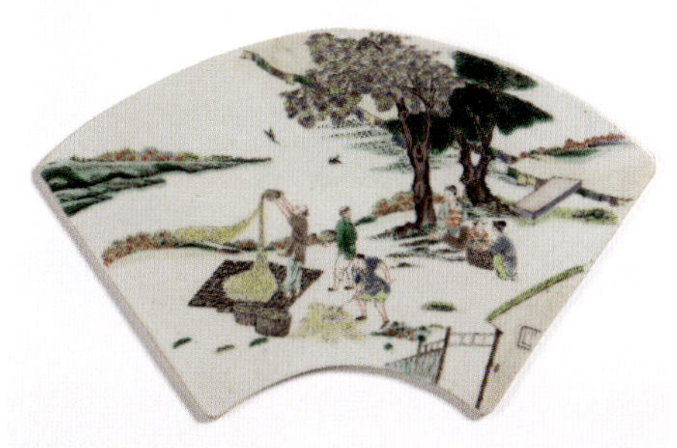

Domestic decoration

These plaques probably once numbered more than three. They formed a set used for domestic decoration. A set of chairs, couches, folding screens or solid partitions could have provided vertical support for the plaques to appear in their total display. The 12th cenury edition of the *Gengzhi tu* included 21 images of agriculture and 24 images of silk production, but it is unlikely that the carpenters who worked with these images cared about reproducing exactly the same total as that of the famous image series.

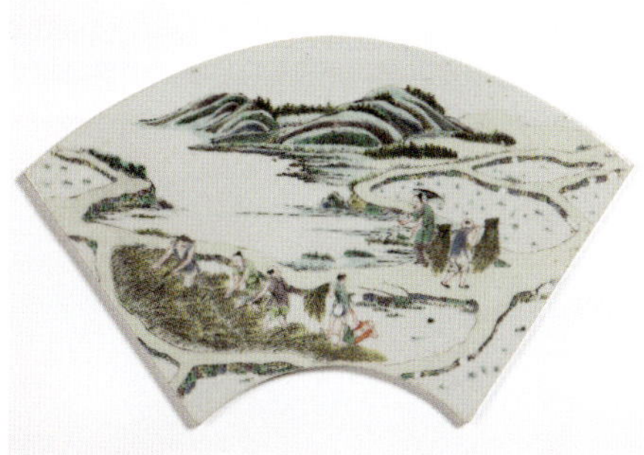

Rich imagery

These plaques exploit several interesting visual references from both art and the world of book publishing. The literary content and its visualization is from books, and the plaques' fan shape is borrowed from a utensil that was conventionally painted or inscribed, not to mention remounted as a page in an album. The larger point is that images in China during the early modern period travelled with increasing rapidity along circuits that crossed and merged with each other. Within this rich image economy certain narrow ranges of visual content were deployed across media and consumed in quite diverse social settings.

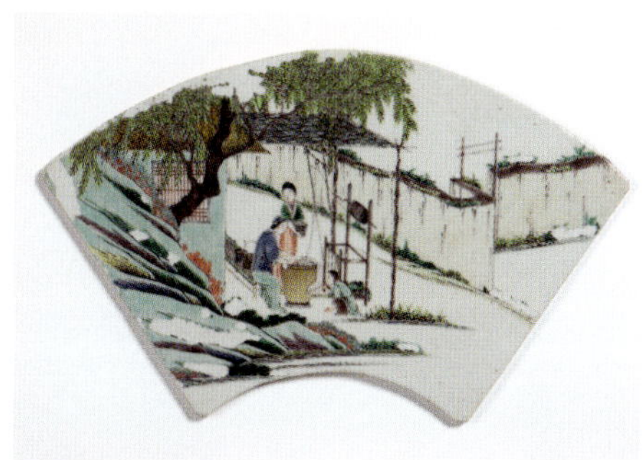

Model of a ball court

Nayarit, Mexico
AD 300-500
8 x 38 x 18 cm
pottery
RMV 4819-1 (1975)

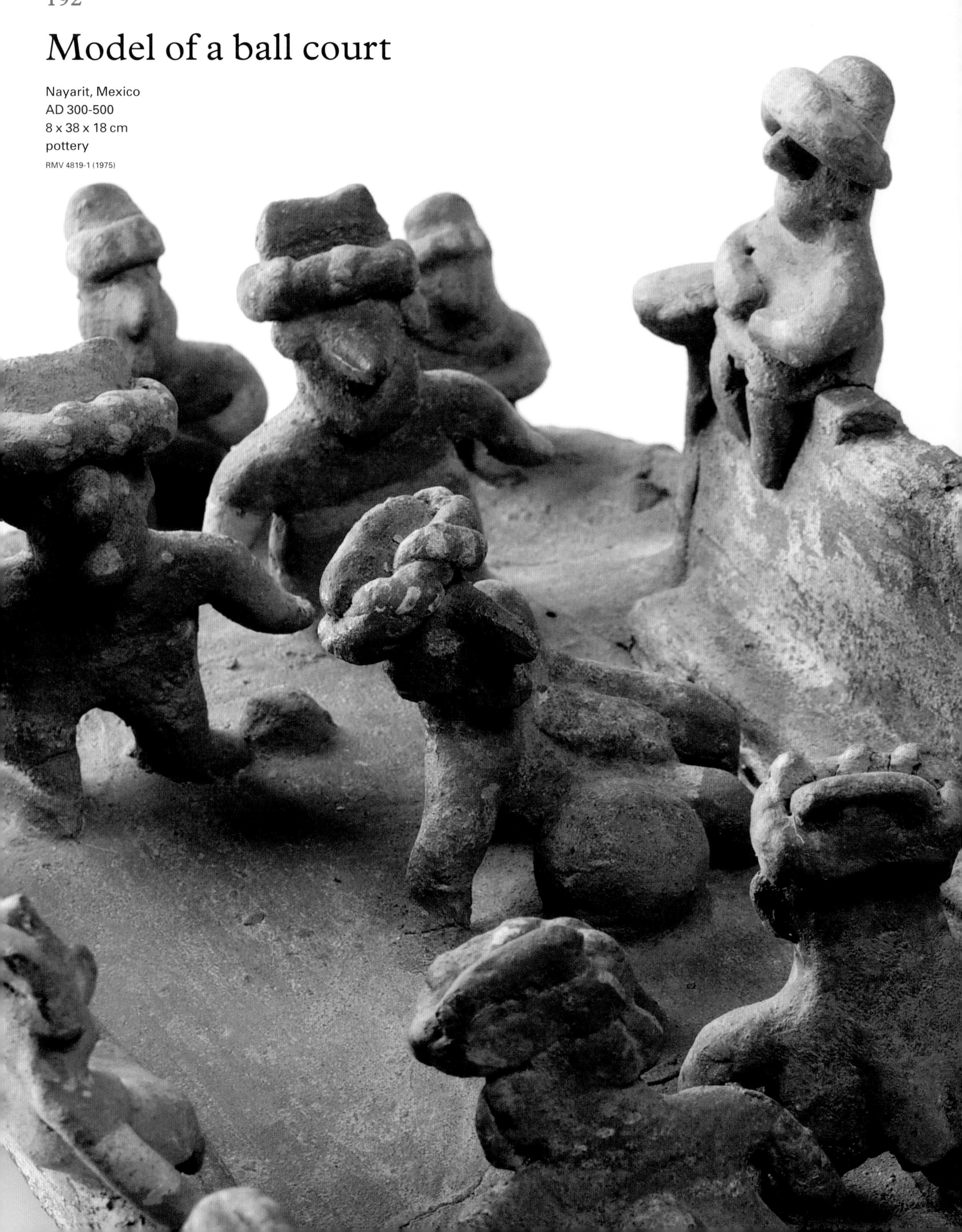

The Mesoamerican ball game

In Mesoamerica, a region that extended from northern Mexico to Costa Rica, the 'Mesoamerican ball game' was played until the arrival of the Spanish. The game was played with a solid rubber ball that could only be touched with the hip. To avoid injury, players wore protective clothing, including chest and hip protectors made of leather or wood. The courts resembled stadiums and were shaped like an elongated capital I. At archaeological sites, they are often found within the ceremonial centre. This tells us that the ball games possessed a certain religious significance as well as an element of play, in which the result was deemed decisive for the future of the gods and the people.

Western Mexico

This miniature comes from a grave in western Mexico and dates from about AD 300 to 500. In the period from about 200 BC to AD 500, the archaeology of western Mexico is characterised by the Nayarit, Colima and Jalisco styles. These pottery styles, of which it is not known for sure whether they belonged to one or several peoples, are part of the shaft tomb tradition of western Mexico, which is known, among other things, for its elaborate cult of the dead.

Shaft tombs

These shaft tombs are vertical shafts, extending to a depth ranging from 3 to an astonishing 20 metres, dug out of the volcanic soil. Bodies lie interred in one or more chambers dug out horizontally at the bottom of each shaft. The deceased were probably members of prominent families or noble 'dynasties'. These tombs are remarkable, quite aside from the enormous effort it must have taken to construct such large shafts and chambers, for the wealth of burial gifts deposited with the dead. These burial gifts consist of a wide variety of small earthenware figurines decorated with scenes from the life of the deceased, such as the ball game, rituals, images of warriors, and processions.

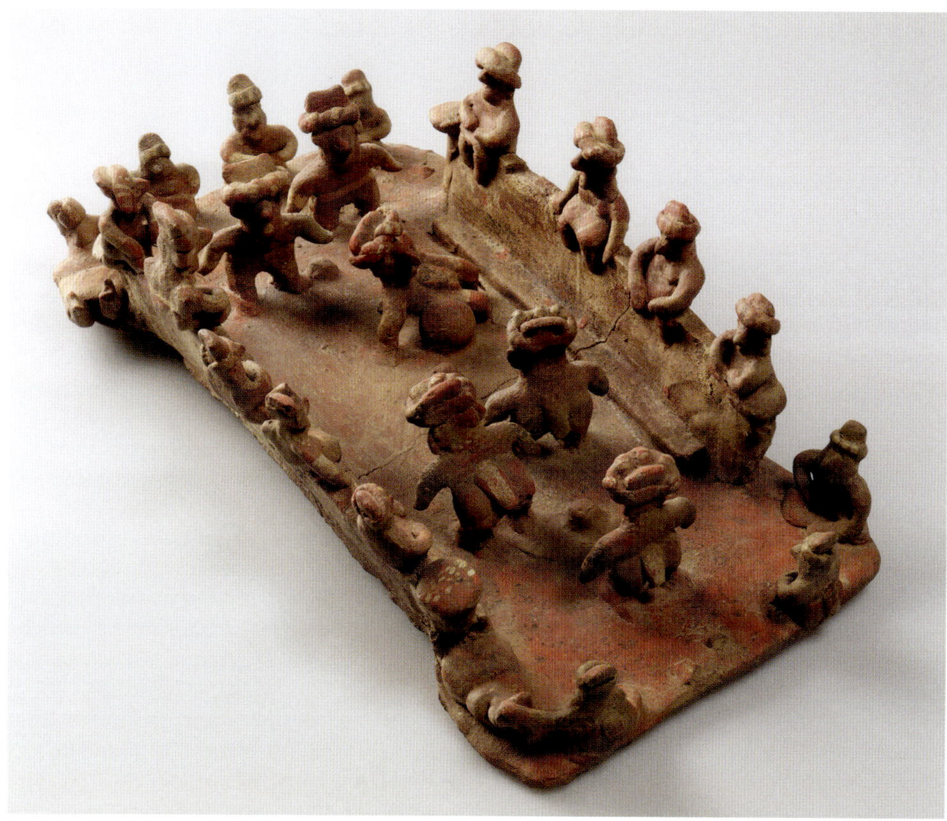

Present-day ball games

Diverse indigenous ball games are still played in Mexico today. The best known is the game *ulama*, which is still played in the state of Sinaloa, in the northwest of Mexico. *Ulama* is a hip ball game that derives directly from the hip ball game played by the Aztecs, who called it *ollama*. Why this ball game has survived into the twenty-first century only in the remote northwest is unknown. The Rijksmuseum Volkenkunde has been carrying out research on the ball game since the 1970s. This research focuses primarily on *ulama* and on the Mixtec ball game and its transnational variants in the US and Mexico.

Ball court

This miniature representation of a ball court shows six players in action. One is playing the ball – depicted exaggeratedly large – across the field with his hip. The court is demarcated with three marking stones. These stones are often found in archaeological contexts. Lengthwise, the court is bounded by tall walls. On these walls, and at the open ends of the court, are seventeen spectators.

Mother-and-child figure

Matjemos; Asmat; Southwest New Guinea, Indonesia
1970
68 cm
wood, lime pigment and red ochre
RMV 4928-9 (1977)

Mother-and-child figure

This statue represents a standing female figure carrying a child on her shoulders. Both figures have their arms raised and clasp their hands together. The child's arms merge seamlessly into a kind of headdress and its legs firmly grip its mother's neck. The statue has been carved from a single piece of light wood and coloured with lime.

Fumeripitsj, the Asmat hero

The statues were originally related to the practice of headhunting, the purpose of which was to safeguard the vital forces of the community. Since the Asmat believe that there are close ties between people and trees, the felling of a tree is likened to the killing of a man. In the creation myth, the heroic Asmat ancestor Fumeripitsj plays a central role in this idea. He built the first men's house and placed wooden statues in it that came to life when he played his drum. When a new men's house is built, dancers act out this creation myth. They start off in a lifeless, squatting pose, and then slowly come to life in response to the rhythm of the drums.

Ancestral figure

Ancestors are often depicted on Asmat carved work such as bis poles, prows and soul ships. This is an independent figure, however, which depicts a specific ancestor. Woodcarvers make ancestral figures at the request of the deceased's relatives. Virtually all the figures in sculptures are depicted either standing or squatting. They provide a material image of the person who has died, and are preserved in the men's house, which is a feature of every Asmat village. In this house, the men of the community discuss village politics, make plans and decisions regarding a range of village affairs, and maintain contact with their ancestors. Because of the tropical climate conditions, each men's house must be rebuilt every three to five years.

The journey to the afterlife

Ancestral statues are used at a range of festivities to reinvigorate the people's contact with the world of the ancestors. After the festivities, the statues are sometimes preserved temporarily in the men's house or left out in the sago forest to rot. One of the celebrations at which ancestral figures play a role is the inauguration of a new men's house. On these occasions, those who have died quite recently, who are present as ancestral figures, will be commemorated. This provides a tangible way for relatives to bid farewell to their loved ones and to send them on their journey to the realm of the ancestors.

Matjemos

This statue by Matjemos was acquired by the anthropologist Adrian A. Gerbrands, who researched the individual stylistic features of Asmat woodcarving in 1961 and 1970. The artistic evolution of Matjemos's style between 1961 and 1970, the year in which this statue was carved, is obvious. Stylistic similarities include the raised arms with the hands clasped together, and the pose of the main figure, as well as the deep-set eyes and sharp mouth. But there are also significant differences: the later statue is far more dynamic and naturalistic, with the child gripping the woman's neck, the space created between the carved feet and the block of wood, and the depiction of the bones of the fingers.

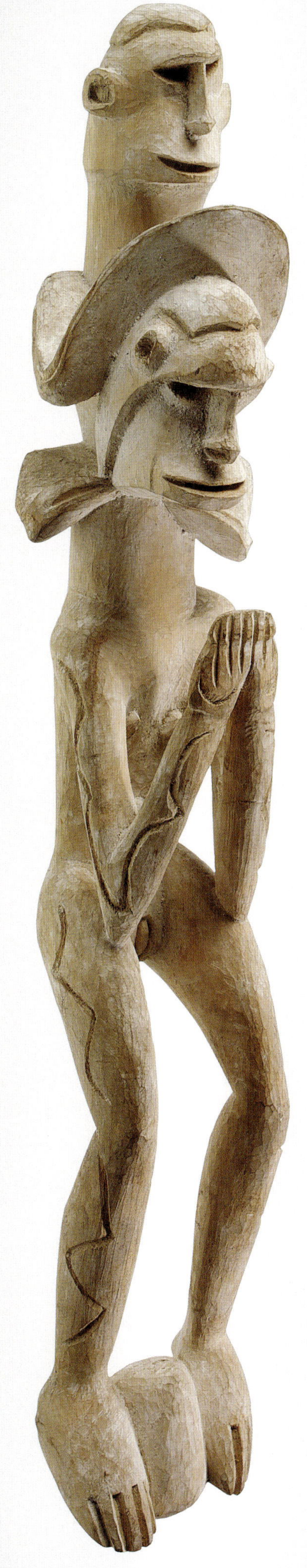

Amulet holder in the form of a pendant

Turkmenistan
late 19th-early 20th century
31 x 32 cm
silver alloy, gold, carnelian, cotton
RMV 5179-1 (1982)

Amulet pendant
Unlike urban women, women from nomadic communities in Turkestan wore their frequently heavy, conspicuous jewellery quite visibly on their clothing. Such items were part of the dowry a girl brought to her marriage, to which she would add new pieces in times of affluence. This impressive item of jewellery, to be worn on the breast, has a religious as well as a decorative function. The tube (*bozbend*) is an amulet holder, and can be used to contain rolled-up pieces of paper with religious texts or small stones. The surface of the amulet-holder is decorated with stylised floral and foliate motifs. The red of the carnelians, which are mounted in silver, stands out against the fire-gilt background and recurs in the cotton strands from which the pendant hangs.

Pounds of extra weight
Women would first wear this type of jewellery at their wedding, as a sign of the transition from girl to married woman. Once they were married, women could show them off on festive occasions, flaunting their status and wealth by wearing jewellery weighing many pounds on their head, neck and back and in their braided hair, as well as in the form of bracelets and rings. This portable silver, gold and carnelian could be turned into currency in times of scarcity. Within the nomadic culture, it was crucial that items of great economic value were easy to transport.

Magical powers
Different kinds of powers were associated with the different shapes of elements of items of jewellery. The triangular upper section, which symbolises a mountain, stands for regeneration. The pointed projections that banish evil refer here to the underworld. And the sound of little bells also serves to keep evil powers at bay. The magical power of the amulet-holder would be enhanced by the addition of religious and medicinal texts, preferably taken from the Qur'an. Colour too confers power. Red carnelian was believed to protect the wearer from miscarriage and disease. In addition, red is associated with joy and fertility.

Turkmens
Large, heavy silver jewellery of this kind was very popular among the women of Turkmen nomad tribes such as the Tekke, Yomud, Ersari, Sarik and their subgroups. To initiates, it conveyed a wealth of information: on the wearer's ethnic identity, her status, social position and circumstances. In this piece, for instance, the combination of fire-gilding and mounts with red carnelians indicates that the item was used within the Tekke tribe. Its size, and above all its weight, reflected the family's assets. In the case of men, their weapons and the use of precious metals in harnesses served to denote their fortune.

Fire-gilding
Tekke jewellery is characterised by the use of fire-gilding on silver and mounts with carnelian semiprecious stones. Fire-gilding involves the application of an amalgam of mercury and gold to the surface of a metal piece of jewellery. Heating the amalgam causes the mercury to evaporate and fixes the layer of gold in place. This form of gilding is highly resistant to oxidation. In the nineteenth century, Turkmen tribes would regularly purchase large quantities of silver jewellery from the proceeds gained from plundering villages. In the same period, tribute imposed to fund war was also often paid in jewellery.

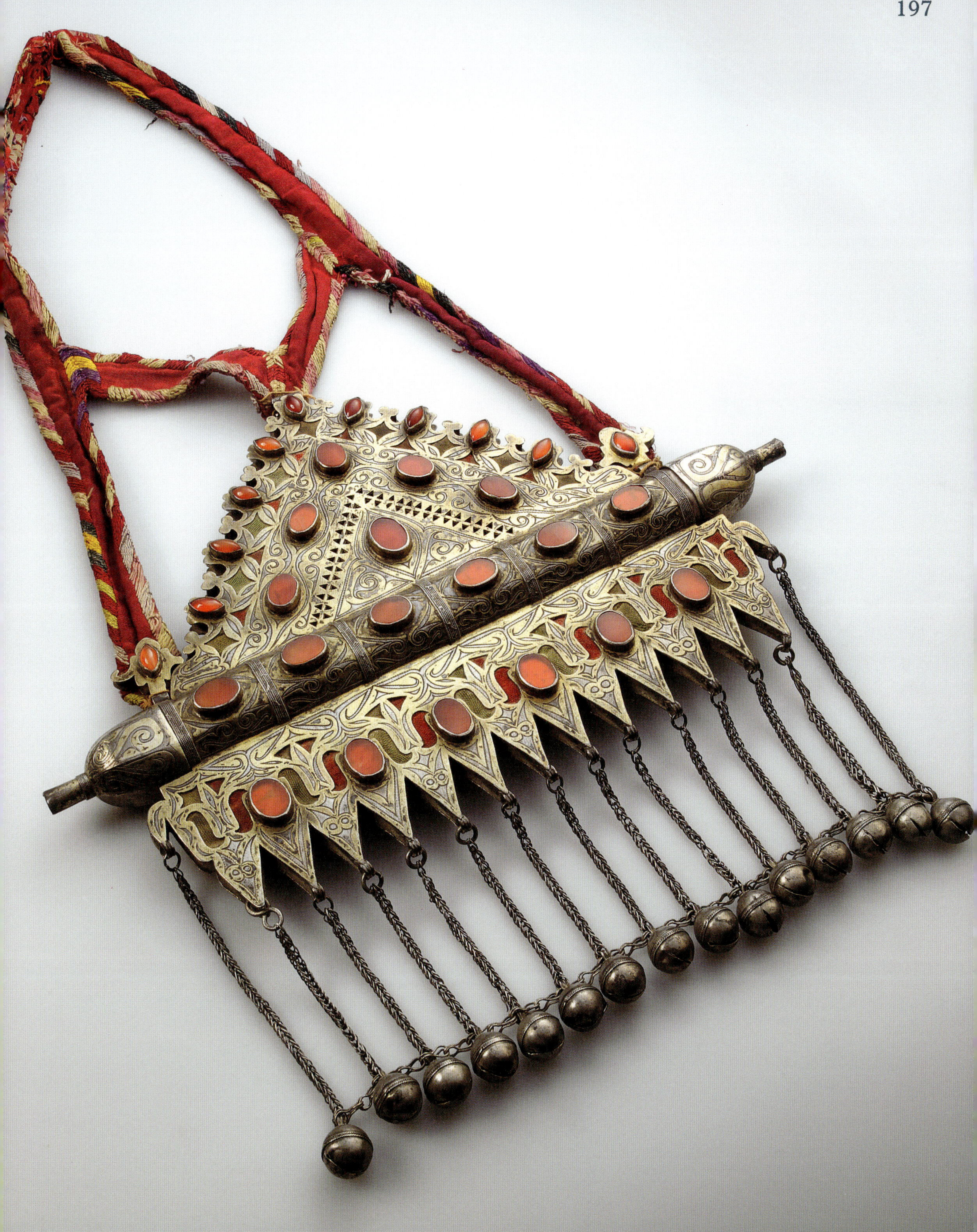

Vedic fire sacrifice set

Kerala, India
1975
16.5 x 28 cm
pottery, *ukha* and *shiras*
RMV 5403-32, RMV 5403-33d (1985)

Agnicayana fire sacrifice

From 12 to 24 April 1975, seventeen priests gathered in the Indian state of Kerala to perform the oldest ritual in the world, Agnicayana. In honour of the Vedic fire god Agni, they recited mantras that are thousands of years old, drank the sacred beverage Soma, and presented their sacrificial offerings, adhering closely to the prescribed rules, in sacrificial altars constructed especially for the purpose, the most important of which was made of bricks and shaped like a large bird with outstretched wings. The duplicate sacrificial implements made on this occasion were given to scholars from Leiden who had attended the ritual and brought to the Rijksmuseum Volkenkunde in 1985.

Media event

One of those present was Frits Staal, who was then professor of South and Southeast Asian Studies at the University of Berkeley in California. Staal studied ancient Vedic texts and was curious to know whether the knowledge they contained was still actively being passed on. He discovered a community of Nambudiri priests in Kerala in which verses that were thousands of years old had been transmitted orally for generations. Staal persuaded them to perform the Agnicayana ritual and obtained their permission to film the event with a group of academics and the filmmaker Robert Gardner. A large proportion of the costs, over 75,000 dollars, was covered by funds raised by Staal. The Rijksmuseum Volkenkunde was one of the sponsors. Several factors turned the ritual into a huge media event.

Controversy

Religious Hindus saw the presence of outsiders at the sacrificial ritual, and the filming of it, as sacrilegious. The event was also criticised by Communists, who protested against the funding by 'Western capitalist big business'. But the biggest controversy of all related to the sacrifice itself. The Vedic scriptures prescribe the sacrifice of a goat, but killing animals is completely contrary to the precepts of present-day Hinduism. The Brahmans decided to modify the ritual, and sacrificed effigies of goats made out of palm leaves and rice instead of live animals.

Frits Staal

Professor Staal (1930-2012) was an outstanding and independent thinker. He studied mathematics, physics and philosophy at the University of Amsterdam in the 1950s, after which he spent three years studying philosophy at a university in Madras. Since he combined Western and Asian philosophy in his thinking, Staal was able to forge innovative relationships between linguistics, mathematics and philosophy. This inspired him to make more advanced comparative studies of centuries-old Indian concepts and aspects of the Western intellectual legacy.

Sacred fire

The ritual involves fire being taken to the sacrificial ground in three pots. One of the most important ritual objects is a clay pot or ukha, in which the fire is lit on the bird-shaped altar. The heads (*shiras*) of a human being and four animals (male goat, bull, ram and horse) also play a role here. The *yajamana* (person who performs the sacrifice and sponsors the ritual) places the *ukha* and *shiras* on the bird-shaped altar, with all the appropriate ritual actions, so that they can be built into it. In a final sacrifice, the altars and all the instruments used – including the *ukha* – are destroyed. Afterwards, three pots of fire are taken to the home of the *yajamana*, who must ensure that the fires are kept burning there. At the time, the set displayed here was made especially for the museum, as an exact duplicate of the original implements.

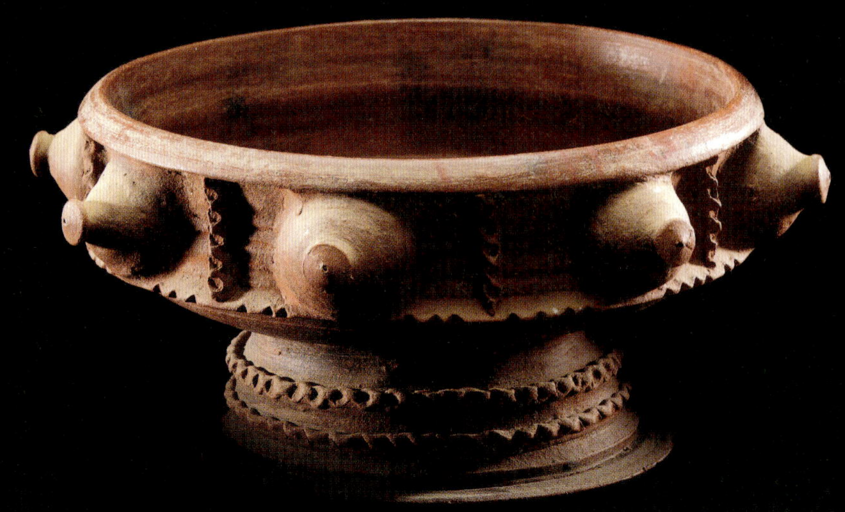

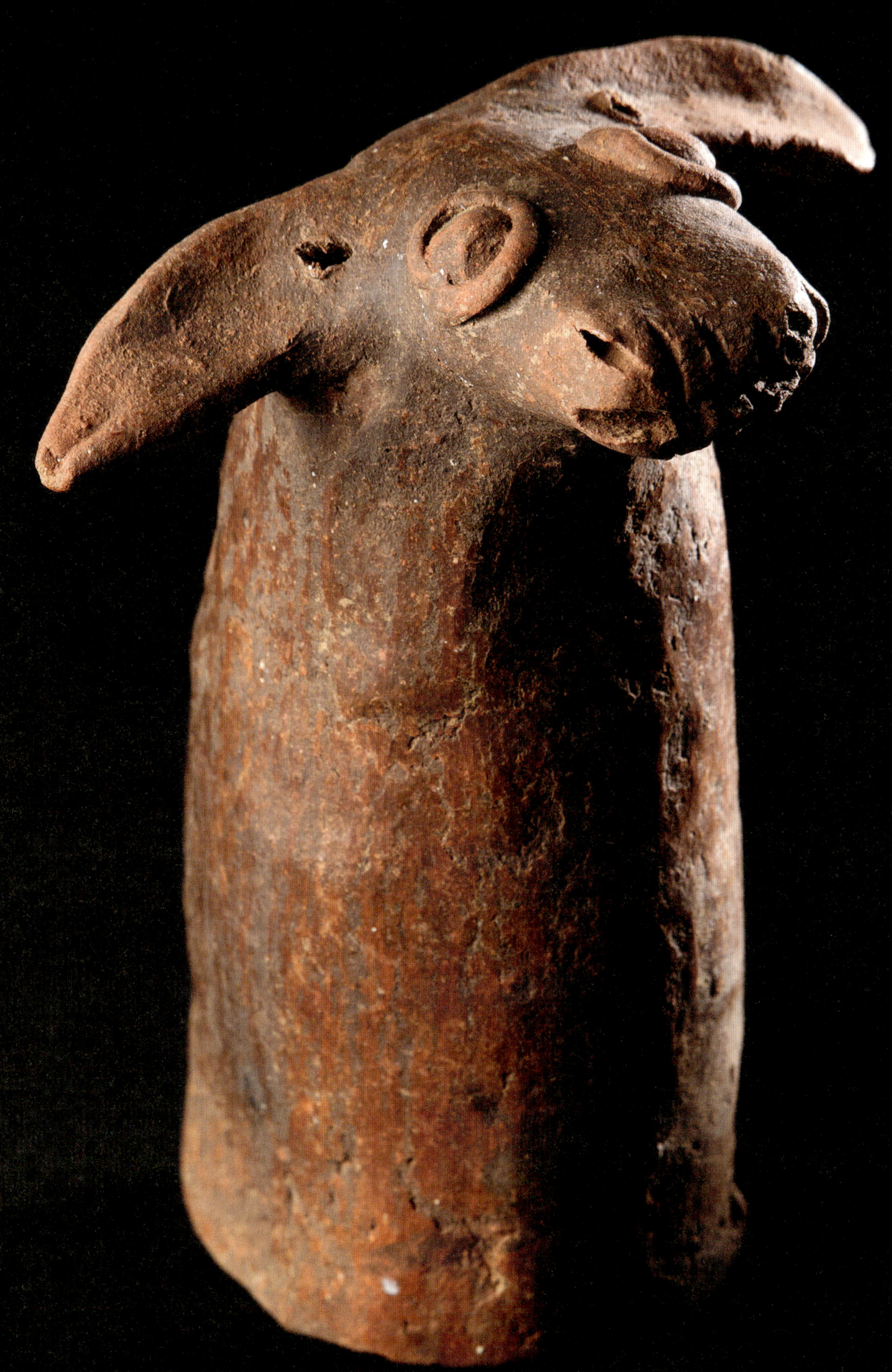

Figure of an organ-grinder (*Calavera*)

Mexico
1990
h. 135 cm, b. 50 cm
papier-mâché
RMV 5658-3a (1991)

Organ-grinder

This skeletal organ-grinder figure is made of papier-mâché. The paper is glued together with a wheat paste. Once the papier-mâché has hardened, a layer of white paint is applied, after which the figure is painted. Figures of this kind were made for the festival of the Day of the Dead in Mexico and are known as *calaveras*. This figure was made by members of the Linares family of Mexico City.

Linares Family

The Linares family is one of Mexico's best-known artist families, and it specialises in papier-mâché figures. Although the family first made these products in the late nineteenth century, it is to Don Pedro Linares (1906-1992) that the family owes its fame. He effected the transition from traditional pieces for village parties to art objects that are displayed in galleries and exhibitions around the world. His sons and grandsons have continued the family business and their figures are in considerable international demand. Their work is so instantly recognisable that the Mexican government uses some of the family's pieces in international contexts as emblems for Mexico.

Día de los Muertos

The festival 'Día de los Muertos' (Day of the Dead), which is celebrated on 1 and 2 November, is Mexico's best-known public holiday. At this festival, the souls of the deceased briefly return to earth. Relatives visit the graves of their loved ones, decorate them with marigolds and other flowers, and leave bread, fruit, drinks and delicacies behind for the dead. It is an occasion for eating the special sweet bread known as *pan de muertos* and little sugar skulls. In addition, the altar at home is embellished with everything the deceased enjoyed, from Coca Cola to whiskey and *tamales*. Graves and home altars are decorated with these *calaveras*. The papier-mâché sculptures depict recognisable scenes and characters, such as an organ-grinder, a taco-seller, or a mariachi band.

Pre-Columbian elements

Although Día de los Muertos is officially a Catholic holiday, its celebrations combine Catholic and pre-Columbian elements. Ancestor worship was an important part of ritual life among the Aztecs. Sixteenth-century Spanish descriptions of Mexico refer to festivities dedicated to ancestors. These include a description of the Aztec festival Miccailhuitl ('Great Feast of the Dead'), at which food and drink were placed on the tombs of the deceased, a ritual that is still common to this day.

Ted J.J. Leyenaar

This piece was acquired by Ted Leyenaar (1935-2009), who studied archaeology at the University of Leiden and specialised in pre-Columbian America. In 1963 he attended the National School of Anthropology and History in Mexico City. After graduation he accepted a position at the Rijksmuseum Volkenkunde in 1965, as curator of Central and South American collections. During his period as curator, he made frequent journeys to the region, especially to Mexico, and the collection grew tenfold. He became interested in present-day cultures, and the ways in which ancient traditions survive in the material culture of the indigenous peoples today. This continuity became the leitmotif of Leyenaar's collecting policy.

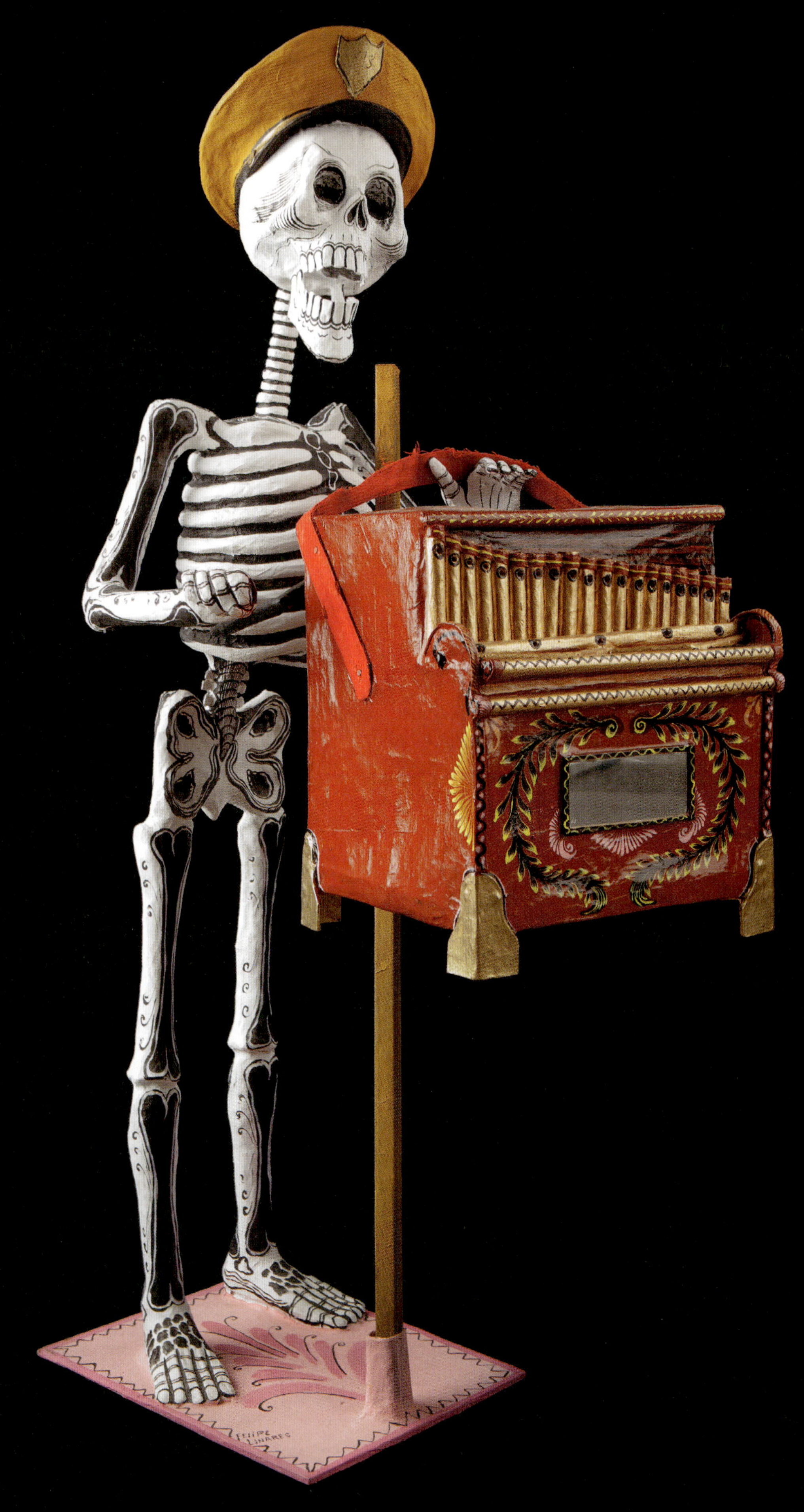

FELIPE LINARES

Mediaeval Tellem cotton

Tellem; Mali
1000-1200, 1100-1300, 1400-1600
83 x 156 cm, 23 x 22 cm, 22 x 19 cm
cotton
RMV B237-755, RMV B237-3287, RMV B237-2023 (1991)

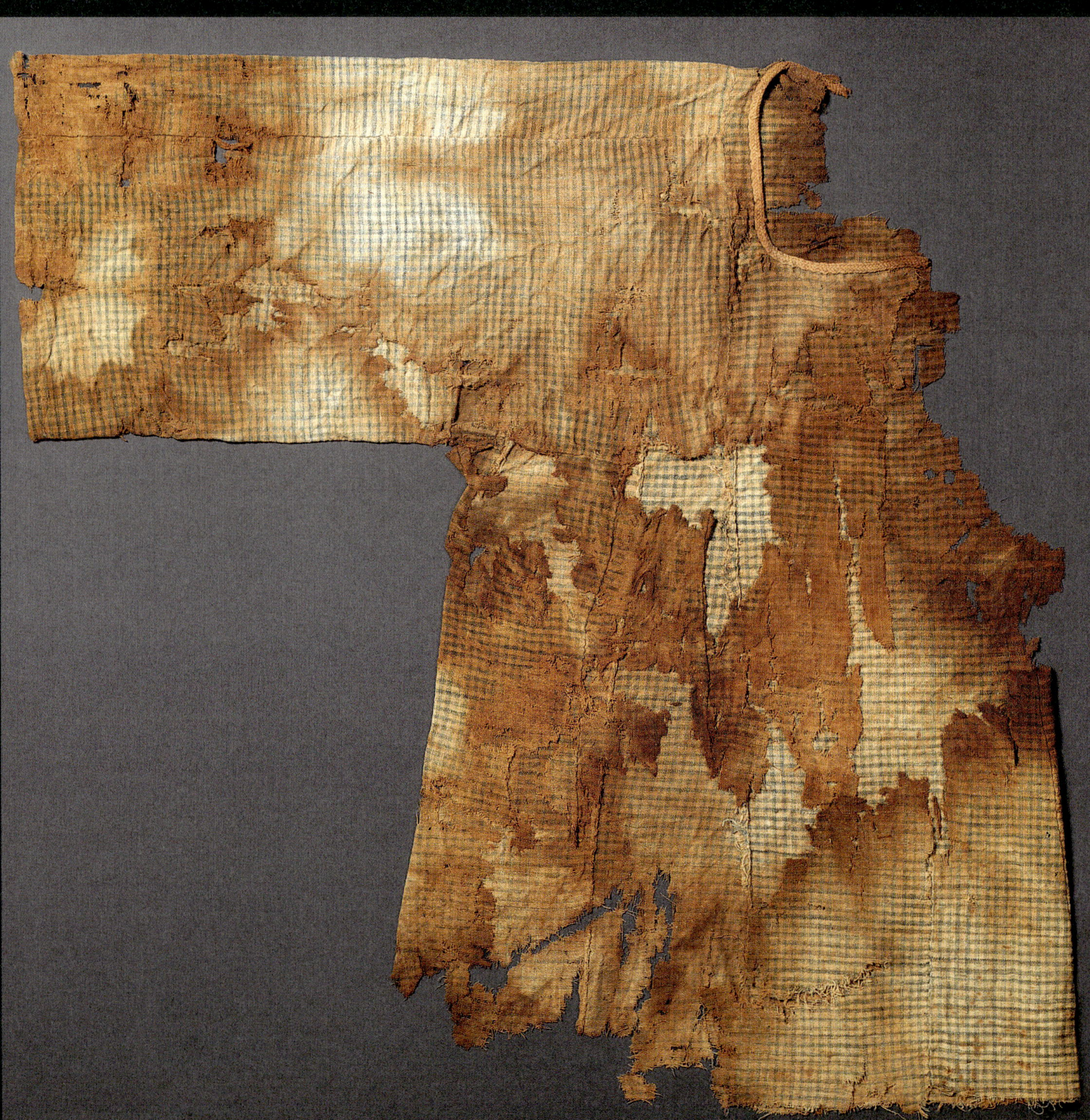

'We found them'

From the eleventh to the sixteenth century, what is now Dogon territory was inhabited by the Tellem, who buried their dead in poorly accessible caves high up in the Cliffs of Bandiagara. The deceased was taken to his or her final resting place wearing clothes, accompanied by a few grave gifts, and wrapped in a blanket. The Tellem objects in these caves, made of perishable materials, are now among the oldest in Sub-Saharan Africa. They have been exceedingly well conserved, making these archaeological finds unique. In the fifteenth century the Tellem people died out. When the Dogon arrived in the region, they met the last living descendants of this people, whom they called *Tellem* – 'we found them'.

The necropolis

The skeletons in the burial caves were jumbled together in chaos, and only in exceptional cases can particular grave gifts be linked to specific individuals. Not everyone was buried with grave gifts. This may suggest a certain differentiation in status. Men and women were often buried in the same cave. No young children have been found, however: they must have been buried elsewhere.

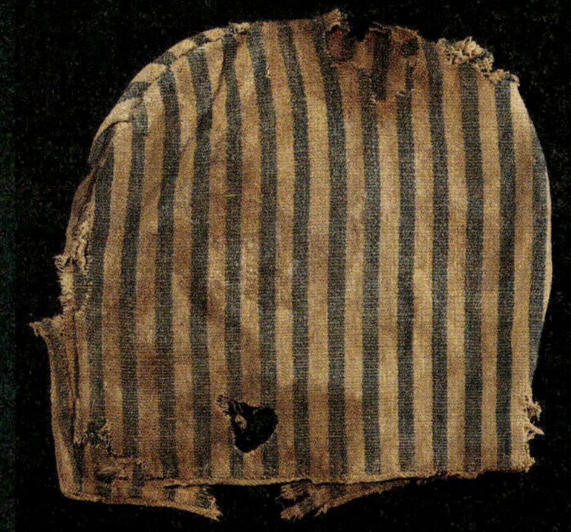

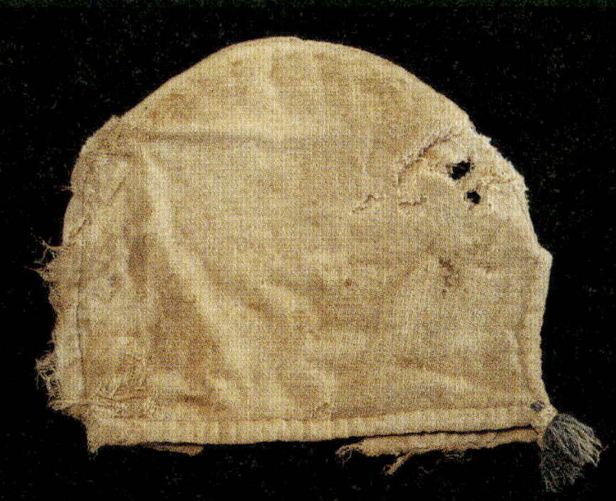

The garments of the dead

The archaeological finds in the burial caves reveal that Tellem women wore loincloths made from vegetable material, while men wore loose-fitting cotton jackets with cotton trousers or leather loincloths. These often have chequered patterns woven into them. The embroidered tunic depicted here was found in a more recent cave. It has wide sleeves and braiding around the neckline. The caps were probably made from pieces of cotton left over from tunics or blankets. Most are semi-circular, the hems generally finished with a little ribbon or a twisted cord with two tassels. They were decorated with patterns woven into the fabric and embroidery. One of the caps found was still on the skull of the deceased.

Restitution

The Rijksmuseum Volkenkunde and the Musée National in Mali have a long history of partnership. In 1989 it was decided to send half of the archaeological Tellem Collection, which the Institute of Anthropobiology of Utrecht University had excavated in the years 1964-74, together with Herman Haan, back to Mali. Mali has agreed to allow the Rijksmuseum Volkenkunde to exhibit the other half on the basis of a long-term loan. This means that both the Malinese and the Dutch people can enjoy these unique treasures.

Weaving

In West Africa, most fabrics were woven from cotton. Before the raw cotton could be spun into thread, it had to be ginned and carded. Spindle whorls were used by both men and women. The weaving was done on a shaft loom. On this loom, which was always operated by a man, narrow strips of fabric are woven, which are later sewn together by hand to produce garments and other cloths (see p. 208-209). Most fabrics are decorated with patterns of stripes and checks woven into the material; either the warp or the weft threads are painted with indigo. Embroidery was used mainly for men's jackets. The Tellem were consummate masters of all these weaving techniques.

Katsinum: Aholi and Dawa

Manfred Susunkewa, Hopi, United States
c. 1990
h. 39.5 cm and 38 cm
wood, dyes, feathers, wool
RMV 5723-3 and RMV 5723-4 (1993)

Cloud People

In the traditional beliefs of the Hopi Indians of Arizona, their spirits or *katsinum* (sing. *katsina*) consist of rain. These are the Cloud People, and they are of vital importance to the Native Americans who live – largely from agriculture – in the semi-desert of the Colorado Plateau. Prayers and gifts are offered to them, in the hope of rain, and hence of fertility and sustenance.

Ceremony

Katsinum are also personified in a large number of figures. These put in regular appearances in the early months of the year as masked dancers in Hopi villages. The boys are initiated into societies, in which they learn about the *katsinum*. Girls learn about the rain spirits through the wooden dolls representing the different spirits that are given to them by the masked dancers.

Dolls

Katsinum dolls are carved from the wood of cottonwood trees. These are soft and have an ideal structure for wood-carving. Many early *katsina* dolls were small, flat, carved in rudimentary shapes, and painted. Later examples were larger, with more rounded forms, with more detailed carving, paintings and decoration. The early *katsina* dolls were static in form and painted simply, but over the years both carving and painting became more detailed: these later figures are sometimes called 'action dolls'.

Manfred Susunkewa

Shortly after 1970, Manfred Susunkewa became one of the first Hopi artists to return to making *katsina* dolls in traditional style: he gave them an erect posture and static pose, and used exclusively traditional tools and mineral and vegetable dyes. This helped him to prevent an artistic burn-out, and ushered in a new phase of his life. Other Hopi artists soon followed his example, such as Philbert Honani, Vernon Mansfield, Manuel Chavarria, Walter Howato and Clark Tenakhongva.

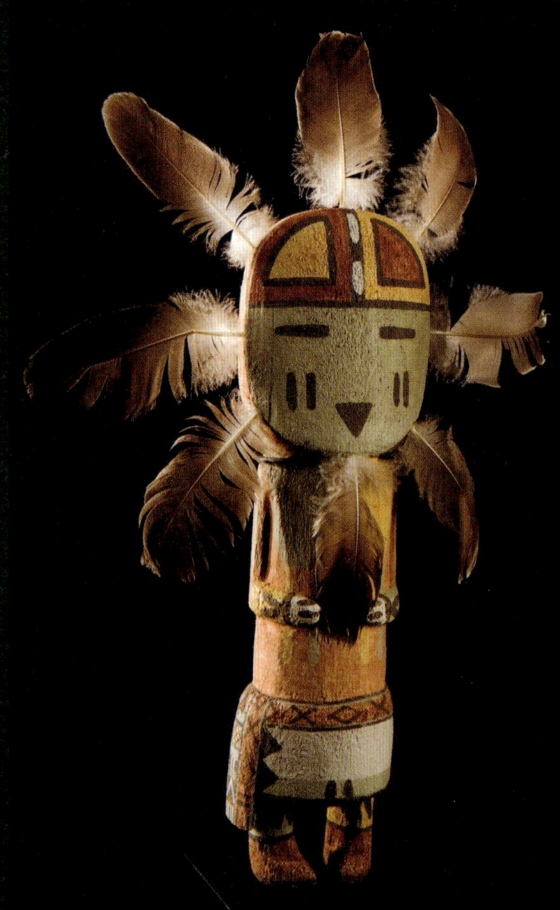

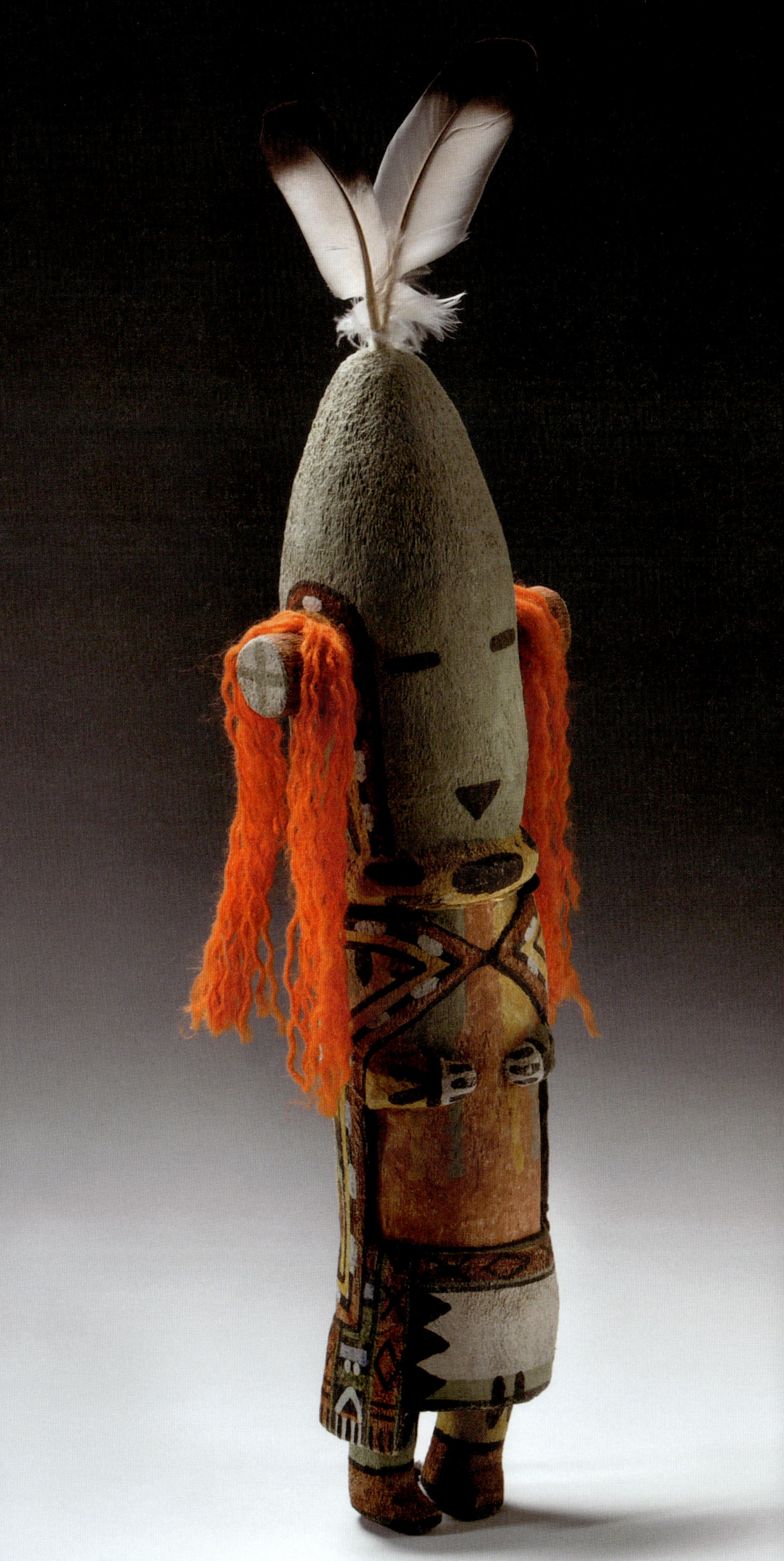

Aholi en Dawa

Aholi's striking features include his conical hat, red tufts of hair in the place of ears, and his blanket, decorated with a stylised image of the Germ God. Aholi appears in the *Powamu* or Bean Dance, as the companion and assistant of Eototo, the chief of the *katsinum* and the leader of the dance. During his visit, Aholi distributes young corn and bean plants. Dawa is the *katsina* that represents the spirit of the sun. Dawa appears in the east every day and traverses the heavens, eventually disappearing into the ocean in the west. He gives life, because people, animals and plants are all dependent on his light and warmth. Dawa is visualised as a young male *katsina* who is kind-hearted and helpful. In the *katsina* dances, Dawa's mask is made of woven yucca fibres, which are largely painted green. The sun is expressed by the corona of eagle feathers around his head.

Market

Around 1870, encouraged by the interest expressed by white people, Hopis started making *katsina* dolls for this external market. Their first customers were soldiers, scholars and government officials. With the advent of the transcontinental railroad, there was a rapid growth in tourism from 1882 onwards. Many tourists took *katsina* dolls home with them as souvenirs of their visit to the American Southwest and the Indians there. Museums and private individuals started to build up collections of objects related to the Native Americans' material culture and art that were in danger of disappearing. Senator Barry Goldwater and the actor John Wayne were among the best-known private collectors of *katsina* dolls.

Vase

Greenland
1997
16 x 9.5 cm
glass
RMV 5882-27 (1997)

Crystal clear

The vase is made of glass, with a mottled brown seal motif. The headless body of a seal is depicted on the inside; its flippers are visible at the bottom of the vase. The seal motif is bounded by colourless, translucent glass. The vase was made for a specific flower, the poppy [Danish *valmue*] and is one in a series of vases designed for Greenland's indigenous flower species. This is the only vase of this type that is included in a museum collection and that is therefore accessible to a wider public.

Royal patronage

Buuti Pedersen is one of Greenland's best-known modern artists, and she is also famous in Denmark. Queen Margrethe of Denmark acquired a seal vase in 2011. Another vase of this type now stands in the Danish royal palace. Buuti Pedersen's work is also displayed at the Danish Embassy in Riyadh in Saudi Arabia, the National Museum of Greenland, the town hall and museum of Narsaq, Kangerlussuaq airport, Greenland's self-government building in Nuuk, Ammassalik Museum, the town hall and hospital of Tasiilaq, and Qaqortoq Museum.

Buuti Pedersen

Buuti (Bodil) Pedersen (1955) is an artist from West Greenland who was based in Ammassalik in East Greenland between 1990 and 2010. In 2010 she moved back to her place of birth, Qaqortoq, together with her husband Ole G. Jensen, former director of the Ammassalik Museum and now director of the museum in Qaqortoq. Buuti Pedersen attended the School of Applied Arts (*Skolen for Brugskunst*) in Copenhagen from 1982 to 1986, and attended a variety of workshops in Studioglas in Strömbergshyttan, Sweden, between 1993 and 2009.

Painting

Besides her designs in glass, Pedersen is also known for her paintings. Her most popular work includes her images of polar bears, which she painted in a wide variety of styles, including a series based on the twelve months of the year. Pedersen designed bear paintings for each month of the year, with apt seasonal motifs. The summer images were dominated by a light yellow sun, while the darker winter versions contain stars, for instance. Her paintings and two-dimensional designs have been depicted on postcards and postage stamps issued by the philatelic society *Grønlands Julemærke*. Pedersen has also designed a number of covers for Greenland's telephone book (1995, 1999, 2000 and 2001), published by Tele Greenland.

Artful glassblowing

The artist Buuti Pedersen from West Greenland made the design and was closely involved in the production process, although the design was executed by her former fellow students, the glassblowers of Studioglas glass factory in Strömbergshyttan, Sweden. The seal motif refers directly to Greenland's ancient hunting culture. The people of Greenland depended for their survival on the meat of seals. The incorporation of this motif shows that even today, traditional aspects of society still possess significance and serve as a source of inspiration.

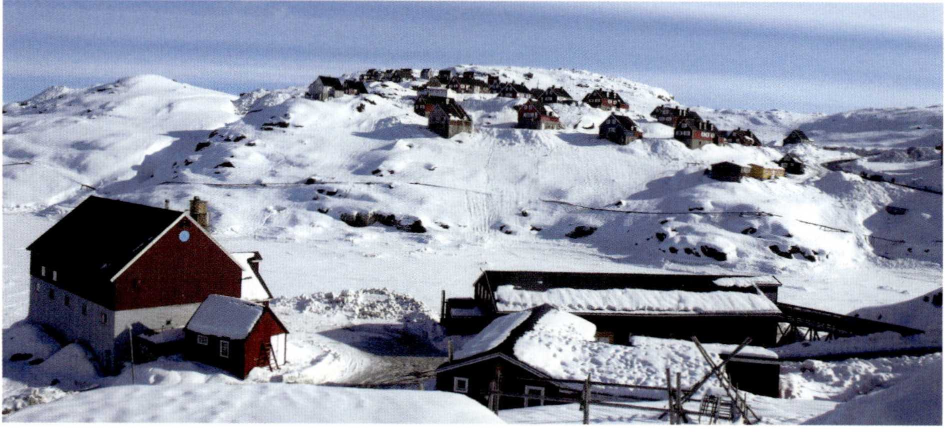

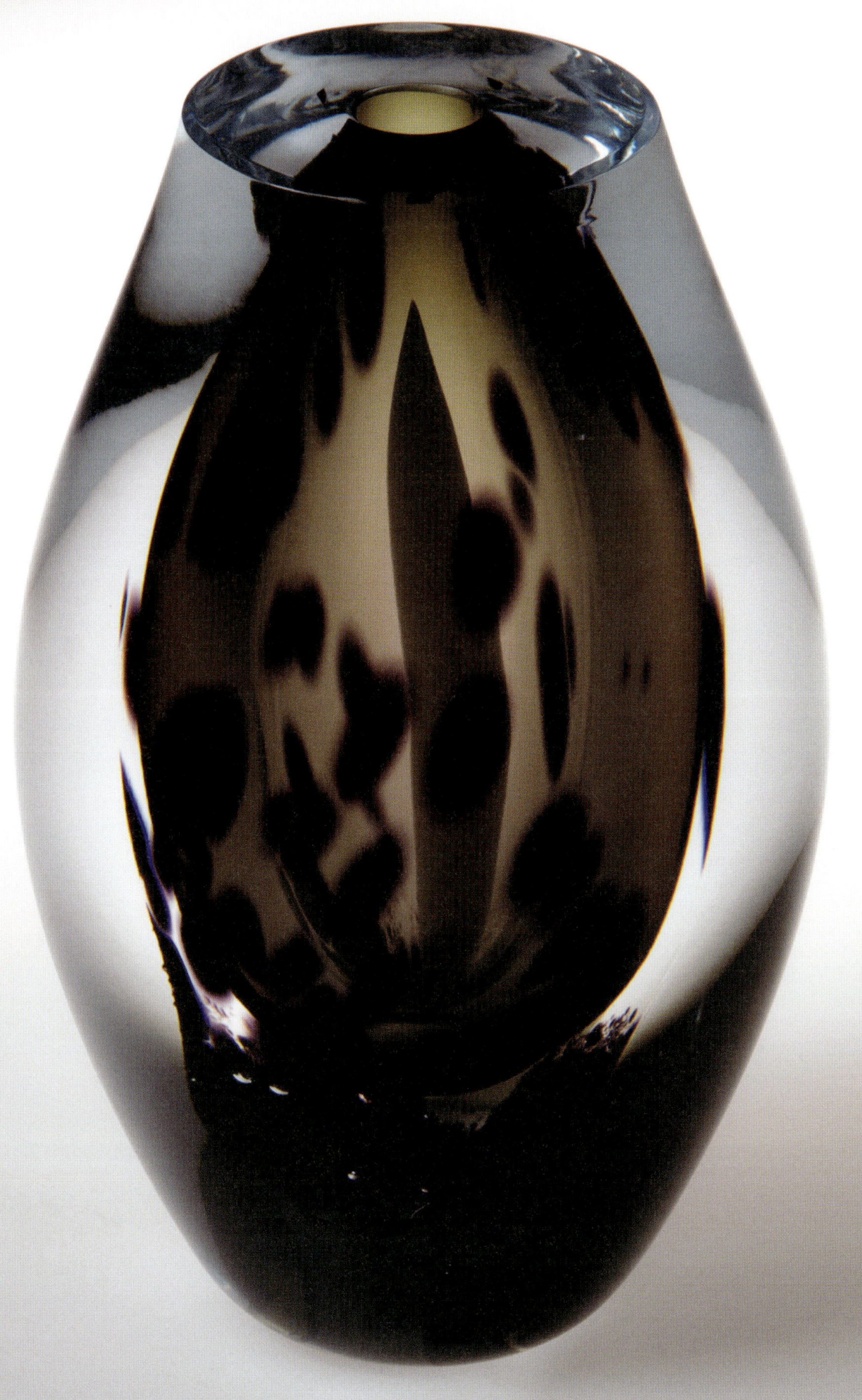

Kente cloth

Ewe, Ghana
early 20th century
157 x 320 cm
cotton, rayon and/or silk
RMV 5899-10 (1998)

National costume

The colourful cotton fabrics of the Asante, an ethnic group in Ghana, are called *kente*, a word probably derived from the Fanti *kenten*, meaning basket. These textiles were taken to the local market in baskets. Women wear the *kente* wrapped around the body, while men wear them rather like togas, leaving the right shoulder bare. *Kente* cloths are regarded by many Ghanaians – including non-Asante – as their national costume. They are exported in large quantities to numerous countries. In the United States, African Americans regard them as symbols of their ancestral homeland.

Specialist weavers

Weaving is a craft held in high esteem among the Asante and their neighbours, the Ewe. Here and throughout West Africa, weavers are men. They use a simple horizontal shaft loom, on which they weave narrow strips of fabric. These strips are then sewn together to make a rectangular piece of material. This traditional *kente* is composed of 23 strips. All the colours and patterns that are woven into the fabric are of symbolic significance. In this piece, numerous figurative motifs are discernible on both sides. Although some are depicted several times, they nonetheless reflect enormous variety. Weaving these complex patterns is a highly specialised task. The *kente* cloth depicted here was worn by a man.

Agotime-Afegame

The words *Le Ekpowu* occur four times in this piece of material, in some cases in reverse image or upside down. According to Nomo Te, one of the oldest weavers from Agotime-Afegame, they should be read as *lekpowu*, which means 'small hill' in Dangme, referring to the place where the people's ancestors found shelter before they settled in Agotime. So it probably comes from Agotime-Afegame. Birgitte Menzel bought it from Ben Atsu Agbelengor in Agotime-Kpetoe in or around 1970.

The collector Brigitte Menzell

Brigitte Menzel was the curator of the Africa Department of Berlin's Museum of Ethnology and director of the German Textile Museum in Krefeld. She became very well known for her research on African textiles, and was one of the first ethnologists to study ethnographic textile collections and more especially the weaving techniques used. The large and well-documented collections she built up in Ghana are of immense significance. Because of her unexpected death in 1998, however, they had scarcely been made accessible for further research. The Rijksmuseum Volkenkunde inherited her legacy.

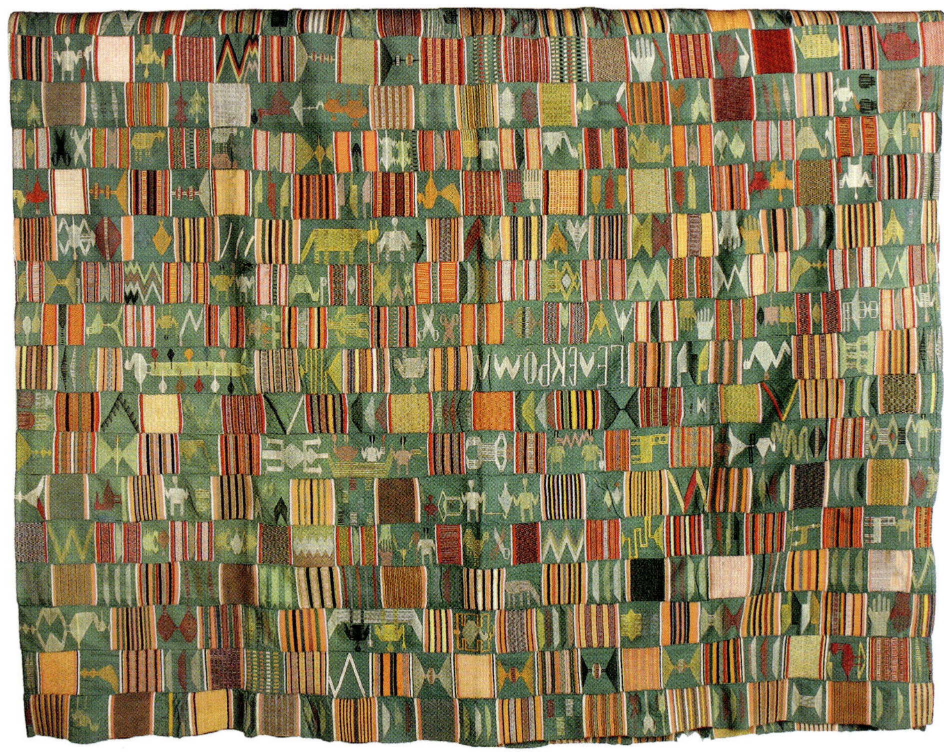

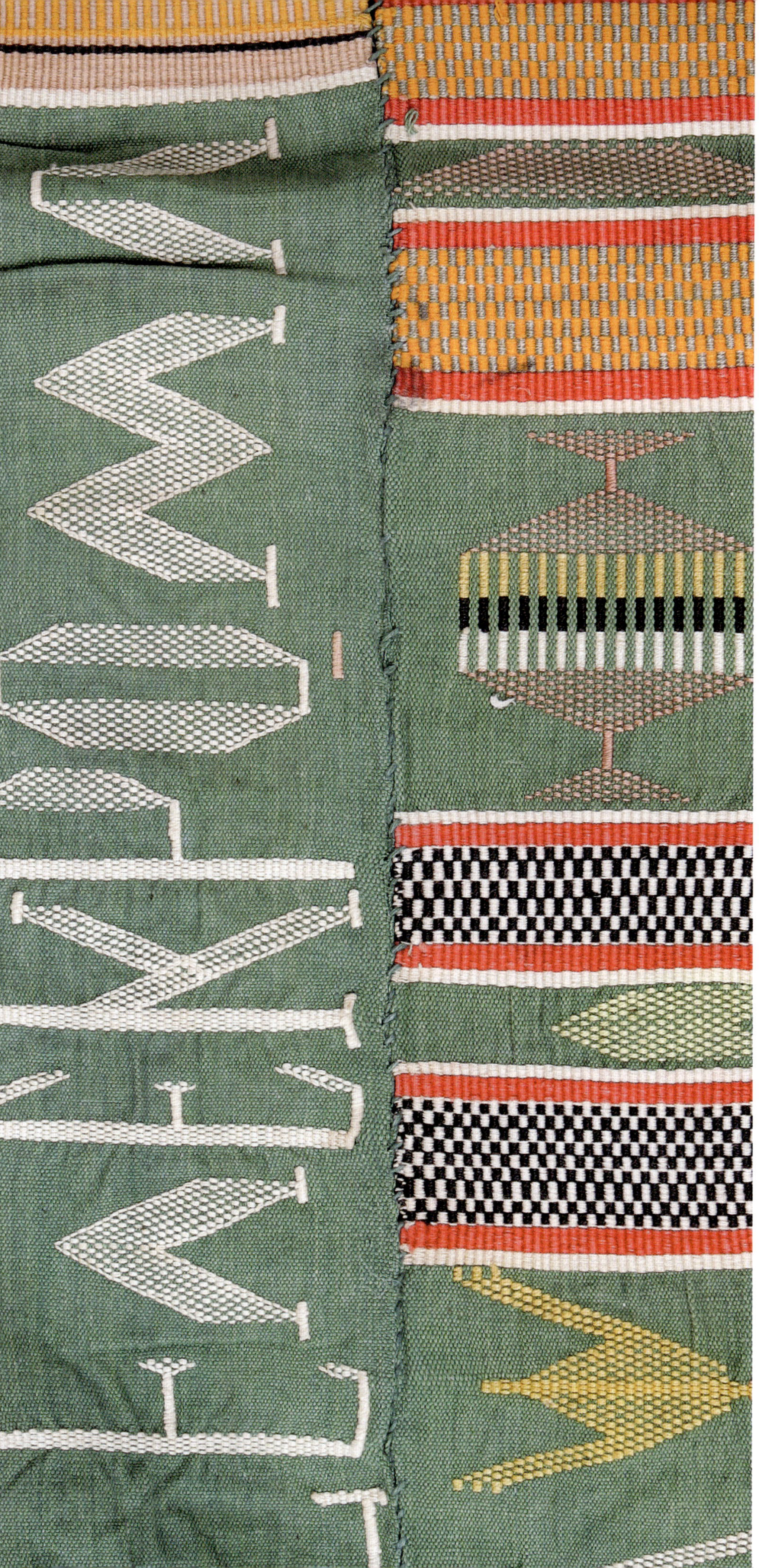

The patronage of Ben Atsu Agbelengor

Ben Atsu Agbelengor werd geboren op 7 april 1922 als zoon van een wever. Omdat zijn vader overleed toen hij nog jong was, heeft zijn oudere broer hem leren weven. Agbelengor was prominent lid van de Evangelische Presbyteriaanse Kerk, die een belangrijke rol speelde bij zijn promotie in het buitenland. Agbelengor won diverse buitenlandse prijzen en ontwikkelde zich als een van de grootste textiel-entrepreneurs in Agotime, onder ander omdat hij krachten bundelde en samenwerkte met wevers uit Agotime en uit de kustgebieden. In zijn privécollectie zaten vijf zeer bijzondere doeken. Omdat hij één van Birgit Menzels belangrijkste informanten was, heeft ze dit doek kunnen kopen. Agbelengor overleed op 4 september 1993.

Garment (*Huipil de tapar*)

Zapotec, Mexico
1930–1939
121 x 119 cm
cotton, silk
RMV 5946-215 (1999)

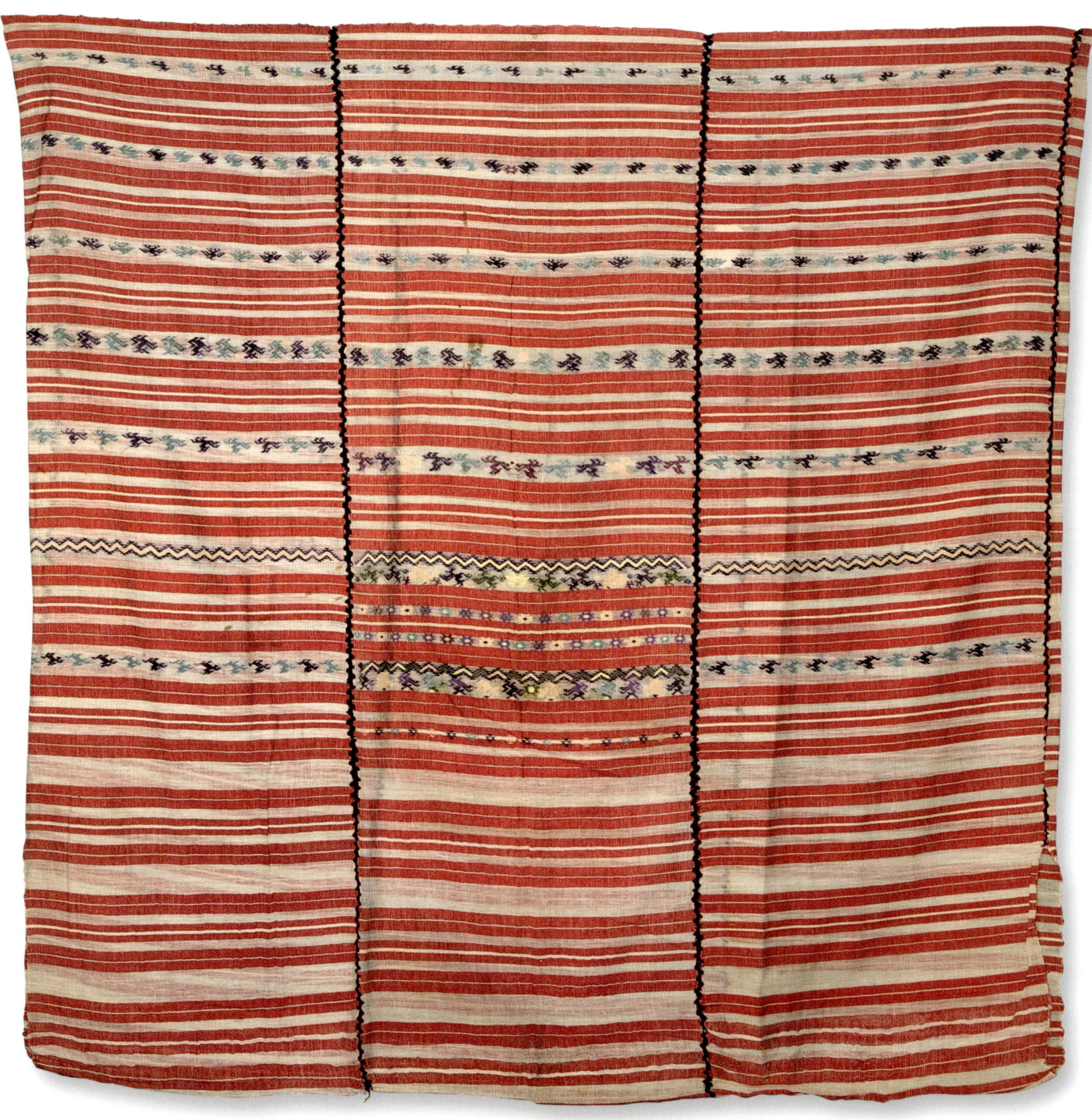

Huipil

The *huipil* (from the Nahuatl word *huipilli* for blouse) is a typical Mesoamerican woman's garment. It is a sleeveless blouse, generally woven from three lengths of fabric that are sewn together, with a central opening for the head. It is worn by girls as well as adult women. Symbols indicate whether the huipil belongs to a married woman or to a girl aged over fifteen. The front of this *huipil de tapar* (covering *huipil*) is embellished with little figures, each with its own symbolic significance. For instance, the image of a deer, explains the Mixtec expert Alejandra Cruz, means: 'May the work of this woman's husband progress as swiftly as a running deer.'

Irmgard Johnson

This *huipil* comes from the Johnson collection, built up by Irmgard Weitlaner-Johnson (1914-2011). Irmgard Weitlaner was born in Philadelphia, and the family moved to Mexico in 1922. In the 1930s she started collecting, on a modest scale, clothing worn by the indigenous Mexican population. In the same period she met Bodil Christensen, with whom she would have a lifelong friendship and with whom she collected. The two women travelled to remote and inaccessible regions and adopted a remarkably systematic approach to collecting. The Johnson Collection would eventually grow to an impressive one thousand-odd pieces, which represent most of Mexico's textile traditions.

Wedding-*huipiles*

Different types of *huipiles* are used for different occasions, such as the special wedding *huipil*. It is the groom's responsibility to pay for his bride's wedding *huipil*. He also determines its appearance, the figures embroidered on it, and the colours of the decorative strips that link the three woven bands of cloth. Traditionally, the decorative bands on a wedding *huipil* are royal blue.

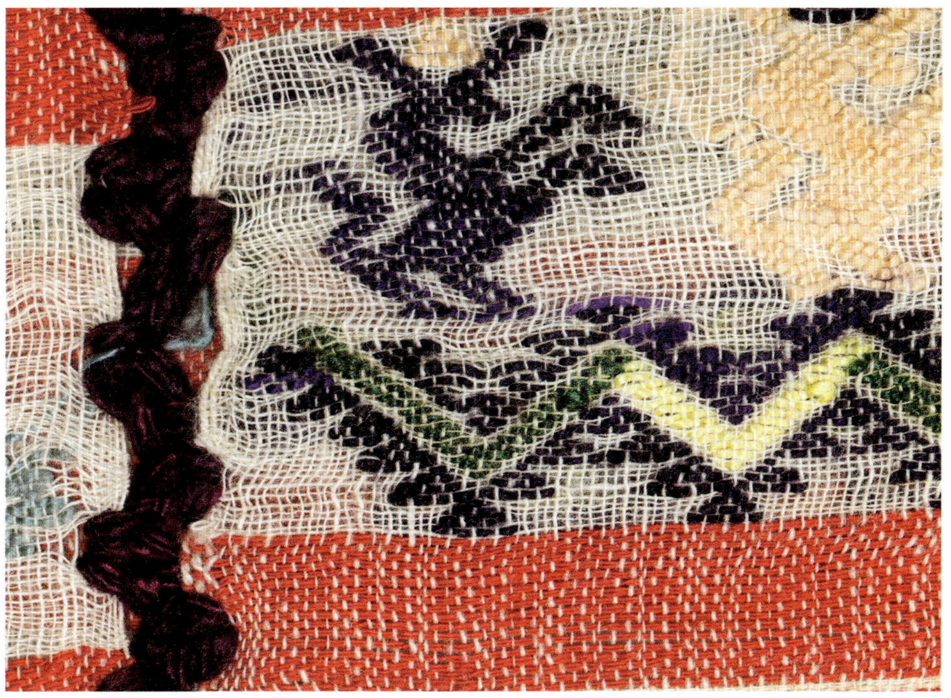

Huipil de Tapar

Making a huipil is very time-consuming work that calls for complex calculations. Certain weaving techniques are passed down from one generation to the next and require years to be taught. All this means that *huipiles* are very expensive. Nowadays they are generally reserved for special occasions such as weddings or public holidays. The *huipil de tapar* is intended for daily use, and generally covers the head, shoulders and chest. In the 1960s, the *huipil de tapar* was sometimes worn for wedding ceremonies; in this case the woman would not use the openings made for the arms. The other openings would only be used when the garment was used to dress a deceased woman. This custom survives to this day on the coast of Oaxaca in southern Mexico.

Mexican textile collection in Leiden

Outside Mexico, the Mexican textile collection of the Rijksmuseum Volkenkunde is the best of its kind. The most important collectors were Irmgard Johnson, Bodil Christensen (1896-1985) and Ted Leyenaar and his wife Paula Leyenaar. What makes the collection so unique is the fact that the items were obtained directly from individual members of the community concerned and that most were collected by women, both of which were quite exceptional for the period. This direct mode of acquisition means that a great deal of documentation has been handed down, on the applicable weaving techniques, materials, and local terminology. The museum also possesses a large number of photographs, dating from 1930 to the late twentieth century, which supply the textiles with context.

Elephant with its attendant

Watanabe Kakushū (with Gensei and Komatsu (?) seals), Edo period, Japan
c. 1813
painting: 42.4 x 56.2 cm; mount: 117 x 79.5 cm silk, ink (sumi)
pigment, mounted as a hanging scroll (*kakejiku*)
RMV 5964-1 (1999)

Pivotal moment in history

However peaceful this scene may appear, it depicts a pivotal moment in the four centuries of Japanese-Dutch relations. In 1813, Thomas Stamford Raffles despatched two ships from British-occupied Batavia to Nagasaki, with the aim of persuading the Japanese to transfer the trading post of Deshima to the British. On board one of the ships was the young Indian elephant depicted here. The animal was five years old and came from Ceylon. To avoid arousing the suspicion of the Japanese and to gain access to the Bay of Nagasaki, the ships flew Dutch flags. Their mission was unsuccessful. The shogun sided with the Dutch.

A Western perspective

Watanabe Kakushū (1778-1830) was born as the son of Watanabe Shūsen (1736-1824), a painter in the guild of official painters and documentalists of foreign imports for the government of Nagasaki, the *goyō eshi*. In 1802 Kakushū too joined the guild. Trained in the naturalistic representation of a wide range of imports, Kakushū clearly drew the elephant from life: the animal is painted anatomically correctly, including details such as, for instance, the characteristic 'finger' in the end of the trunk, which is peculiar to the Indian elephant. He also uses characteristic devices for suggesting depth, such as placing large objects (both the elephant and the pine tree) in the foreground.

Elephant to order

The fact that this painting was executed on silk suggests that it was commissioned privately. The documentary images that Kakushū produced for the authorities were not done on an expensive surface, but drawn on paper. These images too have been preserved, including notes of the elephant's dimensions, which *Opperhoofd* Doeff had recorded. Perhaps this painting was ordered by a wealthy merchant from Nagasaki or by one of the *daimyō* families on Kyūshū.

The Mogul tradition

The way in which the two Ceylonese attendants are painted suggests that Kakushū must have been familiar with Indian miniatures from the Mogul tradition (see p. 160-161). Not only the faces, but also the long fingers, and above all the depiction of the feet – in the Japanese tradition, these were preferably drawn somewhat smaller – and the reduction of clothing to little more than sections of colour all point strongly in that direction.

A second painting

It is known that Kakushū produced a second sumptuous painting of the Ceylon elephant. Set against an identical background, including the ships and the pine tree on the right, the same two attendants are feeding the elephant, which in this second image is without a red blanket. The man who is seated on the elephant's back in the painting shown here is busy bringing over a bunch of hay in the other painting, while the attendant on the left watches on. The image exhibited here is the more interesting of the two, since we have an unobstructed view of the elephant, without the man with the hay disrupting the picture. Furthermore, the design derives a certain dynamic quality from the movement of the elephant, which is raising its trunk to the tropical fruit.

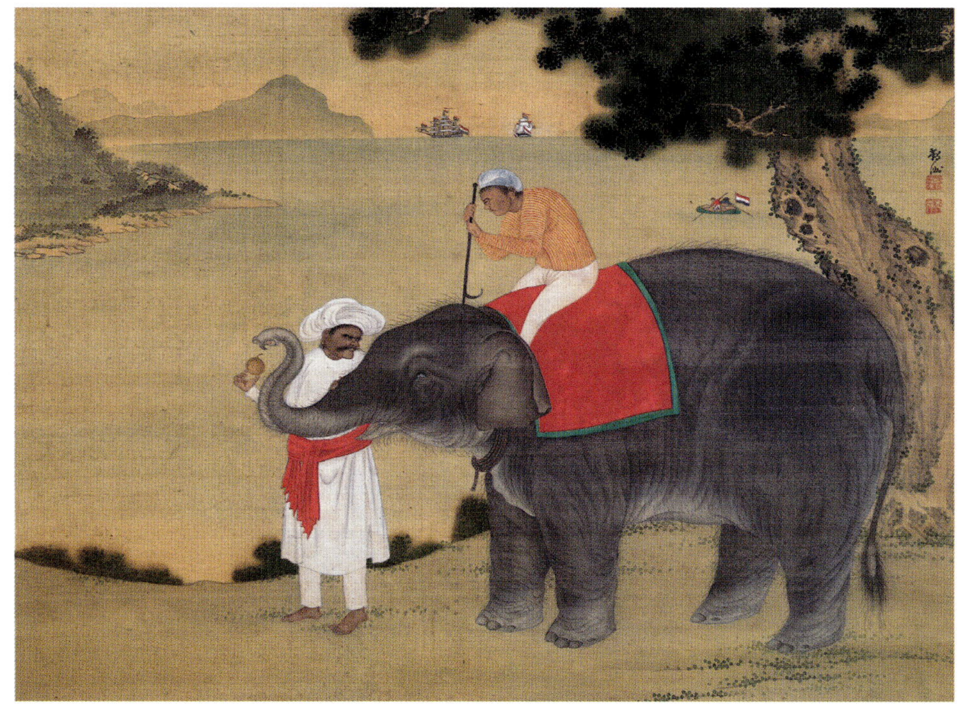

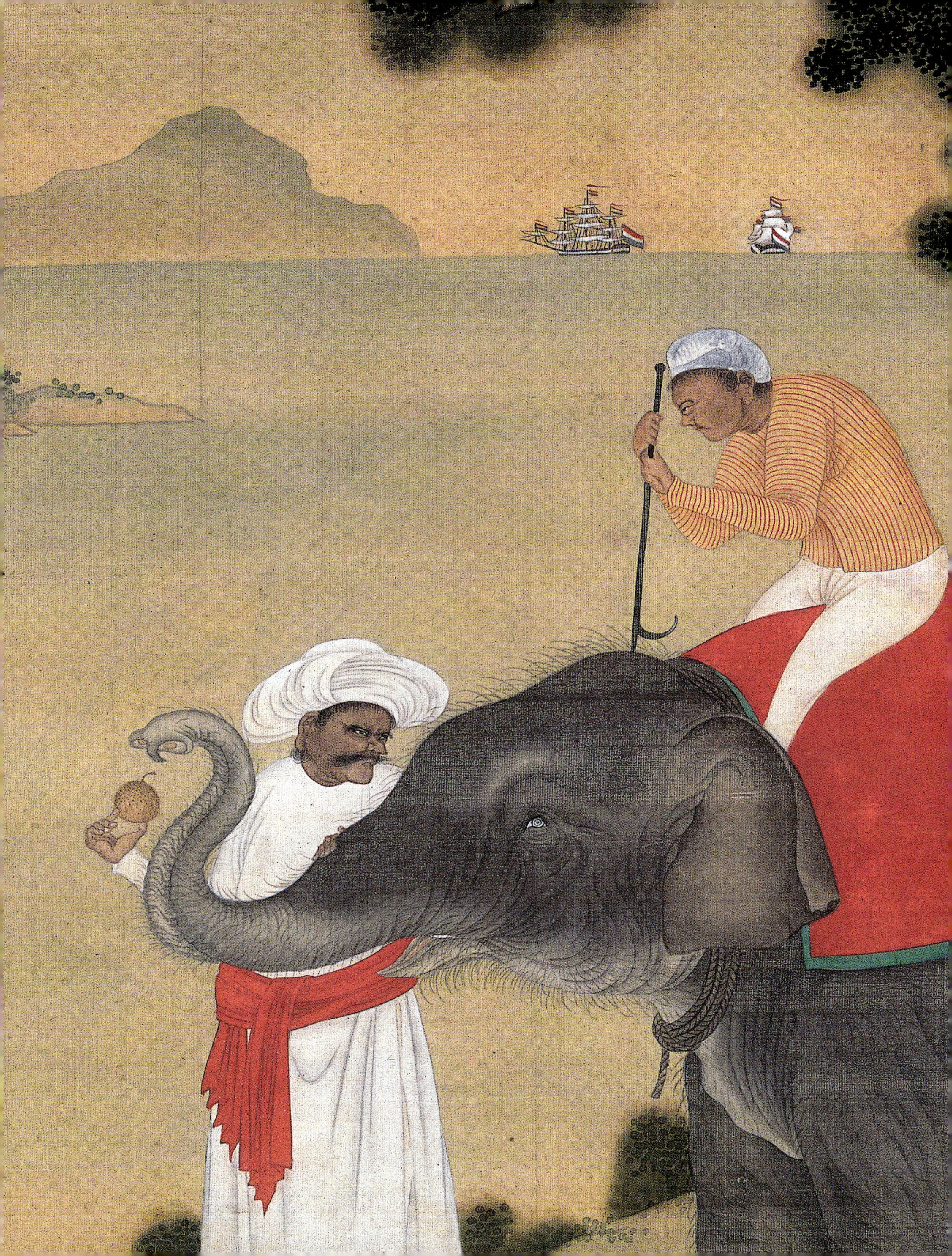

Woman's blouse

Solvej Petersen and Erna Christensen, Skæven sewing atelier; Tunumiit, Tasiilaq, East Greenland
2001
53 x 141 cm
seal fur (saddleback seal, *Phoca groenlandicus*) and arctic fox fur (*Alopex lagopus)*, textile
RMV 5961-16 (2001)

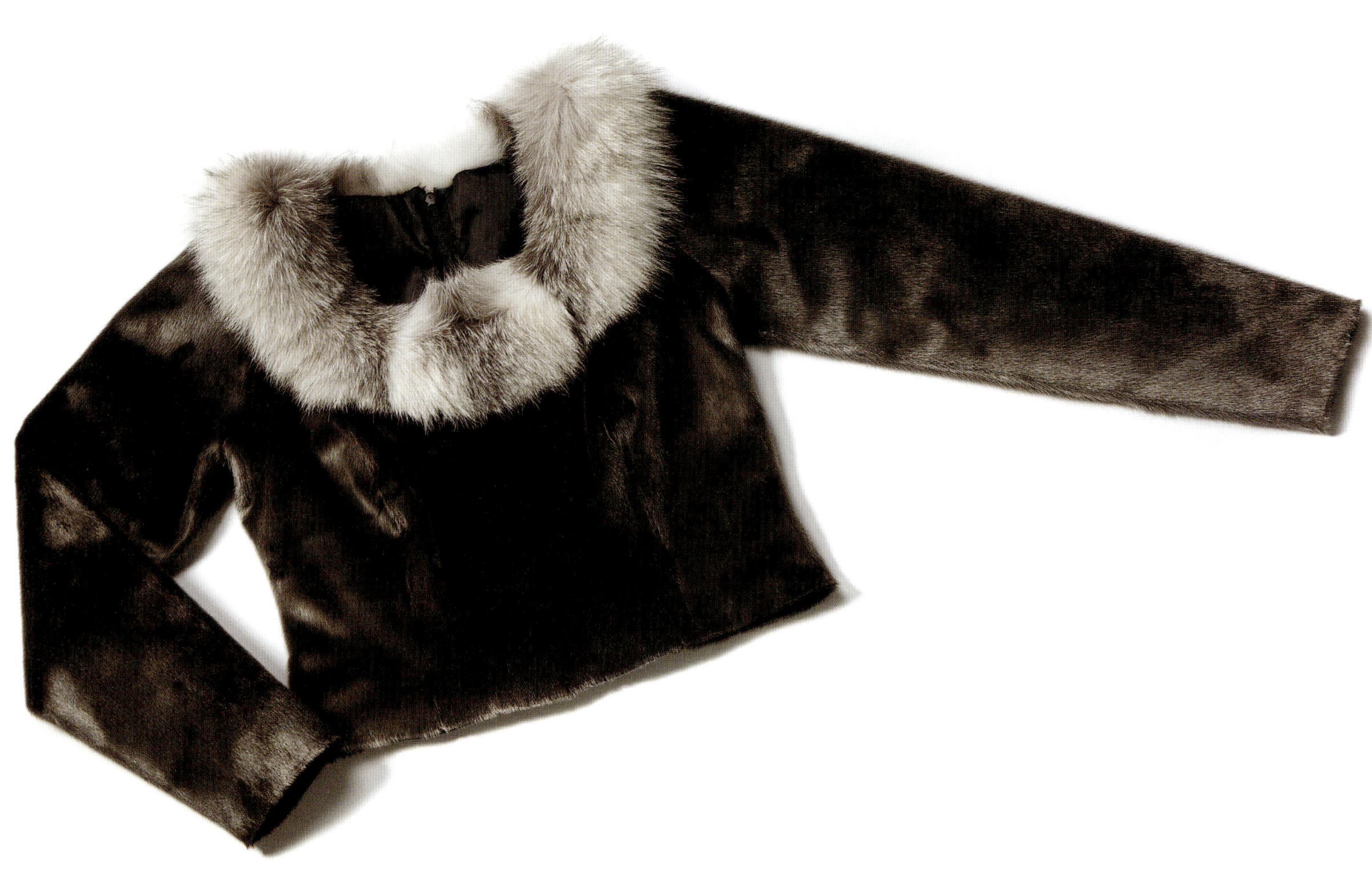

Soft fur

This modern woman's blouse is made from the fur of saddleback seals, tanned and dyed in a factory. It is lined with a smooth synthetic material and trimmed with grey and white arctic fox fur. The garment is relatively short, flatteringly waisted and furnished with darts. It was designed by Solvej Petersen, the Danish director of Skæven sewing atelier in Tasiilaq, Ammassalik, and made by Erna Christensen, one of the leading seamstresses of East Greenland, who is attached to the atelier.

Modern collection

This garment was collected in 2001 by the curator Cunera Buijs, who is continuing the collecting tradition of the Rijksmuseum Volkenkunde. For over forty years, the museum has combined research with collection in Greenland. This approach is exemplified by the work of the social geographer Gerti Nooter, who, as curator of the Arctic and Northern America department, has conducted anthropological research in East Greenland. In the period 1970-1990 he built up a unique, varied collection of items from Greenland. This collection stems from the period of acculturation, when Greenland's material culture was strongly influenced by Danish culture.

A sewing atelier in East Greenland

The sewing atelier *[messertapik* in the language of East Greenland] known as Skæven, in Ammassalik, was founded in 1984 by the municipality of Tasiilaq as an economic initiative to create jobs. Its first director came from West Greenland, after which the directorship passed to a Danish artist. She developed fur products in collaboration with the municipality, which pays close attention to profitability and to assuring a European-oriented price/quality relationship. This approach has enabled the atelier to produce unique items of haute *couture* using ancient Greenland patterns and traditional materials.

What women want

This modern, fashionable woman's blouse can be combined with a long evening skirt of the same material. Garments of this kind are worn at weddings and parties, and on Greenland's national public holiday. Garments such as fur coats, mittens and boots that are styled in modern fashions appeal to a young generation of modern, generally highly-educated, Greenland women, who also wear them to public events with music by local pop groups. In wearing such clothes, women display their status, and their feeling for fashion, innovation, and modernity, while also emphasising their sense of national Greenland identity.

Tanning and dyeing

The sewing atelier employs diverse kinds of sealskins, but it also uses dog fur to line slippers and mittens, as well as the fur of arctic foxes, mountain hares, and rabbits. Various kinds of seal fur are dyed. Such methods are used to transform a wide range of traditional materials from Greenland into modern designs. Non-indigenous materials such as buffalo leather and sheepskin, as well as products made of wool, cotton, and modern materials such as synthetic fabrics, along with plastic buttons and zips and metal hooks, are combined in coats, trousers, bags, and belts.
The sealskins supplied by indigenous hunters are cleaned at home, stored wet at the Skaeven workshop, and shipped to the Great Greenland company and tannery in Qaqortoq, in southern Greenland. Great Greenland supplies factory-tanned and factory-dyed fur to sewing ateliers all over Greenland. The vast majority of the garments and fur products are marketed in Greenland and Denmark. Ten per cent of Greenland's population still depend on seal hunting for basic subsistence. There is too little alternative employment in the villages.

Mountain of immortals (*Xianshan*)

China
19th century
203 x 110 cm
wood, lacquer, gilding
RMV 5970-1 (2002)

Emperor of the void

Called either a *xuhuang* ("emperor of the void") or a *xianshan* ("mountain of immortals"), this rare collection of figures is perhaps the only one in Europe. Another magnificent example is located in the Guangdong Province Museum in Guangzhou. Such awesome iconographies were once more common in Daoist temples. Each figure is mounted on its own mountain ledge, and the combination of all twenty two seems to rise from the single balustraded plinth at the base. The construction is made of lacquered and gilded wood.

Object of study

Where this object was acquired in China is not known. Quite probably it was housed in a temple in one of the southeast coastal provinces of Zhejiang, Fujian or Guangdong. Exchanges between populations in this area and visitors from The Netherlands is one of the longest and most continuous histories of contact between China and Europe. Here too was a stage on which the first ethnographers and their Chinese informants interpreted Chinese religion and customs. Evidence is lacking, but it would be no surprise to discover that this object emanates from a region whose religious life has long been an object of Dutch interest.

Three Pure Ones

The mountainous shape is a standardized form. The number of gods, however, varies. The collection in the Guangdong Museum shows twenty five, and a photograph of a 'mountain' salvaged from a temple in Pudong (now a development area opposite Shanghai) during the Cultural Revolution features twenty. Clearly, different temples adopted diverse compositions of the Daoist pantheon. All mountains of the immortals show three figures at the summit, the "Three Pure Ones" (*san qing*), whose central figure is the deified Lao Zi. Many of the gods lower down in this visual hierarchy owe their identities to historical figures whom popular belief had deified.

Living mountain

The iconography of Daoist gods was more closely tied to native Chinese forms and appearances, unlike Buddhist image which borrowed much from an imagination of ancient India (see p. 158-159). However, the earliest origins of individual figures in Daoist and Buddhist iconographies is not easy to tell apart. Mutual borrowing may have once been quite indiscriminate. Mountains, which Daoist thinking classes as living organisms, are sublime expressions of nature, and they comprise inexhaustible subject for many categories of art.

Lacquered symbols

Daoist altars are conceived as mountains, but a mountain of immortals is the visual furnishing for an altar rather than as the altar itself. A mountain of immortals is deployed during rituals of offering, often displayed with other lacquered wood objects, such as lamps (representing the sun and moon) and symbolic implements associated with particular deities. The immortals in this arrangement and other gods depicted in other art have no sacred function, for the rituals in which they featured can be performed with or without them. Their purpose is primarily to recall the appearance of the deities to whom the performance is devoted.

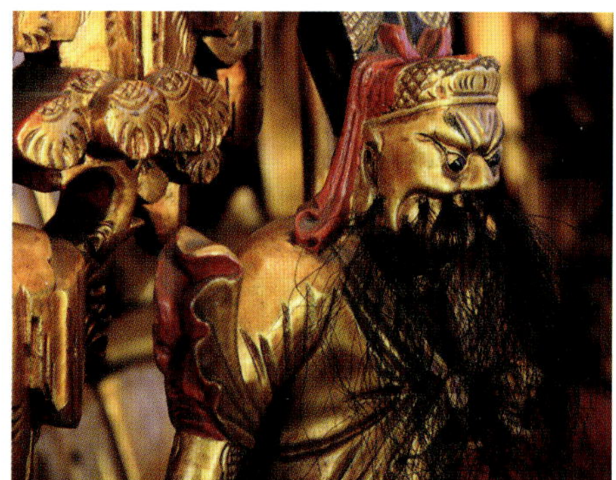

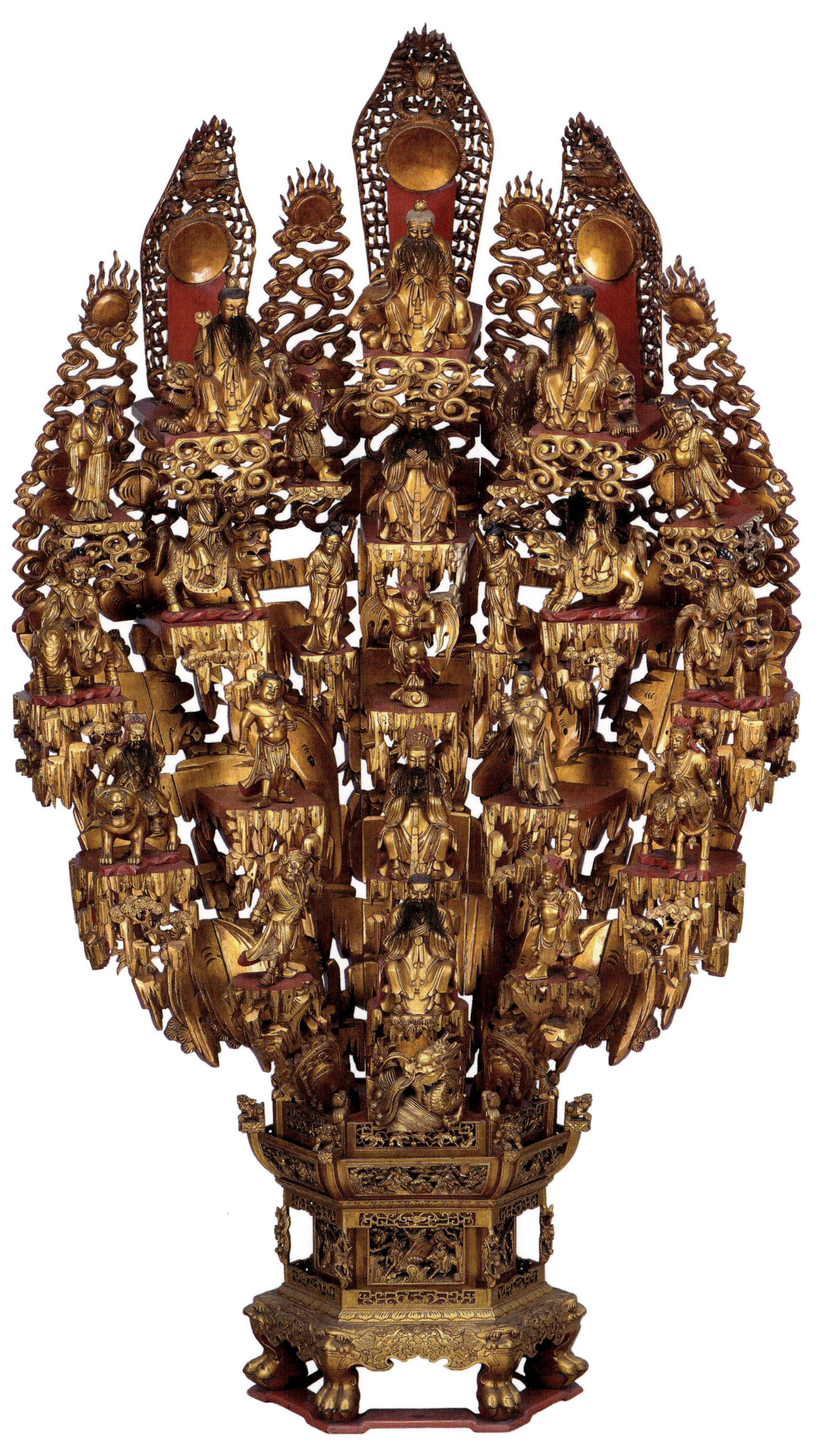

Painting

Karangasem, East Bali, Indonesia
1916
h. 166 cm, l. 455 cm
cotton, paint, gold leaf
RMV 6090-2 (2008)

Cremation ceremony

This huge painting, executed on canvas in the traditional wayang style, was used at the cremation ceremony for I Gusti Gede Djelantik, stadholder of Karangasem (East Bali), on 1 October 1916. It depicts an episode from the *Adiparwa*, the first book of the Indian epic *Mahabharata*, in which gods and demons do battle over the *amrita*, the elixir of immortality. The painting was probably made by artists working at the court of Karangasem, and ordered especially for this ceremony by I Gusti Bagus Djelantik, the old ruler's successor.

Battle and trickery in *wayang* style

The figures in the painting are shaped like *wayang* puppets, in accordance with the iconography of traditional Balinese painting. Two different scenes are depicted. In the lower right corner, Vishnu, disguised as a beautiful woman, has purloined the winged chalice with the elixir of life from the demons. Above this we see Vishnu in the form of a god, holding the chalice in his right hand. Behind him stands Shiva, who can be recognised from his third eye. On the left, gods (recognisable from their halos), demons and their servants are locked in a furious battle to secure the elixir. Vishnu throws his discus (*cakra*).

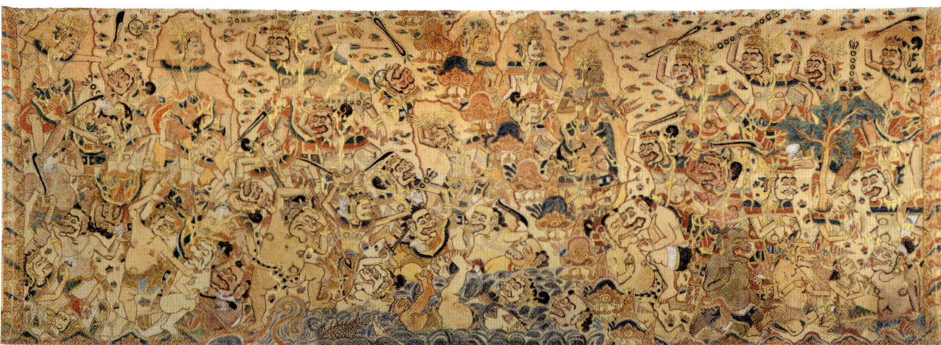

Princely gift

The museum received this painting, along with another one used at the same cremation, as a gift from the Association of Friends of the Kern Institute. The association had acquired the painting in the late 1920s from Mr H.T. Damsté, who had served as Resident of Bali and Lombok from 1919 to 1923. Damsté specialised in collecting objects relating to Balinese painting and death rituals, and published articles on these subjects. He probably acquired this painting during his period as Resident from I Gusti Bagus Djelantik, with whom he had cordial relations.

Ritual decorations

Until recently, traditional painting always had a specific function on Bali, serving as the permanent or temporary decoration of temples or palaces, or of temporary structures erected to mark a particular ritual. Thus, tall towers, in which deceased dignitaries were borne to the cremation site, were covered with painted decorations. The painting shown here hung below the eaves of the temporary structure in which the body of raja I Gusti Gede Djelantik was placed. It was one in a series of paintings depicting scenes from the *Adiparwa*.

Liberation of the soul

This painting, which shows how the gods captured the elixir of life, hung right over the coffin of I Gusti Gede Djelantik at his cremation in 1916. It was highly relevant there, since the very purpose of the Balinese cremation ceremony is to obtain immortality. As the dead person's body is burned and his ashes scattered in the sea, his earthly body returns as a microcosm to the elements of the macrocosm, and his soul is liberated. In performing this ceremony, his descendants fulfil their obligations to the deceased.

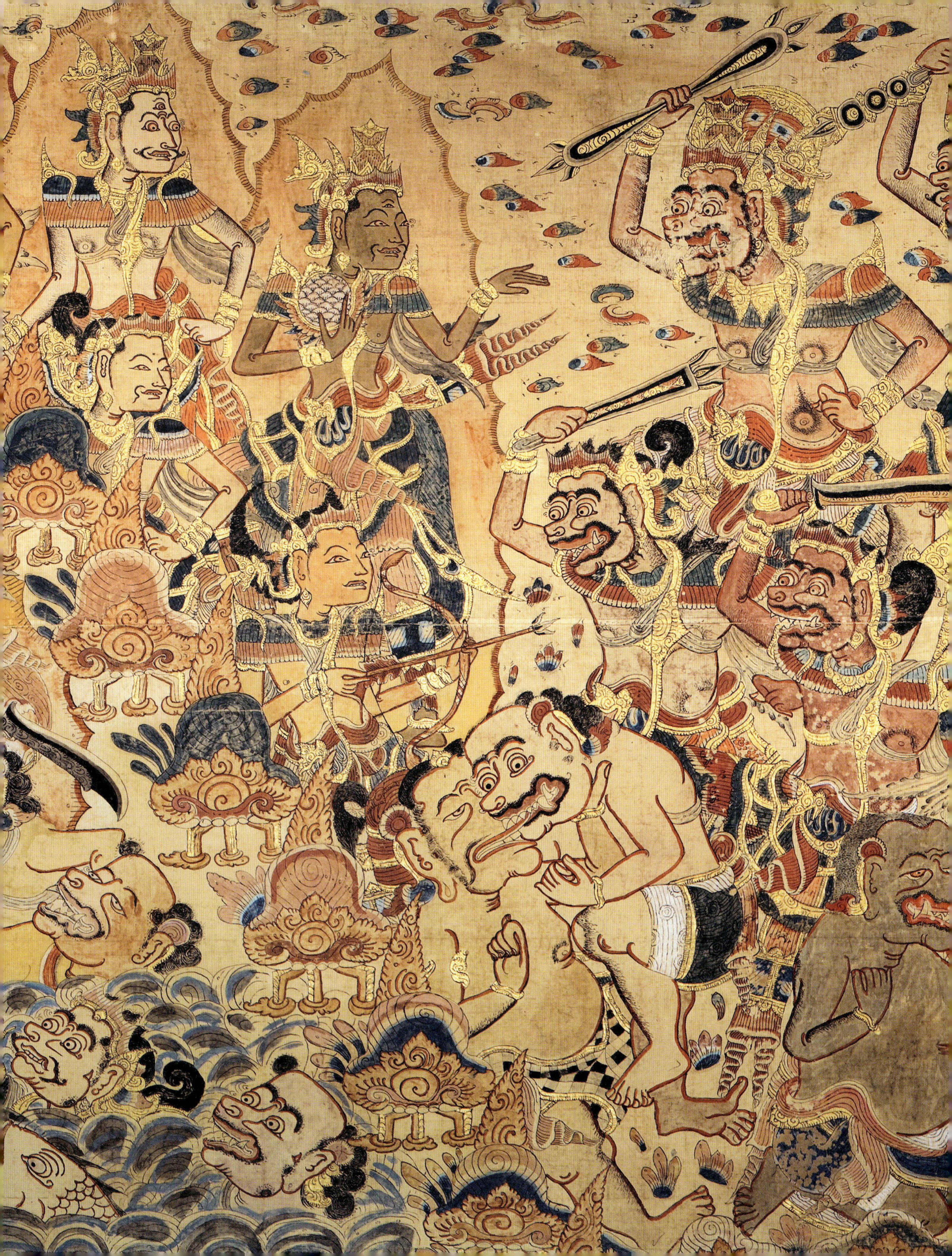

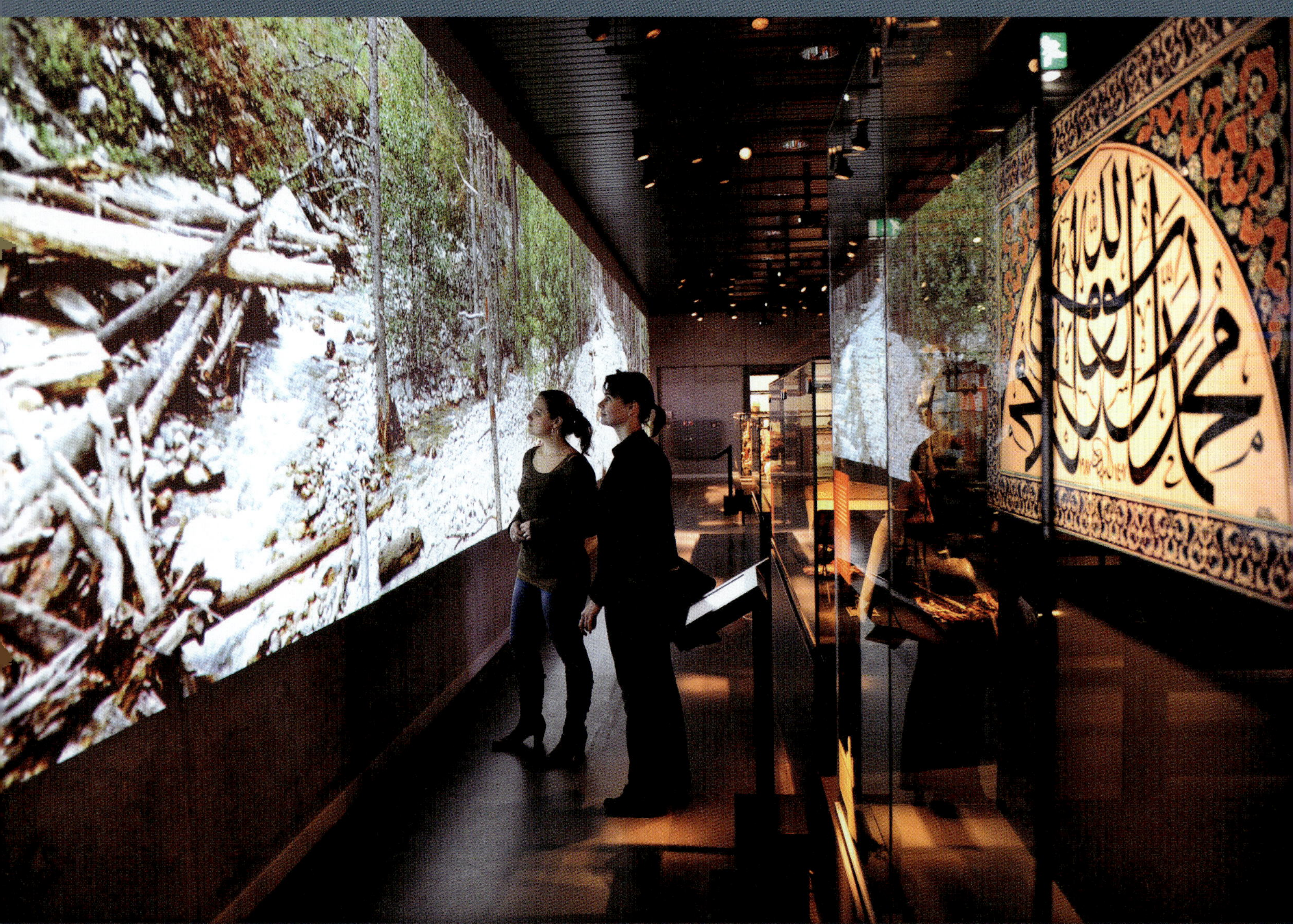

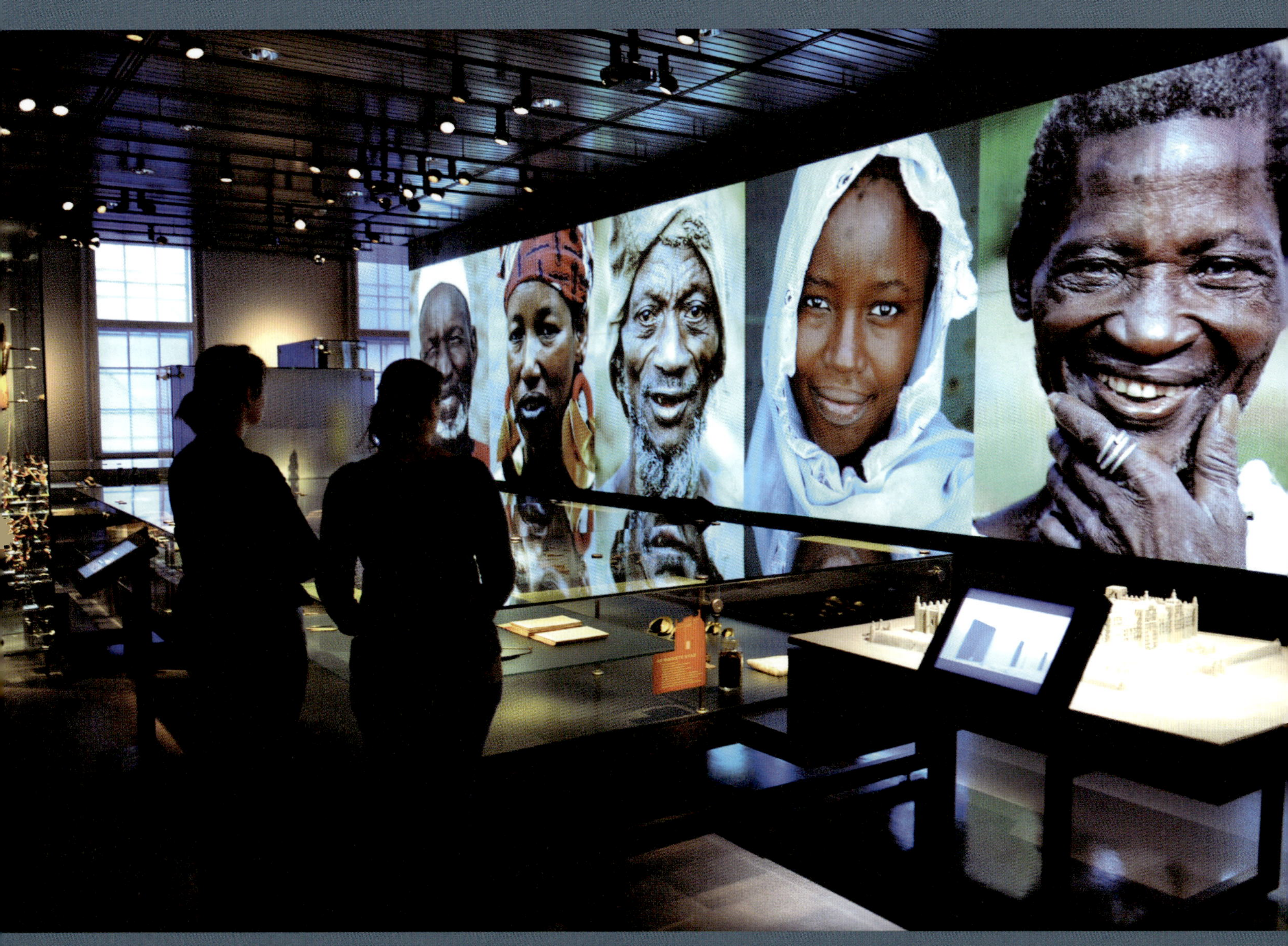

'Shaman bear': transformation sculpture

Padlaya Qiatsuk; Canadian Inuit; Cape Dorset, Nunavut Territory, Canada
1998
33 x 24 x 29 cm
yellow-green 'serpentine' soapstone, feathers, wood
RMV 6094-362 (2009)

Dancing bear

With outstanding craftsmanship and immense aesthetic sensibility, a lightly stylised figure has been carved from soapstone: it depicts a shaman undergoing transformation into a dancing bear. The Inuit see the polar bear as the mythical bringer of culture, who taught the people's ancestors how to survive. The 'dancing bear' developed into a recurrent theme in Inuit art.

Transformation of a polar bear into a shaman

Shamans could travel to 'other worlds' to discover the causes of disasters. They were assisted by animals in the form of spirit helpers. Transformation into the spirit of a polar bear, the most powerful and the most dangerous creature, was an intense and dangerous enterprise, even for experienced shamans. Many myths and legends are told about this process. The relationships between humans, animals and other beings were regulated by a complex system of rules and taboos, related to the Moon Spirit and other supernatural beings. Sila, for instance, was a great spirit that could influence the weather, while Sedna, the Mother of Sea Creatures, exerted power over the sea mammals hunted by the Inuit. She lived on the seabed. There was also a man on the moon, who was one of the sources of supernatural information.

Seer in other worlds

The shamans' hypnotic drum dance was a means of effecting transformation. Here, the light-footed, stylised dance shows that the shaman, who has been transformed into a bear, is on the point of taking off into flight, to move between heaven and earth. In the spirit world he sees a variety of things. The visions that came to the shaman were depicted in art, unless forbidden by a taboo. If he had seen faces, for instance, masks would be made of them. This made it easier to tell and pass on stories in a purely oral culture. These masks with their stories in dancing songs and legends still belong to the living Inuit tradition. They help to determine the form and content of modern Inuit art. 'Shaman/dancing bear' has developed into a well-known genre in the visual art of the Inuit.

Padlaya Qiatsuk

The artist Padlaya Qiatsuk was born on 5 October 1965, in Cape Dorset in Northern Canada. He is one of three brothers whose father was the artist and master carver Lukta Qiatsuk. At twelve years of age, Padlaya started carving bone and soapstone, inspired by his father and other old Inuit sculptors. From his father Padlaya Qiatsuk also learned deep respect for the land and the immense natural world of the surrounding Arctic. Qiatsuk has a preference for figurative work, and his favourite theme is transformational art.

The collector Hans van Berkel

Hans van Berkel's collection is one of the most important private collections of art and objects made by Arctic peoples in the Netherlands. In the 1970s he became involved with the life and fate of the Inuit through his uncle, Leo Mol, who had emigrated to Canada. He realised that by purchasing art and utensils, he could make a positive contribution to this remarkable culture. In 2010, Van Berkel donated his Arctic collection to the Rijksmuseum Volkenkunde.

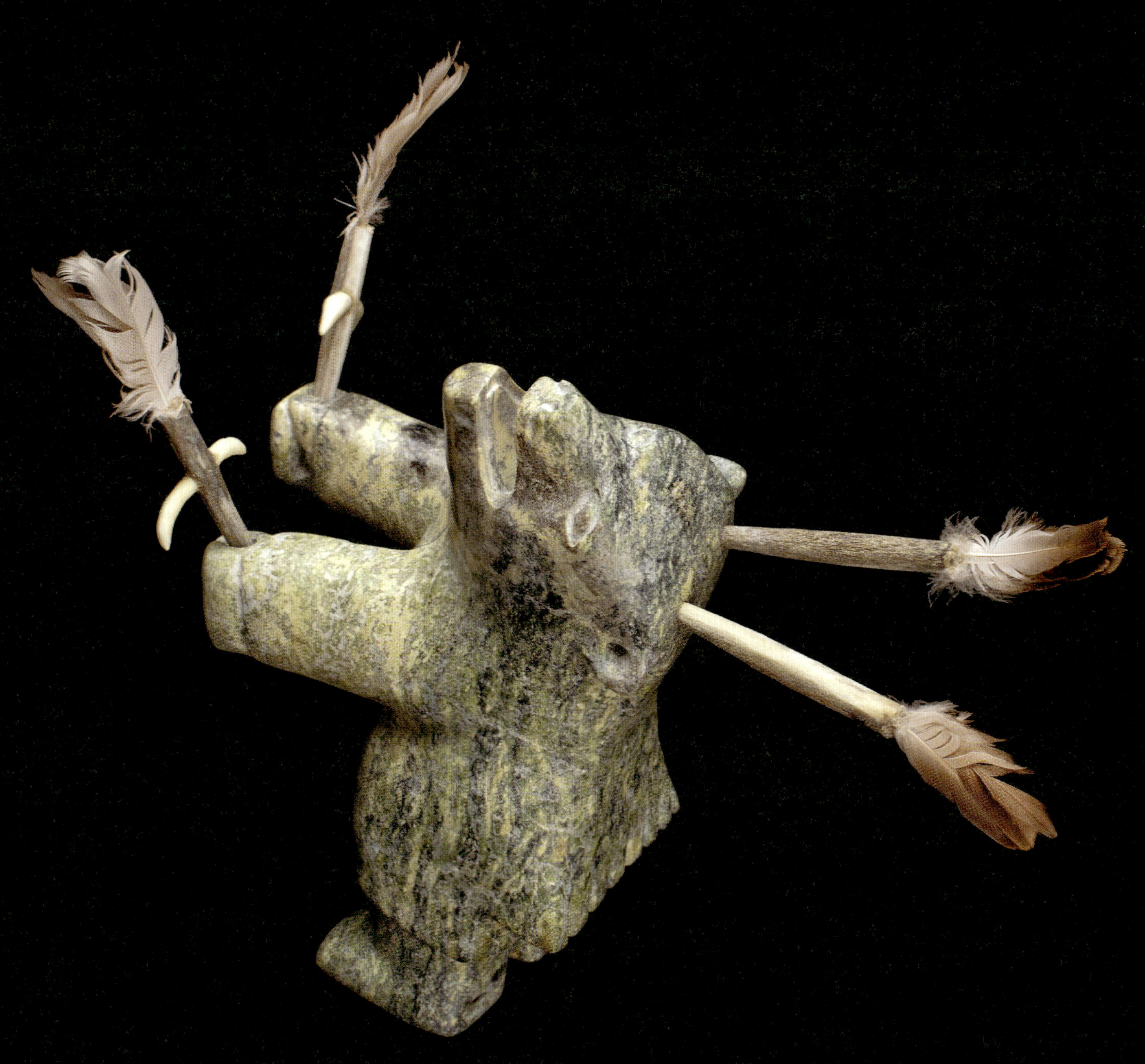

Porcelain serving dish

Edo period, Japan
c. 1813
dish: h. 8.8 cm, diam. 59.7 cm; ring-shaped stand: diam. 34.7 cm
porcelain, glaze, painted
RMV 6096-1 (2009)

Dish with portraits

This large *Imari* porcelain dish shows five different views of the five-year-old Ceylonese elephant that disembarked in Nagasaki on 28 June 1813 (see p. 212-213). The inscription on the bottom of the dish tells us: 'Made in the Seika period of the Great Ming [Dynasty, i.e. 1368-1644], *Ta Min Seika nenzoku.*' This is a fictitious date, typical of nineteenth-century Japanese porcelain.

Drawings by the *goyō eshi*

The remarkable thing about this dish is that the five different views of the elephant are directly based on the original drawings by the *goyō eshi*, the guild of painters and documentalists of foreign imports, now preserved in the National Museum in Tokyo. Like the drawings, this painting in blue glazes deploys chiaroscuro, in that it is done in different shades of blue, in imitation of Western painting techniques, to give the images of the elephant volume and depth.

The little elephant in Japan

Thomas Stamford Raffles, who sent this elephant to Nagasaki in 1813 as a gift to the shōgun, was probably extremely disappointed when Japan declined to accept either the collaborating *Opperhoofd* he nominated, Wardenaar, or the elephant as a gift to the shōgun. Both returned to Batavia that same year. That this incident made a strong impression, or in any case, that the elephant attracted universal interest, is clear from the numerous paintings made of the animal.

A very large dish

With a diameter of 59.7 cm, this dish is a *nishakuzara* – a dish measuring 2 *shaku* (1 *shaku* = 30.3 cm) – probably the largest size that could be produced in the Imari kilns. Both its huge size and its extremely delicate decorations, such as the hues of the elephant in diverse shades of blue, and the minutely elaborated background decorations, make it a truly remarkable piece, displaying great craftsmanship. The quality of the porcelain, both the fired material itself and the remarkably fine glaze, supports the assumption that this piece was made for the domestic Japanese market. As far as is known, this dish is the only one of its kind.

The elephant's backside

Another remarkable feature is that this dish is in absolutely perfect condition, with not the slightest crack or chip to detract from its original quality. As far as its use is concerned, it may well have been used to present slices of raw fish, *sashimi*, on a bed of grated *daikon*. As one continued eating, the elephant would appear from different vantage points. Eventually, as the company became livelier, they would reach the central medallion with the elephant's backside.

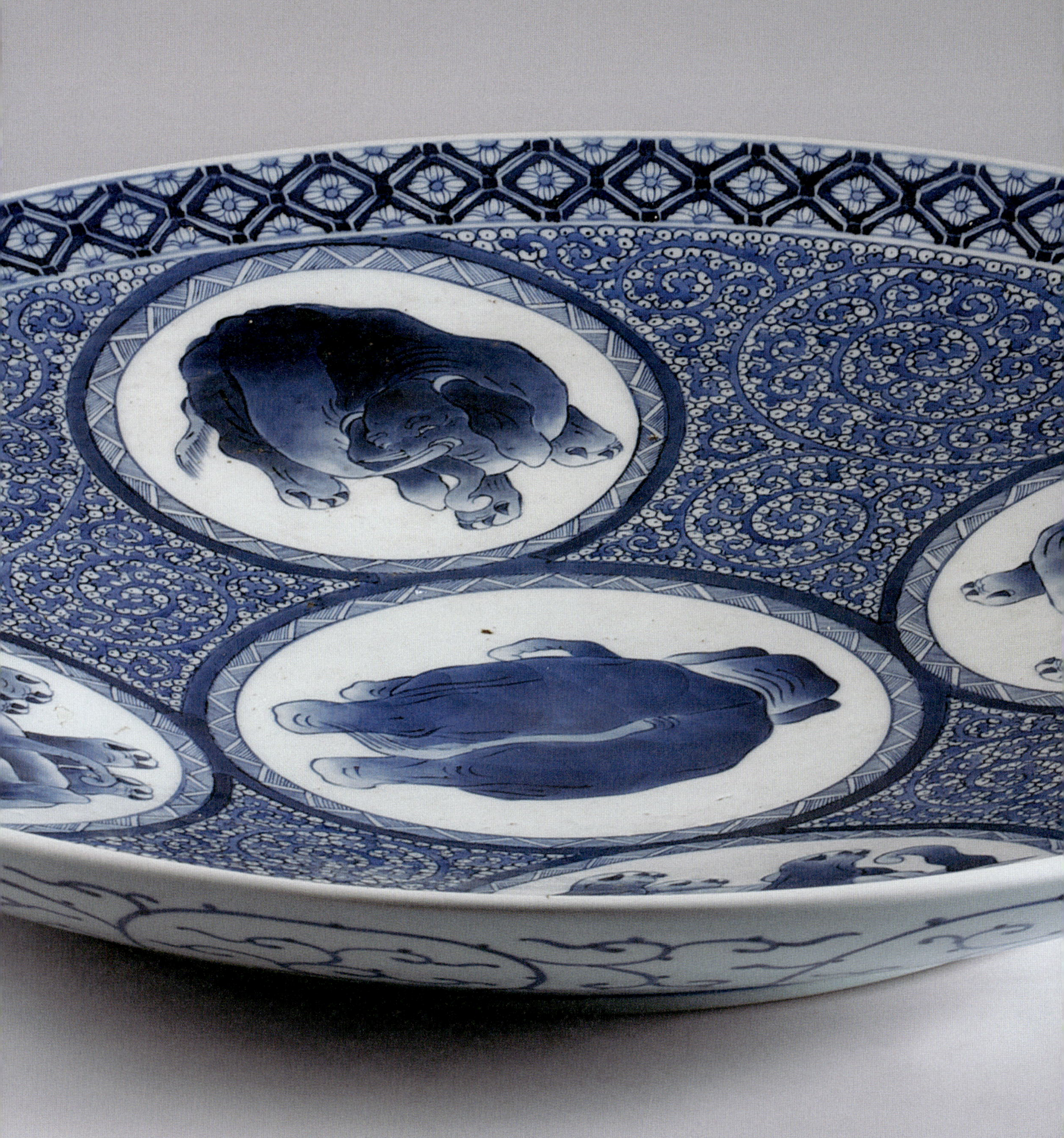

Staff (*Hoeroa*)

Māori, New Zealand
18th century
120 x 7 x 6.5 cm
whalebone
RMV 6107-1 (2009)

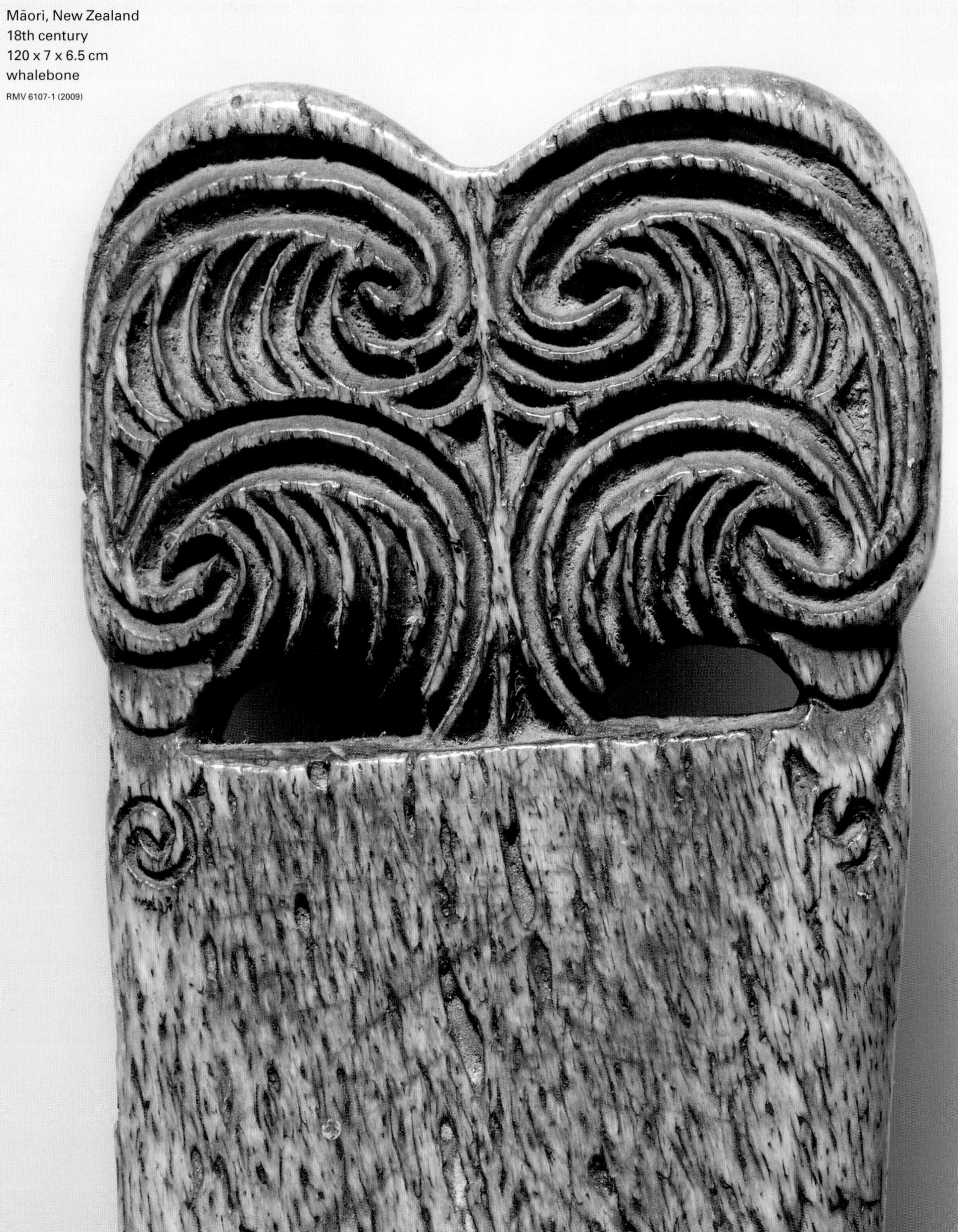

Lower jawbone of a sperm whale

Hoeroa is the indigenous name for a long club made from the lower jaw of a sperm whale. Its sober finish respects the jawbone's natural shape as much as possible. The ajour decorations on the handle include carved spiral motifs evoking the unfolding of fern fronds and referring to the Māori tattoo on the nostrils.

Mana

The staff was used by the Māori of New Zealand in single combat. The warrior could use it to repel, strike or wound his adversary. A *hoeroa* is a prestigious heirloom, with which high-ranking men could assert their personal mana (power and authority). Weapons of this kind are extremely rare: only a handful of specimens are known in museums and private collections. This *hoeroa* is also conspicuous for its outstanding craftsmanship; it is old and possesses a remarkably well-documented and traceable history.

Aesthetics

This weapon's design exemplifies the criteria of beauty that apply among the Māori, who attribute supernatural powers to aesthetics. Only 'beautiful' objects can perform both their practical and symbolic functions efficiently. Master carvers were enormously appreciated and respected, not only for their technical skill but also for their ability to channel supernatural powers.

Metal or stone?

Although this weapon was probably made in the eighteenth century, we cannot say with any certainty whether it was made with metal or stone tools. Quite soon after the arrival of eighteenth-century explorers such as James Cook, Jean-François-Marie de Surville, and Marion du Fresne, inhabitants of the northern coastal regions of New Zealand started fashioning the nails, knives, barrel rings, bayonet blades and axes they acquired into carvers' tools. Some sculptors continued to work with the more traditional nephrite jade (*pounamu*) and other stone implements, however.

A long journey

This *hoeroa* originally belonged to Tāmati Wāka Nene (born around 1780), a great Māori leader from a prominent family. When Nene died in 1871, the Europeans and Māori alike recognised him as a remarkable man with great *mana*. Research has shown that by then his hoeroa had come into the possession of Colonel Dunn, a British man who lived in New Zealand. One of Dunn's descendants offered the object for sale in 1932 to the private collector James Hooper, who found a place for it in his museum in Arundel (Sussex), the Totems Museum. Between 1976 and 1983, Hooper sold his collection through Christie's. By way of the dealer and collector Michael Graham-Stewart, it came into the possession of Rijksmuseum Volkenkunde.

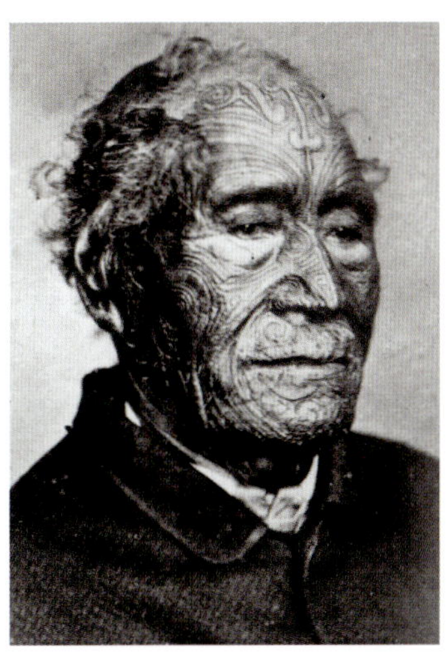

Figurine (*Tupilak*)

Gideon Qeqe; Tunumiit, Tasiilaq, East Greenland
2008
11 x 3.3 x 5.8 cm
sperm whale tooth
RMV 6110-38 (2010)

Gideon Qeqe

A monster or 'tupilak' figure carved from a sperm whale tooth. This figurine was made by Gideon Qeqe, one of East Greenland's leading artists. Gideon Qeqe (b. 1952) learned hunting from Inuit hunters in Tasiilaq, where he was born. He graduated from the local maritime college, worked as an electrician, and did not start making art until he was a mature adult, when an accident left him with a disability. Qeqe draws inspiration from the ancient myths of Greenland. This object was acquired for the museum collection while Cunera Buijs, curator of the Arctic department of the Rijksmuseum Volkenkunde, was conducting anthropological fieldwork in East Greenland.

In the artist's workshop

To meet the growing demand from an international market, the Tasiilaq district developed into the arts and crafts production centre, making objects that are exported by the Royal Greenlandic Trading Company (now Pilsersuisoq A/S). Since the international trade boycott on products made from endangered species introduced at the end of the twentieth century put an end to trade in some of Greenland's materials and products, artists are increasingly working with materials that tourists are permitted to take out of the country without export restrictions, such as wood, reindeer antlers, seal bone and soapstone.

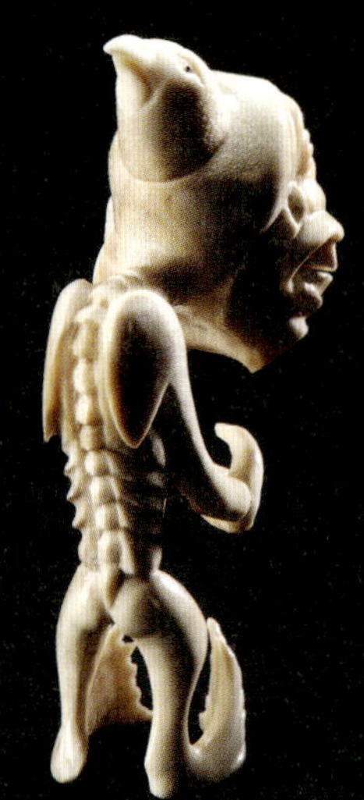

Magical monsters

Well into the nineteenth century, the Inuit resolved conflicts openly in peaceful public drum matches or song duels, but these procedures could not eradicate covert murder and manslaughter altogether. Drum matches were accompanied with black magic: someone would mould animal parts, and sometimes human body parts, into a monster figure or tupilak, blow supernatural power into the figurine, and tell it to kill the rival in love or hunting. When a hunter encountered a tupilak on the ice, or in the water while in his kayak, he could survive only if his own spirit was stronger than the tupilak's. With the advent of the white settlers, the Greenlanders were converted to Lutheranism. Even so, belief in the *tupilak* was still strong in the 1970s. Nowadays, the belief in *tupilat* (plural of *tupilak*) has declined. Traditional festive events have been replaced or fitted into the main events of the Christian calendar, such as Christmas, Epiphany, and Easter. In addition, Greenland's priests and ministers perform Sunday services, baptisms, marriage ceremonies and funeral services at the country's numerous churches and schools.

Artful art

Before Greenland was colonised by Denmark, starting in 1721, the Greenlanders only made objects that had some function within their own community. Contact with whalers, merchants, missionaries, researchers, and tourists gradually generated a demand for art objects that could be taken home as souvenirs, especially masks and sculptures such as tupilat carved from bone, ivory, reindeer antlers, wood and stone. Since the academy of art was founded in the 1970s in Nuuk, Greenland's capital, young Greenlanders have been trained in the modern visual arts. New materials and techniques have been added to the curriculum. Today's students are the second and third generation of skilled creative artists. Both art and crafts play a role in their training and in the experience of a modern Greenland identity.

From bird's head to flippers

The artefact is a combination of bird (bird's head on the back of the figure's head, claw-like front legs), seal (flipper-like back legs) and human (face and torso). The eyes have been blackened with pencil (in the past, soot was used). The head has a characteristic shape, with wrinkles, and is fairly symmetrical. The tiny bulge on the right of the face is a spot or a pimple, according to the artist.

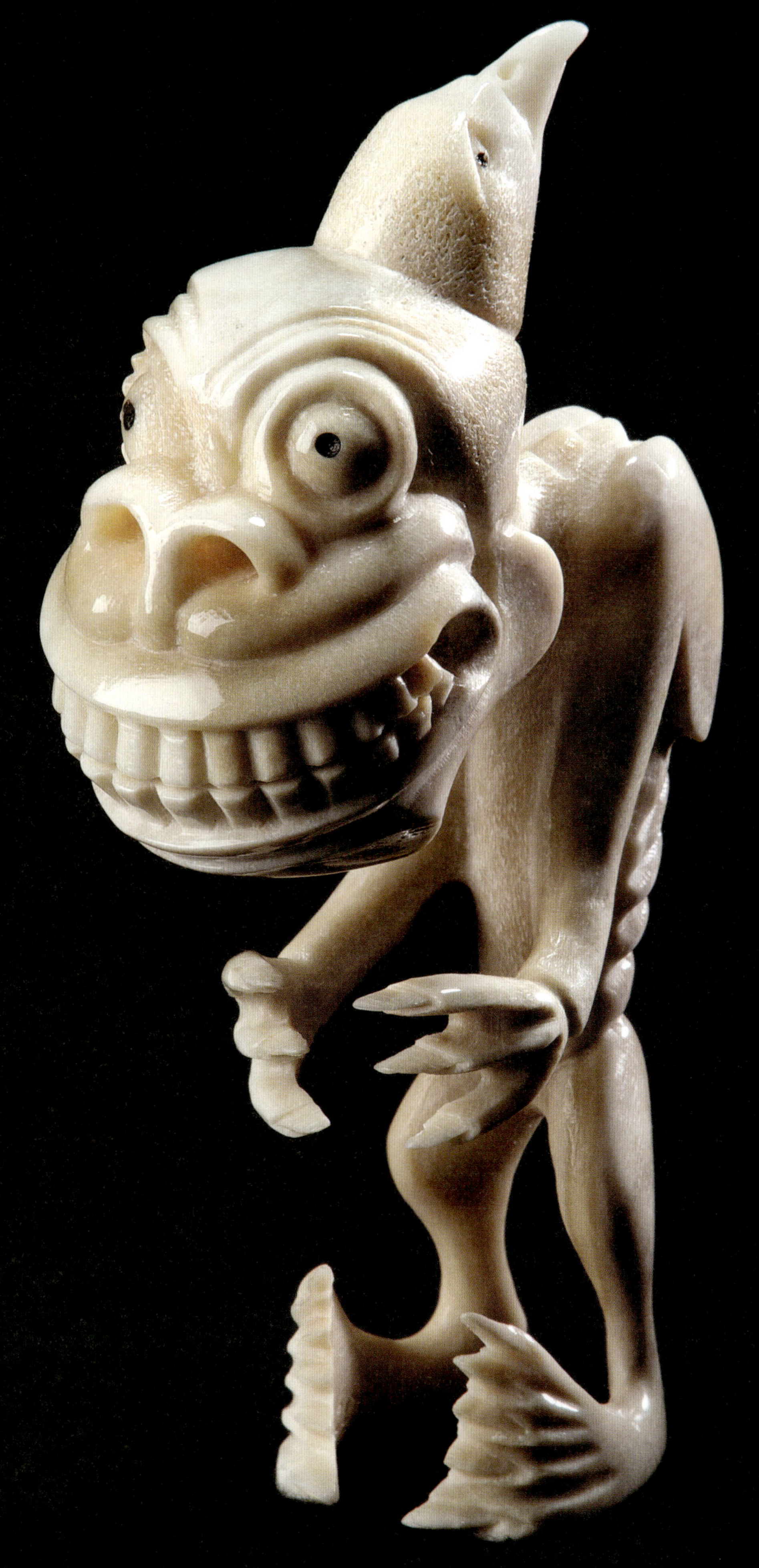

Necklace (*Hasli*)

Rajasthan, Northern India
2011
17.1 x 38.6 cm
gold, enamel, diamond fragments, baby pearls, cotton, gold thread
RMV 6117-1 (2011)

Secret Garden

This kind of necklace is a *hasli*, recognisable from the semicircular ring, made of precious metal. It is to be worn tightly around the neck. The gold (Hindi: *kundan*) mount is studded with diamond fragments and pearls and enamelled on both sides with beautiful floral, foliate and peacock motifs. The back is sometimes called 'the secret garden', a reference to the gardens of paradise of Islam and the gardens of Northern India's rulers, which were enclosed within high walls, hiding them from the gaze of the general population. The peacock is a popular symbol of beauty, grace, and love.

Following the trail of court traditions

In 2007 and 2011, the researcher Saskia Konniger followed the trail of the Mughal and Rajput court traditions, in search of goldsmiths who still possess the skill necessary to work in the famous *kundan* technique. The trail led to the Rajasthan city of Jaipur (a centuries-old centre of the global trade in gemstones), where thousands of merchants from all parts of the world still congregate every day in the precious stones district of Johari Bazar. Konniger discovered hundreds of *kundan* goldsmith families still living in the desert city of Bikaner, trying to earn a living from the ancient craft. She studied the production process and made acquisitions on the museum's behalf. This necklace was purchased from Surana Jewellers of Jaipur.

Indian court cultures

The Mughal and Rajput cultures were closely interrelated. Their works of art, interiors and costumes derived mutual inspiration from each other. Although Rajput rulers preserved an impressive regal ambience characterised by beauty and refinement, none could compete with the Mughal rulers. With an erudite panoply of pomp and circumstance, the Mughal Akbar created a sacred imperial culture. Mughal architecture, poetry, delicate textiles and refined jewellery were renowned far and wide.

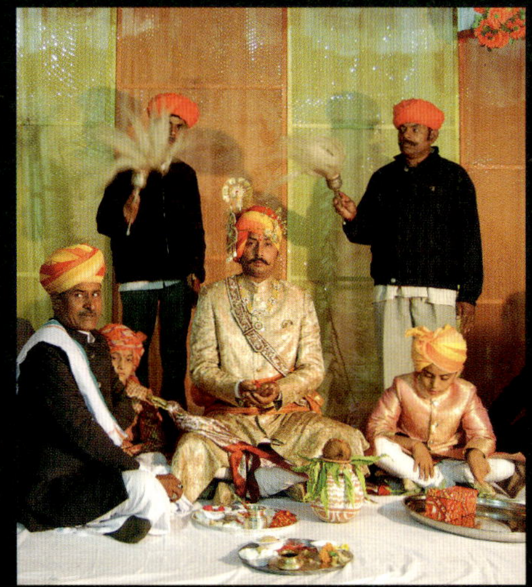

Craftsmanship

Kundan jewellery is made using 22-carat gold. Once the mount is finished, the goldsmith places the gems in a bed of lac (a red mordant dye obtained from the scale insect *Kerria lacca* [aangepast ok??]). The precious stones are placed on a strip of silver paper that has been smoothed out, to enhance the stones' glitter. The piece of jewellery is then finished using a 24-carat gold ribbon, which is pressed around the stones very carefully, without heating. The back is enamelled. For a long time it was customary in India to cut the gems into organic rather than geometrical shapes. The aim was to bring out their glitter to best effect while retaining as much mass as possible. The *kundan* technique enables the goldsmith to modify the mount to fit the shape of the gems.

Taj Mahal

Mughal art still commands considerable interest today, not least because of its abundance of precious stones. Who does not know the Taj Mahal, the marble mausoleum that Akbar's grandson Shah Jahan had built for his deceased wife? Every corner of this immense structure is inlaid with gems, many thousands of them. Besides underscoring the wearer's status and power, jewels were also ideal as a mobile banking system. The Mughul coffers were full of diamonds, pearls, emeralds, and rubies, which were easy to distribute and carry.

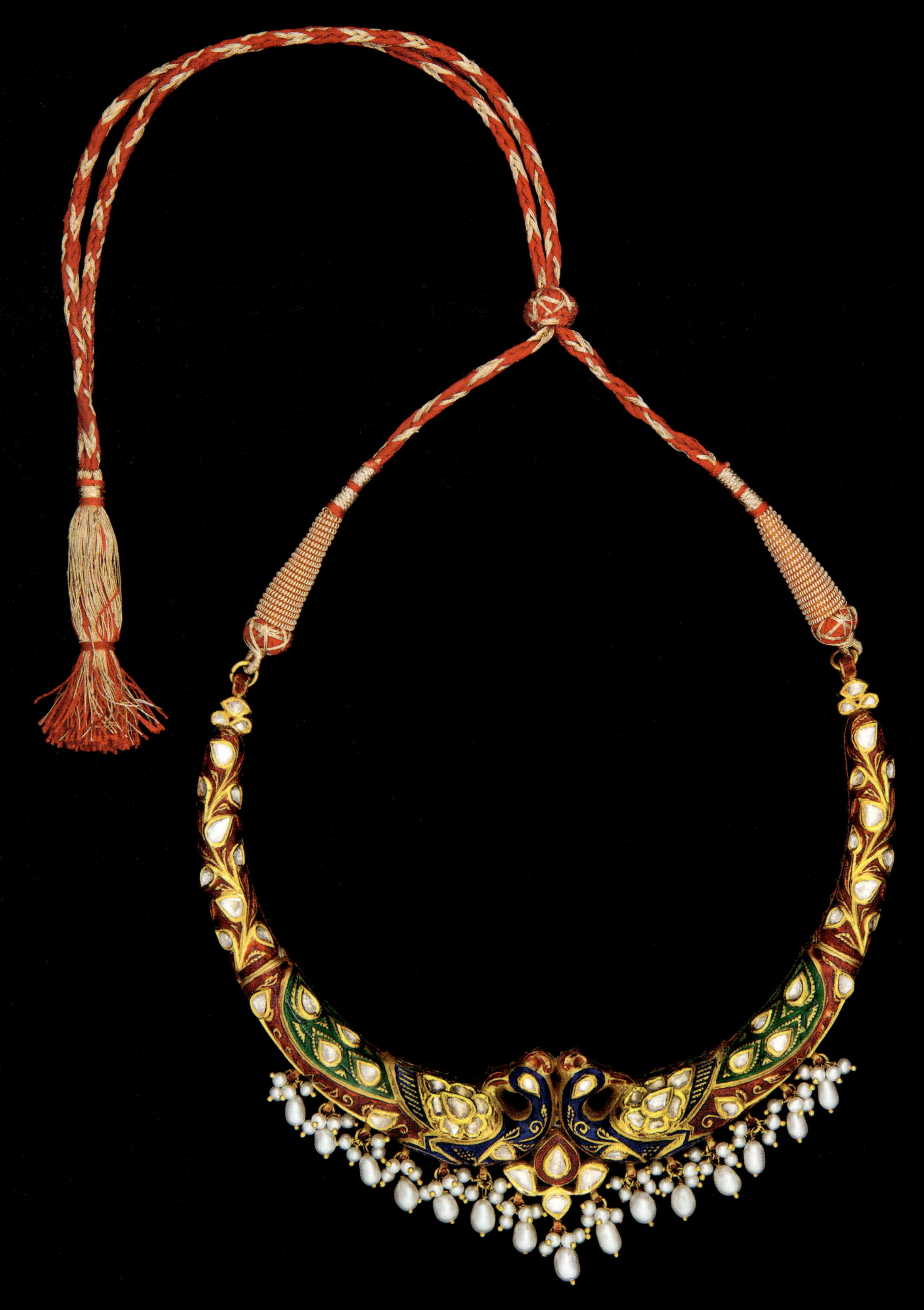

Prow ornament (*Isu, Nguzu nguzu* or *Musu musu*)

New Georgia, Solomon Islands
19th century
25.5 x 30 cm
wood, mother-of-pearl, pigment
RMV 6142-1 (2011)

Canoe decorations

On the island of New Georgia in the Solomon Islands, human figures were carved that consisted of only a head and upper torso with arms. These were often used as figureheads to adorn the prows of war canoes, and are called *toto isu, nguzu nguzu* or *musu musu*. Most were made in the nineteenth century. This remarkably well-finished figure has extremely fine inlaid work, and quite rare inlaid shell earrings.

War, headhunting and religion

These prow ornaments were attached to the prows of war canoes. Though small in relation to the overall canoe size, they were important features and the first objects to capture the attention of the Europeans, who wrote about them from the nineteenth century onwards. The figureheads could be detached from the canoe. They were probably attached to different canoes from time to time, or exchanged between groups. They were evidently major trophies, which would be seized in combat between rival communities when a canoe had been defeated. The use of figureheads is hence closely linked to warfare, head-hunting, and the indigenous religion.

TV celebrity

In 2011 this prow ornament reached the finals in the AVRO television art programme *Hollandse Nieuwe*. The programme revolved around new acquisitions in Dutch museums: what is interesting about them for museum visitors and why do they fit into the museum's collection? Every week, two art lovers went to see two acquisitions at different museums. They were not experts or public figures, but ordinary museum visitors with a passion for art. In the final programme on 11 June, the art lovers chose five acquisitions to be placed in the limelight. The prow ornament was placed at the heart of a special exhibition mounted as a result of this selection.

From talisman to national symbol

The human figures in these prow embellishments were believed to ward off storms and to bring good fortune in war. They often hold a small human head to assure success in headhunting. Alternatively, some figures hold a bird, symbolising successful navigation and a safe return to land. The large staring eyes are said to chase away the evil water spirit kesoko. The patterns on the figure imitate the painted faces of warriors going to combat. Although figureheads like this are no longer used, they remain major symbols of national identity, and since the Solomon Islands gained their independence in 1978 they have featured on the national five-dollar bank notes.

Private collection

This small prow ornament, which was acquired in the 1940s by William G. Schulz and remained in this family until 2011, comes from the Marovo Lagoon in New Georgia in the western Solomon Islands. Similar figureheads were found in other parts of the Solomon Islands such as Choiseul, Santa Isabel, Vella Lavella and the Nggela or Florida Islands.

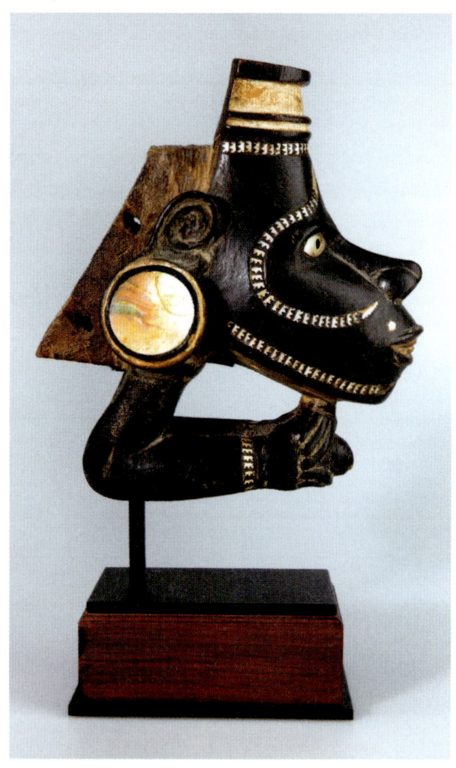

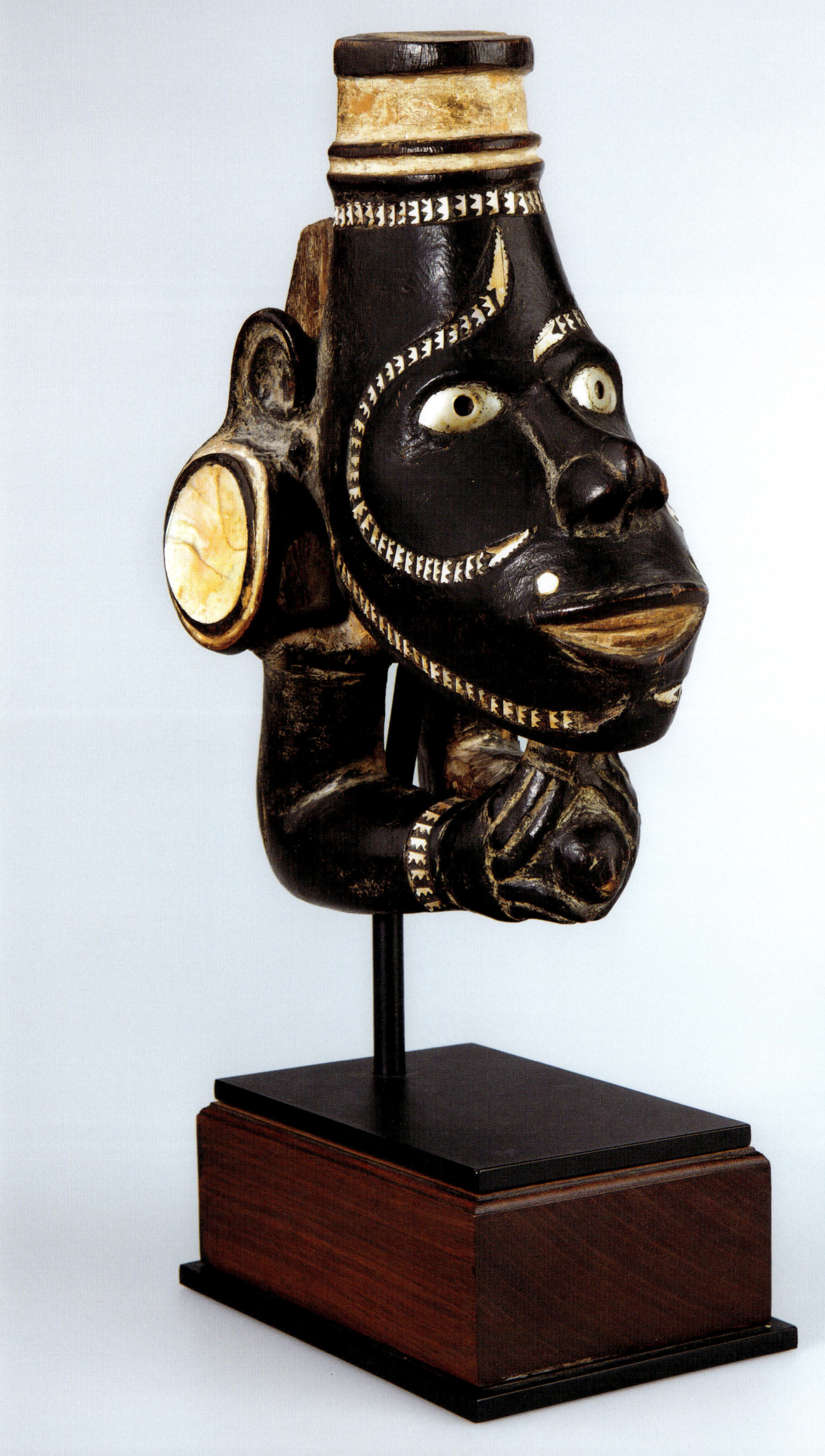

Africa

p. 202

p. 38
p. 46
p. 208

p. 90
p. 94
p. 108

p. 152

p. 148

p. 102

Curator Africa, Dr. Annette M. Schmidt wrote the texts for the masterpieces from Africa.

Further reading

Bassani, E. & M. McLeod (eds) (2000), African Art and artefacts in European collections 1400-1800. British Museum Press, London.

Bassani, E. & W.B. Fagg (1988), *Africa and the Renaissance: Art in Ivory.* New York: The Center for African Art.

Bedaux, R.M.A. & J. Smits (1992), 'A seventeenth century ivory figure in the Rijksmuseum voor Volkenkunde in Leiden', *African Arts* 15: 76-77.

Bolland, R. (1991), *Tellem textiles; archaeological finds from burial caves in Mali's Bandiagara Cliff. Mededelingen van het Rijksmuseum voor volkenkunde, Leiden no. 27.* Amsterdam, Leiden and Bamako: Royal Tropical Institute.

Cole, H.M. & D.H. Ross (1977), *The arts of Ghana.* Regents of the University of California.

Duchâteau, A. (1990), Benin; vroege hofkunst uit Afrika. Gemeentekrediet, Brussel. Rijksmuseum voor Volkenkunde Leiden.

Kramer, M. (2005), *Colourful changes: two hundered years of social and design history in the hand-woven textiles of the Ewe-speaking regions of Ghana and Togo (1800-2000),* Unpublished PhD.

Lahuard, R. (1977), *Les phemba du mayombe.* Arnouville: Arts d'Afrique Noire.

MacGaffey, W. & M. Harris (eds.) (1993), *Astonishment and Power.* Washington and London: National Museum of African art; Smithsonian Institution Press.

Marquart, J. (1913), Die Benin-Sammlung des Reichsmuseums für Völkerkunde in Leiden. Brill, Leiden.

Plankersteiner, B. (ed.) (2007), *Benin Kings and Rituals: Court Arts from Nigeria.* Snoeck Publishers & Kunsthistorisches Museum mit RMVK und ÖTM.

Schmidt, A.M. & P. Westerdijk (2006), *The Cutting Edge: West Central African 19th century throwing knives in the national Museum of Ethnology Leiden.* Leiden: National Museum of Ethnology & C. Zwartenkot Art Books.

Willis, W.B. (1998), *The Adrinkra Dictonary.* The Pyramid complex: Washington.

China

Curator China, Dr. Oliver J. Moore wrote the texts for the masterpieces from China.

Further reading

Benn, C. (2002), *China's Golden Age: Everyday Life in the Tang Dynasty.* New York: Oxford University Press.

Campen, J. van (2000), *Royers Chinese cabinet.* Amsterdam: Rijksmuseum.

Clunas, C. (1997), *Pictures and Visuality in Early Modern China.* London: Reaktion Books.

Fiskesjö, M. & C. Xingcan (2004), *China before China: Johan Gunnar Andersson, Ding Wenjiang, and the Discovery of China's Prehistory.* Stockholm: Östasiatiska museet.

Hay, J. (2010), *Sensuous Surfaces: The Decorative Object in Early Modern China.* London: Reaktion Books.

Kuchiki, Y. (2011) 朽木ゆり子「ハウス・オブ・ヤマナカ、東洋の至宝を欧米に売った美術商」 (House of Yamanaka: Art Dealer Who Sold Oriental Treasures to America and Europe). Tokyo: Shinchosha.

Lai, Chi Tim et al. (2008), *The Studio and the Altar: Daoist Art in China.* Hong Kong: Chinese University of Hong Kong.

Moore, O. (2011), 'Vertier en plezier', in Benoît Mater (ed.), *De Gouden Eeuw van China – Tang dynastie (618 907 na Chr.),* 137 170. Assen: Drents Museum.

Schipper, K. (1988), *Tao: De Levende Religie van China.* Amsterdam: Meulenhoff.

Siren, O. (1927/28), 'Studien zur chinesischen Plastik der Post T'angzeit', *Ostasiatische Zeitschrift* 1/2: 1 20.

Ströber, E. (2001), *"La Maladie de porcelaine": Ostasiatische Porzellan aus der Sammlung Augusts des Starken.* Dresden: Staatliche Kunstsammlungen.

Wilson, V. (1986), *Chinese Dress.* London: Victoria & Albert Museum.

Wu, H. (1986), 'Buddhist Elements in Early Chinese Art (2nd and 3rd Centuries A.D.)', *Artibus Asiae* 47 (3/4): 263-352.

Circumpolar region

Curator circumpolar region, Dr. Cunera Buijs wrote the texts for the masterpieces from the Circumpolar region.

Further reading

Arima, E.Y. (1987), *Inuit Kayaks in Canada: A Review of Historical Records and Construction, Based Mainly on the Canadian Museum of Civilization's Collection,* Mercury Series, Canadian Ethnology Service 110, Ottawa: Canadian Museum of Civilization / National Museums of Canada.

Bettenhaussen, P. & R. Kerkhoven (1991), *Eskimoland, verleden, heden en toekomst van de Groenlandse Inuit.* Den Haag/Abcoude: Museon/Uitgeverij Unipers.

Black, L. (1991), *Glory Remembered, Wooden Headgear of Alaska Sea Hunters.* Junea: Alaska Sate Museum.

Buijs, C. (2005), 'Bont rond het vege lijf, Kleding van Oost-Groenland'. Leiden : Rijksmuseum voor Volkenkunde, e-publicatie www.volkenkunde.nl.

Crandall, R.C. (2000), *Inuit Art. A History.* North Carolina: Jefferson.

Diószegi, V. & M. Hoppál (1996), *Shamanism in Siberia.* Budapest: Akadémia Kiadó.

Fienup-Riordan, A. (2008), *The Way we Genuinely Live, Masterworks of Yup'ik Science and Survival.* Anchorage Museum at Rasmussen Center.

Fitzhugh, W.W. & A. Crowell (eds.), (1988), *Crossroads of Continents. Cultures of Siberia and Alaska.* Washington: Smithsonian Institution Press.

Franchesci, G., T. Møbjerg, J. Rosing, A. Jørn (n.d.), *Folk Art in Greenland throughout a Thousand Years,* Köln: Verlag der Buchhandlung Walther König.

Golden, H. (2006), *Kayaks in Greenland. The History and Development of the Greenlandic Hunting Kayak, 1600-2000.* Portland: White House Grocery Press.

Kaalund, B. (1983, reprint 2011) *Art of Greenland: Sculpture, Crafts, Painting,* Berkeley: University of California Press.

Konovalov, A. & V. Gorbacheva (eds.) (2006), *Between Worlds, Shamanism of the Peoples of Siberia.* Moscow: Khudozhnik I Kniga.

Petersen, H.C. (1986), *Skinboats of Greenland.* Roskilde: The National Museum of Denmark, The Museum of Greenland & The Viking Ship Museum in Roskilde.

Rajagopalan, S. (2005), *Layers of meaning, Clothing of the Amur.* www.volkenkunde.nl e-publicatie Manker, E (1965), People of eight seasons. London: Watts.

VanStone, J.W. (1985), 'An Ethnographic Collection from Northern Sakhalin Island', *Fieldiana* New Series 8: 1-67

p. 70

p. 214
p. 206
p. 228

p. 222

p. 12

p. 60

p. 18

p. 92

Insular Southeast Asia

Curator Insular Southeast Asia, Francine Brinkgreve (M.A.) wrote the texts for the masterpieces from Insular Southeast Asia.

Further reading

Brinkgreve, F. (2005), 'Vorsten van Bali en koloniaal gezag. Collectievorming en politiek', in E. Sri Hardiati & P. ter Keurs (eds.), *Indonesia. De ontdekking van het verleden*, 122-145. Amsterdam: KIT Publishers.

Brinkgreve, F. & R. Miedema (2008), 'Doeken voor een dode vorst', *Aziatische kunst* 38, 4: 8-21.

Duuren, D. van (1998), *The kris: an earthly approach to a cosmic symbol*. Wijk en Aalburg: Pictures Publishers.

Ernawati, W. (2007), 'The Lombok treasure', in P, ter Keurs (ed.), *Colonial collections revisited*, 186-202. Leiden: CNWS Publications. (Mededelingen van het Rijksmuseum voor Volkenkunde, Leiden, no. 36)

Jonge, N. de & T. van Dijk (1995), *Forgotten islands of Indonesia: the art & culture of the Southeast Moluccas*. Hong Kong: Periplus Editions.

Keurs, P. ter (2002), 'Manipa's world: Enggano: sources, culture and material culture (part 2)', *Tribal arts* 28 (summer/autumn 2002): 106-133.

Klokke, A.H. (1994), 'Oorsprongsmythen en afbeeldingen van de Ngaju-Dayak *Mihing*: de achtergrond van een bestaande methode van visvangst', *Bijdragen tot de Taal-, Landen Volkenkunde* 150: 67-109.

Nieuwenhuis, A.W. (1904-07), *Quer durch Borneo: Ergebnisse seiner Reisen in den Jahren 1894*, 1896-97 und 1898-1900. Leiden: Brill.

Nieuwenkamp, W.O.J. (1947), *Bouwkunst en beeldhouwkunst van Bali*. 's-Gravenhage: Leopold's Uitgevers-Maatschappij.

Prager, M. & P. ter Keurs (ed.) (1998), *W.H. Rassers and the Batak magic staff*. Leiden: Rijksmuseum voor Volkenkunde. (Mededelingen van het Rijksmuseum voor Volkenkunde, Leiden, no. 29).

Reichle, N. (ed.) (2010), *Bali: art, ritual, performance*. San Francisco: Asian Art Museum

Serrurier, L. (1896), *De wajang poerwa: eene ethnologische studie*. Leiden: Brill.

Vatter, E. (1934), 'Der Schlangendrache auf Alor und verwandte Darstellungen in Indonesien, Asien und Eropa', *Ipek*: 119-148.

Veldhuisen, H.C. (1993), *Batik Belanda 1840-1940: Dutch influence in batik from Java: history and stories*. Jakarta: Gaya Favorit Press.

Wassing-Visser, R. (1995), *Koninklijke geschenken uit Indonesië: historische banden met het Huis Oranje-Nassau (1600-1938)*. Den Haag: Stichting Historische Verzameling van het Huis Oranje-Nassau. Zwolle: Waanders Uitgevers.

Japan and Korea

Curator Japan and Korea, Prof Dr. Matthi Forrer wrote the texts for the masterpieces from Japan and Korea.

Further reading

Asakura M. (無声) (1992), *Misemono kenky – shimaihen*. Tokyo: Heibonsha.

Calza, Gian Carlo (ed.) (2003), *Hokusai*. London & New York: Phaidon.

Chaiklin, M. (2010), 'Simian Amphibians: The Mermaid Trade in Early Modern Japan', in N. Yoko (ed.), *Large and broad. The Dutch impact on early modern Asia.* (Toyo Bunko Research Library, 13), 241-273. Tokyo: The Toyo Bunko.

Davey, N.K. (1972), *Netsuke. A comprehensive study based on the M.T. Hindson collection.* London: Sotheby's Parke Bernet Publishing.

Donovan, E. (1823), *The naturalist's repository of exotic natural history; consisting of seventy-two elegantly coloured plates, with appropriate scientific and general descriptions, of the most curious, scarce, and beautiful quadrupeds, birds, fishes, insects, shells, marine productions, and other interesting objects of natural history, the produce of foreign climates.* Volume II. London.

Kikuchi M. (1993), *Mankoku kaibutsu daihakurankai.* Tokyo: Nanpōdō.

Edmunds, W. H. (1934), *Pointers and Clues to the Subjects of Chinese and Japanese Art.* London: Martson & Co.

Forrer, M. (1996), *Edo no k gei. An exhibition of Japanese crafts focusing on the Jan Cock Blomhoff collection.* Himeji: Enzan kinen Nihon kōgei bijutsukan, 24.

Forrer, M. (2007), 'Katsushika Hokusai meeting with Siebold,' in M. Forrer, H. Kamiya, N. Wagatsuma (eds.), *Siebold & Hokusai and his tradition*, 3-20. Tokyo: Tokyo Shinbun.

Goncourt, E. de (1896), *Hokousaï.* Paris: Bibliothèque Charpentier

Forrer, M. & K. Vos (1986), *Griezelen in Japan.* Leiden: Rijksmuseum voor Volkenkunde.

Forrer, M. (1997), 'Long leg and long arm fishing', *Andon* 57: 41-46.

Hizō Nihon bijutsu taikan (1993), Vol. 9: *Raiden Kokuritsu Minzokugaku Hakubutsukan.* Tokyo: Kōdansha.

Imaizumi, M. (1990), *Nabeshima. Nihon tōki taikei*, 21. Tokyo: Heibonsha.

Kagesato, T. (ed.) (1978), *Oranda Kokuritsu Minzokugaku Hakubutsukan. Shiiboruto korekushon. Hizō ukiyoe.* Tokyo: Kōdansha.

Nabeshima, N. (ed.) (1954), *Nabeshima hanū no kenkū.* Kyoto: Heiandō.

Overmeer Fisscher, J.F. van (1833), *Bijdrage tot de kennis van het Japansche Rijk.* Amsterdam: J. Müller & Comp.

Rein, J.J. (1889), *The industries of Japan, together with an account of its agriculture, forestry, arts, and commerce.* London: Hodder and Stoughton.

Schiermeier, K. & M. Forrer (2006), *Pronkstukken uit keizerlijk Japan. Meiji-kunst uit de Khalili collectie.* Zwolle: Waanders Uitgevers.

Siebold, Ph.F. von (n.d.), *Nippon. Archiv zur Beschreibung von Japan und dessen Neben- und Schutzländern.* Vol. II, Leiden.

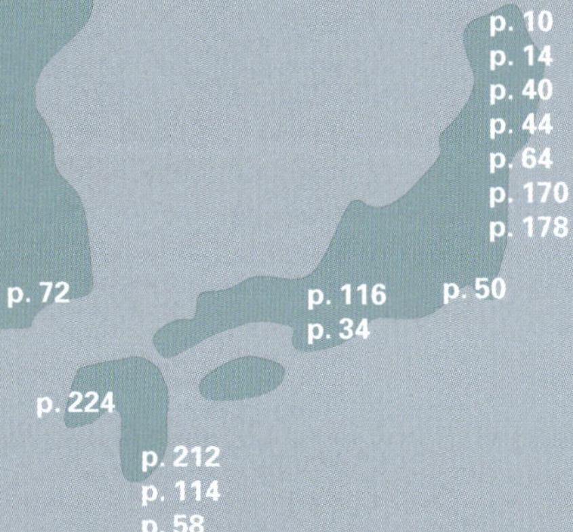

Central and South America

Chief curator and curator Central and South America, Dr. Laura Van Broekhoven and junior curator Central and South America, Martin Berger (M.A.) wrote the texts for the masterpieces from Central and South America.

Further reading

Bock, E.K. de (1999), Appendix B: The Van den Bergh Collection. In C.B. Donnan & D. McClelland (eds.), *Moche Fineline Painting. Its Evolution and its Artists*, 301-303. Los Angeles: UCLA Fowler Museum of Cultural History.

Bourget, S. & K.L. Jones (eds.) (2008), *The Art and Archaeology of the Moche: An Ancient Andean Society of the Peruvian North Coast.* Austin: University of Texas Press.

Brandes, S. (2006), *Skulls to the Living, Bread to the Dead.* Malden, MA: Blackwell Publishing

Duin, R.S. (2009), *Wayana Socio-Political Landscapes: Multi-scalar regionality and temporality in Guiana.* PhD thesis, University of Florida.

Epstein, D. J. (1975), 'The Folk Banjo: A Documentary History', *Ethnomusicology* 19 (3): 347-371.

Golden, C.W. (2003), 'The Politics of Warfare in the Usumacinta Basin: La Pasadita and the Realm of Bird Jaguar', in M.K. Brown & T. Stanton (eds.), *Ancient Mesoamerican Warfare*, 31-48. Walnut Creek, CA: Alta Mira Press.

Interview met Kapitein Samé, 12-08-2010 door S. Konniger.

Jackson, M.A. (2008), *Moche Art and Visual Culture in ancient Peru.* Albuquerque: University of New Mexico Press.

Masuoka, S.N. (1994), *En Calavera: The Papier-Mâché Art of the Linares Family.* Los Angels: UCLA Fowler Museum.

Medendorp, C. (2008), *Kijkkasten uit Suriname.* Amsterdam: KIT Publishers.

Stedman, J.G. (1799-1800), *Reize naar Surinamen, en door de binnenste gedeelten van Guiana* (Volume 3). Amsterdam: Johannes Allart.

Urton, G. (2003), *Signs of the Inka Khipu: Binary Coding in the Andean Knotted-String Records.* Austin: University of Texas Press.

Van Broekhoven, L. (ed.) (2003), *Met Kuifje naar de Inca's : strijdbaar heden, roemrijk verleden.* Brussel : Éditions Moulinsart.

Van Broekhoven, L. (n.d.), *Weefsels van het volk van de regen*, E-Publicaties Rijksmuseum Volkenkunde, http://www.volkenkunde.nl/publicaties/22Mixteeks_textiel/n/fr_pub.html

Van den Hoek, C. (1986), 'Surinaams kaartgeld', *Muntkoerier* 15: 34-35.

Von Winning, H. & O. Hammer (1972), *Anecdotal Sculpture of Ancient West Mexico.* Los Angeles: Ethnic Arts Council of Los Angeles.

Webster, D. (2000), 'The Not So Peaceful Civilization: A Review of Maya War', *Journal of World Prehistory* 14(1): 65-119.

Zorich, Z. (2011), 'Defending a Jungle Kingdom', *Archaeology*: 64(5), consulted online at http://www.archaeology.org/1109/features/maya_warfare_yaxchilan_piedras_negras.html

North America

Curator North America, Dr. Pieter Hovens wrote the texts for the masterpieces from North America.

Further reading

Brasser, T. (1961), 'War Clubs', *American Indian Tradition* 7 (3): 77-83.

Busby, S. & R. Reeder (2003), *Spruce Root Basketry of the Tlingit and Haida*. Seattle: University of Washington Press.

Ferg, A., (ed.) (1987), *Western Apache Material Culture*, Tuscon: Arizona State Museum.

Griffith, J.S. & F.S. Molina (1980), *Old Men of the Fiesta: an Introduction to the Pascola Arts*, Phoenix: Heard Museum.

Hail, B. & K.C. Duncan (1989), *Out of the North*. Seattle: University of Washington Press.

Horse Capture, G.P. (1992), 'The Warbonnet: a Symbol of Honor', in E. Maurer (ed.), *Native American Heritage*, 60-67. Chicago: Chicago Art Institute.

King, J. (2007), 'Ball-Headed Clubs in 19th Century Europe', in J. King & C.F. Feest (eds.), *Three Centuries of Woodlands Indian Art*, 75-84. Altenstadt: ZKF Publishers.

Kolaz, T. (1985), 'Yaqui Pascola Masks', *American Indian Art Magazine* 11 (1): 38-45.

Markoe, G. (ed.) (1986), *Vestiges of a Proud Nation*. Burlington: Robert H. Fleming Museum.

Peterson, S. (1989), *The Living Tradition of Maria Martinez*. Tokio and New York: Kodansha International.

Secacuku R. (1995), *Following the Sun and Moon: Hopi Kachina Tradition*. Flagstaff: Northland Press.

p. 16

p. 184

p. 82

p. 36

p. 204

p. 130

p. 80

p. 54

p. 62

Oceania

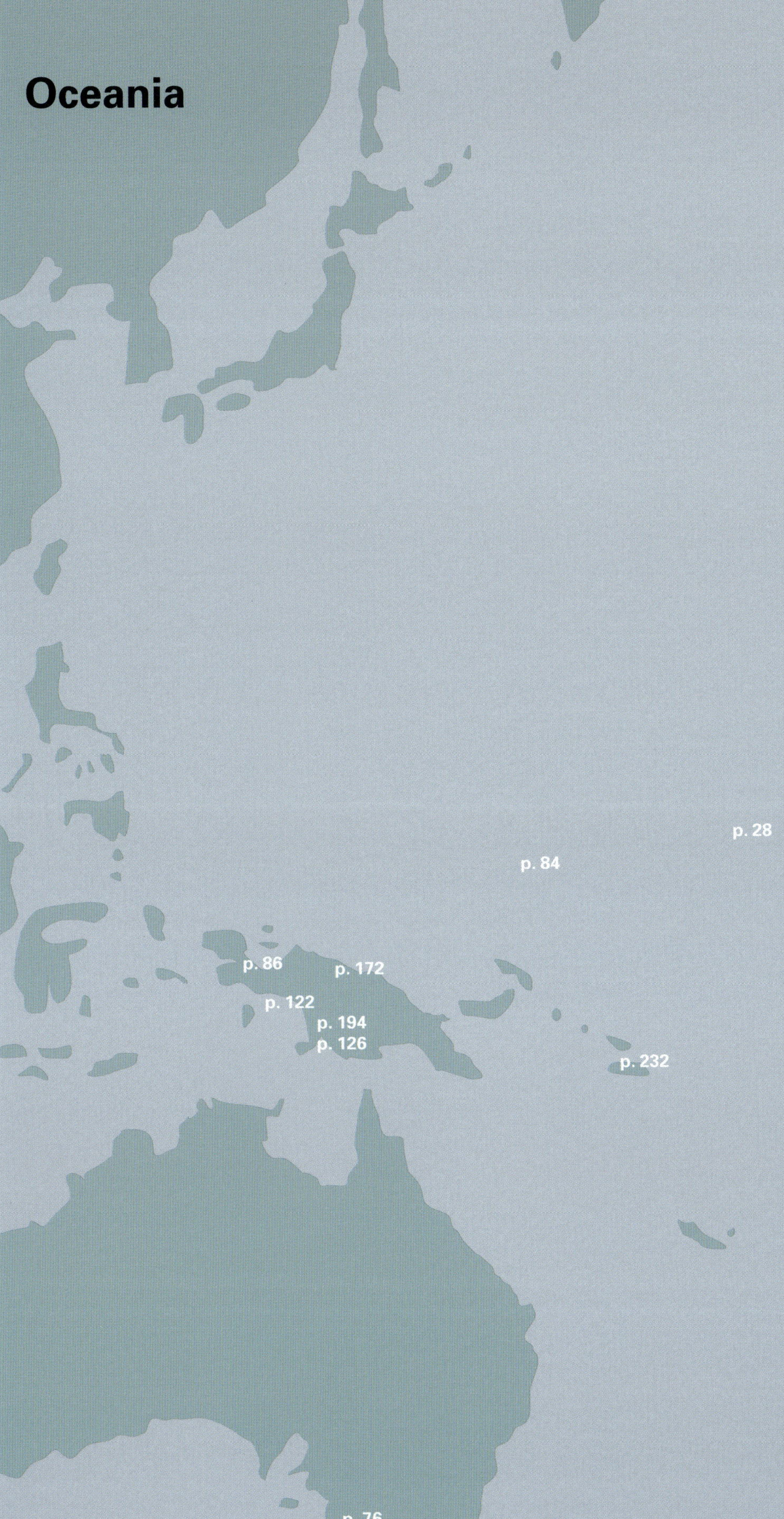

Curator Oceania, Dr. F. Wonu Veys wrote the texts for the masterpieces from Oceania.

Further reading

Dongen, van P.L.F., M. Forrer & W.R. van Gulik (eds.), (1987), *Topstukken uit het Rijksmuseum voor Volkenkunde. Masterpieces from the National Museum of Ethnology*, 264. Leiden: Rijksmuseum voor Volkenkunde.

Gerbrands, A.A. (1967), *Wow-Ipits: eight Asmat Woodcarvers of New Guinea*. The Hague-Paris: Mouton & Co.

Greub, S. (ed.) (1992), *Art of Northwest New Guinea: from Geelvink Bay, Humboldt Bay, and Lake Sentani*. New York: Rizzoli.

Heermann, I. (ed.) (2009), *Südseeoasen. Leben und überleben im Westpazifik*. Stuttgart: Linden Museum Stuttgart. Staatliches Museum für Völkerkunde.

Hooper, S. (2006), *Pacific Encounters. Art & Divinity in Polynesia 1760-1860*. London: The British Museum Press.

Jones, P. (1996), Boomerang. *Behind an Australian Icon*. Berkeley, California: Ten Speed Press.

Jones, P. (2012), *Some observations on the Australian boomerang, no. 680-9, National Museum of Ethnology, Leiden* [unpublished notes]

Kaeppler, A. (2008), *The Pacific Arts of Polynesia & Micronesia*. Oxford: Oxford University Press.

Kooijman, S. (1959), *The art of Lake Sentani*. New York: The Museum of Primitive Art.

Morphy, H. (1998), *Aboriginal Art*. New York: Phaidon.

Neich, R. & F. Pereira (2004), *Pacific Jewelry and Adornment*. Honolulu: University of Hawai'i Press.

Pouwer, J. (1955), *Enkele aspecten van de Mimika-cultuur (Nederlands Zuidwest Nieuw Guinea)*. 's Gravenhage: Staatsdrukkerij en Uitgeversbedrijf.

Smidt, D. (ed.) (1993), *Asmat Art. Woodcarvings of Southwest New Guinea*. Hong Kong: Perliplus Editions Ltd.

Smidt, D. (ed.) (2003), *Kamoro Art, Tradition and Innovation is a New Guinea culture*. Amsterdam: KIT Publishers.

Veys, F.W. (2010), *Mana Maori. De kracht van Nieuw-Zeelands eerste bewoners*. Leiden: Leiden University Press.

Waite, D. & K. Conru (2008), *Solomon Islands Art*. The Conru Collection. Milan: 5 Continents Editions.

India and Sri Lanka

Junior curator India, Saskia Konniger (M.A.) wrote the texts for the masterpieces from India and Sri Lanka.

Further reading

Ahjuwalia, R. (2008), *Rajput Painting, Romantic, Divine and Courtly Art from India*. London: The British Museum Press.

Chuttiwongs, N. (n.d.), *Gemoedsstemmingen van Liefde*, digitale publicatie op de website van Rijksmuseum Volkenkunde.

Draaisma, A. (2007), 'Ganjifa: kaarten met de goden', *India NU*, sept/okt.

Gschwend, A.J. & J. Beltz (2010), *Elfenbeine aus Ceylon, Luxusgüter für Katharina von Habsburg (1507-1578)*. Zürich: Museum Rietberg.

Gupte, R.S. (1980), *Iconography of the Hindus, Buddhists and Jains*. Bombay: D.B. Taraporevala Sons & Co.

Jacobs, E.M. (2000), *Koopman in Azië, De handel van de Verenigde Oost-Indische Compagnie tijdens de 18de eeuw*. Zutphen: Walburg Pers.

Konniger, S. (2011), *De Verborgen Tuin, Goudsmeden in Noord-India*. Amsterdam: KIT Publishers.

Schechner, R. (1986), 'Wrestling Against Time: The Performance Aspects of Agni', *Journal of Asian Studies*, 45(2): 359-363.

Staal, F. (1983), *Agni: The Vedic Ritual of the Fire Altar*, Volume 1. Berkeley: CA: Asian Humanities Press.

Staal, F. (2008), *Discovering the Vedas, Origins, Mantras, Rituals, Insights*. India: Penguin Books.

Stutley, M. & J. (1997), *Harper's Dictionary of Hinduism, Its Mythology, Folklore, Philosophy, Literature, and History*. New York: Harper & Row.

Theuns-de Boer, G. (2008), *A Vision of Splendour, Indian Heritage in the Photographs of Jean Philippe Vogel, 1901-1913*. Leiden: Mapin publishing and the Kern Institute.

Von Leyden, R. (1982), *Ganjifa, the playing cards of India*. Londen: Victoria & Albert Museum.

p. 188
p. 230
p. 160

p. 198

p. 56

Middle East, West and Central Asia

Curator Middle East, West and Central Asia, Dr. Luit Mols wrote the texts for the masterpieces from the Middle East, West and Central Asia.

Further reading

Déroche, F. (2005), *Islamic Codicology. An Introduction to the Study of Manuscripts in Arabic Script*, London: Al-Furqān Islamic Heritage Foundation.

Farmer, H.G. (1929), 'Meccan Musical Instruments', *The Journal of the Royal Asiatic Society of Great Britain and Ireland* 61(3): 489-505.

Ferdowsi, A. (2006), *Shahnameh. The Persian Book of Kings, A New Translation by Dick Davies*. New York: Penguin.

James, D. (1992), *After Timur. Qur'ans of the 15th and 16th Centuries. The Nasser D. Khalili Collection of Islamic Art* III. London: Nour Foundation/Azimuth Press/Oxford University Press.

Kalter, J. (1984), *The Arts and Crafts of Turkestan*. Londen: Thames and Hudson.

Menzel, T. (1932), 'Beiträge sur Kenntnis der Derwisch-tāğ', in T. Menzel (ed.), *Festschrift Georg Jacob zum siebsigsten Geburtstag 26 Mai 1932*, 174-199. Leipzig: Harrassowitz.

Mojan, M. Al- (2010), *The Honorable Kabah. Architecture and Kiswah*. Mekka: Al-Kawm Center.

Munneke, R. (1990), *Van Zilver, goud en kornalijn. Turkmeense sieraden uit Centraal-Azië*. Leiden/Breda: Rijksmuseum voor Volkenkunde.

Poché, C. (1985), 'Qanbūs', in S. Sadie (ed.) *The New Grove Dictionary of Musical Instruments* (3 volumes). London: Macmillan Publishers Limited.

Porter, V. (2012), 'Textiles of Mecca and Medina', in V. Porter (ed.), *Hajj. Journey to the heart of Islam*, 256-265. Londen: The British Museum Press.

Schimmel, A. (1975) *Mystical Dimensions of Islam*. Chapel Hill: The University of North Carolina Press.

Schletzer, D. & R. Schletzer (1983), *Old Silver Jewellery of the Turcoman*. Berlijn: Dietrich Reimer.

Sims, E. (2002), *Peerless Images. Persian Painting and its Sources*. New Haven/London: Yale University Press.

Snouck Hurgronje, C. (2007), *Mekka. Vertaald en ingeleid door Jan Just Witkam*. Amsterdam/Antwerpen: Atlas.

Classical South and Southeast Asia

Curator Classical South and Southeast Asia, Prof. Dr. Marijke J. Klokke wrote the texts for the masterpieces from Classical South and Southeast Asia.

Further reading

Brandes, J.L.A. (1909), *Beschrijving van Tjandi Singasari en de wolkentooneelen van Panataran*. 's-Gravenhage: Nijhoff; Batavia: Albrecht.

Fontein, J. (1990), *The sculpture of Indonesia*. Washington: National Gallery of Art; New York: Abrams.

Klokke, M. (1996), 'Drie Javaanse watervaten in hun religieuze context', *Aziatische Kunst* 26 (1): 45-51.

Klokke, M.J. (2000), 'Stone images of the Singhasari and Majapahit periods', *Arts of Asia* 30(6): 60-68.

Lunsingh Scheurleer P. & M.J. Klokke (1988), *Divine Bronze: Ancient Indonesian Bronzes from 600-1600*. Leiden: Brill.

Lunsingh Scheurleer, P. (2001), 'The kamandalu containing the amrta: the transformation and reinterpretation of an Indian water vessel in ancient Java', in M.J. Klokke & K.R. van Kooij (eds.), *Fruits of Inspiration: studies in honour of Prof. J.G. de Casparis*, 257-289. Groningen: Forsten.

Lunsingh Scheurleer, P. (2005), 'De schat van Wonoboyo in de Nieuwe Kerk', *Aziatische Kunst* 35(4): 14-41.

Lunsingh Scheurleer, P. (2005), 'Singosari-beelden in de Nieuwe Kerk', *Aziatische Kunst* 35(4): 42-72.

Moeller, V. (1985), *Javanische Bronzen*. Berlin: Staatliche Museen Preussischer Kulturbesitz.

Schoterman, J.A. (1994), 'A surviving Amoghapasa sadhana: its relation to the five main statues of Candi Jago', in: Marijke J. Klokke & Pauline Lunsingh Scheurleer (eds.), *Ancient Indonesian sculpture*, 154-177. Leiden: KITLV Press.

Sedyawati, E. (1994), *Ganesa statuary of the Kadiri and Sinhasari periods: a study of art history*. Leiden: KITLV Press.

Zin, M. (2003), 'The usnisa as a physical characteristic of the Buddha's relatives and successors', *Silk Road Art and Archaeology* 9: 107-129.

Pakistan and the Himalayas

Curator Classical South and Southeast Asia, Prof. Dr. Marijke J. Klokke and junior curator India, Saskia Konniger (M.A.) wrote the texts for the masterpieces from Pakistan en the Himalayas.

Further reading
Beer, R. (2004), *The encyclopedia of Tibetan symbols and motifs*. Chicago: Serindia.
Behrendt, K.A. (2007), *The art of Gandhara in the Metropolitan Museum of Art*. New York: The Metropolitan Museum of Art.
Donaldson, T. E. (2001), *Iconography of the Buddhist sculpture of Orissa*. New Delhi: Indira Gandhi National Centre for the Arts.
Estournel, J.-L. (1992), 'Rus-pa'i-rgyan: parures rituelles tibétaines en os humain', *Histoire de l'Art* 20: 39-49. (http://www.aaoarts.com/asie/RPRG/rprg.html).
Kooij, K. R. van & P. Lunsingh Scheurleer (eds.) (1997), *A companion to Buddhist art*. Leiden: Working Group Art and Material Culture, Faculty of Arts.
Laufer, B. (1923), *The use of human skulls and bones in Tibet*. Chicago: Field Museum of Natural History.
Linrothe, R. & J. Watt (2004), *Demonic Divine: Himalayan art and beyond*. New York: Rubin Museum of Art.
Lipton, B. & N. Dorjee Ragnubs (1996), *Treasures of Tibetan art: collections of the Jacques Marchais Museum of Tibetan Art*. Staten Island, NY: Jacques Marchais Museum of Tibetan Art; New York [etc.]: Oxford University Press.
Pal, P. (1990), *Art of Tibet: a catalogue of the Los Angeles County Museum of Art collection*. Los Angeles: Los Angeles County Museum of Art.
Pott, P.H. (1951), *Introduction to the Tibetan collection of the National Museum of Ethnology*, Leiden. Leiden: Brill.
Salomon, R. (2009), 'Why did the Gandharan Buddhists bury their manuscripts?', in S.C. Berkwitz, J. Schober & C. Brown (eds.), *Buddhist manuscript cultures: knowledge, ritual, and art*, 19-34. London and New York: Routledge.
Snellgrove, D. L. (1987), *Indo-Tibetan Buddhism: Indian Buddhists and their Tibetan successors*. London: Serindia.

COLOPHON

Photograph captions
p. 22
Batak ritual with use of magic staff, ca. 1910.
Photographer: Albert Grubauer
(RMV A83-13).
p. 54
The Apache camp in San Carlos, Arizona,
July 1883. Photographer: Duhem
(RMV A50-64).
p. 58
Page from a Japanese encyclopaedia (From a
Japanese Encyclopaedia of Arts & Sciences.
London Published by E. Donovan & Messns
Simpkin & Marshall October 1, 1823).
p. 62
Portrait of a Yaqui Indian carrying a yoke with
two chicken baskets, ca. 1880. Photographer:
Alfredo Laurent (RMV A50-18).
p. 68
Portrait of a seated Dervish, 1910.
Photographer: Antoine Sevruguin
(RMV A6-45).
p. 88
Ritual dance with *hudoq* masks carried out by
Kayan-Dayak men on the occasion of a sowing
festival, 1896. Photographer: unknown
(RMV A10-181).
p. 92
Nivch family fishing for its own subsistence,
east coast of Sakhalin Island, Siberia, July,
2007. Photographer: Herman de Boer.
p. 142
Display in the Netherlands of part of the
Lombok treasure, 1897-1898. Photographer:
unknown (RMV A330-1).
p. 170
Portrait of an elderly man made by Katsushika
Hokusai (1760-1849), 1779-1849 (RMV 2736-2).
p. 186
Dr. Arnoud Klokke, ca. 1950. Photographer:
unknown.
p. 206
Tasiilaq, capital city of the East Greenland
district in the snow, April 2007. Photographer:
Herman de Boer.
p. 226
Tāmati Wāka Nene, ca. 1870. Photographer:
Elizabeth Pulman (Alexander Turnbull Library,
No.PA2-1357).
p. 230
Rajput wedding, the groom and his entourage,
Jaipur, 2007. Photographer: Saskia Konniger.

Masterpieces of Rijksmuseum Volkenkunde

Publisher:
KIT Publishers
Mauritskade 63
Postbus 95001
1090 HA Amsterdam
E-mail: publishers@kit.nl
www.kitpublishers.nl

©2013 Rijksmuseum Volkenkunde

Concept and coordination:
John Sijmonsbergen and Fanny Wonu Veys
Translation: Beverley Jackson
General editor: Saskia Konniger
Copy editor Japan and Korea: Wietske du Pon
Managing editor: Fanny Wonu Veys
Object photography: Lourens Smak, Ben Grishaaver
Design: stoopmanvos, Rotterdam
Production: High Trade BV, Zwolle

ISBN 978 94 6022 2542

All rights reserved. No part of this publication
may be reproduced, stored in a retrieval system,
or transmitted in any form, or by any means,
electronic or otherwise, without the prior written
permission of the Rijksmuseum Volkenkunde.